VIZ GRAPHIC NOVEL

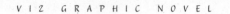

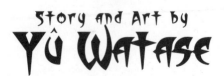

CERES
Celestial Legend™
VOL. 4: CHIDORI

Story and Art by
Yû Watase

CERES™
Celestial Legend
Volume 4: Chidori
Shôjo Edition

This volume contains the CERES: CELESTIAL LEGEND installments
from Part 4, issue 1, through Part 4, issue 4, in their entirety.

STORY & ART BY YÛ WATASE

English Adaptation/Gary Leach
Translation/Lillian Olsen
Touch-up Art & Lettering/Melanie Lewis
Cover Design & Layout/Hidemi Sahara
Editor — 1st Edition/Andy Nakatani
Shôjo Edition Editors/Elizabeth Kawasaki & Frances E. Wall

Managing Editor/Annette Roman
Editor-in-Chief/Alvin Lu
Sr. Director of Licensing & Acquisitions/Rika Inouye
Production Manager/Noboru Watanabe
Vice President of Sales/Joe Morici
Vice President of Marketing/Liza Coppola
Executive Vice President/Hyoe Narita
Publisher/Seiji Horibuchi

© 1997 Yuu Watase/Shogakukan, Inc. First published by Shogakukan, Inc. in Japan as "Ayashi no Ceres."
New and adapted artwork and text © 2004 VIZ, LLC. All rights reserved.

Printed in Canada

Published by VIZ, LLC
P.O. Box 77010
San Francisco CA 94107

Shôjo Edition

10 9 8 7 6 5 4 3 2 1

First printing, July 2004
First English edition, May 2003

store.viz.com

www.viz.com

www.animerica-mag.com

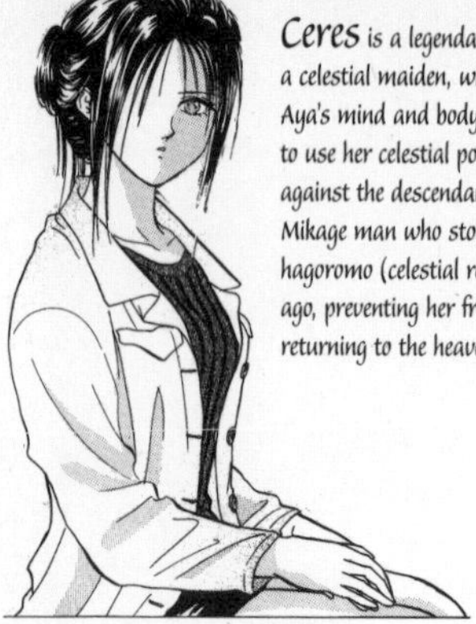

Ceres is a legendary tennyo, a celestial maiden, who inhabits Aya's mind and body. She vows to use her celestial powers against the descendants of the Mikage man who stole her hagoromo (celestial robe) ages ago, preventing her from returning to the heavens.

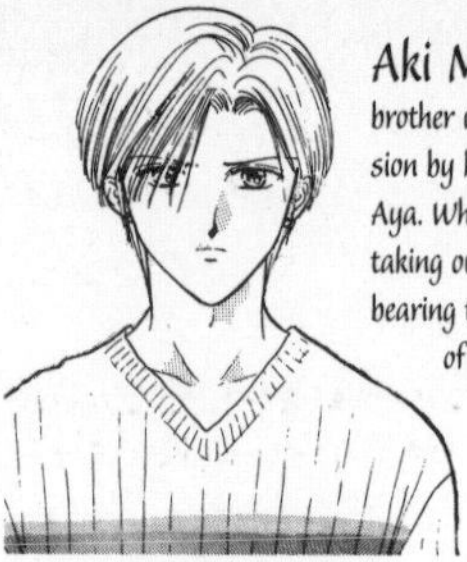

Aki Mikage is Aya's nice-guy twin brother who is taken into protective seclusion by his family to separate him from Aya. While the consciousness of Ceres is taking over Aya, Aki is showing signs of bearing the consciousness of the founder of the Mikage family line (the man who stole Ceres' robes).

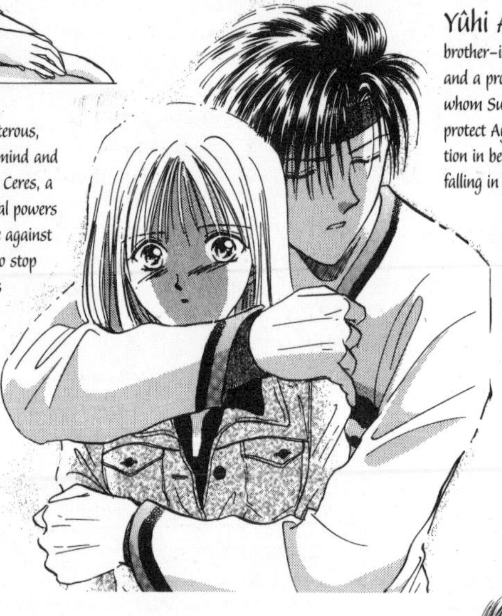

Yûhi Aogiri is Suzumi's brother-in-law, an aspiring chef and a proficient martial artist whom Suzumi has ordered to protect Aya. Despite his frustration in being Aya's guardian, he's falling in love with her.

Aya Mikage is a boisterous, modern 16-year-old whose mind and body are being taken over by Ceres, a heavenly maiden with celestial powers who is obsessed with revenge against the Mikage family. In order to stop Ceres, Aya's own family tries to kill her. Amid the chaos, Aya falls for Tôya, a man hired by the Mikages to keep an eye on her.

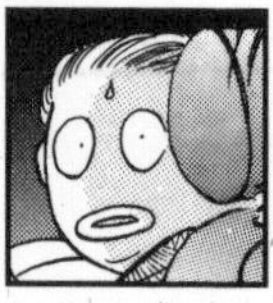

Mrs. Q (Oda Kyû) is the bizarre but faithful servant of Suzumi's household who occasionally provides comic relief.

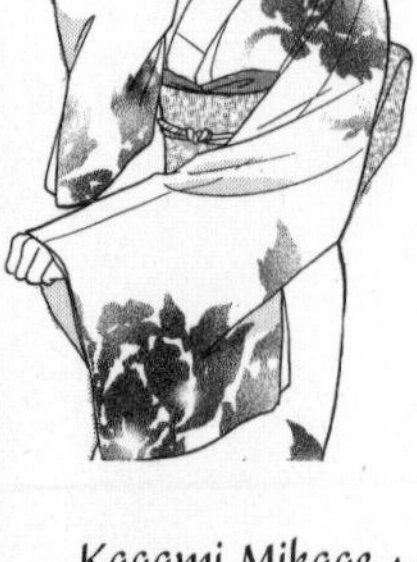

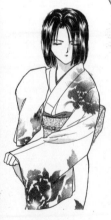

Suzumi Aogiri is a Japanese dance teacher and a descendant of a tennyo. She takes Aya into her home and tries to support and protect her, along with her brother-in-law Yûhi and faithful servant Mrs. Q. In volume three, Kagami's henchmen trapped Suzumi in a hallucinatory dream-state. While Ceres manages to save her, Suzumi's psyche may forever be trapped in an illusory world.

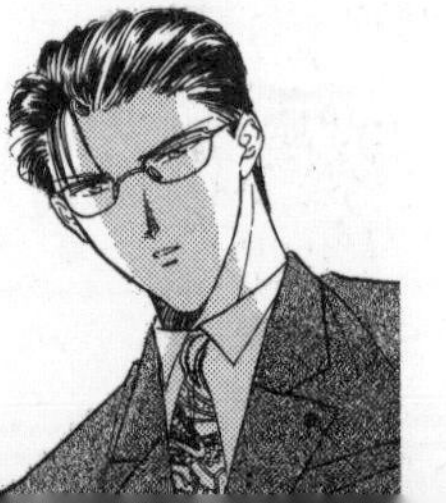

Kagami Mikage, Aya's cousin, has plans for Aya, Aki and Tôya. The Mikage family wants to kill Ceres through Aya, but as the head of Mikage International's research and development team, Kagami masterminds the C-Project, a plan to further his own agenda through the descendants of tennyo.

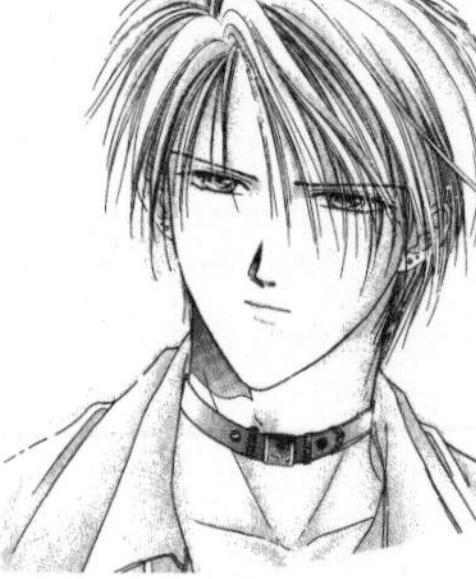

Tôya, a handsome but mysterious stranger who has amnesia, works for the Mikages with the hope that their advanced technology can help him regain his memory. However, he always feels compelled to help Aya escape dangerous situations.

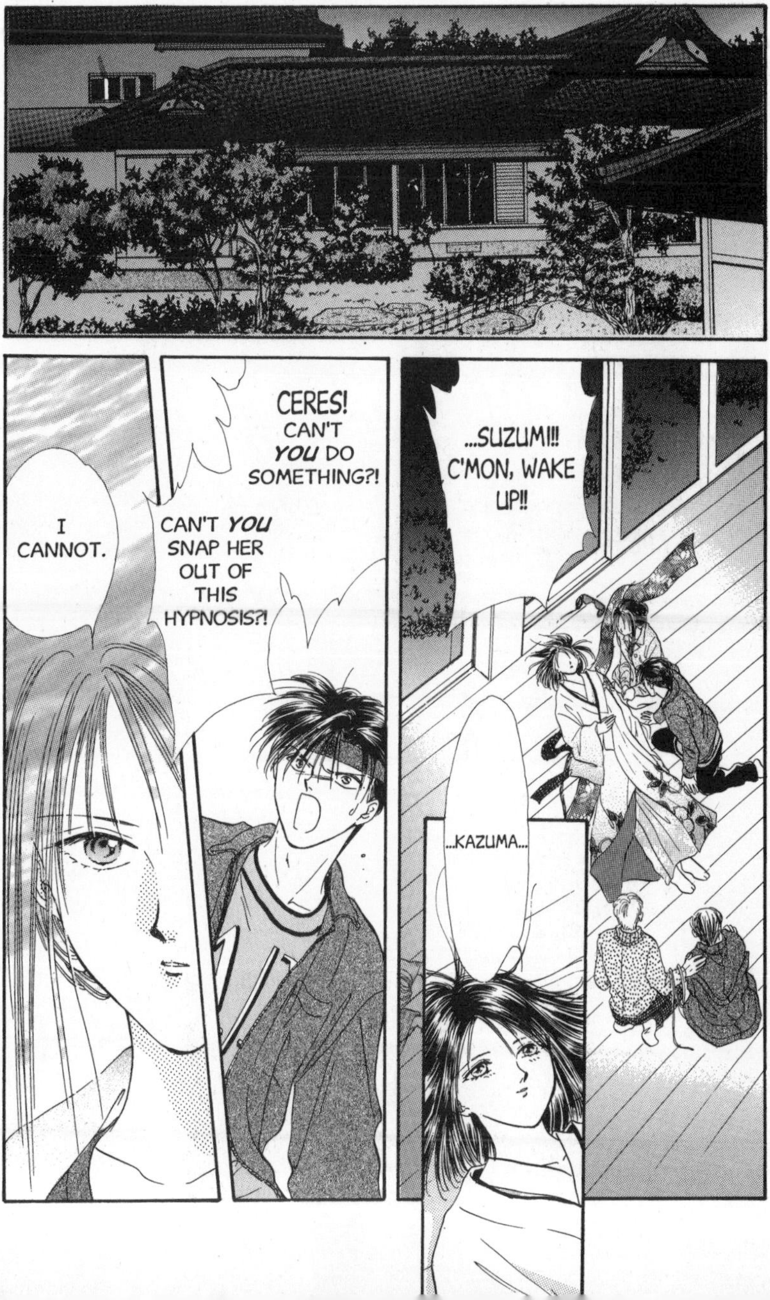
...SUZUMI!! C'MON, WAKE UP!!
...KAZUMA...
CERES! CAN'T *YOU* DO SOMETHING?!
CAN'T *YOU* SNAP HER OUT OF THIS HYPNOSIS?!
I CANNOT.

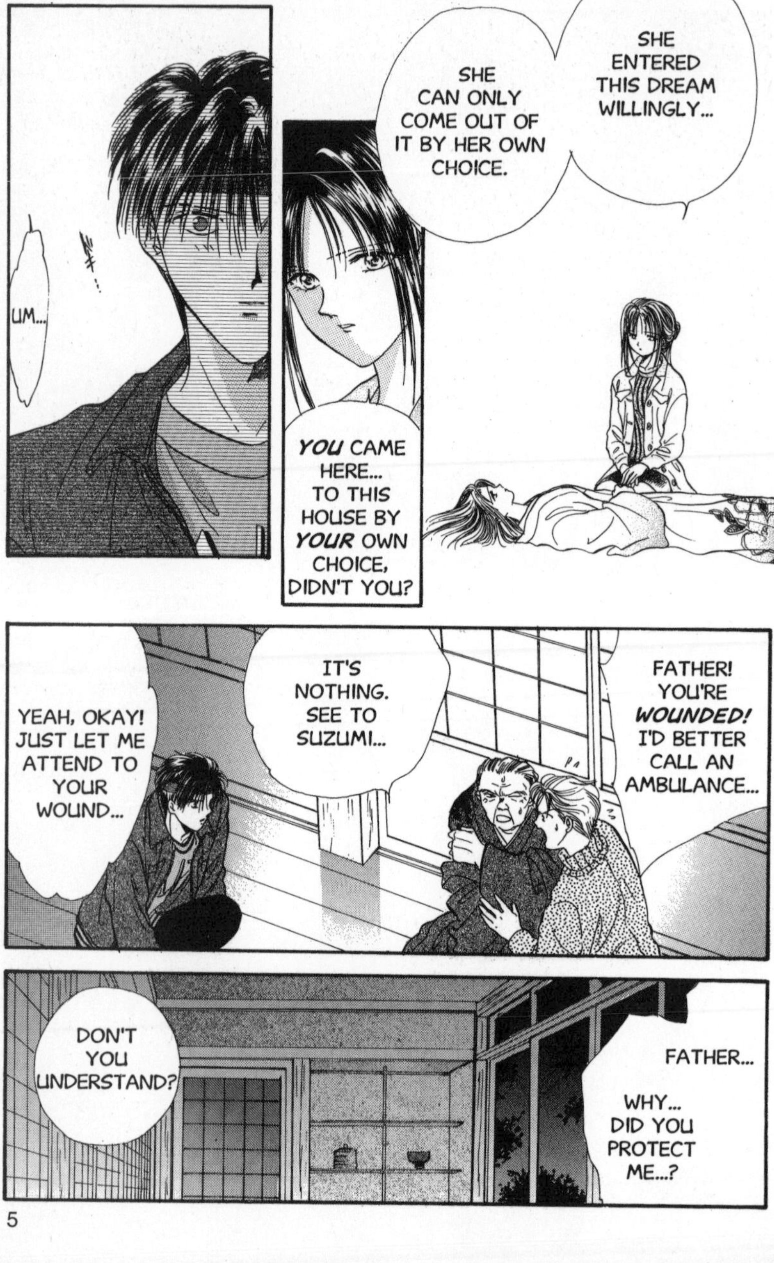
SHE ENTERED THIS DREAM WILLINGLY...
SHE CAN ONLY COME OUT OF IT BY HER OWN CHOICE.
YOU CAME HERE... TO THIS HOUSE BY *YOUR* OWN CHOICE, DIDN'T YOU?
UM...
FATHER! YOU'RE *WOUNDED!* I'D BETTER CALL AN AMBULANCE...
IT'S NOTHING. SEE TO SUZUMI...
YEAH, OKAY! JUST LET ME ATTEND TO YOUR WOUND...
FATHER...
WHY... DID YOU PROTECT ME...?
DON'T YOU UNDERSTAND?

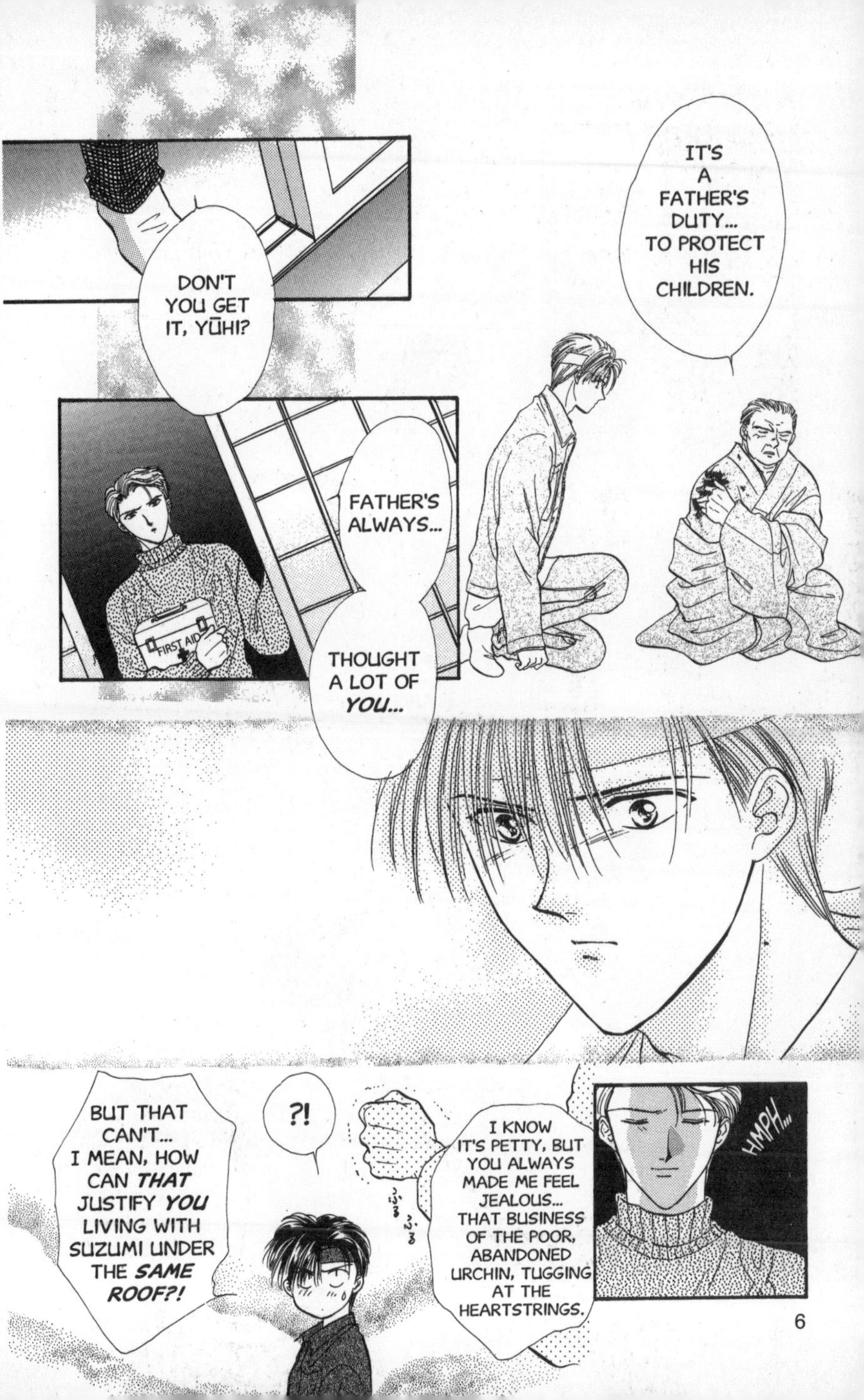
IT'S A FATHER'S DUTY... TO PROTECT HIS CHILDREN.
DON'T YOU GET IT, YŪHI?
FATHER'S ALWAYS...
THOUGHT A LOT OF *YOU*...
HMPH...
I KNOW IT'S PETTY, BUT YOU ALWAYS MADE ME FEEL JEALOUS... THAT BUSINESS OF THE POOR, ABANDONED URCHIN, TUGGING AT THE HEARTSTRINGS.
?!
BUT THAT CAN'T... I MEAN, HOW CAN *THAT* JUSTIFY *YOU* LIVING WITH SUZUMI UNDER THE *SAME* *ROOF*?!

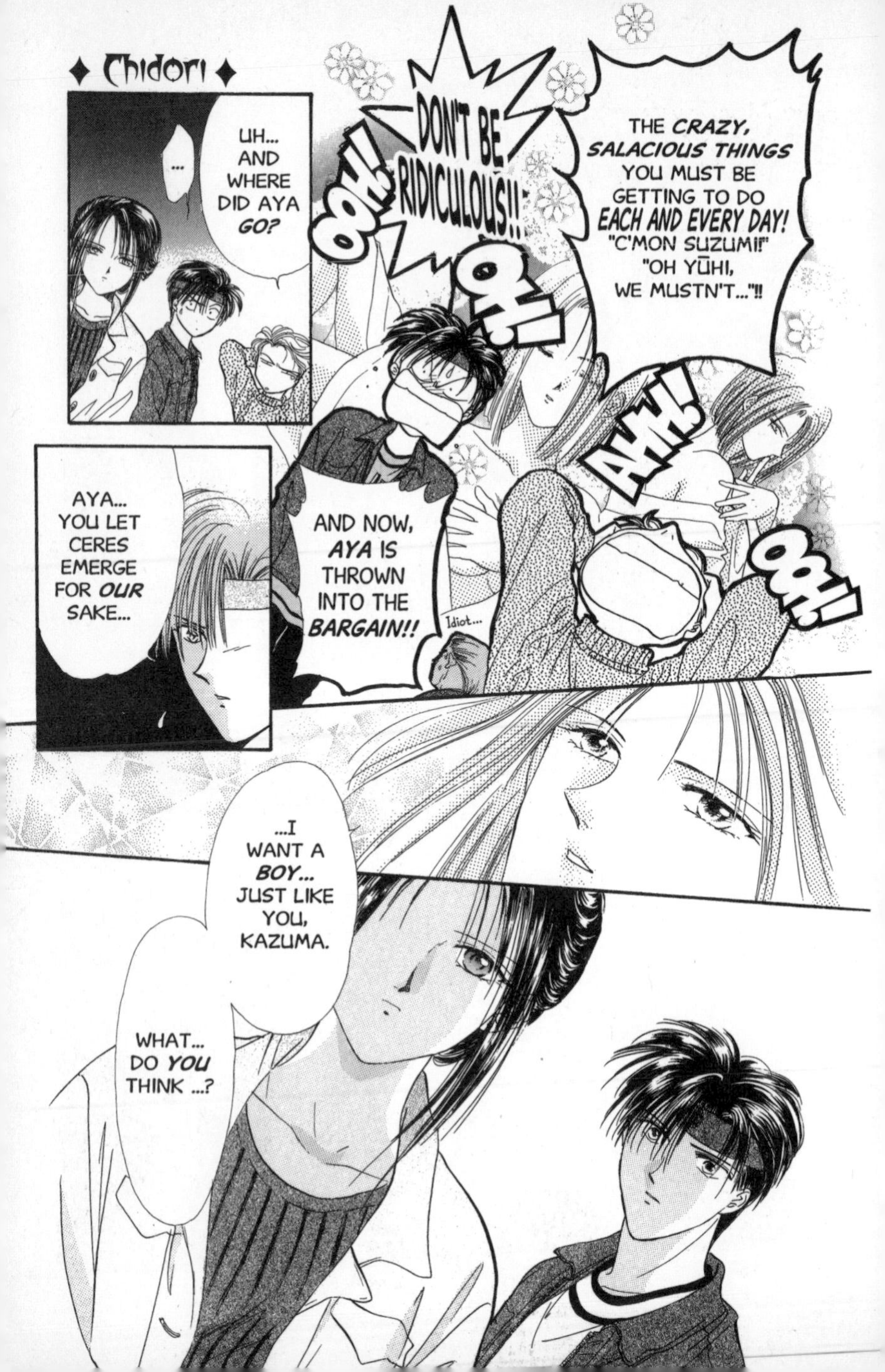
THE CRAZY, SALACIOUS THINGS YOU MUST BE GETTING TO DO EACH AND EVERY DAY! "C'MON SUZUMI!" "OH YŪHI, WE MUSTN'T..."!!
DON'T BE RIDICULOUS!!
OOH!
OH!
AHH!
OOH!
AND NOW, AYA IS THROWN INTO THE BARGAIN!!
Idiot...
UH... AND WHERE DID AYA GO?
...
AYA... YOU LET CERES EMERGE FOR OUR SAKE...
...I WANT A BOY... JUST LIKE YOU, KAZUMA.
WHAT... DO YOU THINK ...?

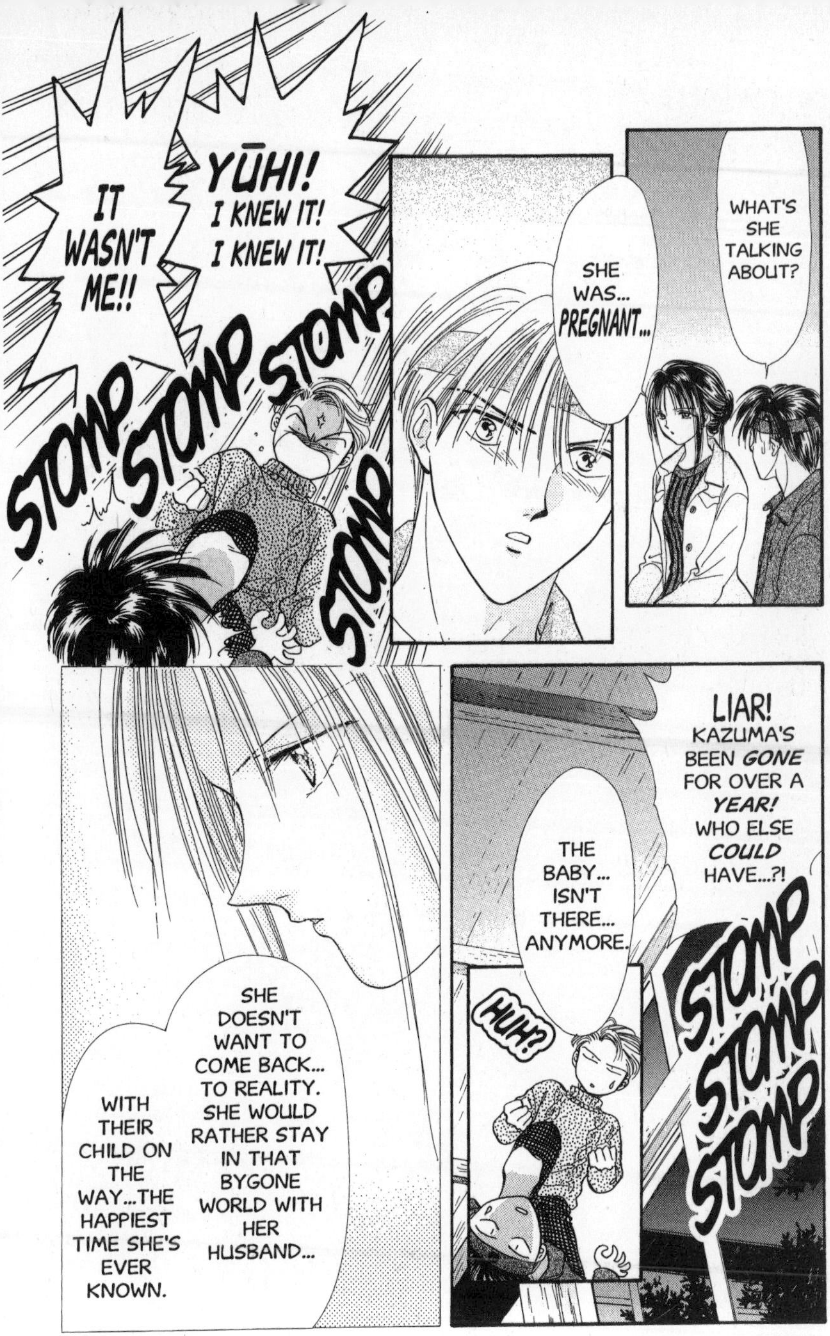
WHAT'S SHE TALKING ABOUT?
SHE WAS... PREGNANT...
YŪHI! I KNEW IT! I KNEW IT!
IT WASN'T ME!!
STOMP STOMP STOMP STOMP
LIAR! KAZUMA'S BEEN GONE FOR OVER A YEAR! WHO ELSE COULD HAVE...?!
THE BABY... ISN'T THERE... ANYMORE.
STOMP STOMP STOMP
HUH?
SHE DOESN'T WANT TO COME BACK... TO REALITY. SHE WOULD RATHER STAY IN THAT BYGONE WORLD WITH HER HUSBAND...
WITH THEIR CHILD ON THE WAY...THE HAPPIEST TIME SHE'S EVER KNOWN.

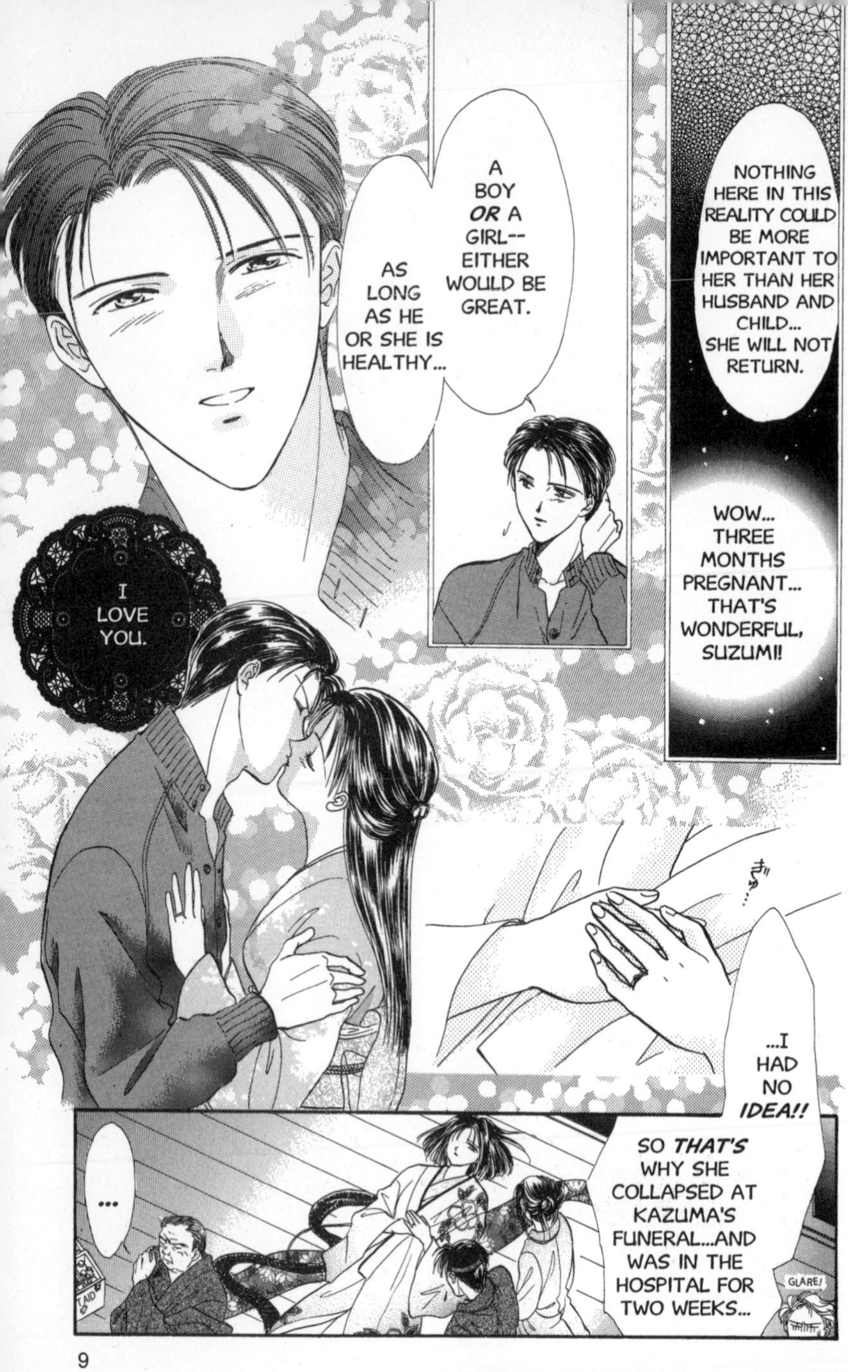
NOTHING HERE IN THIS REALITY COULD BE MORE IMPORTANT TO HER THAN HER HUSBAND AND CHILD... SHE WILL NOT RETURN.
WOW... THREE MONTHS PREGNANT... THAT'S WONDERFUL, SUZUMI!
A BOY *OR* A GIRL-- EITHER WOULD BE GREAT.
AS LONG AS HE OR SHE IS HEALTHY...
I LOVE YOU.
...I HAD NO *IDEA!!*
SO *THAT'S* WHY SHE COLLAPSED AT KAZUMA'S FUNERAL...AND WAS IN THE HOSPITAL FOR TWO WEEKS...
GLARE!
...

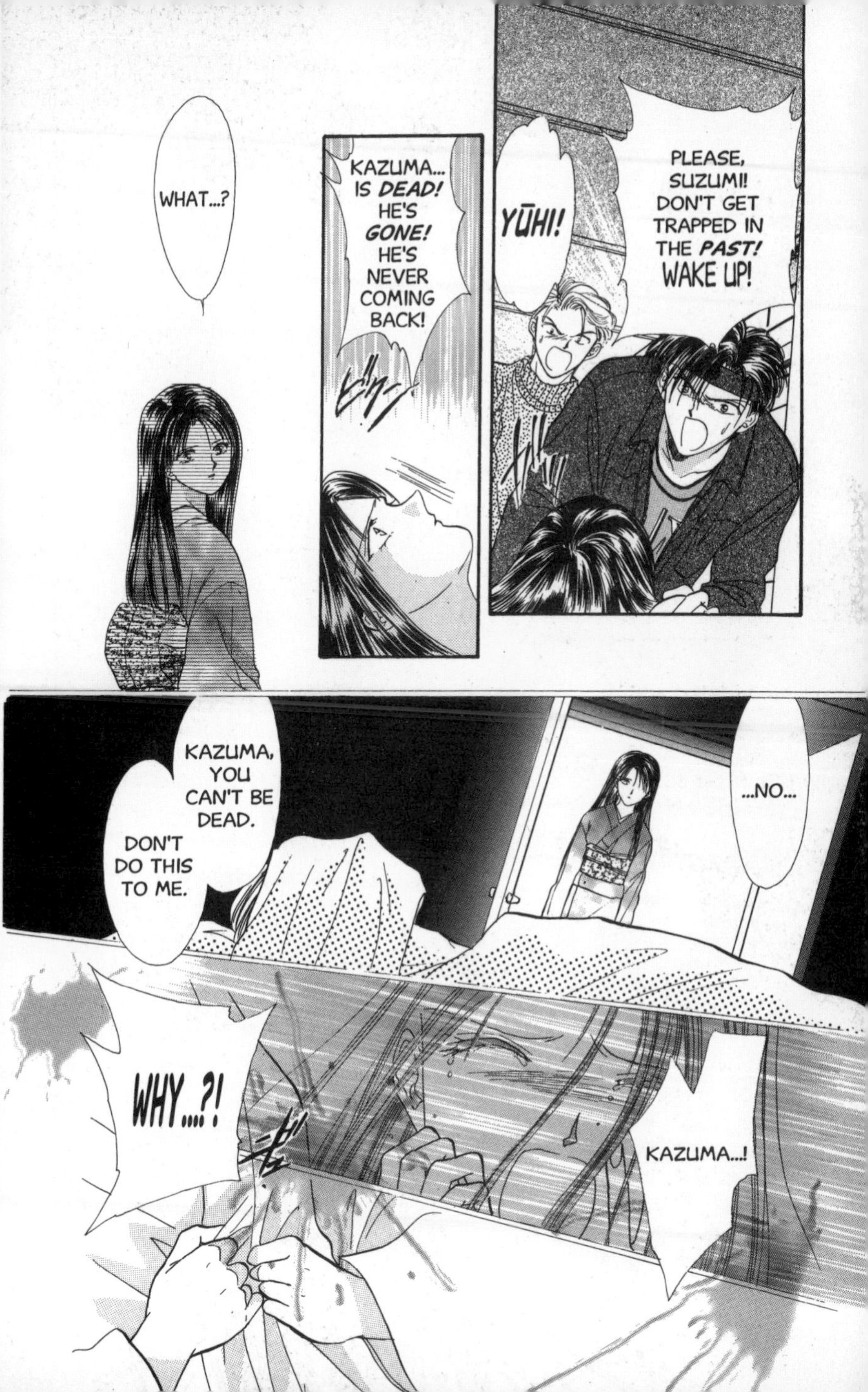
PLEASE, SUZUMI! DON'T GET TRAPPED IN THE *PAST!* WAKE UP!
YŪHI!
KAZUMA... IS *DEAD!* HE'S *GONE!* HE'S NEVER COMING BACK!
WHAT...?
...NO...
KAZUMA, YOU CAN'T BE DEAD.
DON'T DO THIS TO ME.
KAZUMA...!
WHY...?!

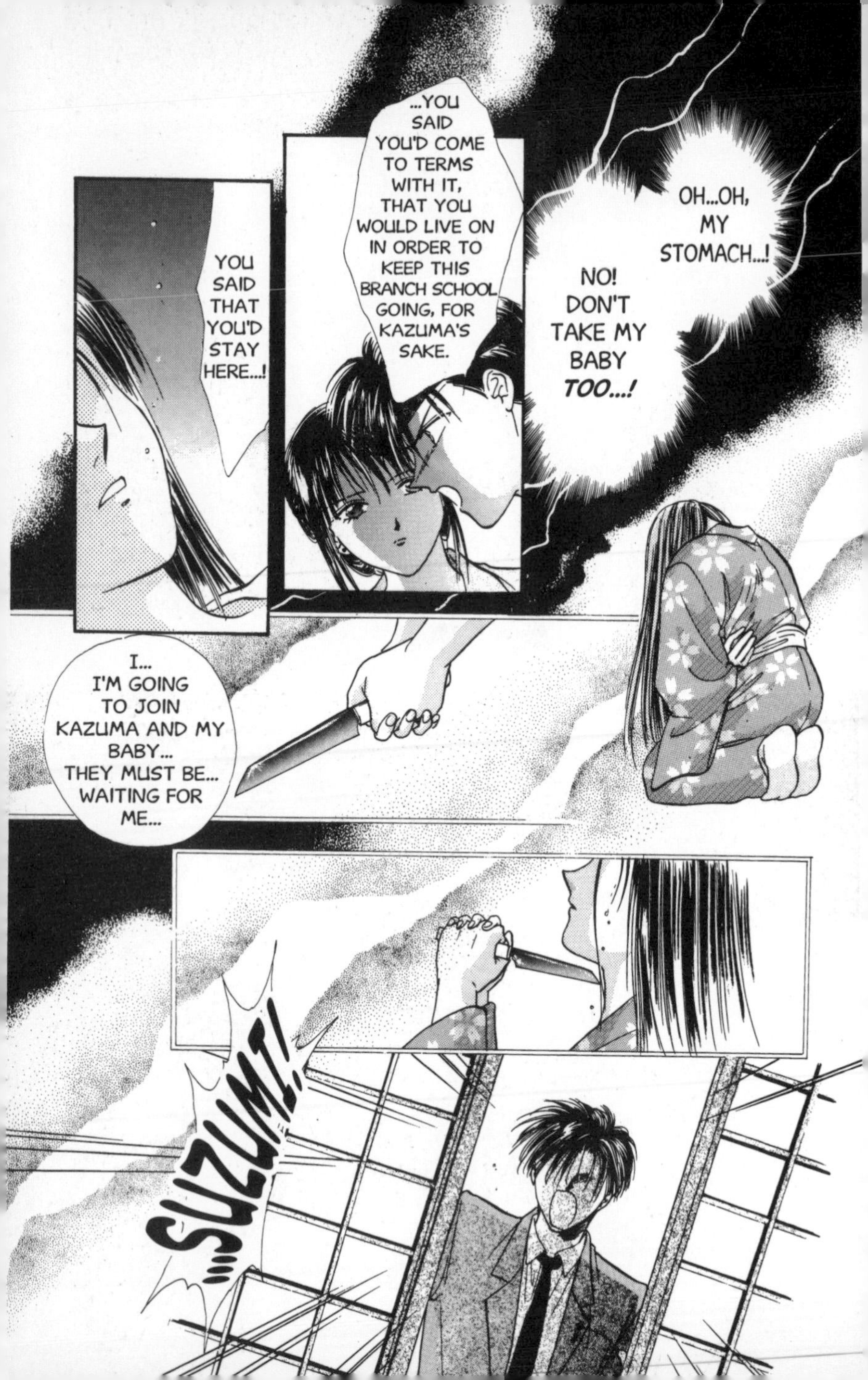
OH...OH, MY STOMACH...!
NO! DON'T TAKE MY BABY TOO...!
...YOU SAID YOU'D COME TO TERMS WITH IT, THAT YOU WOULD LIVE ON IN ORDER TO KEEP THIS BRANCH SCHOOL GOING, FOR KAZUMA'S SAKE.
YOU SAID THAT YOU'D STAY HERE...!
I... I'M GOING TO JOIN KAZUMA AND MY BABY... THEY MUST BE... WAITING FOR ME...
SUZUMI!

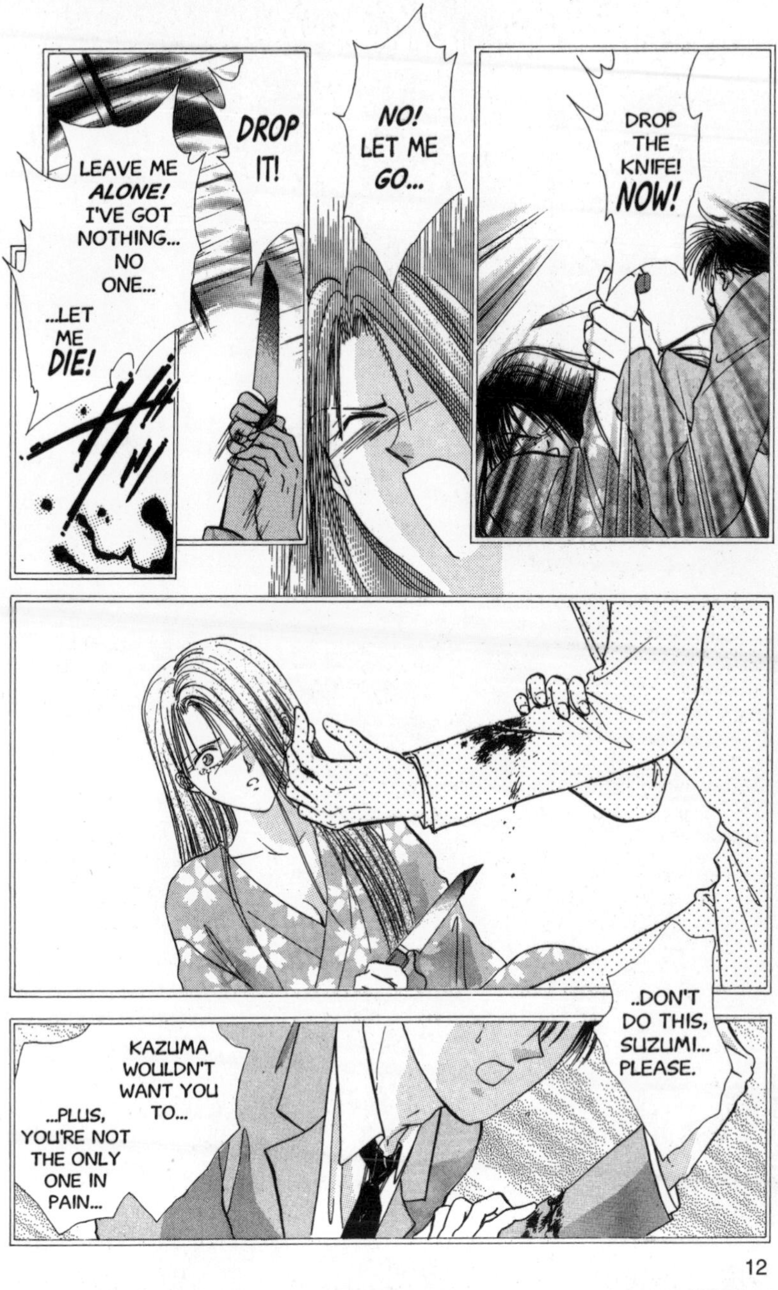
DROP THE KNIFE! NOW!
NO! LET ME GO...
DROP IT!
LEAVE ME ALONE! I'VE GOT NOTHING... NO ONE... ...LET ME DIE!
..DON'T DO THIS, SUZUMI... PLEASE.
KAZUMA WOULDN'T WANT YOU TO...
...PLUS, YOU'RE NOT THE ONLY ONE IN PAIN...

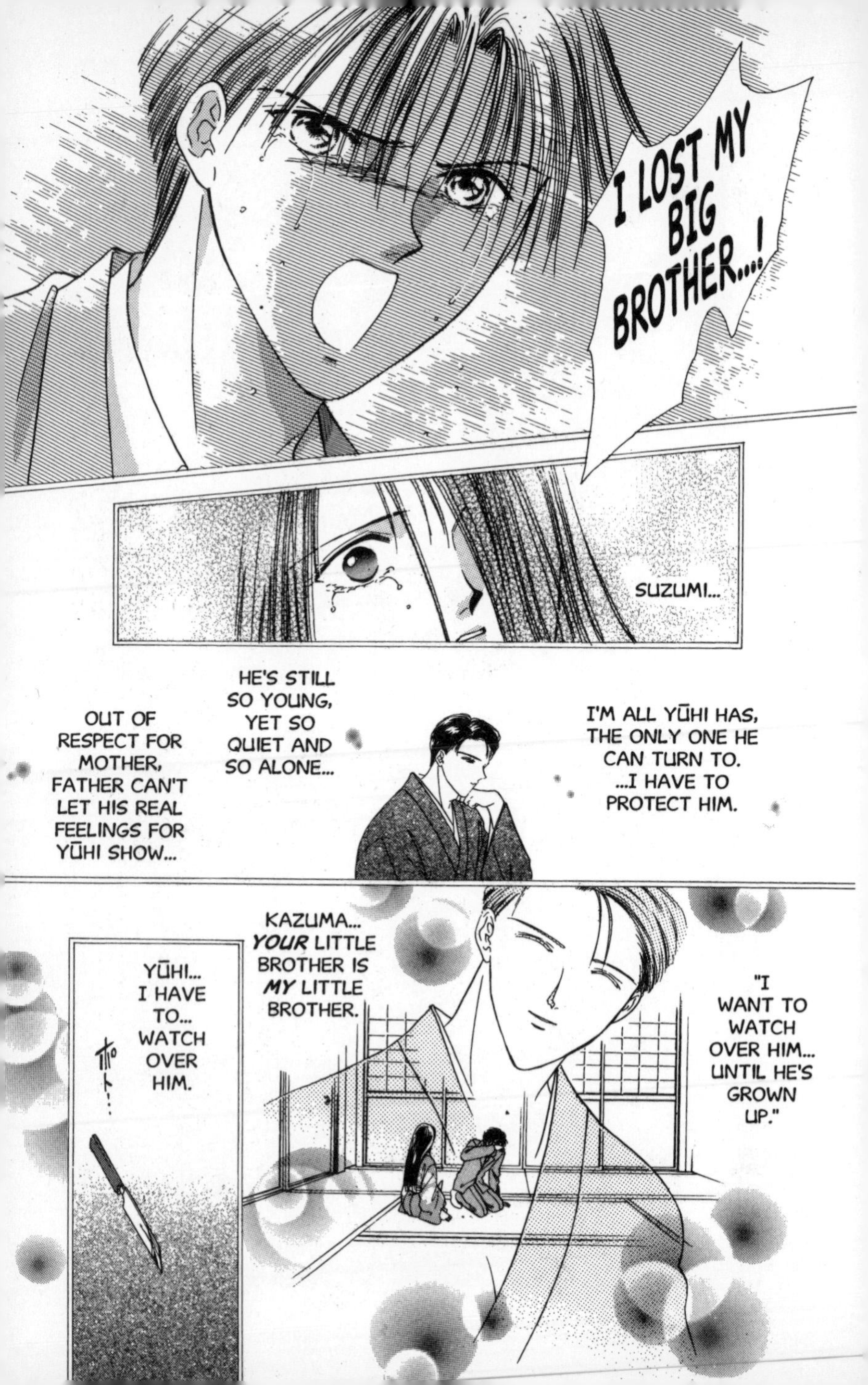

I LOST MY BIG BROTHER...!
SUZUMI...
I'M ALL YŪHI HAS, THE ONLY ONE HE CAN TURN TO. ...I HAVE TO PROTECT HIM.
HE'S STILL SO YOUNG, YET SO QUIET AND SO ALONE...
OUT OF RESPECT FOR MOTHER, FATHER CAN'T LET HIS REAL FEELINGS FOR YŪHI SHOW...
"I WANT TO WATCH OVER HIM... UNTIL HE'S GROWN UP."
KAZUMA... *YOUR* LITTLE BROTHER IS *MY* LITTLE BROTHER.
YŪHI... I HAVE TO... WATCH OVER HIM.
ポト…

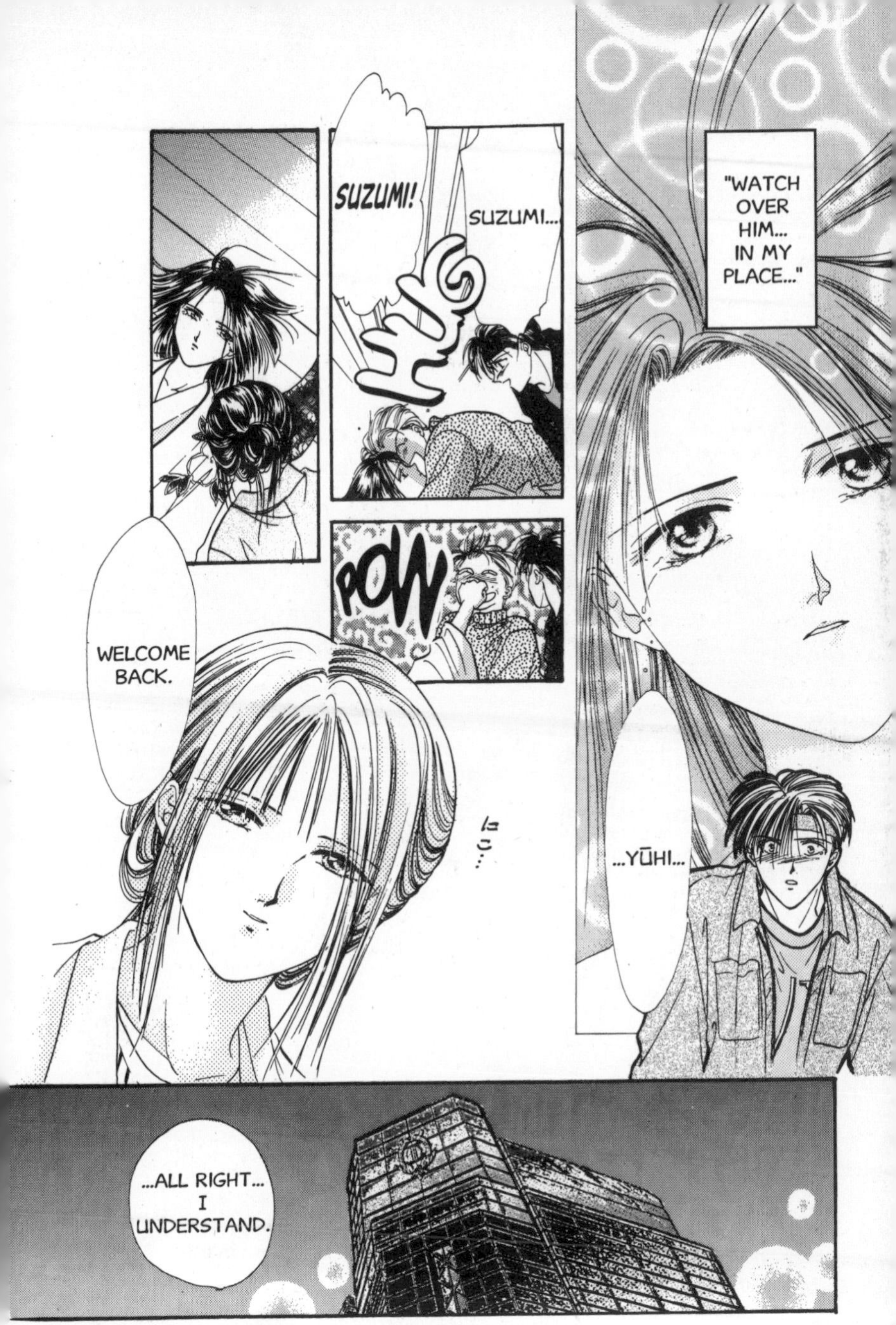
"WATCH OVER HIM... IN MY PLACE..."
...YŪHI...
SUZUMI!
SUZUMI...
POW
WELCOME BACK.
にこ…
...ALL RIGHT... I UNDERSTAND.

Ceres: 4

Hello and welcome to the 4th volume of Ceres! Little by little, I'm giving out hints of foreshadowing here and there, but don't mind them - just keep reading. And while I'm working on this series, some sad incidents have been happening, a child has murdered other children and I feel so bluer than blue... I'm feeling dark blue. So I was talking about it all with my assistants, and our opinion was that "It's unreasonable for adults to try to understand what a child is thinking." People forget as they get older that they had unexpected dark sides to themselves when they were in middle school and high school. That's because as adults we're too concerned with making a living. As I was talking with my assistants about how we ourselves used to think back when we were children, I remembered that I wanted psychic powers. I wanted powers others didn't have that would let me get back at people I didn't like. I wanted to become a completely different person, and I really wished that there could be someone who could truly understand me, even if it were a ghost or goblin. I had totally forgotten about all that. After I realized that psychic powers wouldn't bring me happiness, I turned those ideas into concepts for manga. Maybe that's what it means to grow up? Anyway, now I wonder where all that middle school anger swirling inside me like hot magma came from. Last time, I said, "You should go to school"... but I can say that in retrospect, because I don't have to go to school anymore. I **hated** school. I liked studying -well, I didn't mind it- but the social life just wasn't my thing. Is that just because I don't like to cooperate with others? They do say that people with blood type B aren't the best team players...
Why am I talking about such heavy stuff...?
Well, I'll continue in the next sidebar...

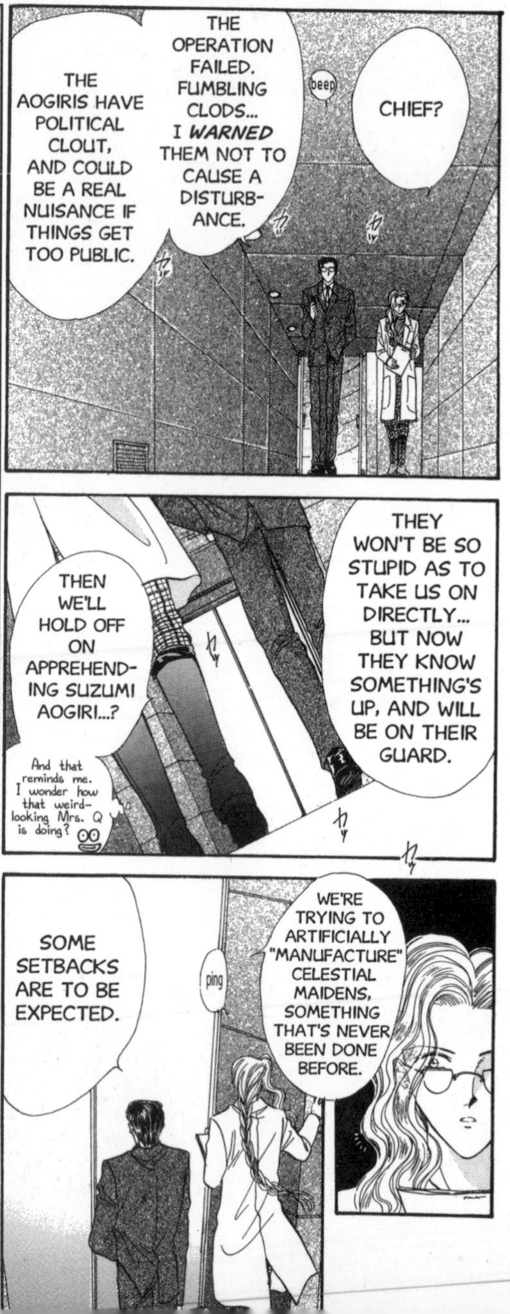
CHIEF?
beep
THE OPERATION FAILED. FUMBLING CLODS... I *WARNED* THEM NOT TO CAUSE A DISTURB-ANCE.
THE AOGIRIS HAVE POLITICAL CLOUT, AND COULD BE A REAL NUISANCE IF THINGS GET TOO PUBLIC.
THEY WON'T BE SO STUPID AS TO TAKE US ON DIRECTLY... BUT NOW THEY KNOW SOMETHING'S UP, AND WILL BE ON THEIR GUARD.
THEN WE'LL HOLD OFF ON APPREHEND-ING SUZUMI AOGIRI...?
And that reminds me. I wonder how that weird-looking Mrs. Q is doing?
WE'RE TRYING TO ARTIFICIALLY "MANUFACTURE" CELESTIAL MAIDENS, SOMETHING THAT'S NEVER BEEN DONE BEFORE.
ping
SOME SETBACKS ARE TO BE EXPECTED.

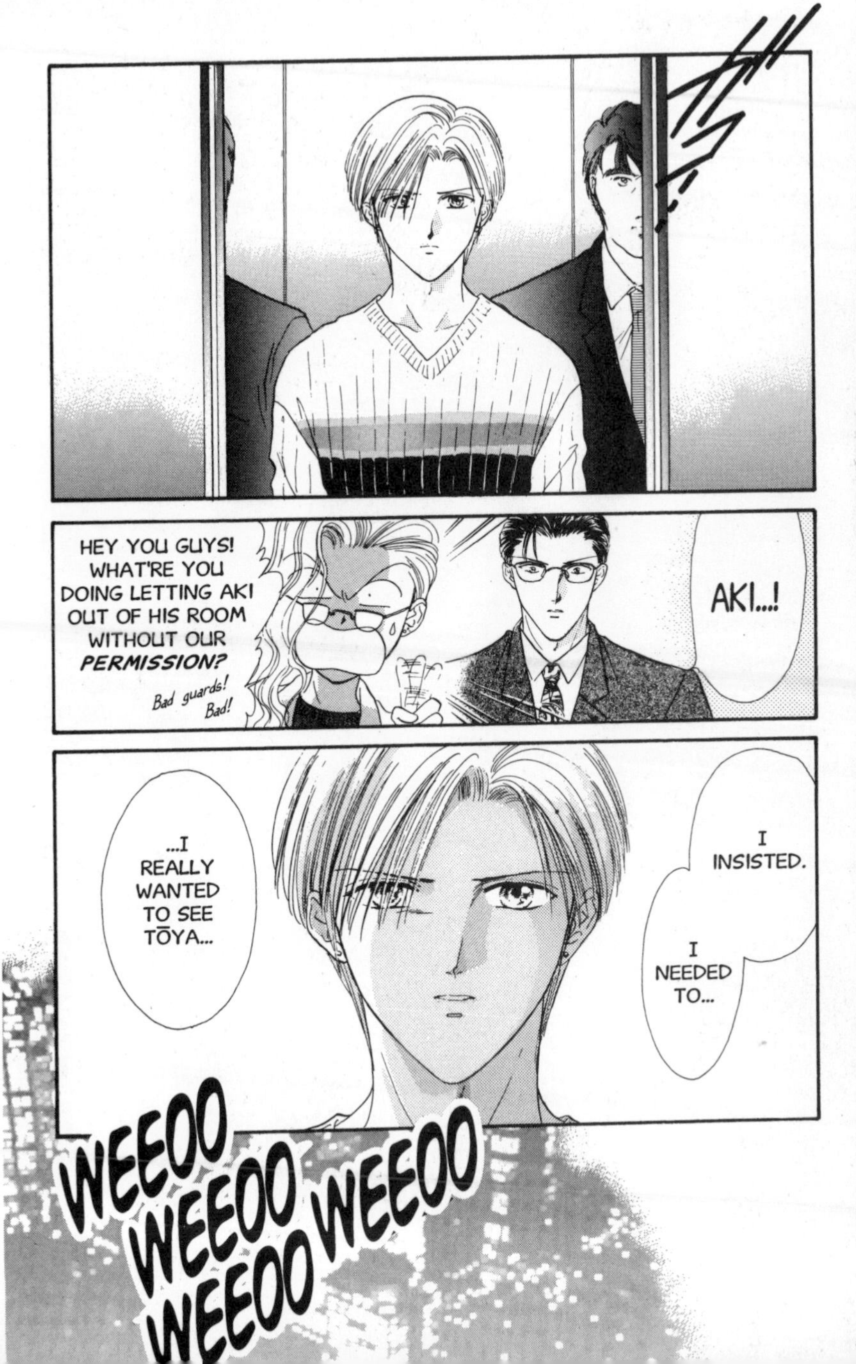
AKI...!
HEY YOU GUYS! WHAT'RE YOU DOING LETTING AKI OUT OF HIS ROOM WITHOUT OUR **PERMISSION?**
Bad guards! Bad!
I INSISTED.
I NEEDED TO...
...I REALLY WANTED TO SEE TŌYA...
WEEOO WEEOO WEEOO WEEOO

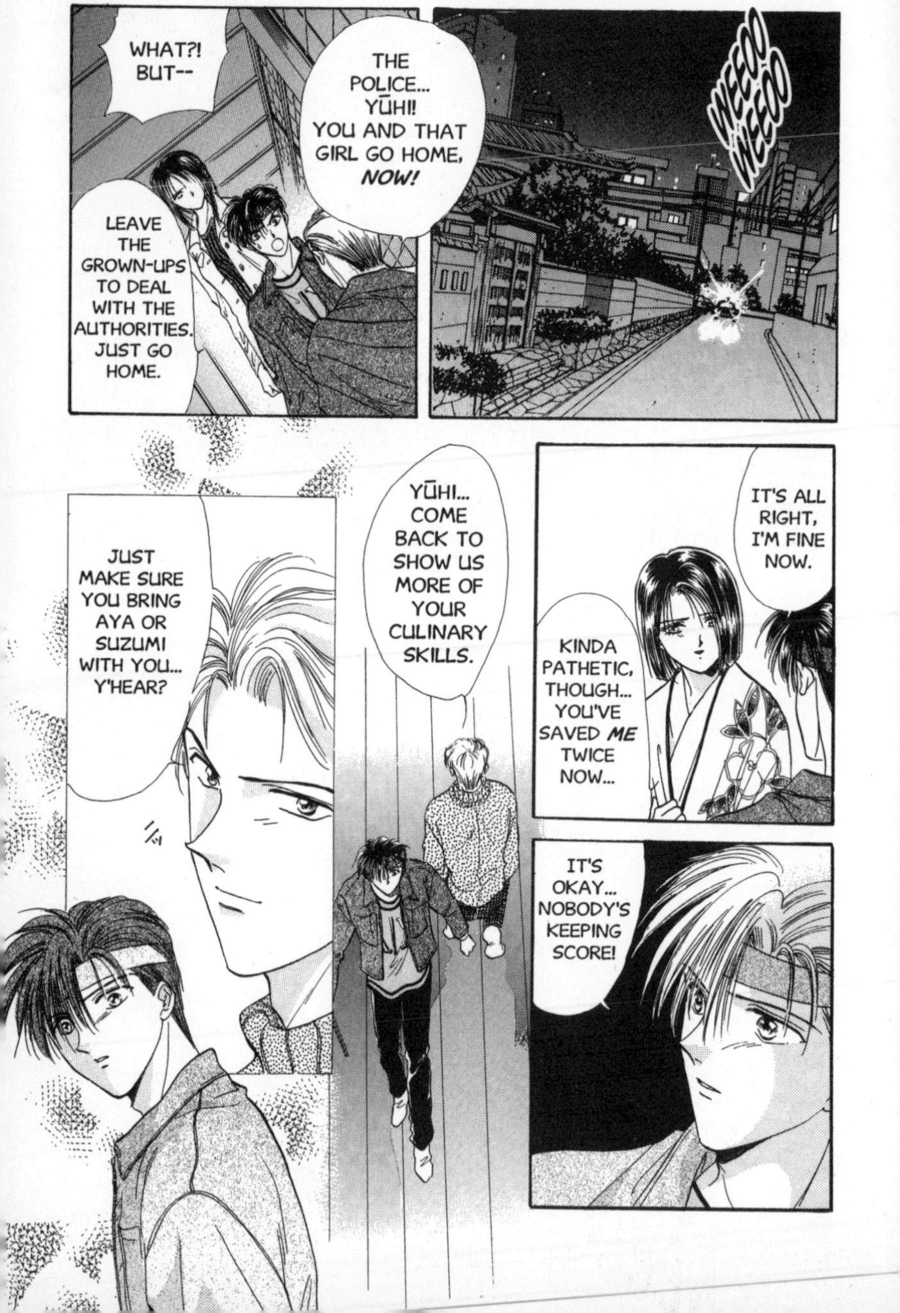
WEEOO WEEOO
THE POLICE... YŪHI! YOU AND THAT GIRL GO HOME, NOW!
WHAT?! BUT--
LEAVE THE GROWN-UPS TO DEAL WITH THE AUTHORITIES. JUST GO HOME.
IT'S ALL RIGHT, I'M FINE NOW.
KINDA PATHETIC, THOUGH... YOU'VE SAVED ME TWICE NOW...
IT'S OKAY... NOBODY'S KEEPING SCORE!
YŪHI... COME BACK TO SHOW US MORE OF YOUR CULINARY SKILLS.
JUST MAKE SURE YOU BRING AYA OR SUZUMI WITH YOU... Y'HEAR?

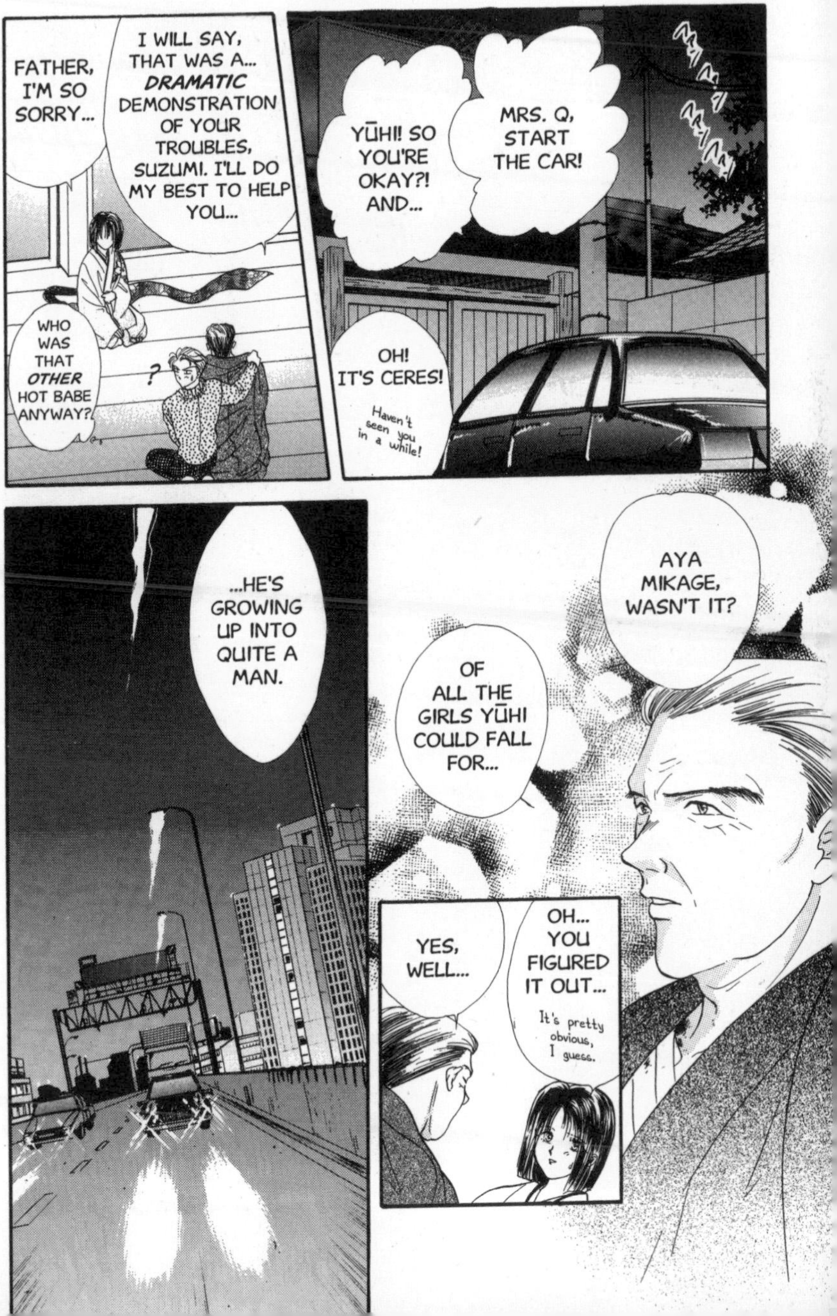
MRS. Q, START THE CAR!
YŪHI! SO YOU'RE OKAY?! AND...
OH! IT'S CERES!
Haven't seen you in a while!
I WILL SAY, THAT WAS A... *DRAMATIC* DEMONSTRATION OF YOUR TROUBLES, SUZUMI. I'LL DO MY BEST TO HELP YOU...
FATHER, I'M SO SORRY...
WHO WAS THAT *OTHER* HOT BABE ANYWAY?
AYA MIKAGE, WASN'T IT?
OF ALL THE GIRLS YŪHI COULD FALL FOR...
OH... YOU FIGURED IT OUT...
It's pretty obvious, I guess.
YES, WELL...
...HE'S GROWING UP INTO QUITE A MAN.

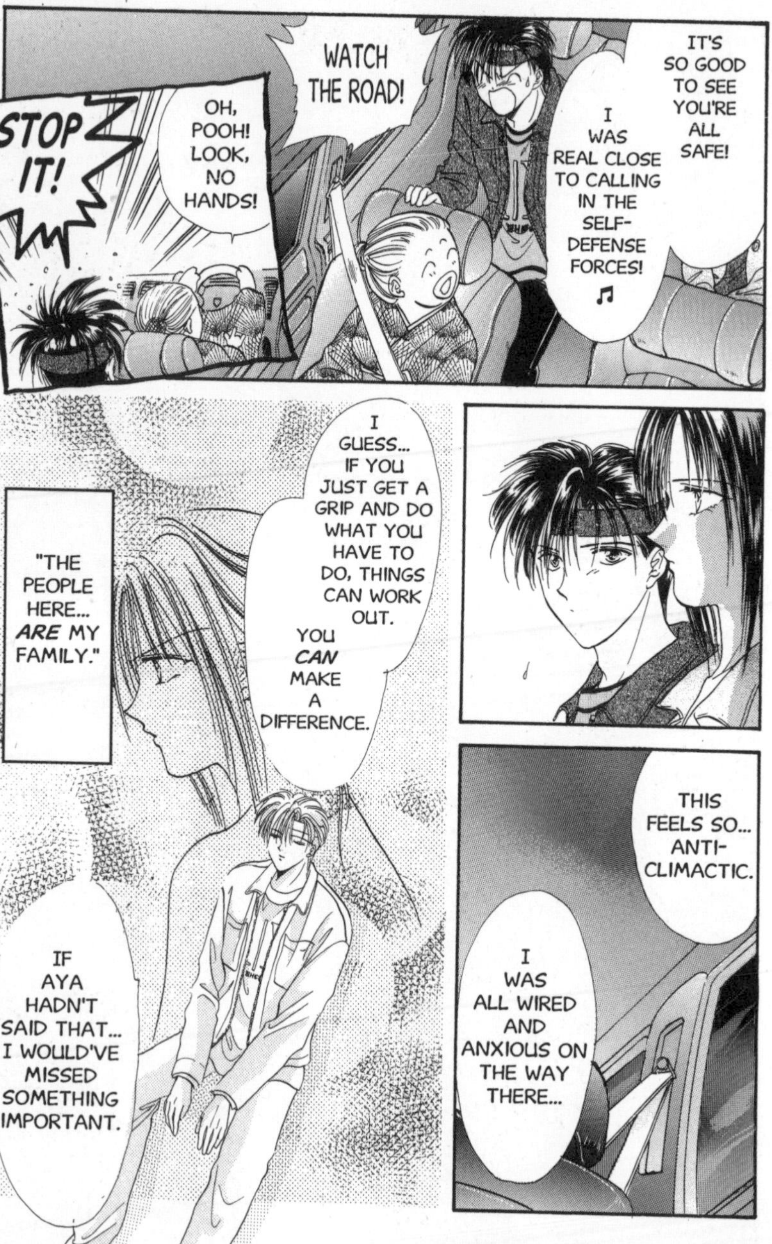
IT'S SO GOOD TO SEE YOU'RE ALL SAFE!
I WAS REAL CLOSE TO CALLING IN THE SELF-DEFENSE FORCES! ♪
WATCH THE ROAD!
OH, POOH! LOOK, NO HANDS!
STOP IT!
THIS FEELS SO... ANTI-CLIMACTIC.
I WAS ALL WIRED AND ANXIOUS ON THE WAY THERE...
I GUESS... IF YOU JUST GET A GRIP AND DO WHAT YOU HAVE TO DO, THINGS CAN WORK OUT.
YOU *CAN* MAKE A DIFFERENCE.
"THE PEOPLE HERE... *ARE* MY FAMILY."
IF AYA HADN'T SAID THAT... I WOULD'VE MISSED SOMETHING IMPORTANT.

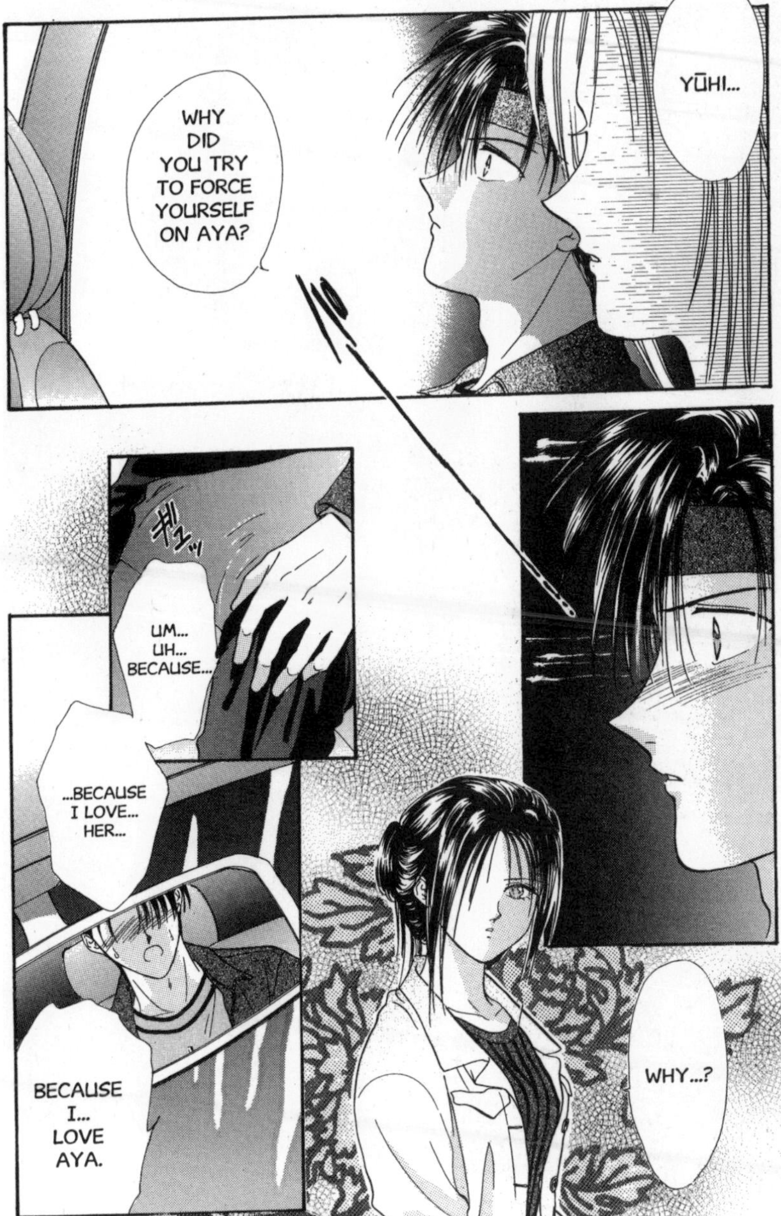
YŪHI...
WHY DID YOU TRY TO FORCE YOURSELF ON AYA?
ギュッ
UM... UH... BECAUSE...
...BECAUSE I LOVE... HER...
BECAUSE I... LOVE AYA.
WHY...?

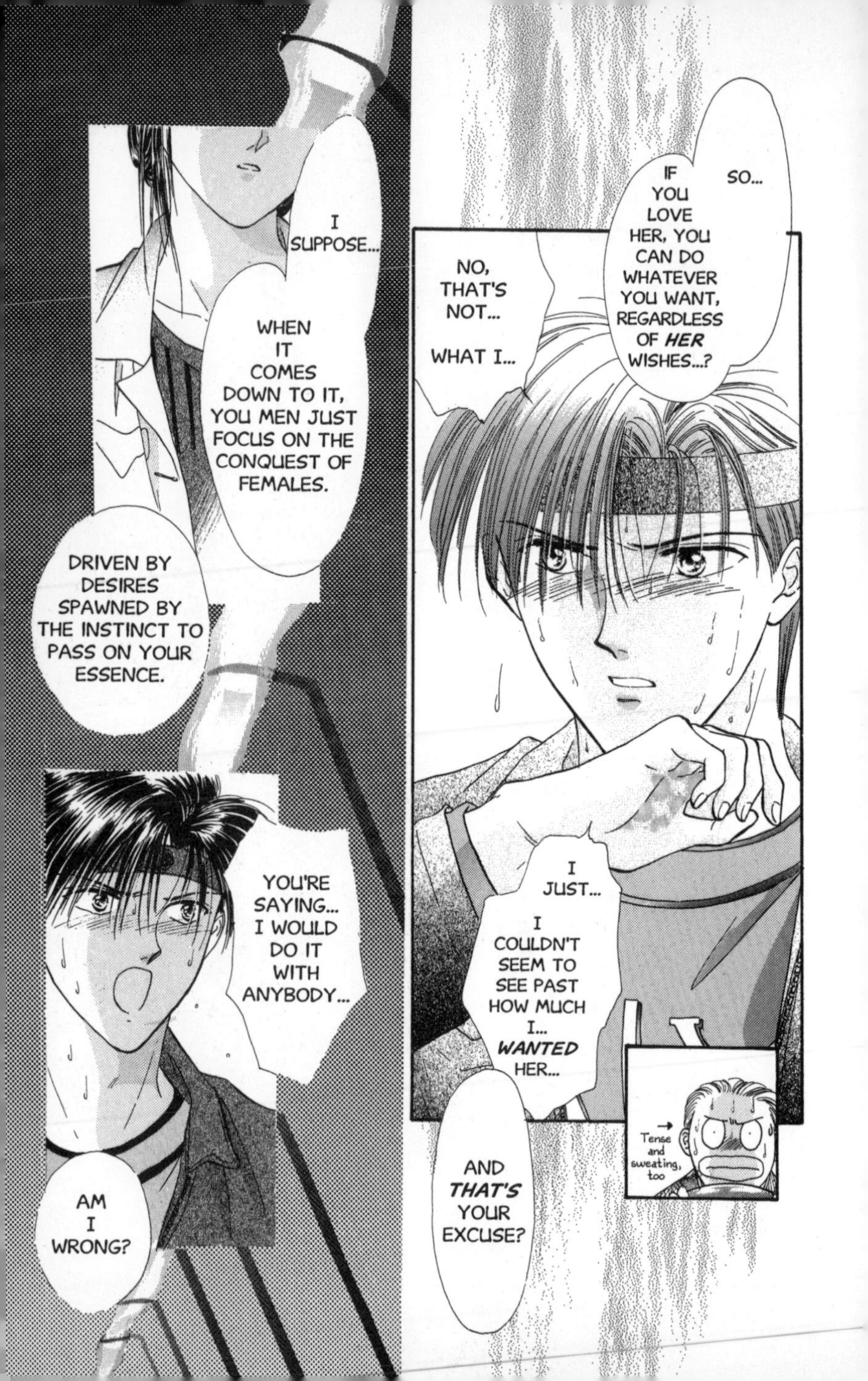
I SUPPOSE...
WHEN IT COMES DOWN TO IT, YOU MEN JUST FOCUS ON THE CONQUEST OF FEMALES.
DRIVEN BY DESIRES SPAWNED BY THE INSTINCT TO PASS ON YOUR ESSENCE.
YOU'RE SAYING... I WOULD DO IT WITH ANYBODY...
AM I WRONG?
SO... IF YOU LOVE HER, YOU CAN DO WHATEVER YOU WANT, REGARDLESS OF *HER* WISHES...?
NO, THAT'S NOT... WHAT I...
I JUST... I COULDN'T SEEM TO SEE PAST HOW MUCH I... *WANTED* HER...
AND *THAT'S* YOUR EXCUSE?
Tense and sweating, too

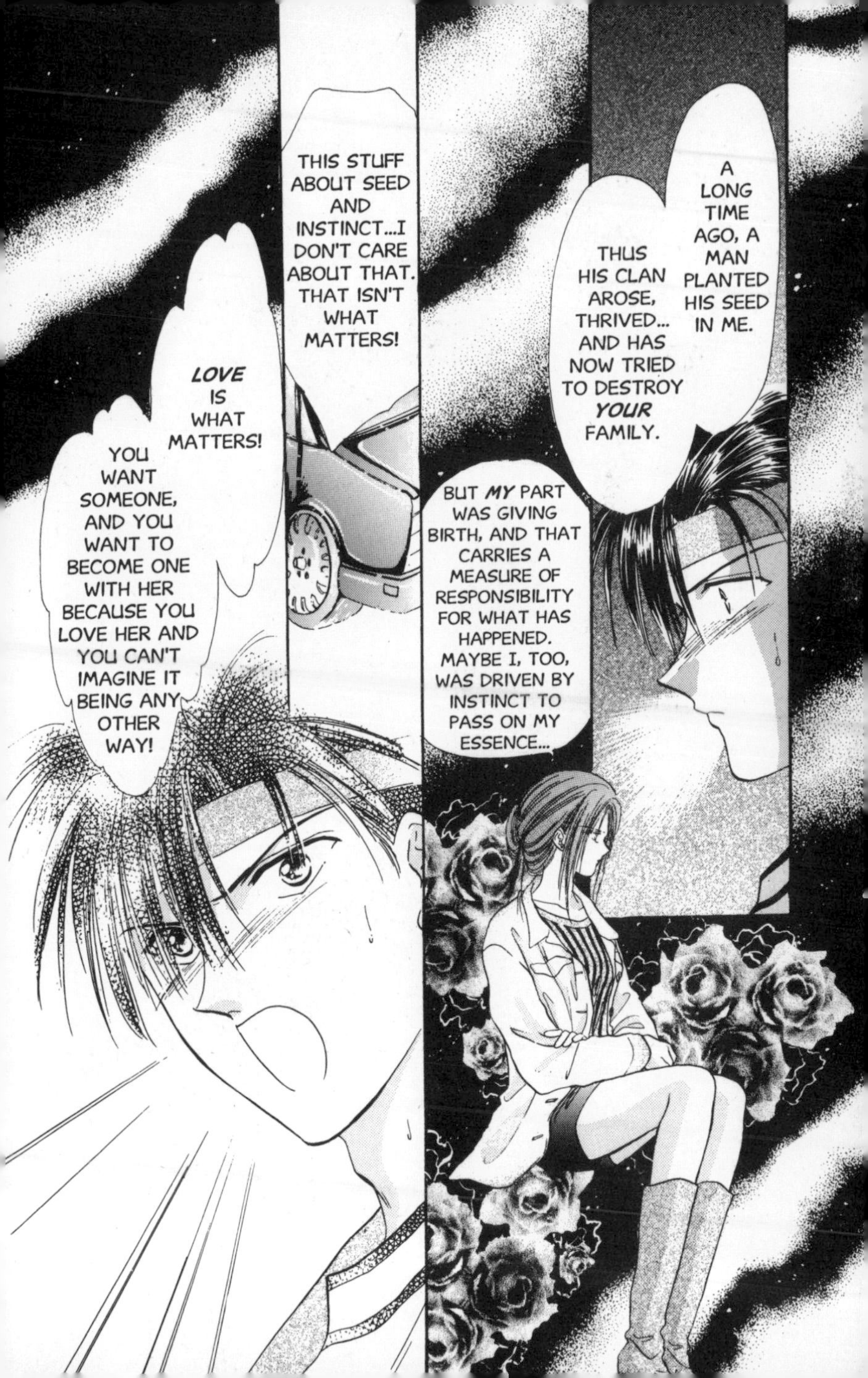
A LONG TIME AGO, A MAN PLANTED HIS SEED IN ME.
THUS HIS CLAN AROSE, THRIVED... AND HAS NOW TRIED TO DESTROY *YOUR* FAMILY.
BUT *MY* PART WAS GIVING BIRTH, AND THAT CARRIES A MEASURE OF RESPONSIBILITY FOR WHAT HAS HAPPENED. MAYBE I, TOO, WAS DRIVEN BY INSTINCT TO PASS ON MY ESSENCE...
THIS STUFF ABOUT SEED AND INSTINCT...I DON'T CARE ABOUT THAT. THAT ISN'T WHAT MATTERS!
LOVE IS WHAT MATTERS!
YOU WANT SOMEONE, AND YOU WANT TO BECOME ONE WITH HER BECAUSE YOU LOVE HER AND YOU CAN'T IMAGINE IT BEING ANY OTHER WAY!

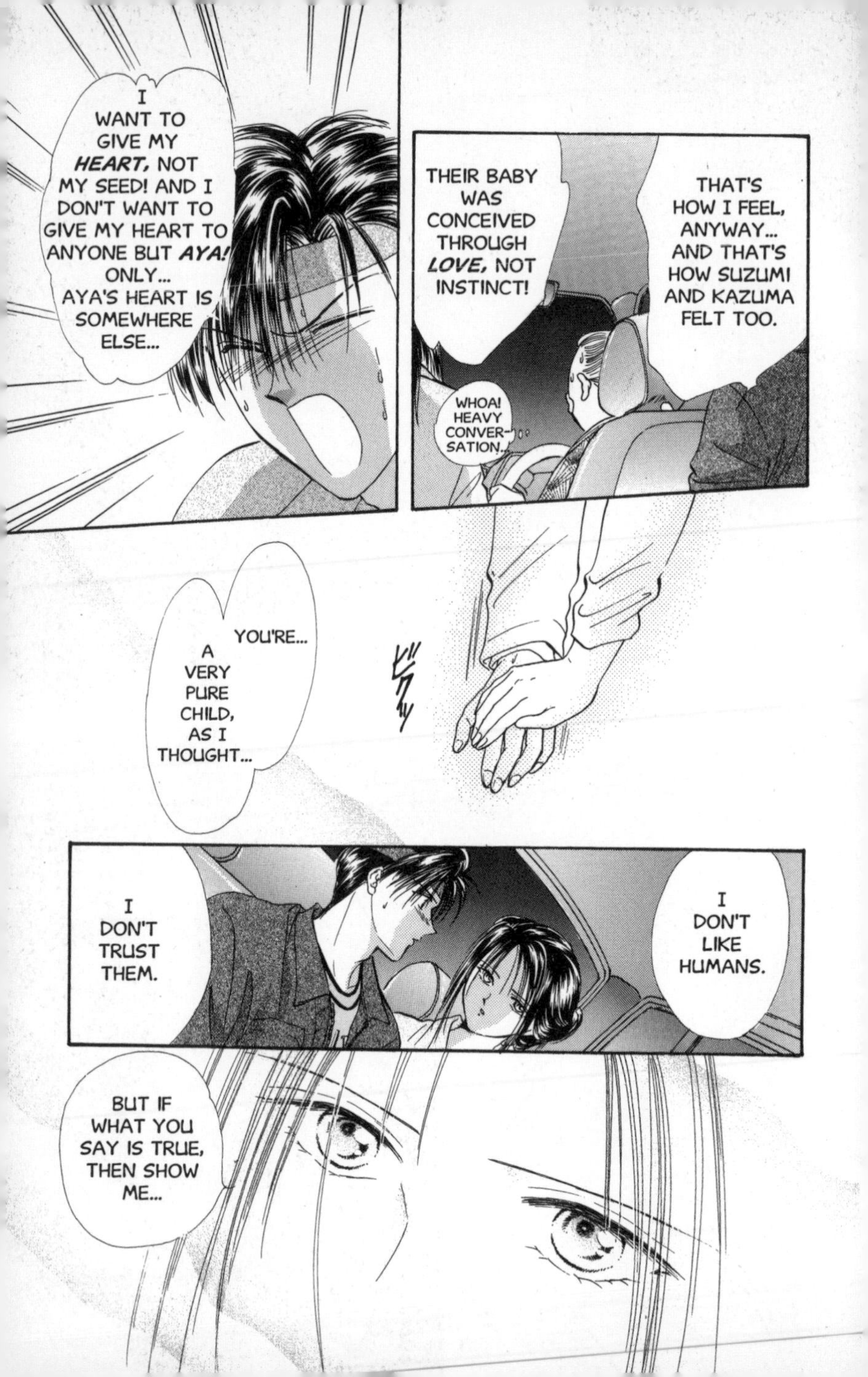
THEIR BABY WAS CONCEIVED THROUGH *LOVE,* NOT INSTINCT!
THAT'S HOW I FEEL, ANYWAY... AND THAT'S HOW SUZUMI AND KAZUMA FELT TOO.
WHOA! HEAVY CONVER-SATION...
I WANT TO GIVE MY *HEART,* NOT MY SEED! AND I DON'T WANT TO GIVE MY HEART TO ANYONE BUT *AYA!* ONLY... AYA'S HEART IS SOMEWHERE ELSE...
ビクッ
YOU'RE... A VERY PURE CHILD, AS I THOUGHT...
I DON'T LIKE HUMANS.
I DON'T TRUST THEM.
BUT IF WHAT YOU SAY IS TRUE, THEN SHOW ME...

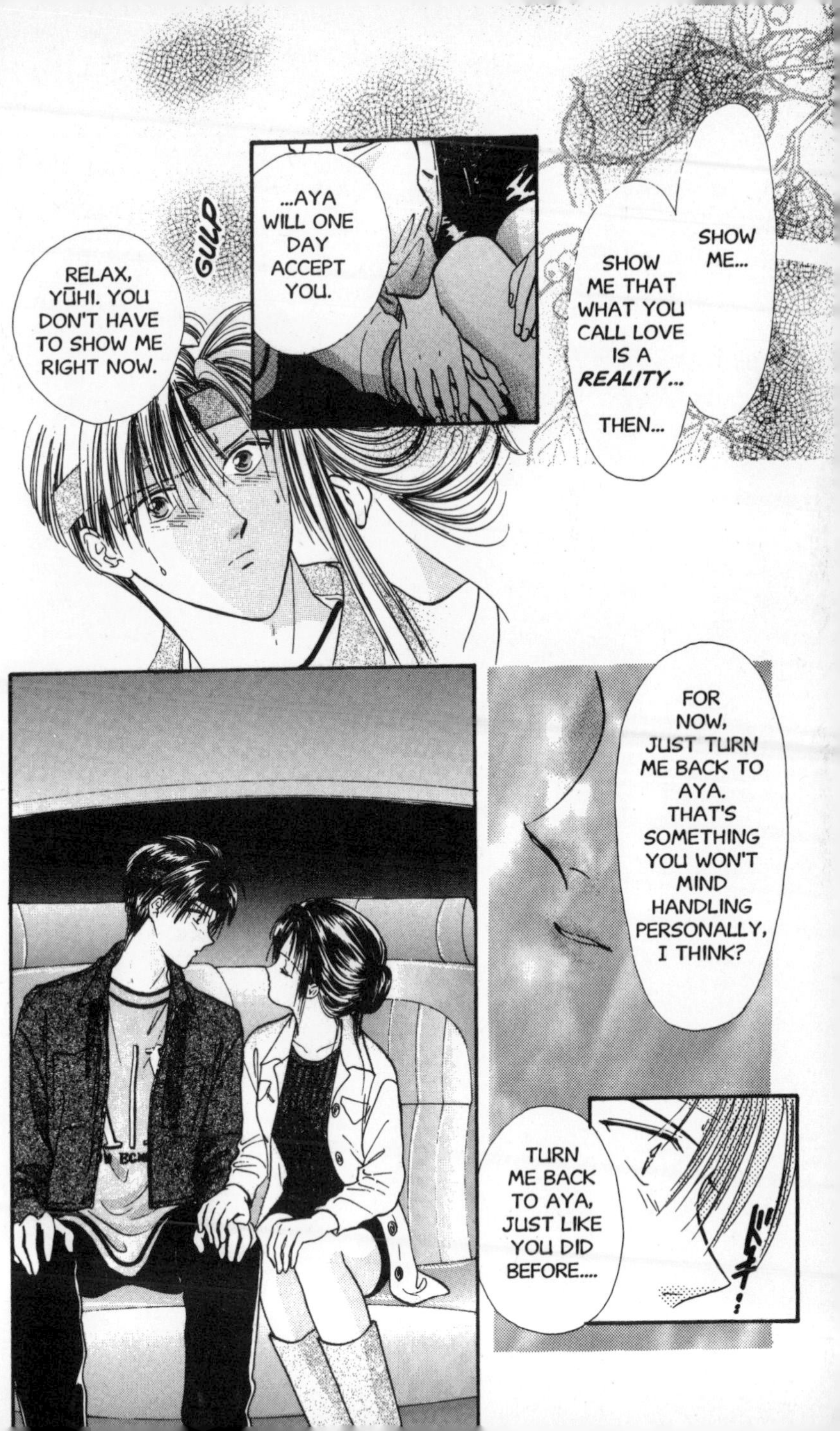
SHOW ME...
SHOW ME THAT WHAT YOU CALL LOVE IS A *REALITY*...
THEN...
...AYA WILL ONE DAY ACCEPT YOU.
GULP
RELAX, YŪHI. YOU DON'T HAVE TO SHOW ME RIGHT NOW.
FOR NOW, JUST TURN ME BACK TO AYA. THAT'S SOMETHING YOU WON'T MIND HANDLING PERSONALLY, I THINK?
TURN ME BACK TO AYA, JUST LIKE YOU DID BEFORE....

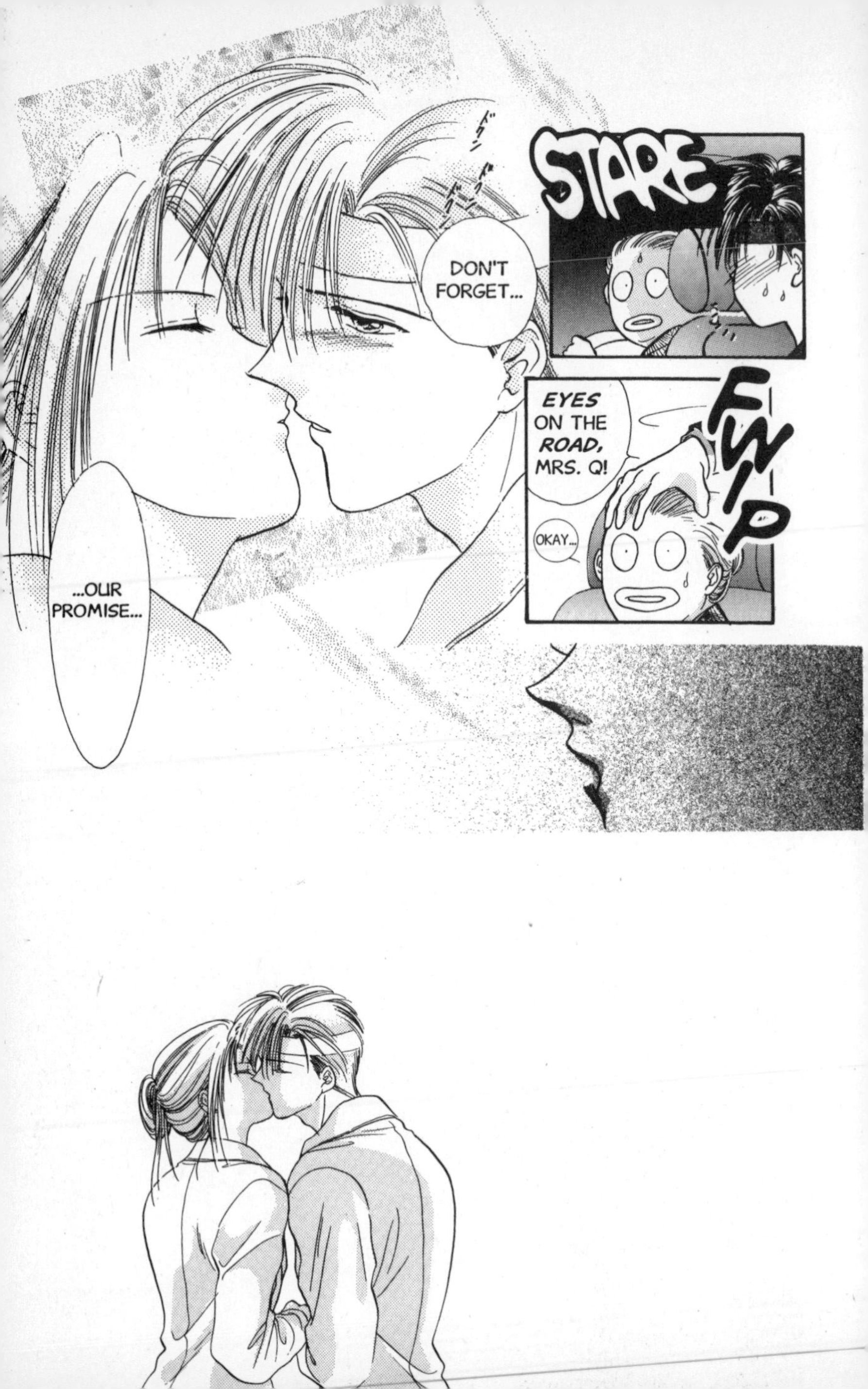
STARE
EYES ON THE ROAD, MRS. Q!
FWIP
OKAY...
DON'T FORGET...
...OUR PROMISE...

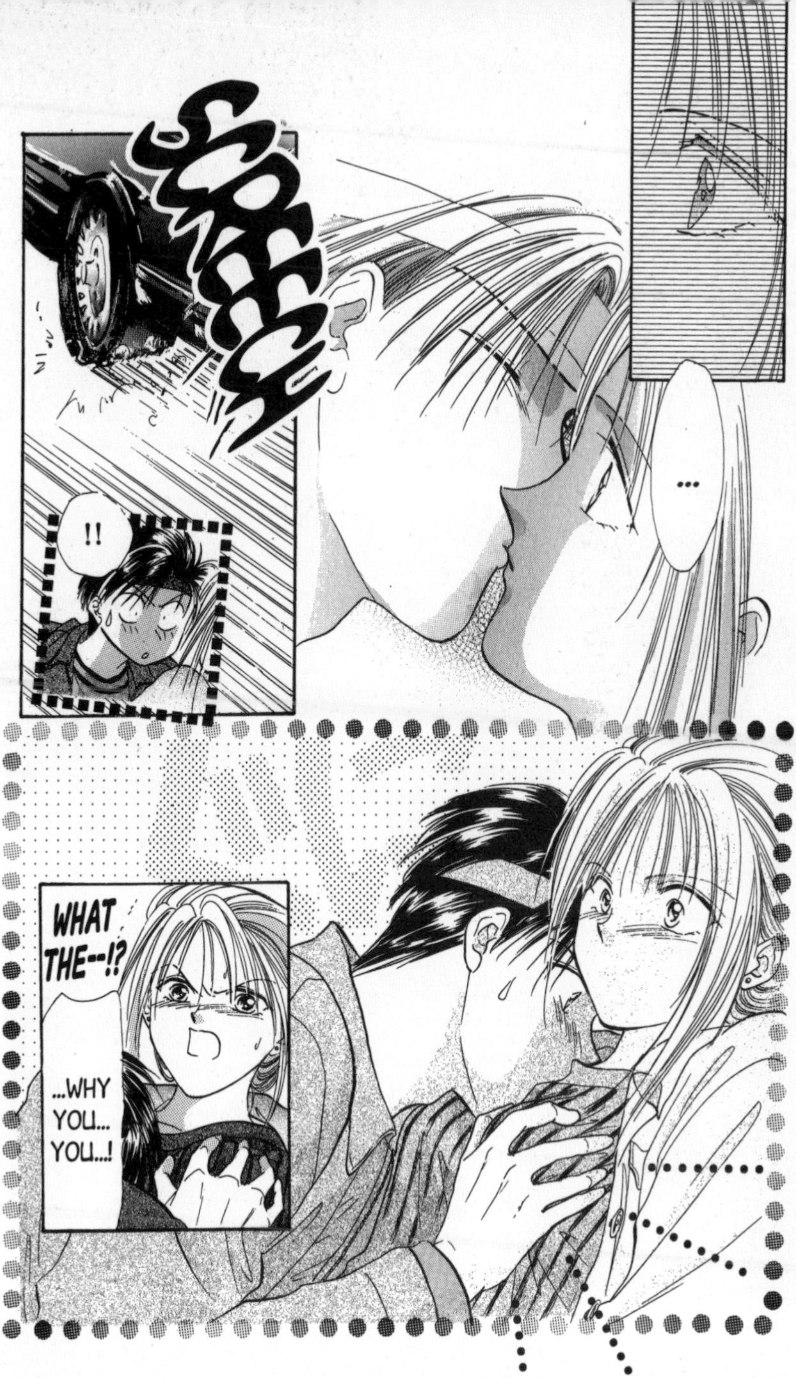
...
SCREECH
!!
WHAT THE--!?
...WHY YOU... YOU...!

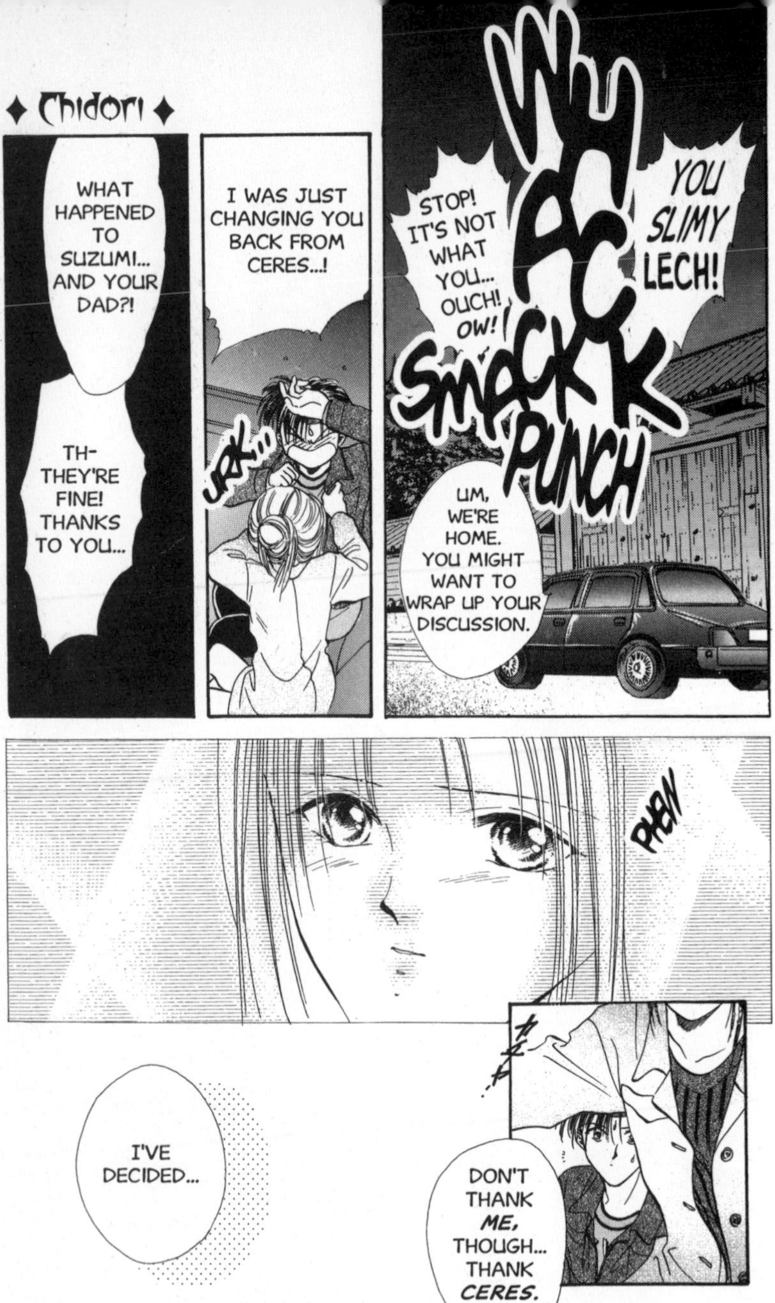
WHACK
YOU SLIMY LECH!
STOP! IT'S NOT WHAT YOU... OUCH! OW!
SMACK
PUNCH
UM, WE'RE HOME. YOU MIGHT WANT TO WRAP UP YOUR DISCUSSION.
I WAS JUST CHANGING YOU BACK FROM CERES...!
JRK...
WHAT HAPPENED TO SUZUMI... AND YOUR DADA?!
TH-THEY'RE FINE! THANKS TO YOU...
PHEW
DON'T THANK *ME,* THOUGH... THANK *CERES.*
I'VE DECIDED...

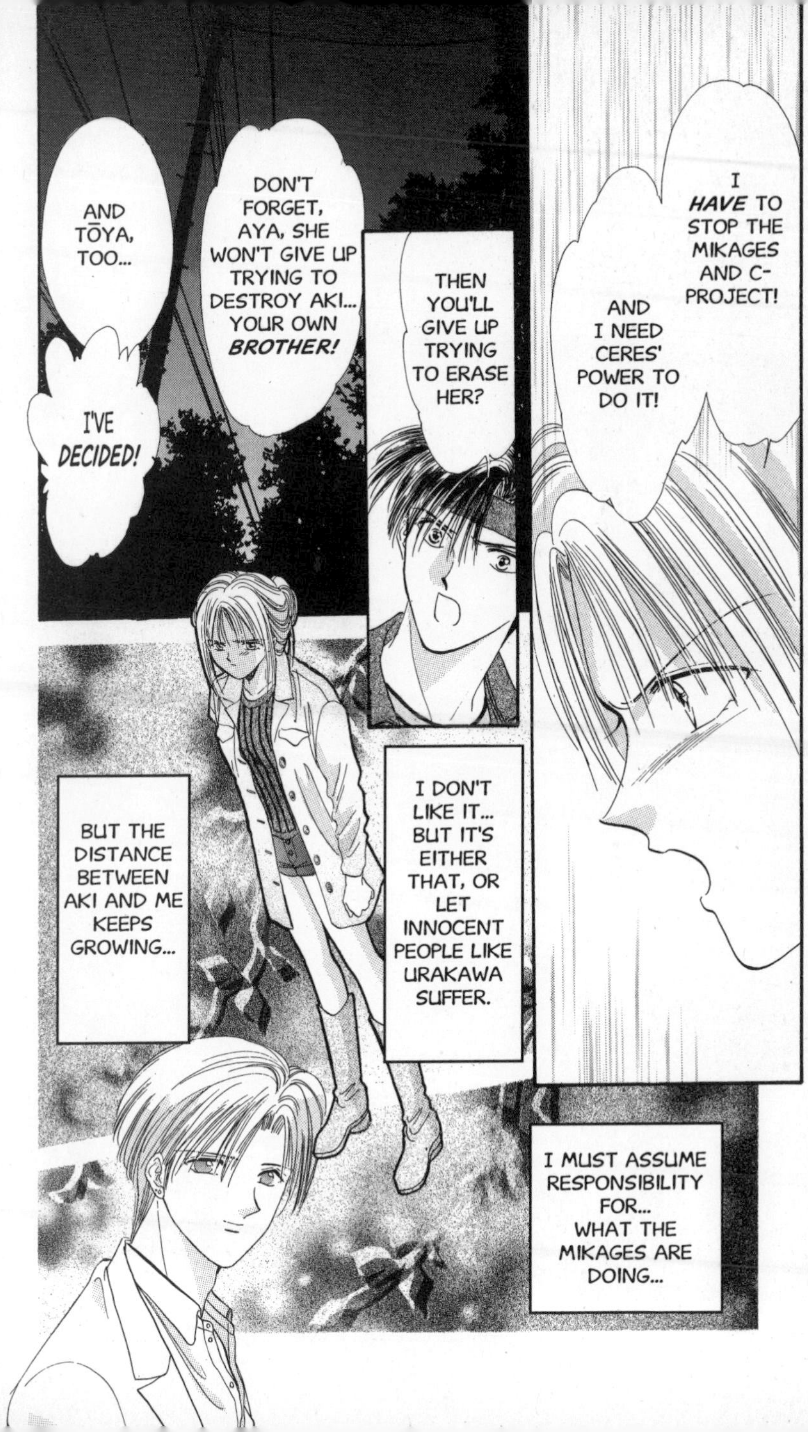
I *HAVE* TO STOP THE MIKAGES AND C-PROJECT!
AND I NEED CERES' POWER TO DO IT!
THEN YOU'LL GIVE UP TRYING TO ERASE HER?
DON'T FORGET, AYA, SHE WON'T GIVE UP TRYING TO DESTROY AKI... YOUR OWN *BROTHER!*
AND TŌYA, TOO...
I'VE *DECIDED!*
I DON'T LIKE IT... BUT IT'S EITHER THAT, OR LET INNOCENT PEOPLE LIKE URAKAWA SUFFER.
BUT THE DISTANCE BETWEEN AKI AND ME KEEPS GROWING...
I MUST ASSUME RESPONSIBILITY FOR... WHAT THE MIKAGES ARE DOING...

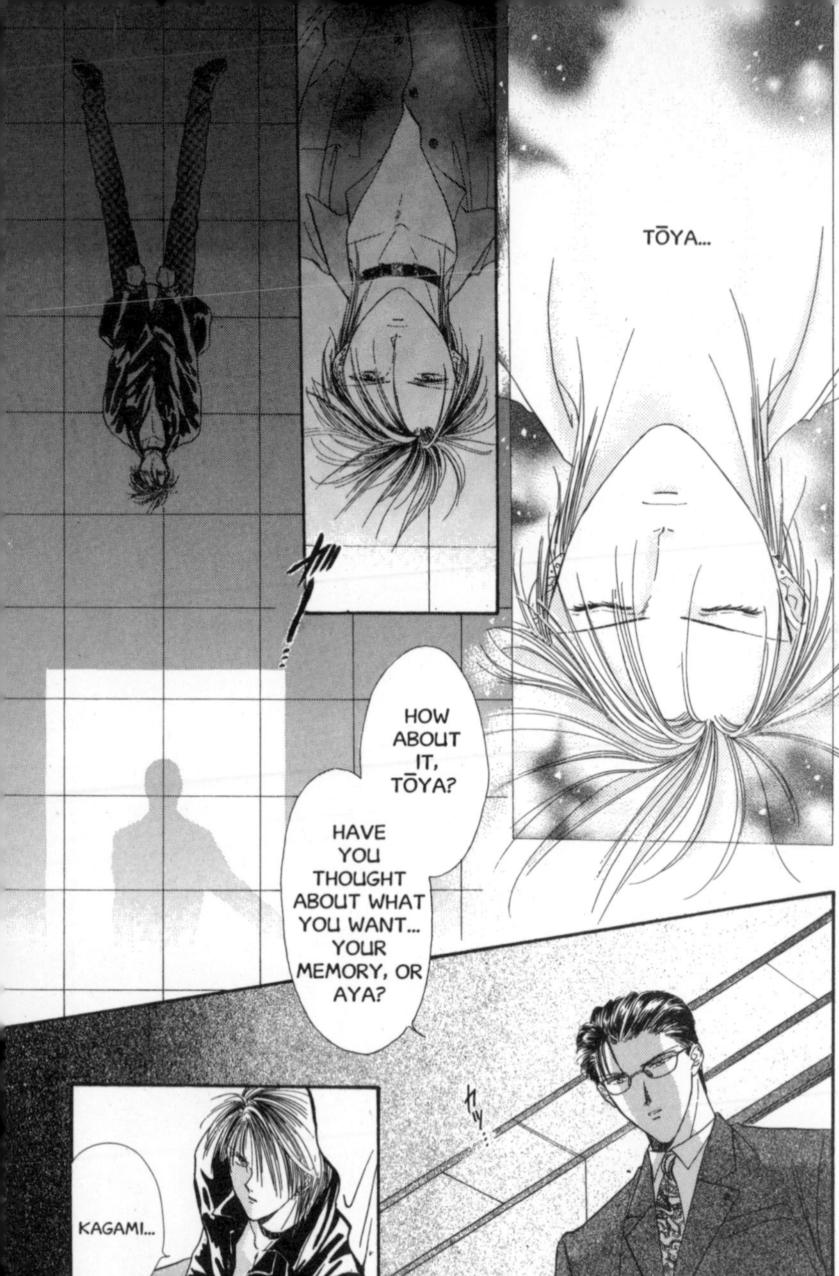
TŌYA...
HOW ABOUT IT, TŌYA?
HAVE YOU THOUGHT ABOUT WHAT YOU WANT... YOUR MEMORY, OR AYA?
KAGAMI...

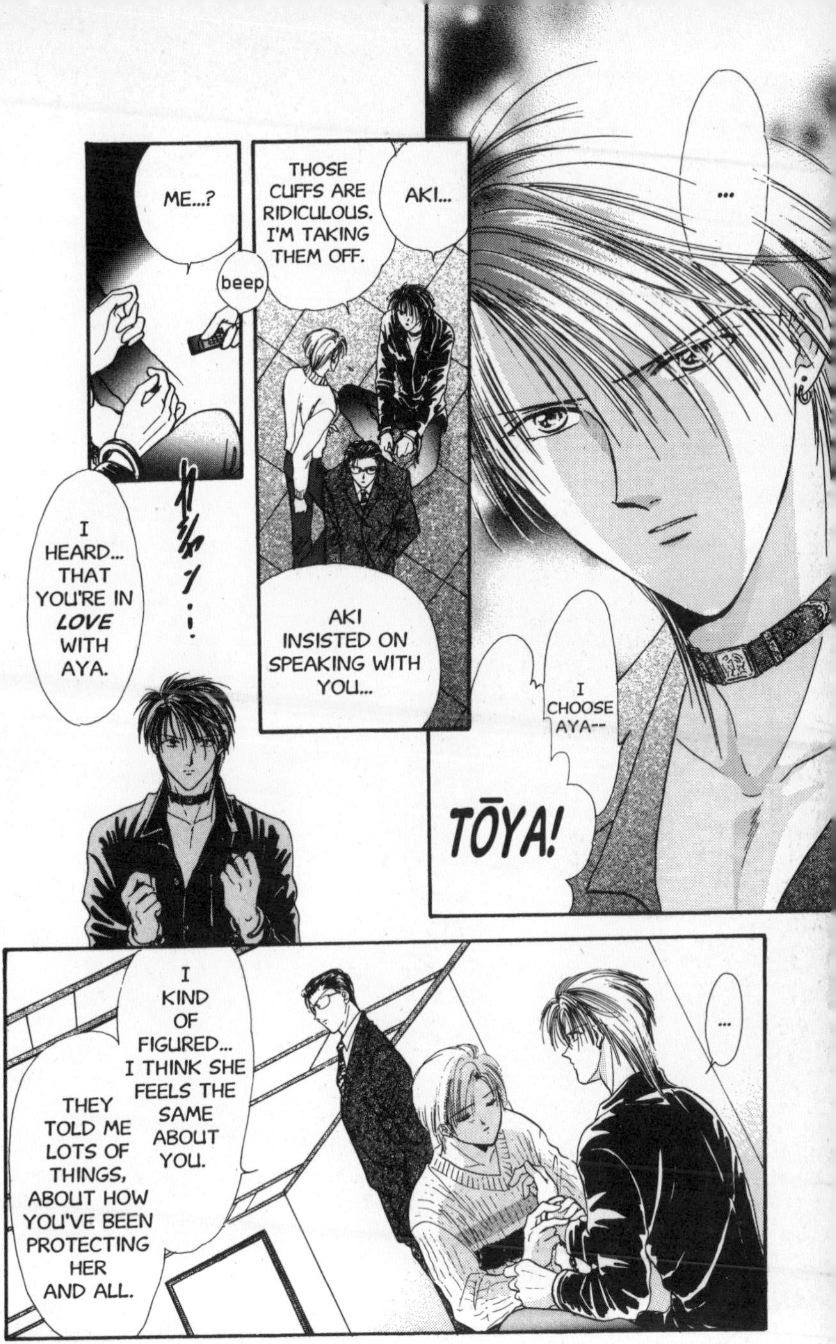
...
I CHOOSE AYA--
TŌYA!
AKI...
THOSE CUFFS ARE RIDICULOUS. I'M TAKING THEM OFF.
AKI INSISTED ON SPEAKING WITH YOU...
ME...?
beep
I HEARD... THAT YOU'RE IN *LOVE* WITH AYA.
...
I KIND OF FIGURED... I THINK SHE FEELS THE SAME ABOUT YOU.
THEY TOLD ME LOTS OF THINGS, ABOUT HOW YOU'VE BEEN PROTECTING HER AND ALL.

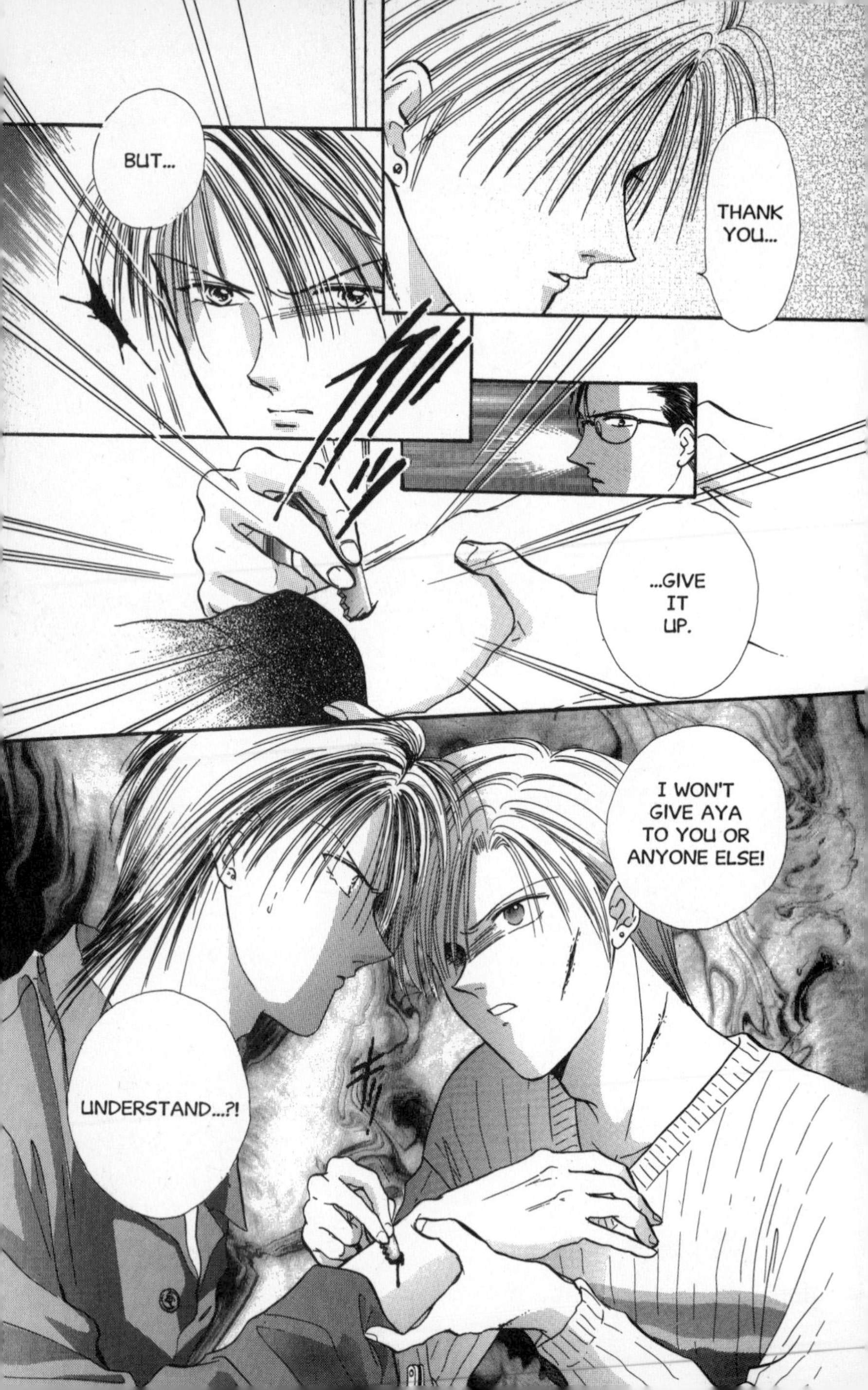
THANK YOU...
BUT...
...GIVE IT UP.
I WON'T GIVE AYA TO YOU OR ANYONE ELSE!
UNDERSTAND...?!

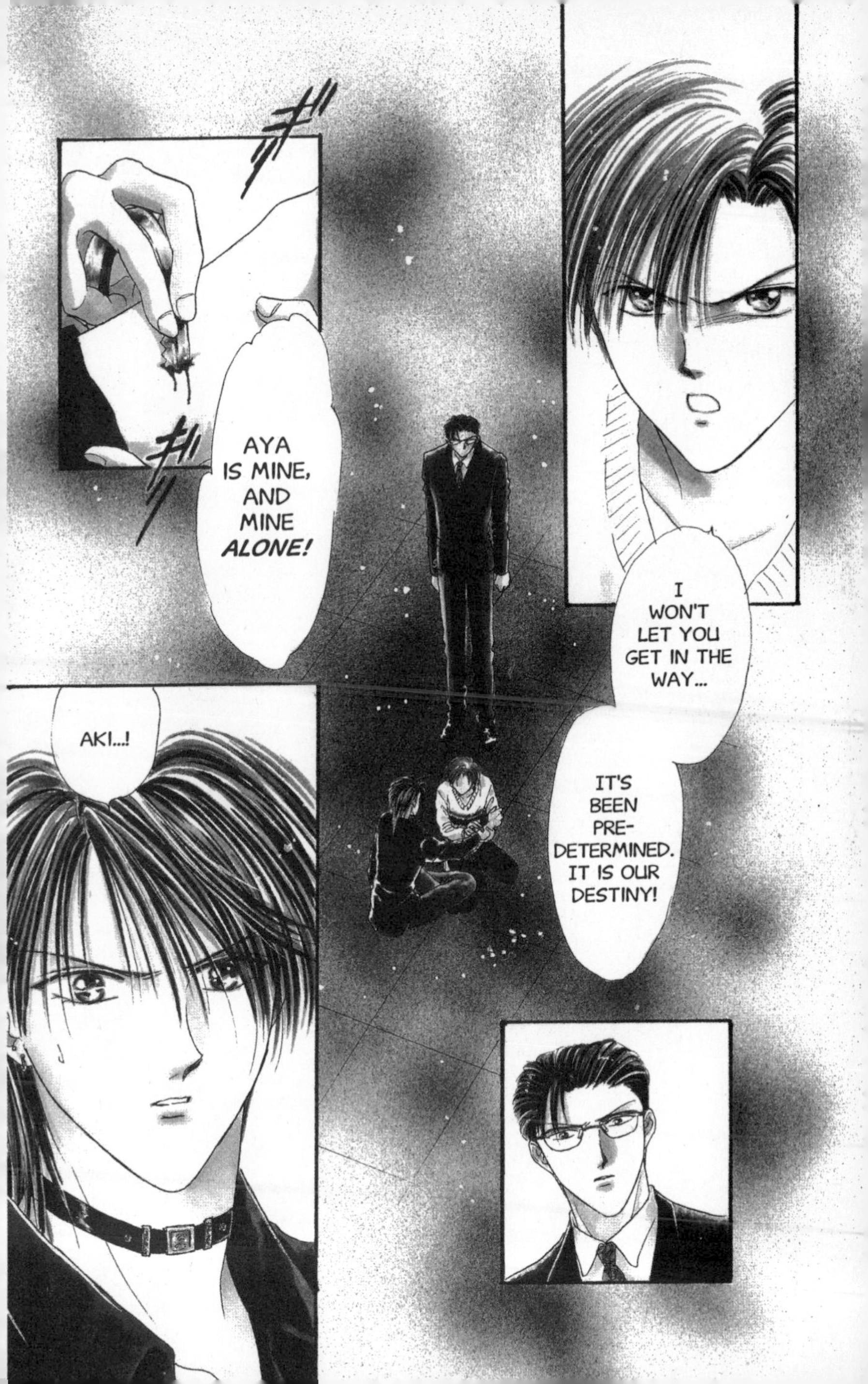
AYA IS MINE, AND MINE ALONE!
I WON'T LET YOU GET IN THE WAY...
IT'S BEEN PRE-DETERMINED. IT IS OUR DESTINY!
AKI...!

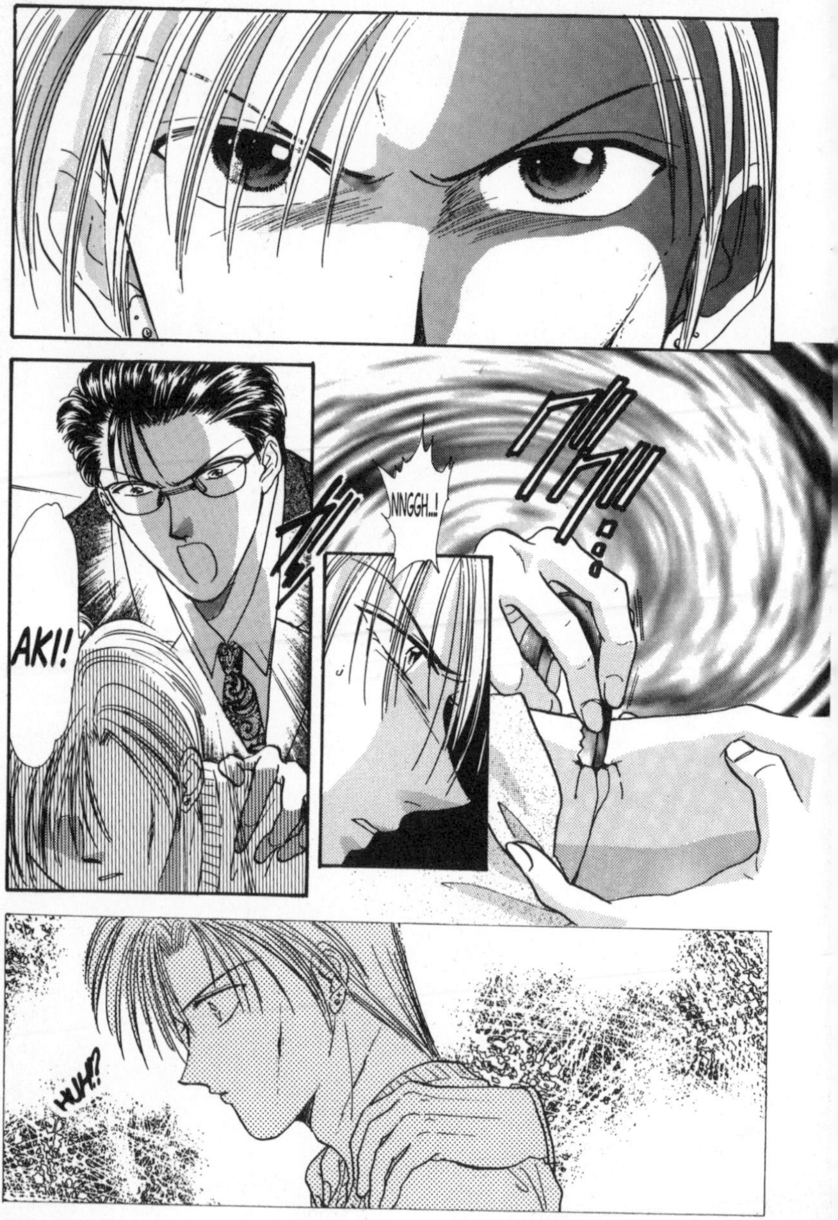
NNGGH..!
AKI!
HUH?

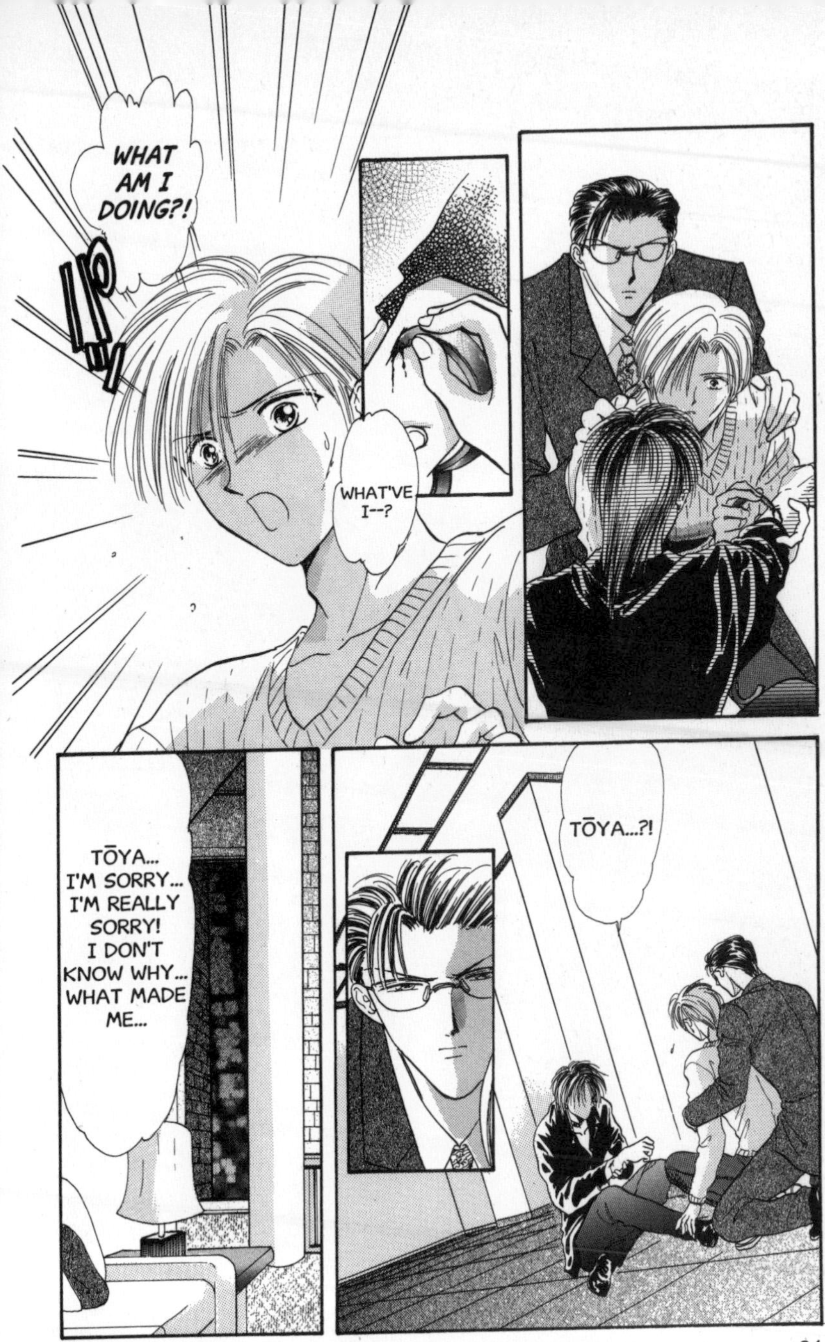
WHAT'VE I--?
WHAT AM I DOING?!
TŌYA...?!
TŌYA... I'M SORRY... I'M REALLY SORRY! I DON'T KNOW WHY... WHAT MADE ME...

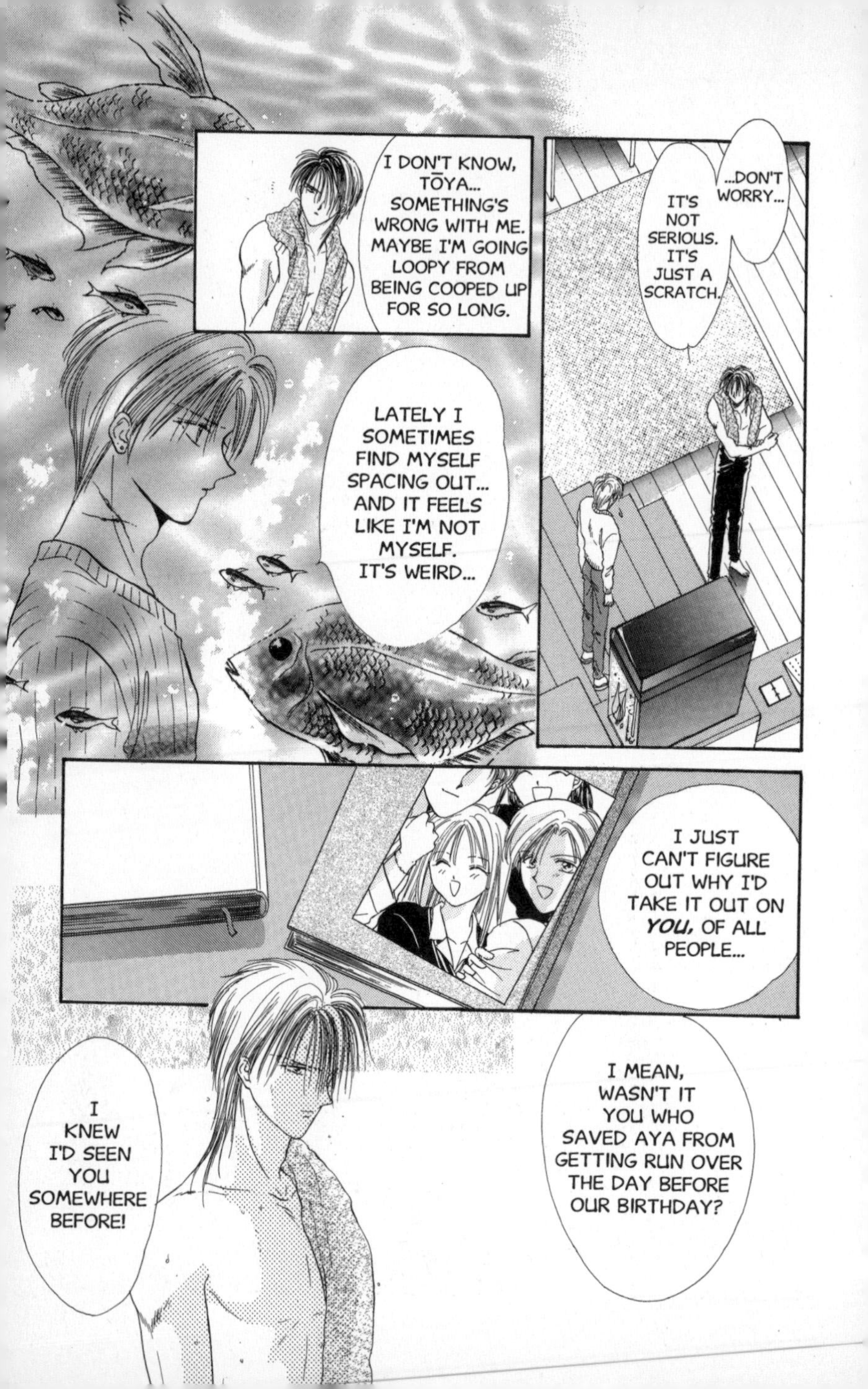

...DON'T WORRY...
IT'S NOT SERIOUS. IT'S JUST A SCRATCH.
I DON'T KNOW, TŌYA... SOMETHING'S WRONG WITH ME. MAYBE I'M GOING LOOPY FROM BEING COOPED UP FOR SO LONG.
LATELY I SOMETIMES FIND MYSELF SPACING OUT... AND IT FEELS LIKE I'M NOT MYSELF. IT'S WEIRD...
I JUST CAN'T FIGURE OUT WHY I'D TAKE IT OUT ON *YOU,* OF ALL PEOPLE...
I MEAN, WASN'T IT YOU WHO SAVED AYA FROM GETTING RUN OVER THE DAY BEFORE OUR BIRTHDAY?
I KNEW I'D SEEN YOU SOMEWHERE BEFORE!

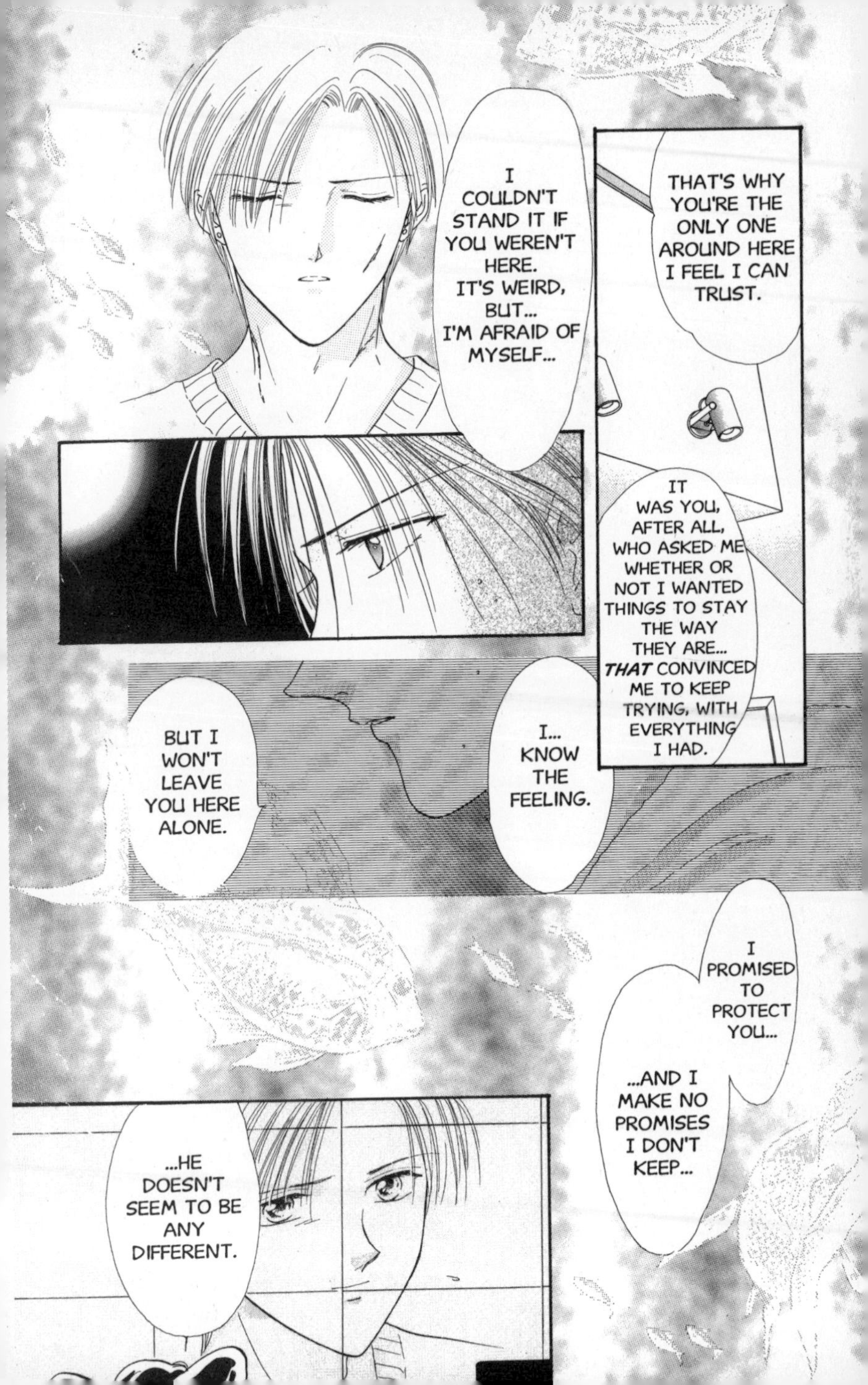
THAT'S WHY YOU'RE THE ONLY ONE AROUND HERE I FEEL I CAN TRUST.
I COULDN'T STAND IT IF YOU WEREN'T HERE. IT'S WEIRD, BUT... I'M AFRAID OF MYSELF...
IT WAS YOU, AFTER ALL, WHO ASKED ME WHETHER OR NOT I WANTED THINGS TO STAY THE WAY THEY ARE... *THAT* CONVINCED ME TO KEEP TRYING, WITH EVERYTHING I HAD.
I... KNOW THE FEELING.
BUT I WON'T LEAVE YOU HERE ALONE.
I PROMISED TO PROTECT YOU...
...AND I MAKE NO PROMISES I DON'T KEEP...
...HE DOESN'T SEEM TO BE ANY DIFFERENT.

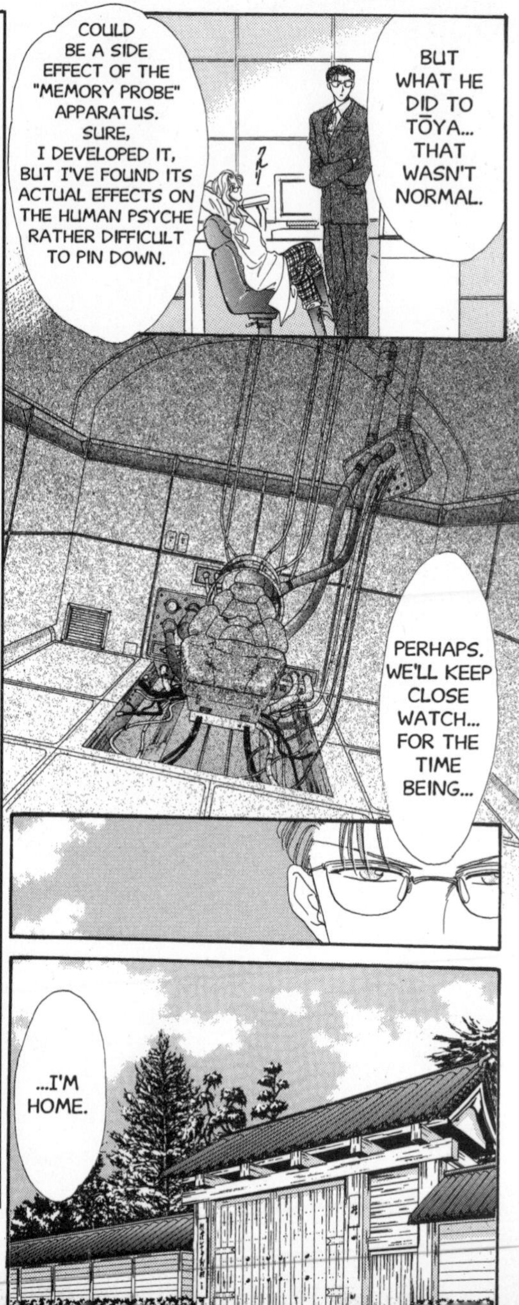
BUT WHAT HE DID TO TŌYA... THAT WASN'T NORMAL.
COULD BE A SIDE EFFECT OF THE "MEMORY PROBE" APPARATUS. SURE, I DEVELOPED IT, BUT I'VE FOUND ITS ACTUAL EFFECTS ON THE HUMAN PSYCHE RATHER DIFFICULT TO PIN DOWN.
PERHAPS. WE'LL KEEP CLOSE WATCH... FOR THE TIME BEING...
...I'M HOME.

♦ Chidori ♦

Oh, I'd been thinking about how I said in a previous sidebar that **Ceres** is rather dark, and then I realized - this is a contemporary drama. I guess this is what happens when I try to set the story in the present day. The present day as I see it is gloomy and gray (at least Japan is). People as a whole, even children, are depressed. They look tired. Even high school girls, those hordes of look-a-like clones, who are said to represent the present day, look like they lack spirit to me and my assistants. It's like they're living a lie, without realizing it, by acting so incredibly chipper. But I guess it's okay, as long as they're having fun. And if I focus on that, the series is probably going to be really dark, but there are still lots of things that show it's not all bad for mankind. Also, those girls labeled kogals might look flighty on the outside,

but they could be pretty serious inside. Really?

It's not good when people just go by outward appearances. The media is making too much of a big deal. And there are way too many stupid adults around! Still, I hope young boys and girls don't lose heart. You can change the future. Each of you has that power. Wait until you are older to start thinking about the futility of it all. And I'll have Aya keep doing her best, too. This is an age when parents and children kill each other, and people with money and power use underhanded methods to get what they want. The Mikage Family is representative of those things for me. And as you may have realized, the theme is the same as my previous series. My next series will also probably inherit the same theme too. Just like genes.

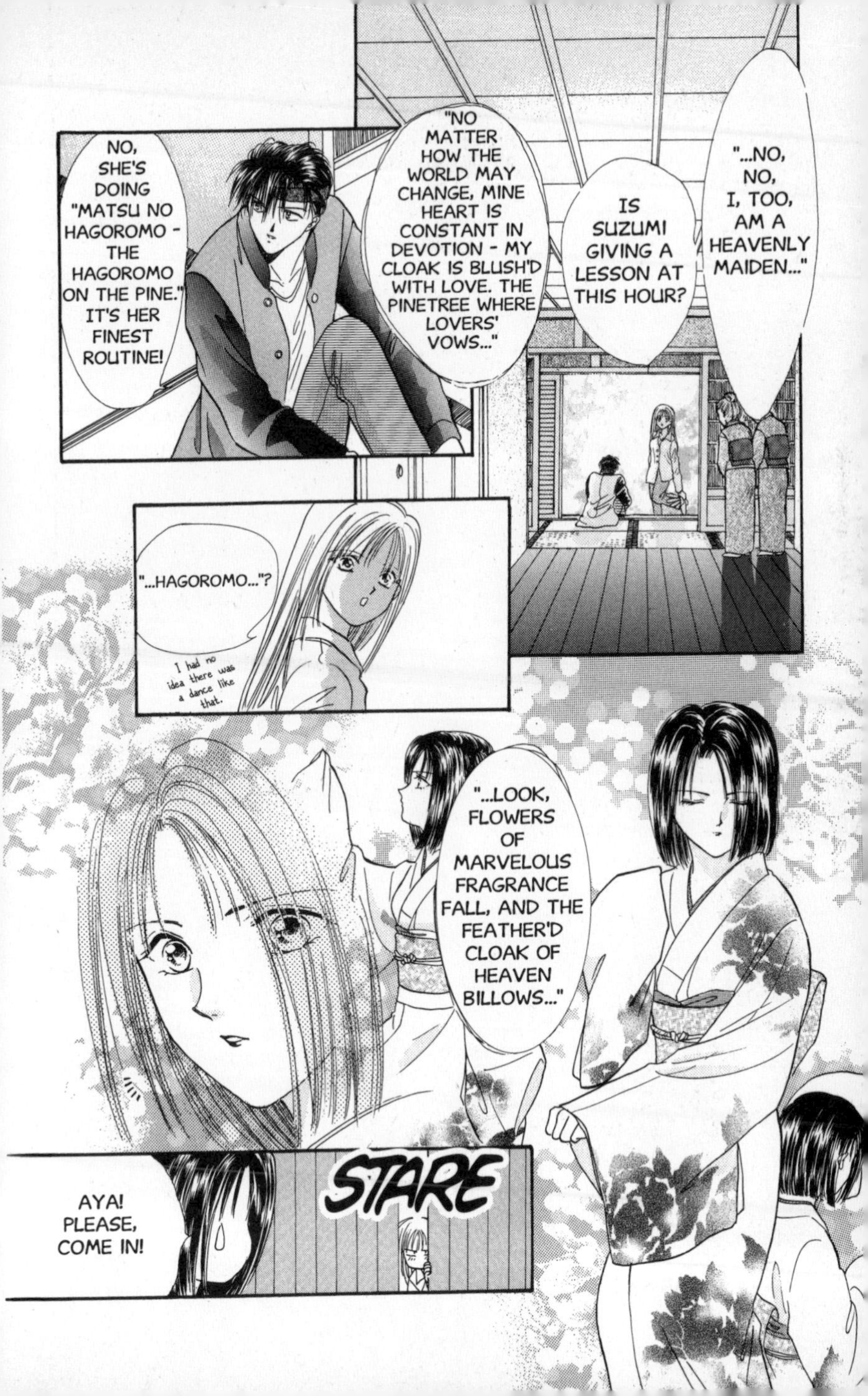
"...NO, NO, I, TOO, AM A HEAVENLY MAIDEN..."
IS SUZUMI GIVING A LESSON AT THIS HOUR?
"NO MATTER HOW THE WORLD MAY CHANGE, MINE HEART IS CONSTANT IN DEVOTION - MY CLOAK IS BLUSH'D WITH LOVE. THE PINETREE WHERE LOVERS' VOWS..."
NO, SHE'S DOING "MATSU NO HAGOROMO - THE HAGOROMO ON THE PINE." IT'S HER FINEST ROUTINE!
"...HAGOROMO..."?
I had no idea there was a dance like that.
"...LOOK, FLOWERS OF MARVELOUS FRAGRANCE FALL, AND THE FEATHER'D CLOAK OF HEAVEN BILLOWS..."
STARE
AYA! PLEASE, COME IN!

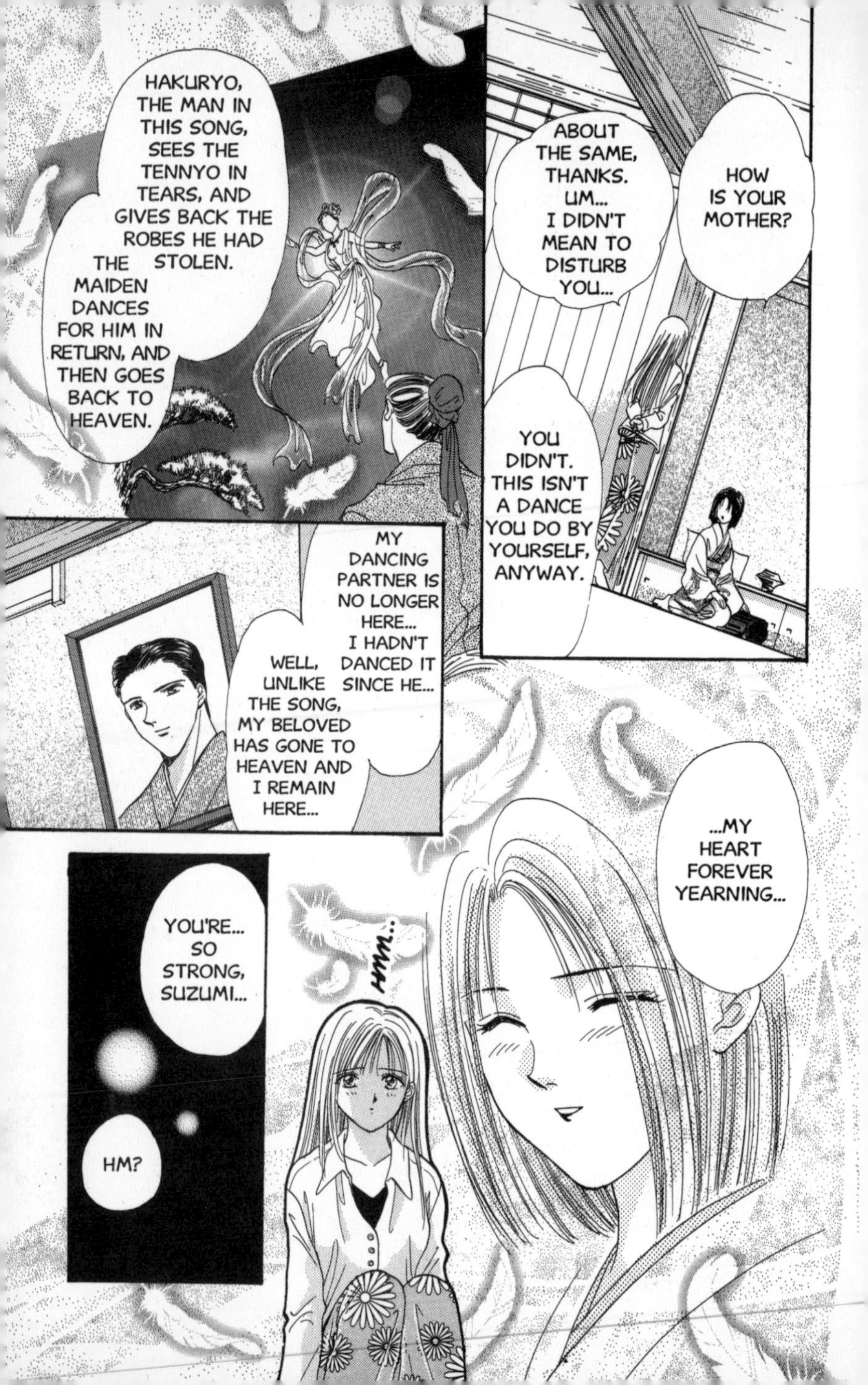
HOW IS YOUR MOTHER?
ABOUT THE SAME, THANKS. UM... I DIDN'T MEAN TO DISTURB YOU...
YOU DIDN'T. THIS ISN'T A DANCE YOU DO BY YOURSELF, ANYWAY.
HAKURYO, THE MAN IN THIS SONG, SEES THE TENNYO IN TEARS, AND GIVES BACK THE ROBES HE HAD STOLEN.
THE MAIDEN DANCES FOR HIM IN RETURN, AND THEN GOES BACK TO HEAVEN.
MY DANCING PARTNER IS NO LONGER HERE... I HADN'T DANCED IT SINCE HE...
WELL, UNLIKE THE SONG, MY BELOVED HAS GONE TO HEAVEN AND I REMAIN HERE...
...MY HEART FOREVER YEARNING...
HMM...
YOU'RE... SO STRONG, SUZUMI...
HM?

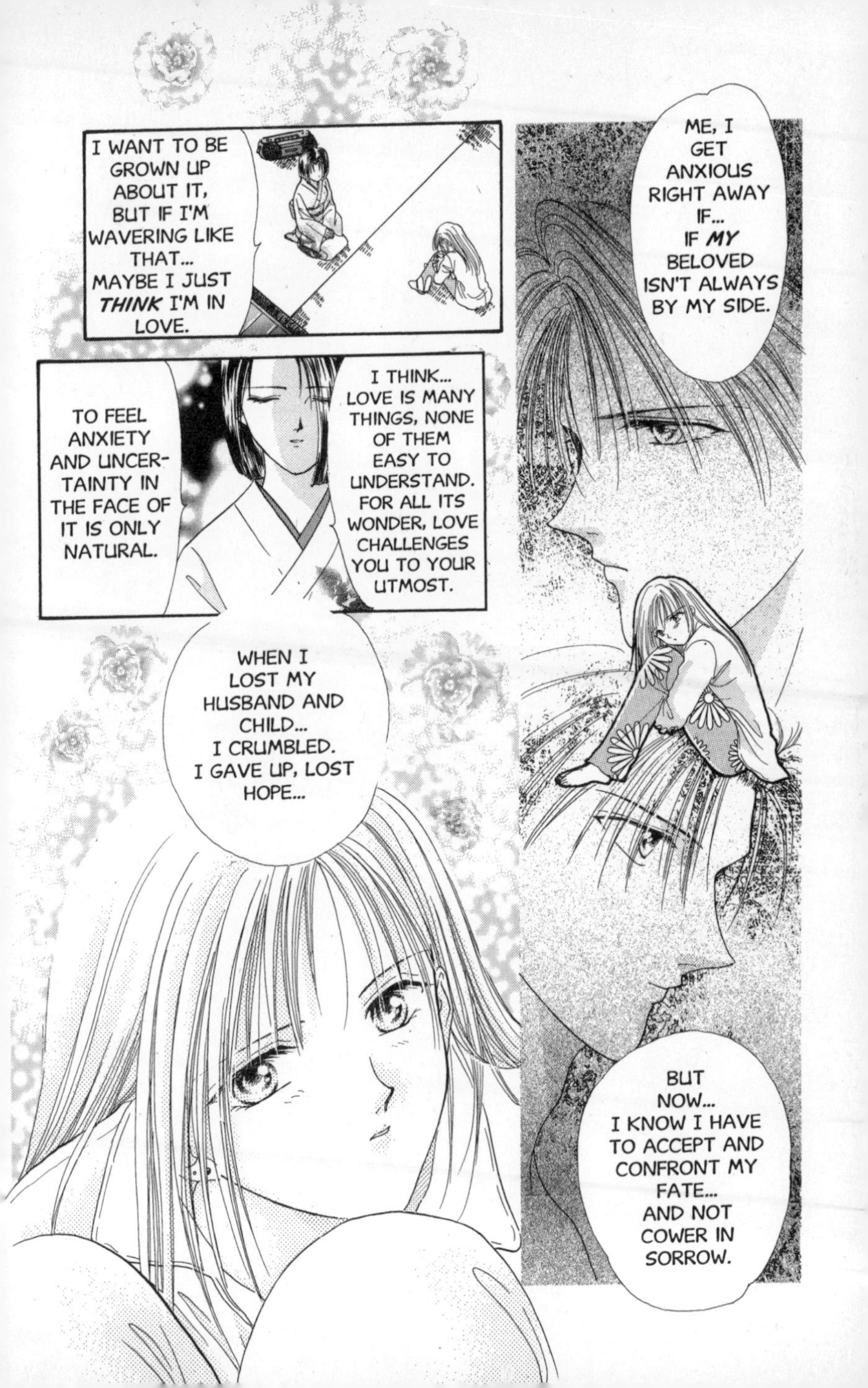
ME, I GET ANXIOUS RIGHT AWAY IF... IF *MY* BELOVED ISN'T ALWAYS BY MY SIDE.
BUT NOW... I KNOW I HAVE TO ACCEPT AND CONFRONT MY FATE... AND NOT COWER IN SORROW.
I WANT TO BE GROWN UP ABOUT IT, BUT IF I'M WAVERING LIKE THAT... MAYBE I JUST *THINK* I'M IN LOVE.
I THINK... LOVE IS MANY THINGS, NONE OF THEM EASY TO UNDERSTAND. FOR ALL ITS WONDER, LOVE CHALLENGES YOU TO YOUR UTMOST.
TO FEEL ANXIETY AND UNCERTAINTY IN THE FACE OF IT IS ONLY NATURAL.
WHEN I LOST MY HUSBAND AND CHILD... I CRUMBLED. I GAVE UP, LOST HOPE...

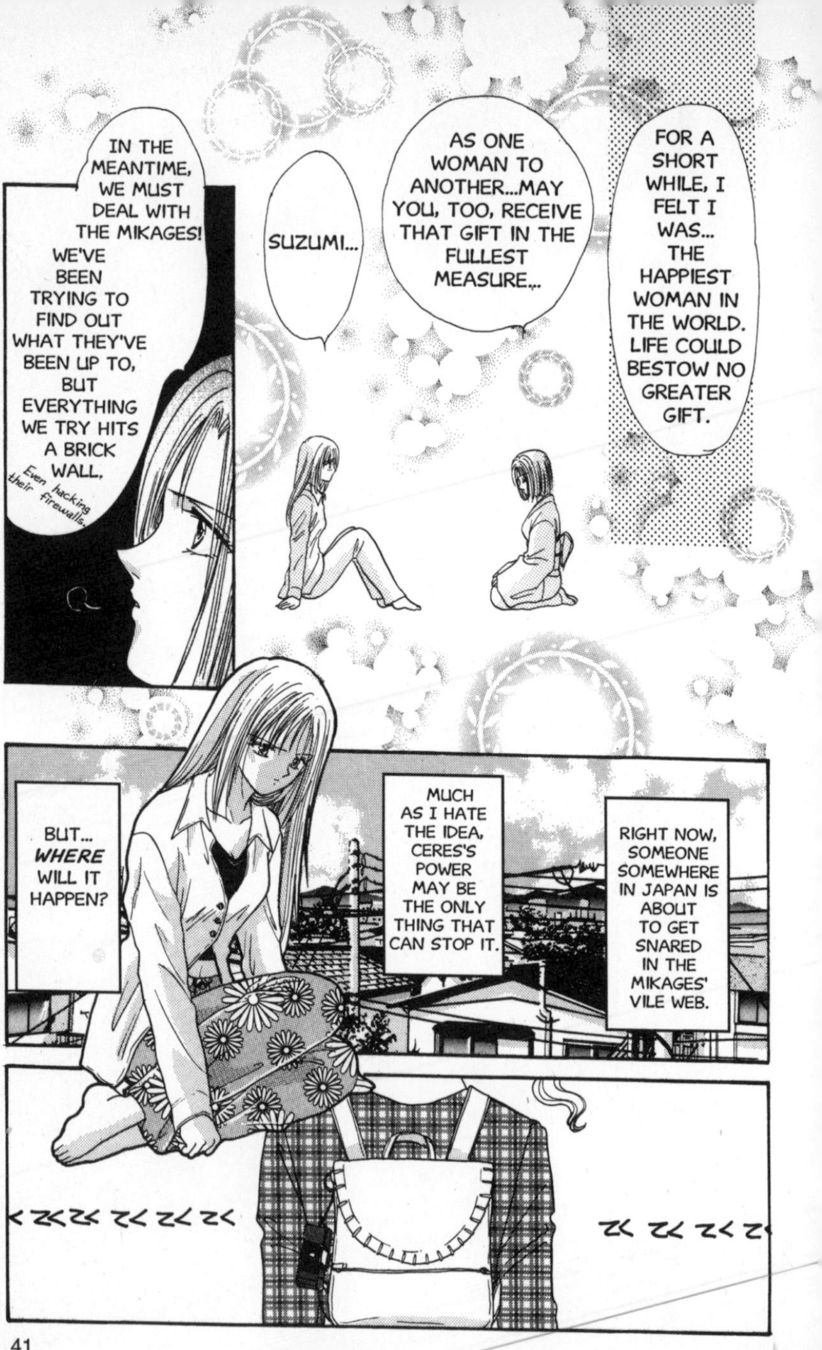
FOR A SHORT WHILE, I FELT I WAS... THE HAPPIEST WOMAN IN THE WORLD. LIFE COULD BESTOW NO GREATER GIFT.
AS ONE WOMAN TO ANOTHER...MAY YOU, TOO, RECEIVE THAT GIFT IN THE FULLEST MEASURE...
SUZUMI...
IN THE MEANTIME, WE MUST DEAL WITH THE MIKAGES!
WE'VE BEEN TRYING TO FIND OUT WHAT THEY'VE BEEN UP TO, BUT EVERYTHING WE TRY HITS A BRICK WALL.
Even hacking their firewalls.
RIGHT NOW, SOMEONE SOMEWHERE IN JAPAN IS ABOUT TO GET SNARED IN THE MIKAGES' VILE WEB.
MUCH AS I HATE THE IDEA, CERES'S POWER MAY BE THE ONLY THING THAT CAN STOP IT.
BUT... *WHERE* WILL IT HAPPEN?

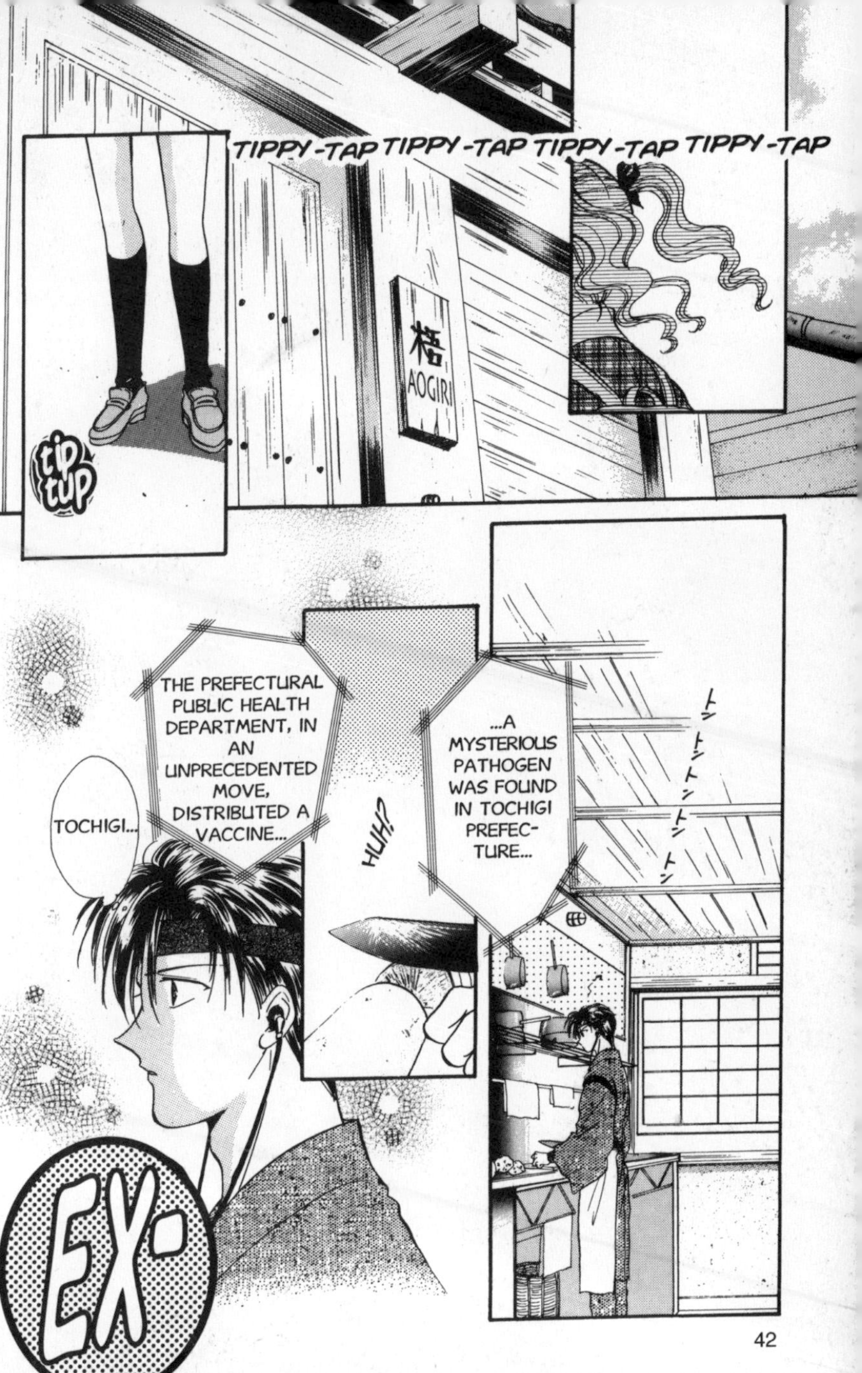
TIPPY-TAP TIPPY-TAP TIPPY-TAP TIPPY-TAP
AOGIRI
tip tup
トントントントン
...A MYSTERIOUS PATHOGEN WAS FOUND IN TOCHIGI PREFEC-TURE...
HUH?
THE PREFECTURAL PUBLIC HEALTH DEPARTMENT, IN AN UNPRECEDENTED MOVE, DISTRIBUTED A VACCINE...
TOCHIGI...
EX-

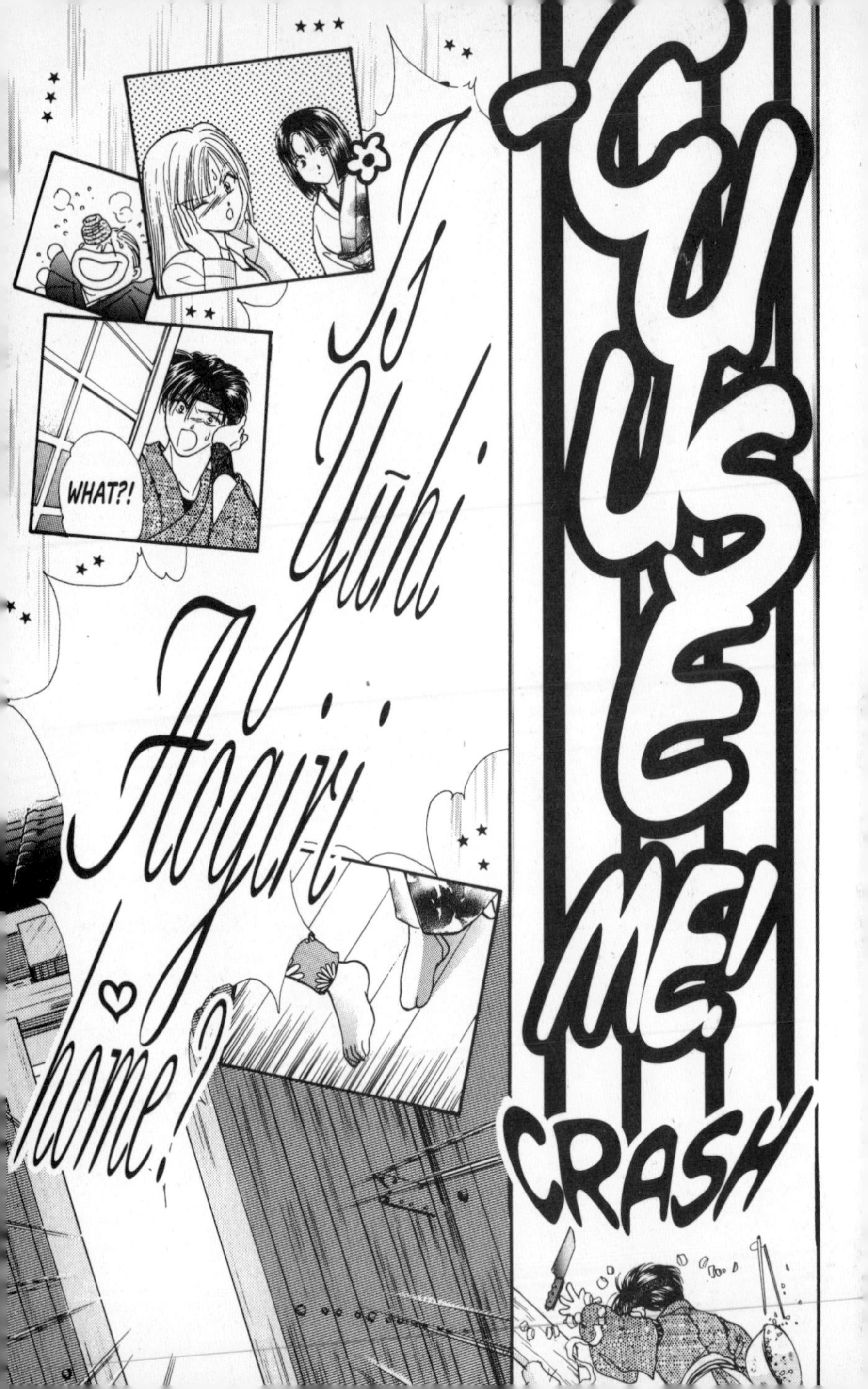
'CUSE ME!
CRASH
Is Yuki Agari home? ♡
WHAT?!

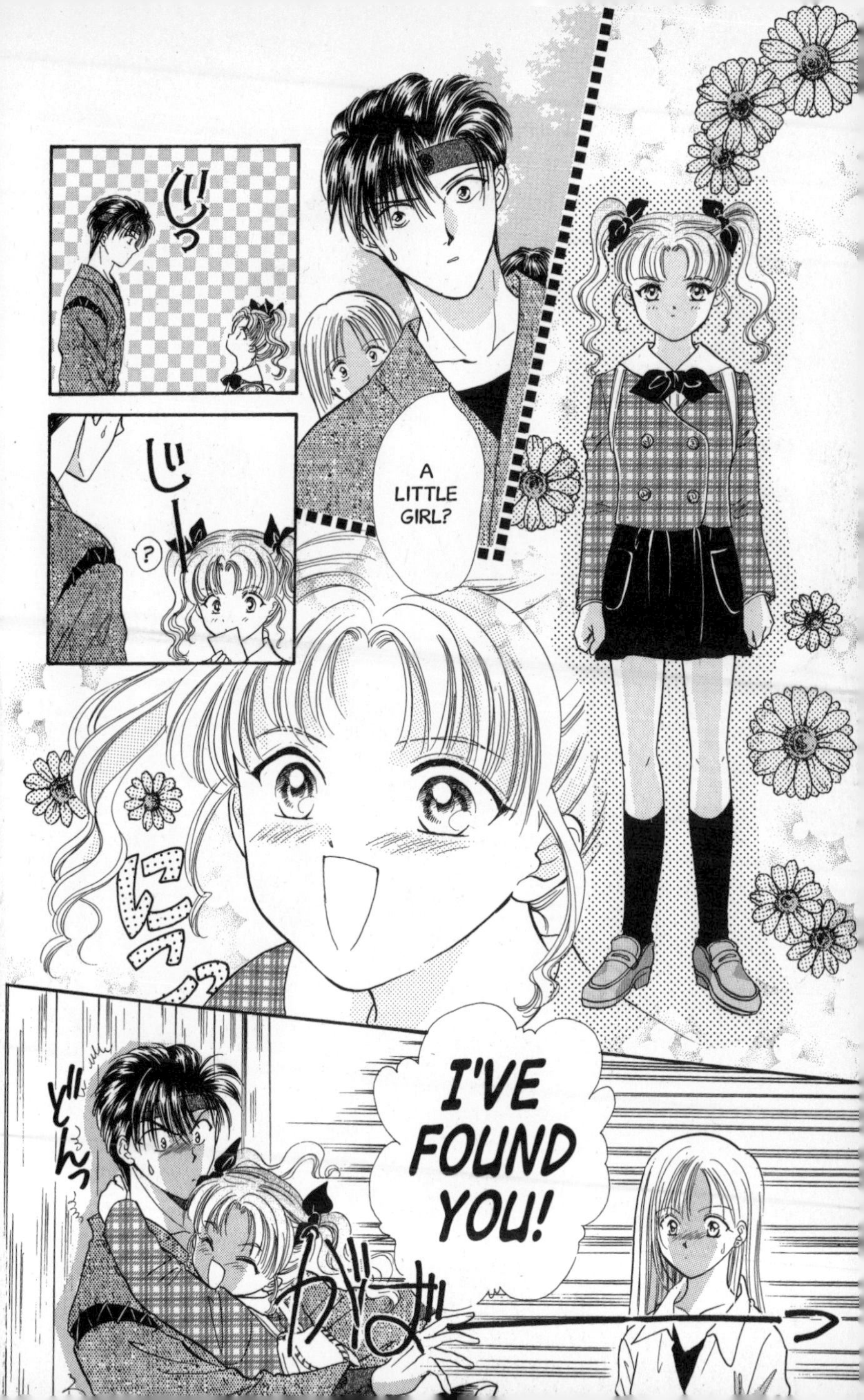
A LITTLE GIRL?
じいっ
じー
?
にこっ
I'VE FOUND YOU!
がばっ
どんっ

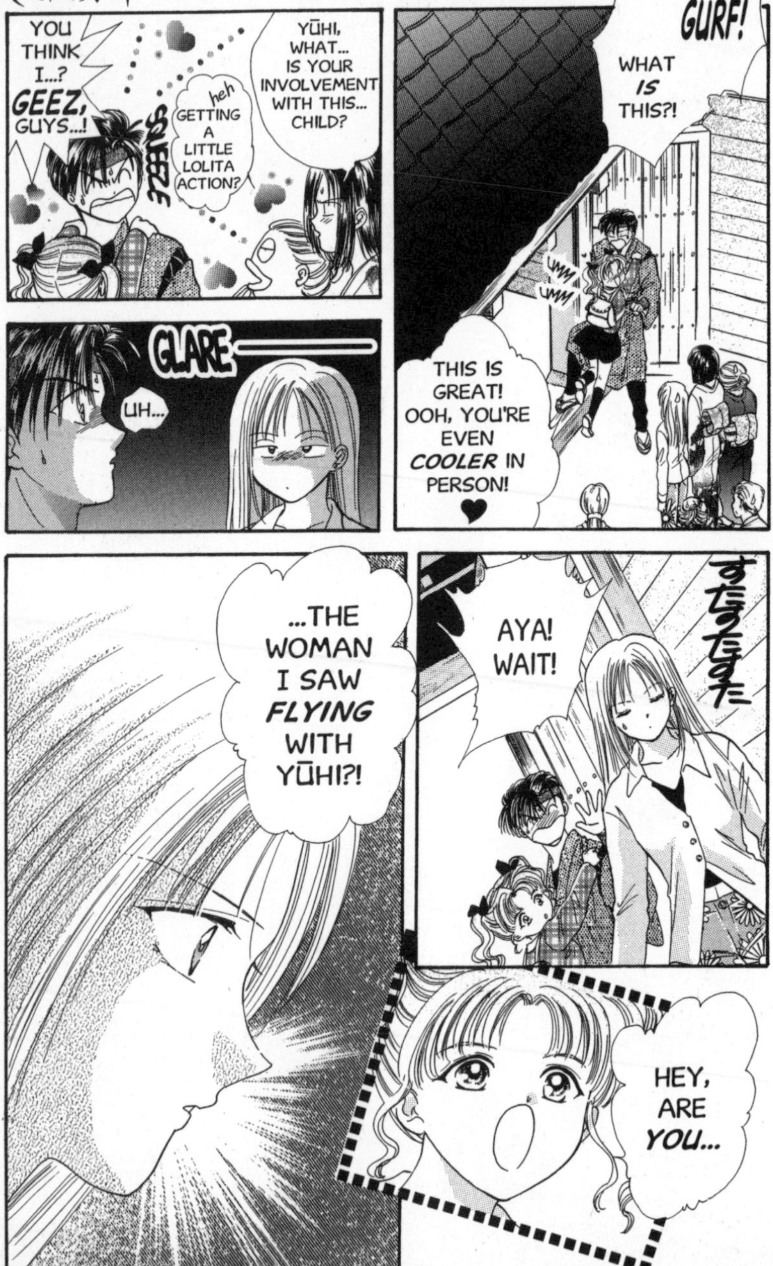
GURF!
WHAT *IS* THIS?!
UMM UMM
THIS IS GREAT! OOH, YOU'RE EVEN *COOLER* IN PERSON! ♥
YŪHI, WHAT... IS YOUR INVOLVEMENT WITH THIS... CHILD?
heh GETTING A LITTLE LOLITA ACTION?
SQUEEZE
YOU THINK I...? *GEEZ,* GUYS...!
GLARE
UH...
すたすたすた
AYA! WAIT!
HEY, ARE *YOU*...
...THE WOMAN I SAW *FLYING* WITH YŪHI?!

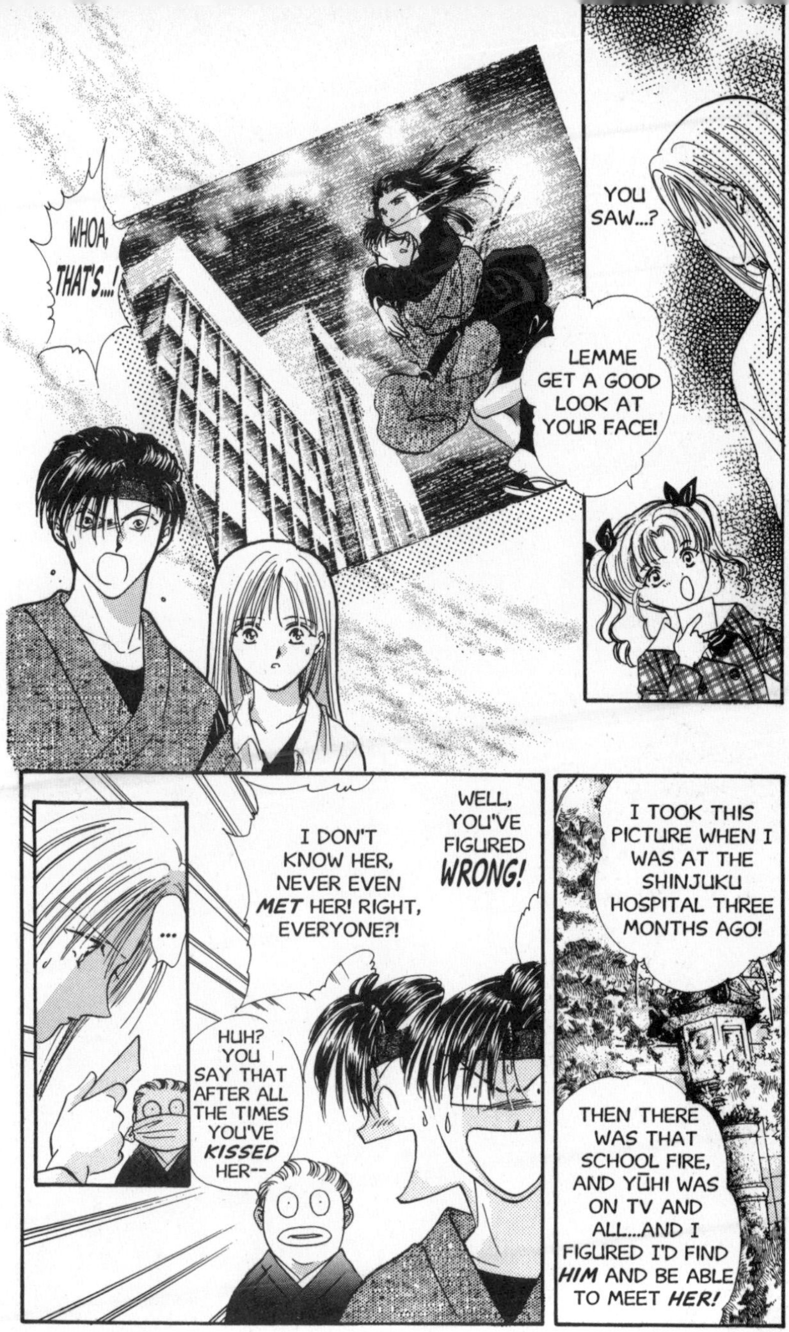
YOU SAW...?
LEMME GET A GOOD LOOK AT YOUR FACE!
WHOA, THAT'S...!
I TOOK THIS PICTURE WHEN I WAS AT THE SHINJUKU HOSPITAL THREE MONTHS AGO!
THEN THERE WAS THAT SCHOOL FIRE, AND YŪHI WAS ON TV AND ALL...AND I FIGURED I'D FIND HIM AND BE ABLE TO MEET HER!
WELL, YOU'VE FIGURED WRONG!
I DON'T KNOW HER, NEVER EVEN MET HER! RIGHT, EVERYONE?!
...
HUH? YOU SAY THAT AFTER ALL THE TIMES YOU'VE KISSED HER--

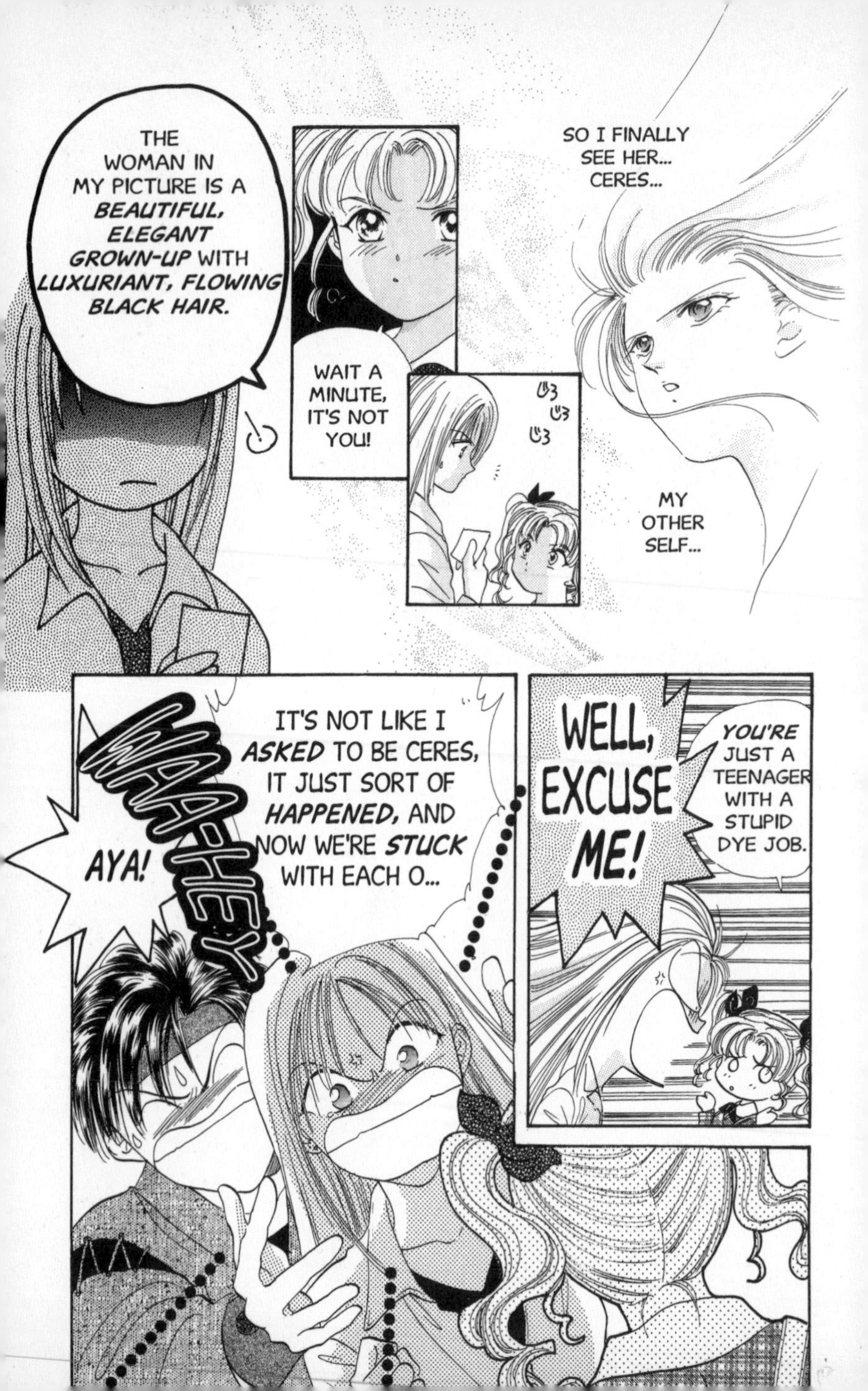

SO I FINALLY SEE HER... CERES...
MY OTHER SELF...
WAIT A MINUTE, IT'S NOT YOU!
じろ
じろ
じろ
THE WOMAN IN MY PICTURE IS A BEAUTIFUL, ELEGANT GROWN-UP WITH LUXURIANT, FLOWING BLACK HAIR.
YOU'RE JUST A TEENAGER WITH A STUPID DYE JOB.
WELL, EXCUSE ME!
IT'S NOT LIKE I ASKED TO BE CERES, IT JUST SORT OF HAPPENED, AND NOW WE'RE STUCK WITH EACH O...
WAA-HEY
AYA!

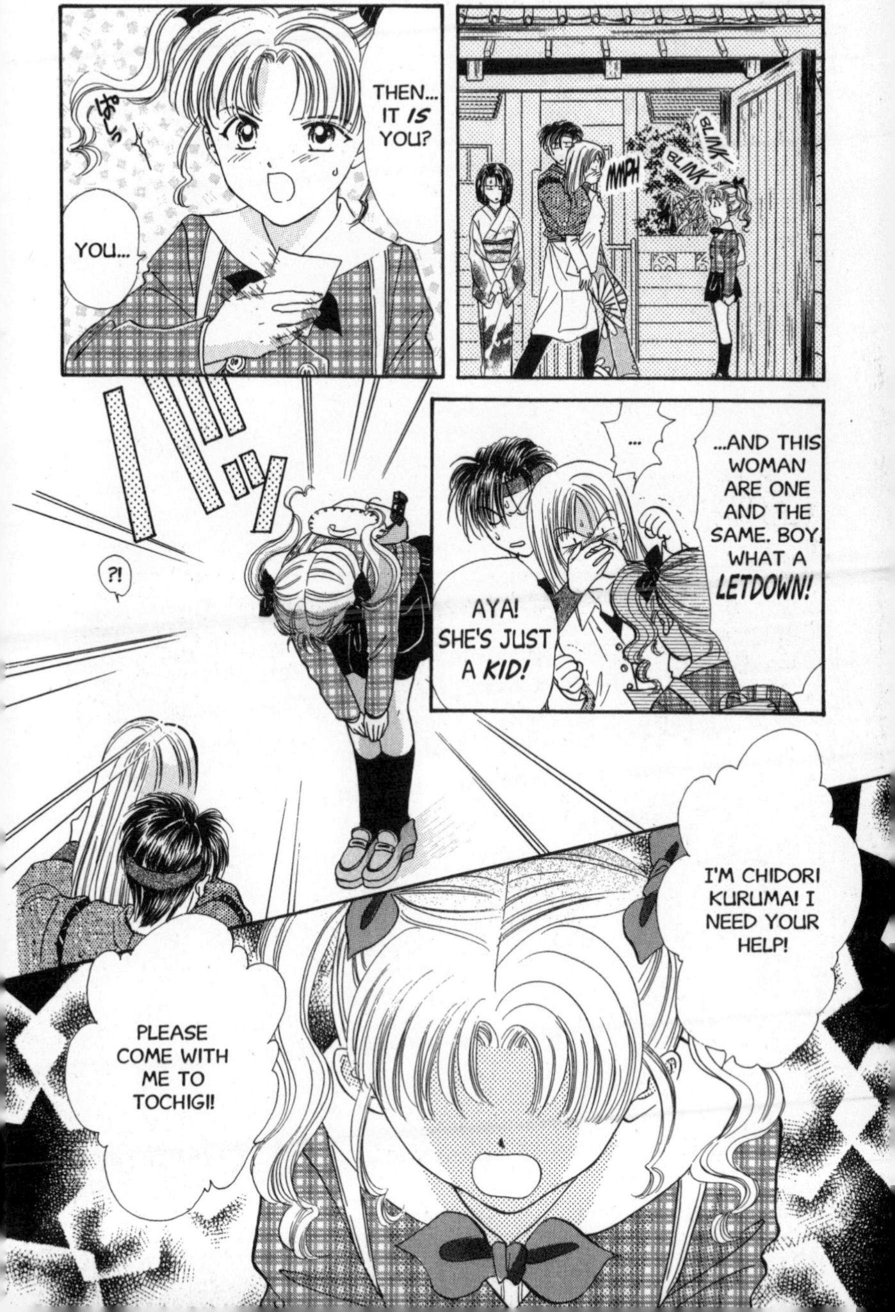
BLINK
BLINK
MMPH
THEN... IT IS YOU?
ぱしっ
YOU...
...
...AND THIS WOMAN ARE ONE AND THE SAME. BOY, WHAT A LETDOWN!
AYA! SHE'S JUST A KID!
?!
I'M CHIDORI KURUMA! I NEED YOUR HELP!
PLEASE COME WITH ME TO TOCHIGI!

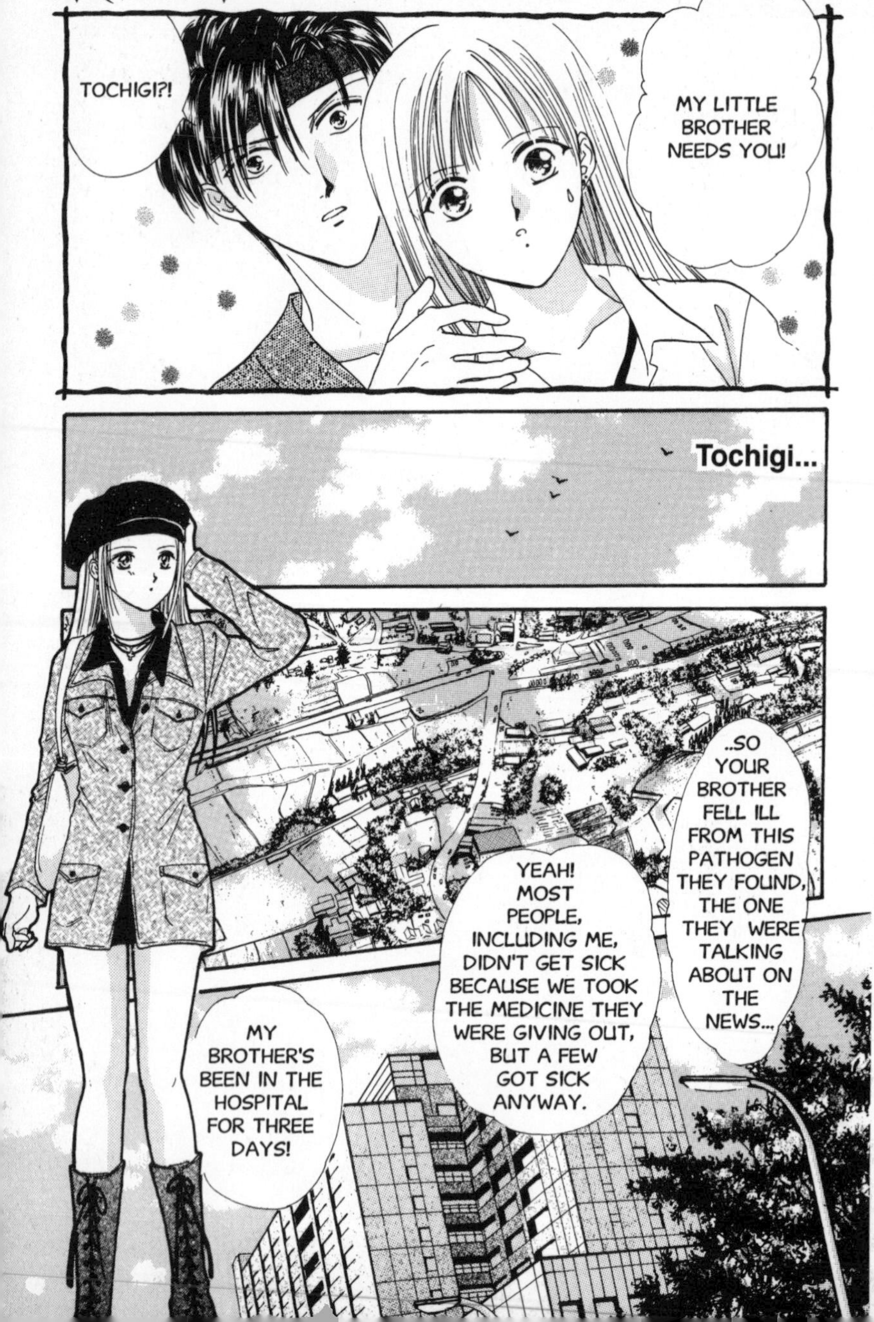
MY LITTLE BROTHER NEEDS YOU!
TOCHIGI?!
Tochigi...
..SO YOUR BROTHER FELL ILL FROM THIS PATHOGEN THEY FOUND, THE ONE THEY WERE TALKING ABOUT ON THE NEWS...
YEAH! MOST PEOPLE, INCLUDING ME, DIDN'T GET SICK BECAUSE WE TOOK THE MEDICINE THEY WERE GIVING OUT, BUT A FEW GOT SICK ANYWAY.
MY BROTHER'S BEEN IN THE HOSPITAL FOR THREE DAYS!

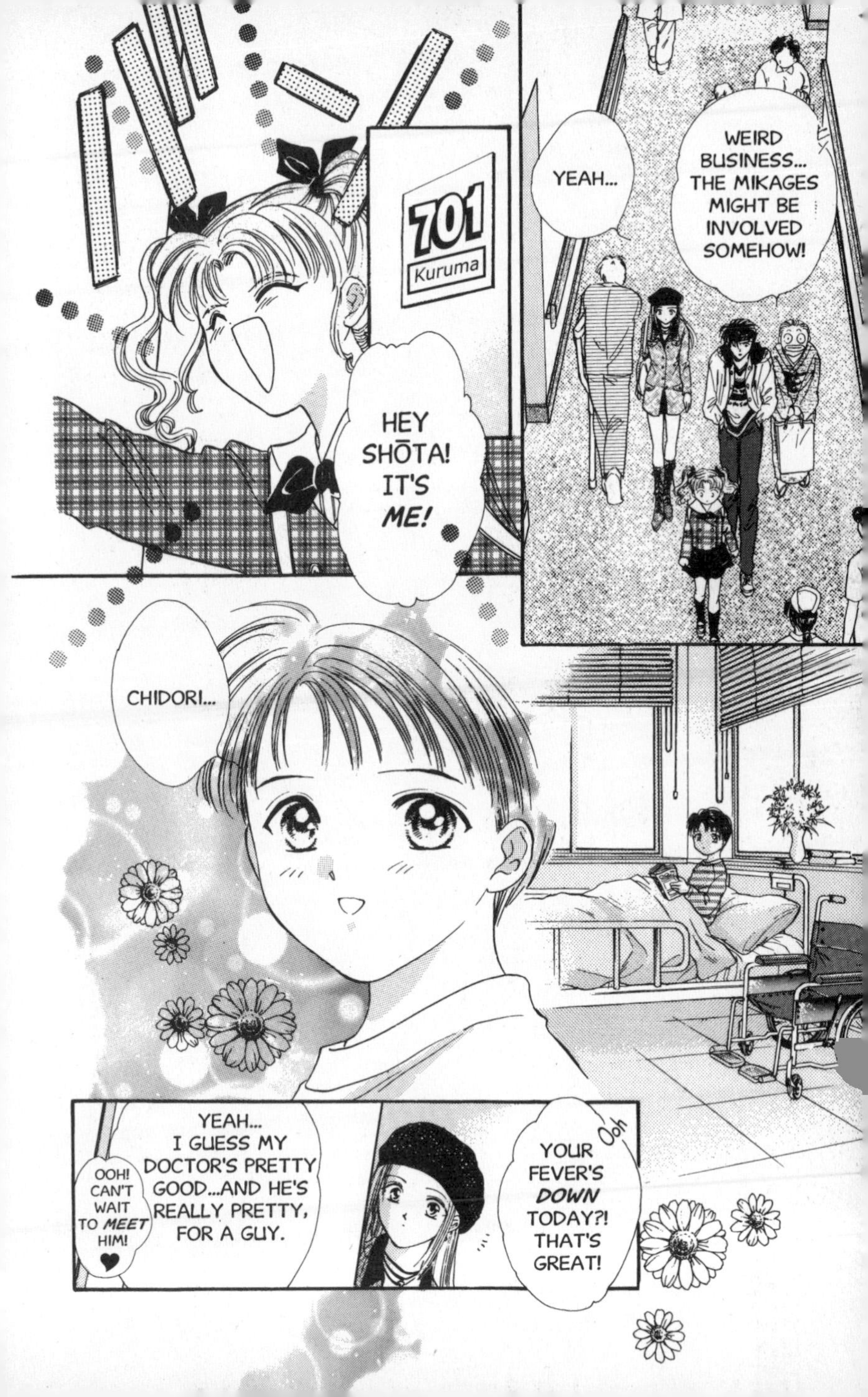
WEIRD BUSINESS... THE MIKAGES MIGHT BE INVOLVED SOMEHOW!
YEAH...
701
Kuruma
HEY SHŌTA! IT'S *ME!*
CHIDORI...
Ooh
YOUR FEVER'S *DOWN* TODAY?! THAT'S GREAT!
YEAH... I GUESS MY DOCTOR'S PRETTY GOOD...AND HE'S REALLY PRETTY, FOR A GUY.
OOH! CAN'T WAIT TO *MEET* HIM! ♥

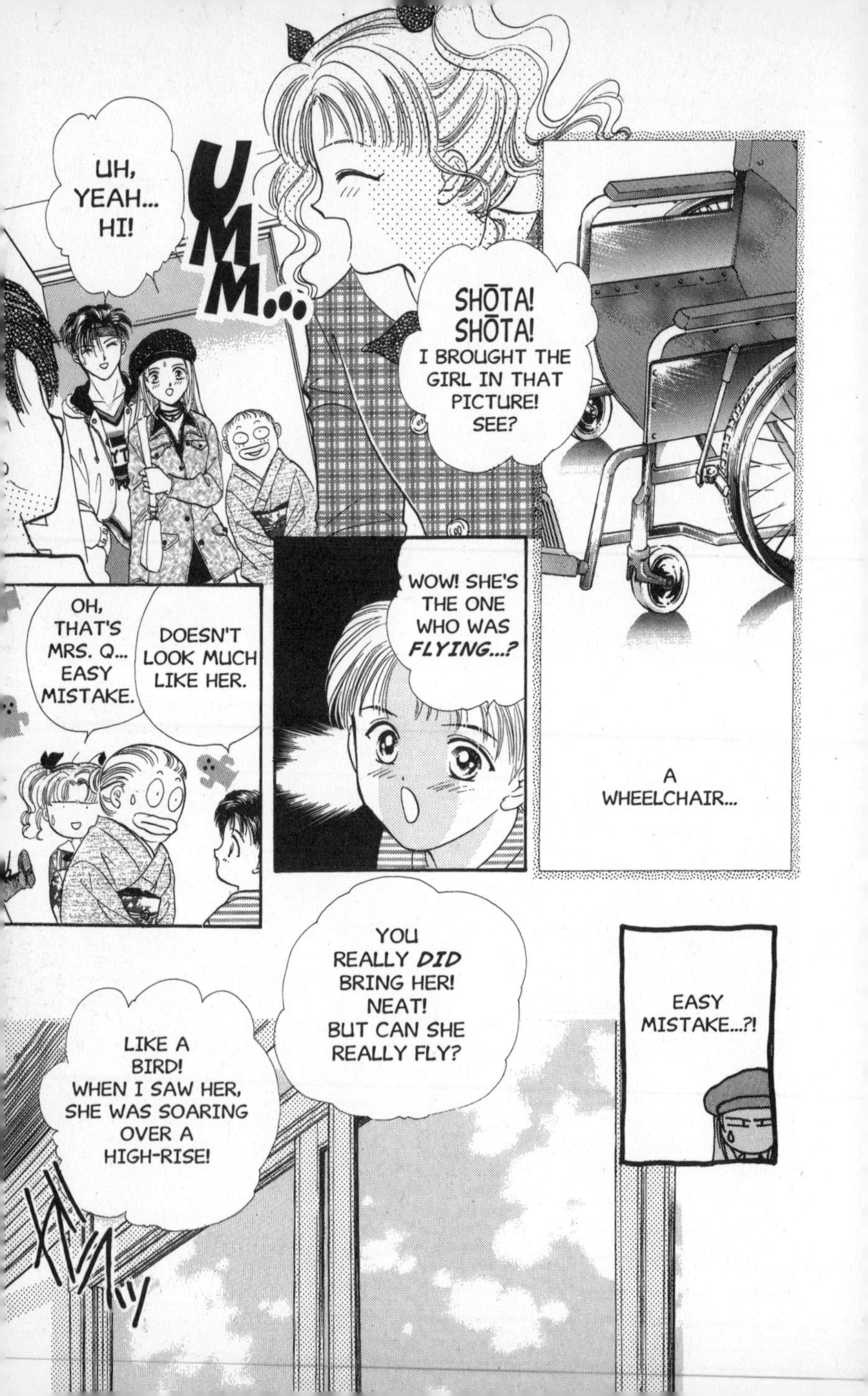
SHŌTA! SHŌTA! I BROUGHT THE GIRL IN THAT PICTURE! SEE?
UMM...
UH, YEAH... HI!
A WHEELCHAIR...
WOW! SHE'S THE ONE WHO WAS *FLYING...?*
DOESN'T LOOK MUCH LIKE HER.
OH, THAT'S MRS. Q... EASY MISTAKE.
EASY MISTAKE...?!
YOU REALLY *DID* BRING HER! NEAT! BUT CAN SHE REALLY FLY?
LIKE A BIRD! WHEN I SAW HER, SHE WAS SOARING OVER A HIGH-RISE!

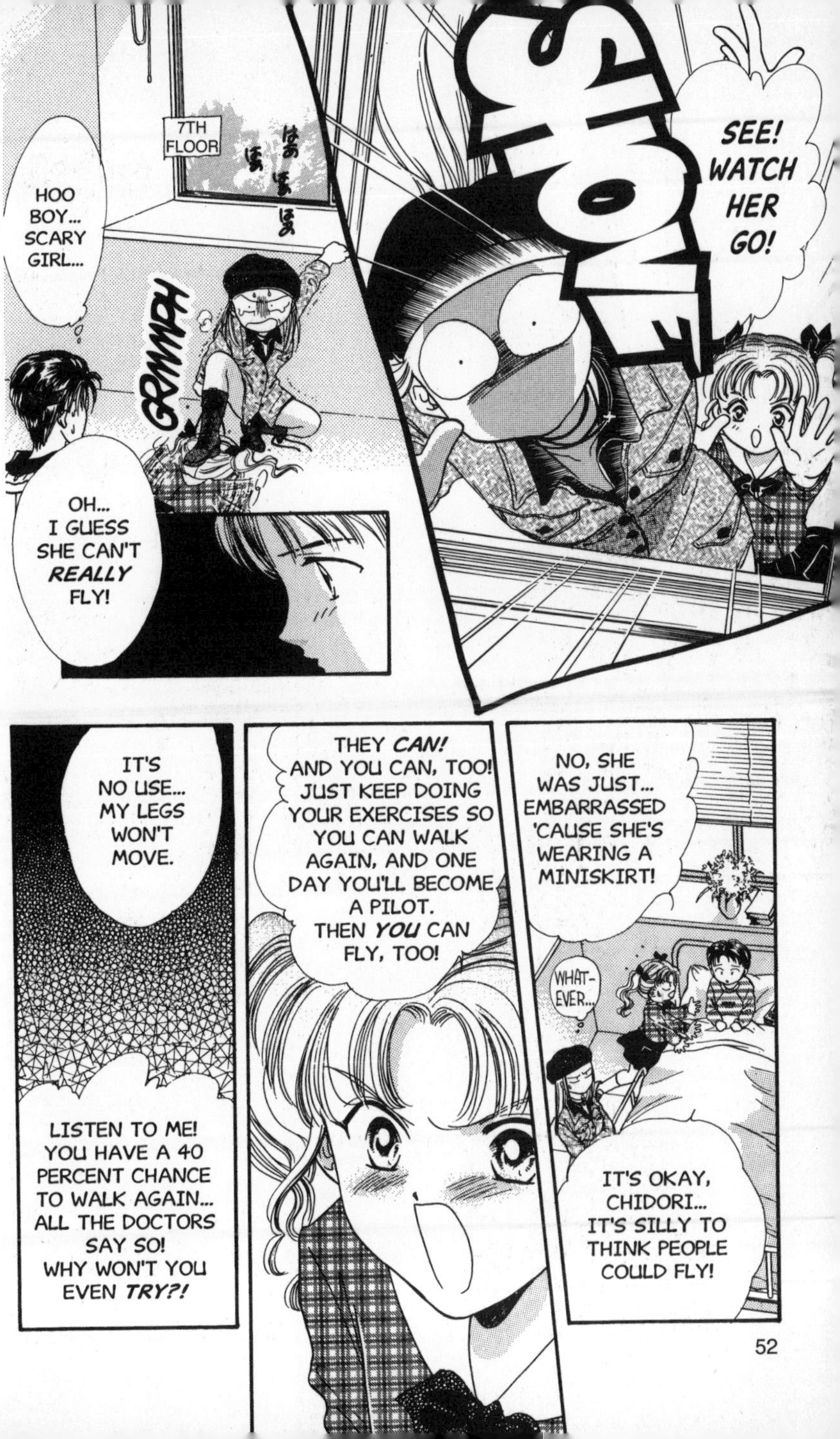
SEE! WATCH HER GO!
7TH FLOOR
HOO BOY... SCARY GIRL...
GRMMPH
OH... I GUESS SHE CAN'T REALLY FLY!
NO, SHE WAS JUST... EMBARRASSED 'CAUSE SHE'S WEARING A MINISKIRT!
WHAT-EVER...
IT'S OKAY, CHIDORI... IT'S SILLY TO THINK PEOPLE COULD FLY!
THEY CAN! AND YOU CAN, TOO! JUST KEEP DOING YOUR EXERCISES SO YOU CAN WALK AGAIN, AND ONE DAY YOU'LL BECOME A PILOT. THEN YOU CAN FLY, TOO!
IT'S NO USE... MY LEGS WON'T MOVE.
LISTEN TO ME! YOU HAVE A 40 PERCENT CHANCE TO WALK AGAIN... ALL THE DOCTORS SAY SO! WHY WON'T YOU EVEN TRY?!

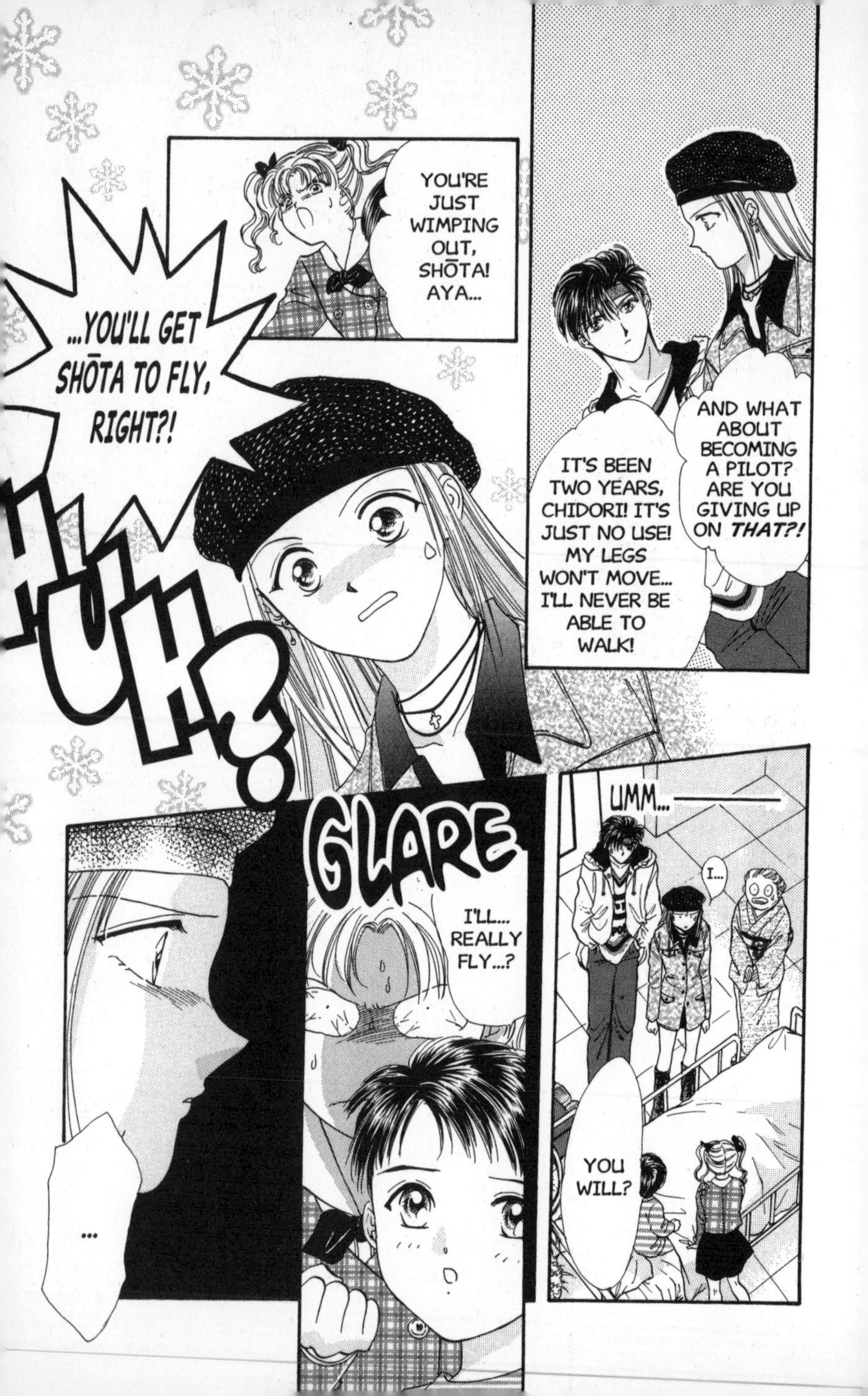
AND WHAT ABOUT BECOMING A PILOT? ARE YOU GIVING UP ON *THAT?!*
IT'S BEEN TWO YEARS, CHIDORI! IT'S JUST NO USE! MY LEGS WON'T MOVE... I'LL NEVER BE ABLE TO WALK!
YOU'RE JUST WIMPING OUT, SHŌTA! AYA...
...YOU'LL GET SHŌTA TO FLY, RIGHT?!
HUH?!
UMM...
I...
YOU WILL?
GLARE
I'LL... REALLY FLY...?
...

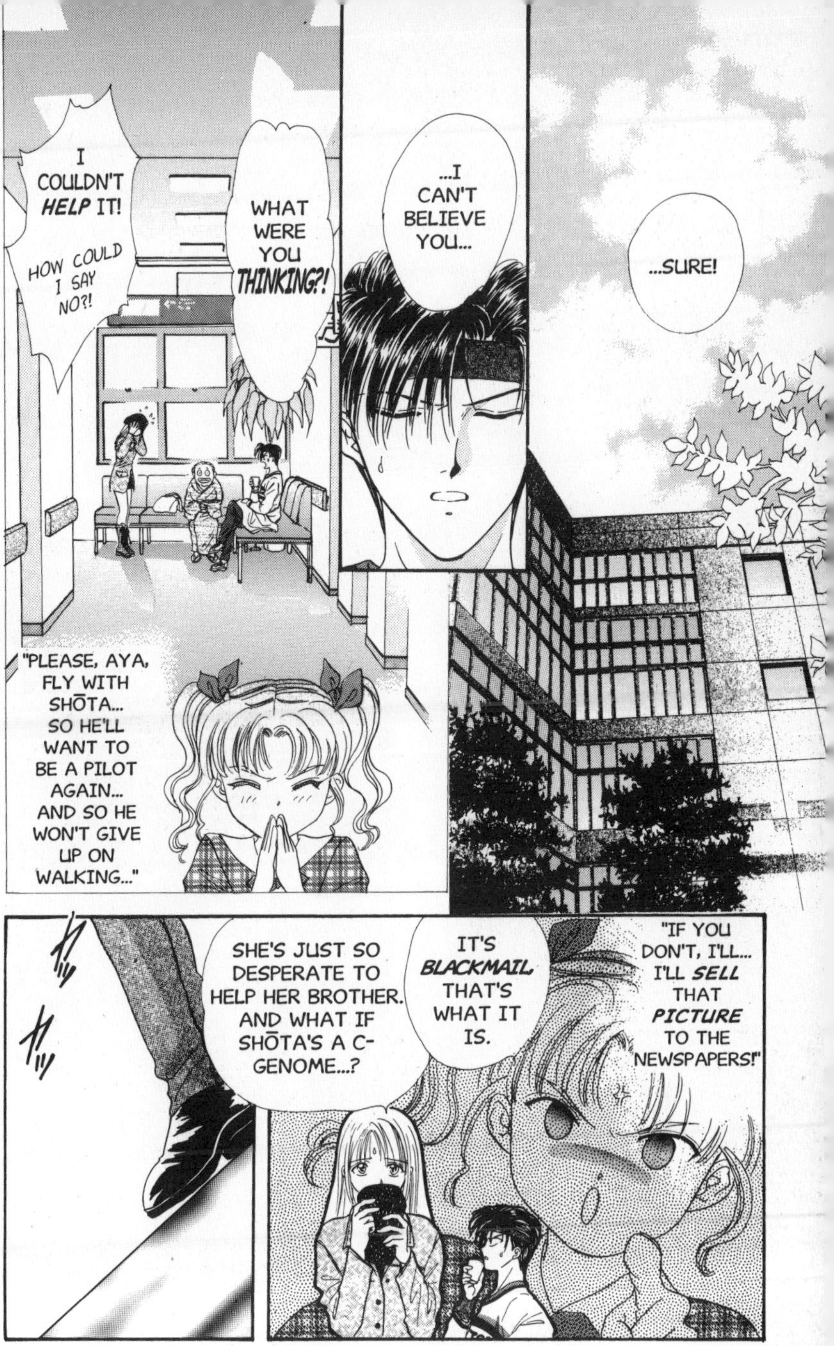
...SURE!
...I CAN'T BELIEVE YOU...
WHAT WERE YOU THINKING?!
I COULDN'T HELP IT!
HOW COULD I SAY NO?!
"PLEASE, AYA, FLY WITH SHŌTA... SO HE'LL WANT TO BE A PILOT AGAIN... AND SO HE WON'T GIVE UP ON WALKING..."
"IF YOU DON'T, I'LL... I'LL SELL THAT PICTURE TO THE NEWSPAPERS!"
IT'S BLACKMAIL THAT'S WHAT IT IS.
SHE'S JUST SO DESPERATE TO HELP HER BROTHER. AND WHAT IF SHŌTA'S A C-GENOME...?

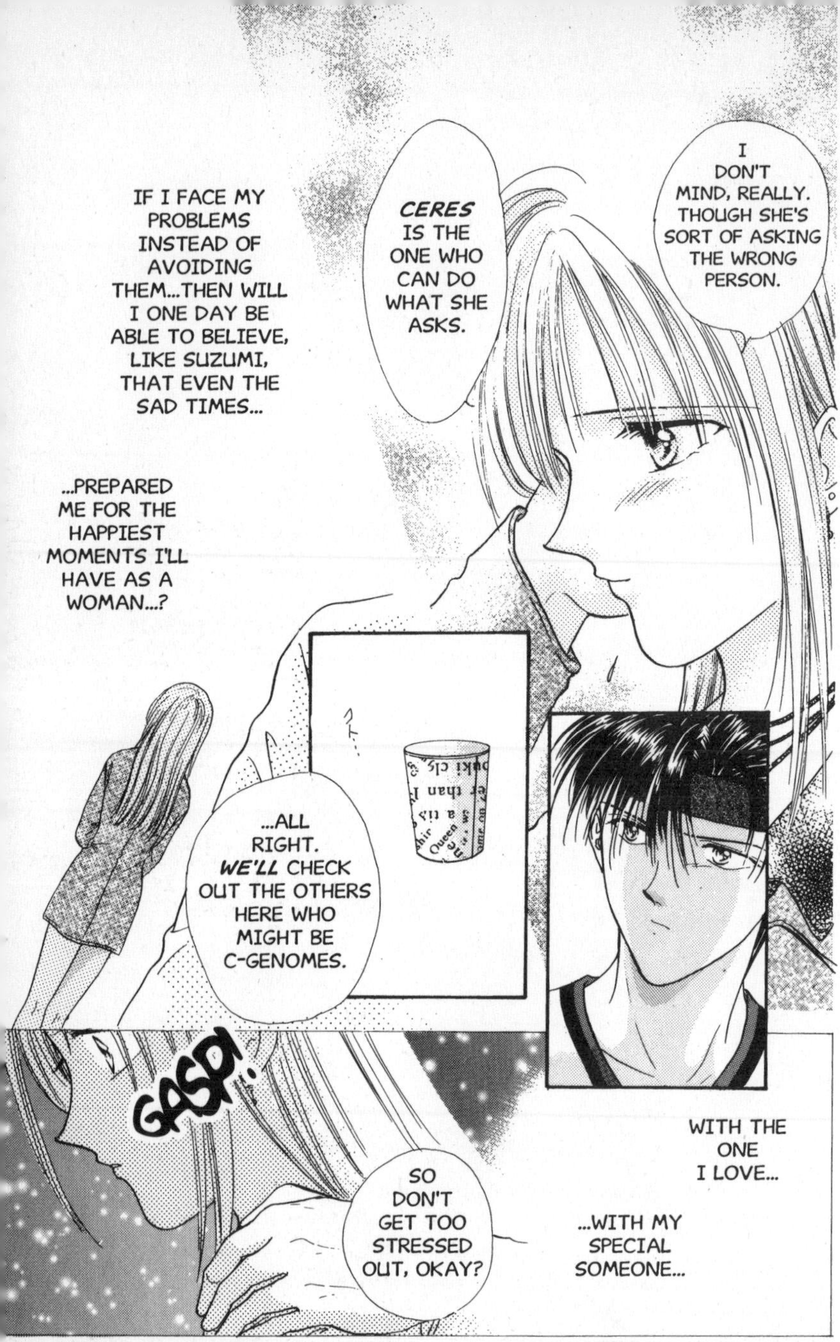
I DON'T MIND, REALLY. THOUGH SHE'S SORT OF ASKING THE WRONG PERSON.
CERES IS THE ONE WHO CAN DO WHAT SHE ASKS.
IF I FACE MY PROBLEMS INSTEAD OF AVOIDING THEM...THEN WILL I ONE DAY BE ABLE TO BELIEVE, LIKE SUZUMI, THAT EVEN THE SAD TIMES...
...PREPARED ME FOR THE HAPPIEST MOMENTS I'LL HAVE AS A WOMAN...?
...ALL RIGHT. WE'LL CHECK OUT THE OTHERS HERE WHO MIGHT BE C-GENOMES.
WITH THE ONE I LOVE...
...WITH MY SPECIAL SOMEONE...
SO DON'T GET TOO STRESSED OUT, OKAY?
GASP!

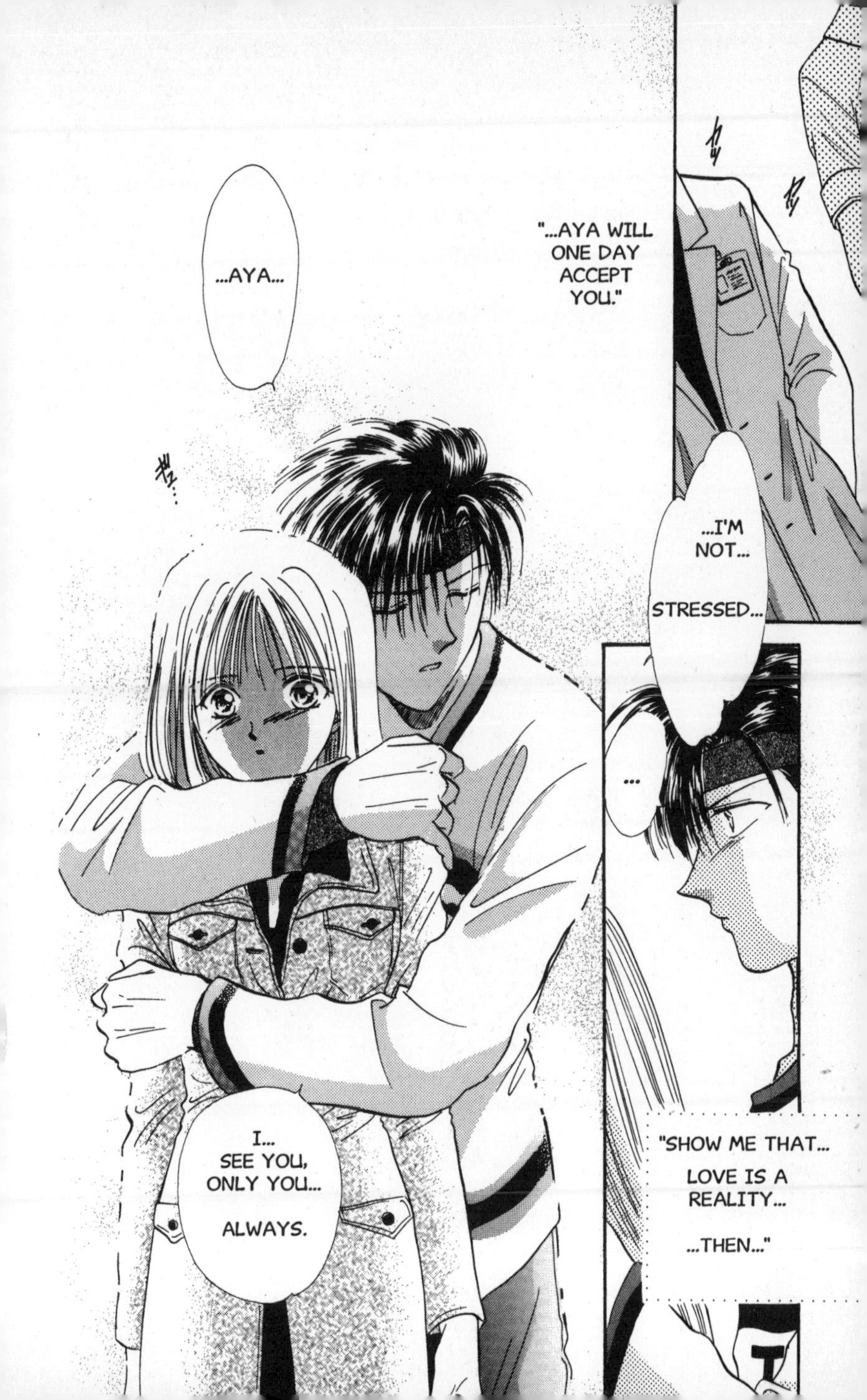

...I'M NOT... STRESSED...
...
"SHOW ME THAT... LOVE IS A REALITY... ...THEN..."
"...AYA WILL ONE DAY ACCEPT YOU."
...AYA...
I... SEE YOU, ONLY YOU... ALWAYS.

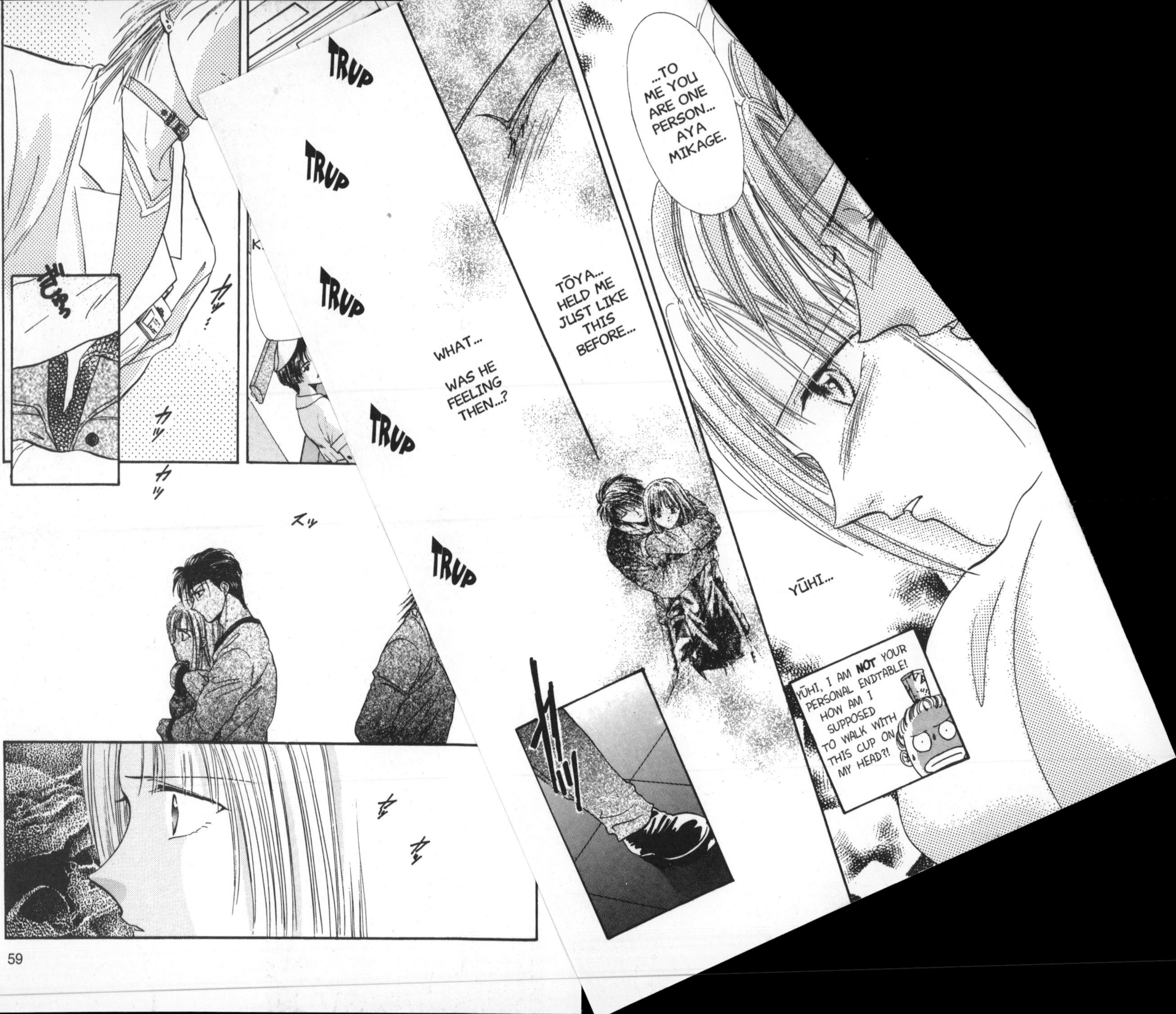
...TO ME YOU ARE ONE PERSON... AYA MIKAGE.
YŪHI...
YŪHI, I AM NOT YOUR PERSONAL ENDTABLE! HOW AM I SUPPOSED TO WALK WITH THIS CUP ON MY HEAD?!
TŌYA... HELD ME JUST LIKE THIS BEFORE...
WHAT...
WAS HE FEELING THEN...?
TRUP
TRUP
TRUP
TRUP
TRUP
K...
カッ
カッ
スッ

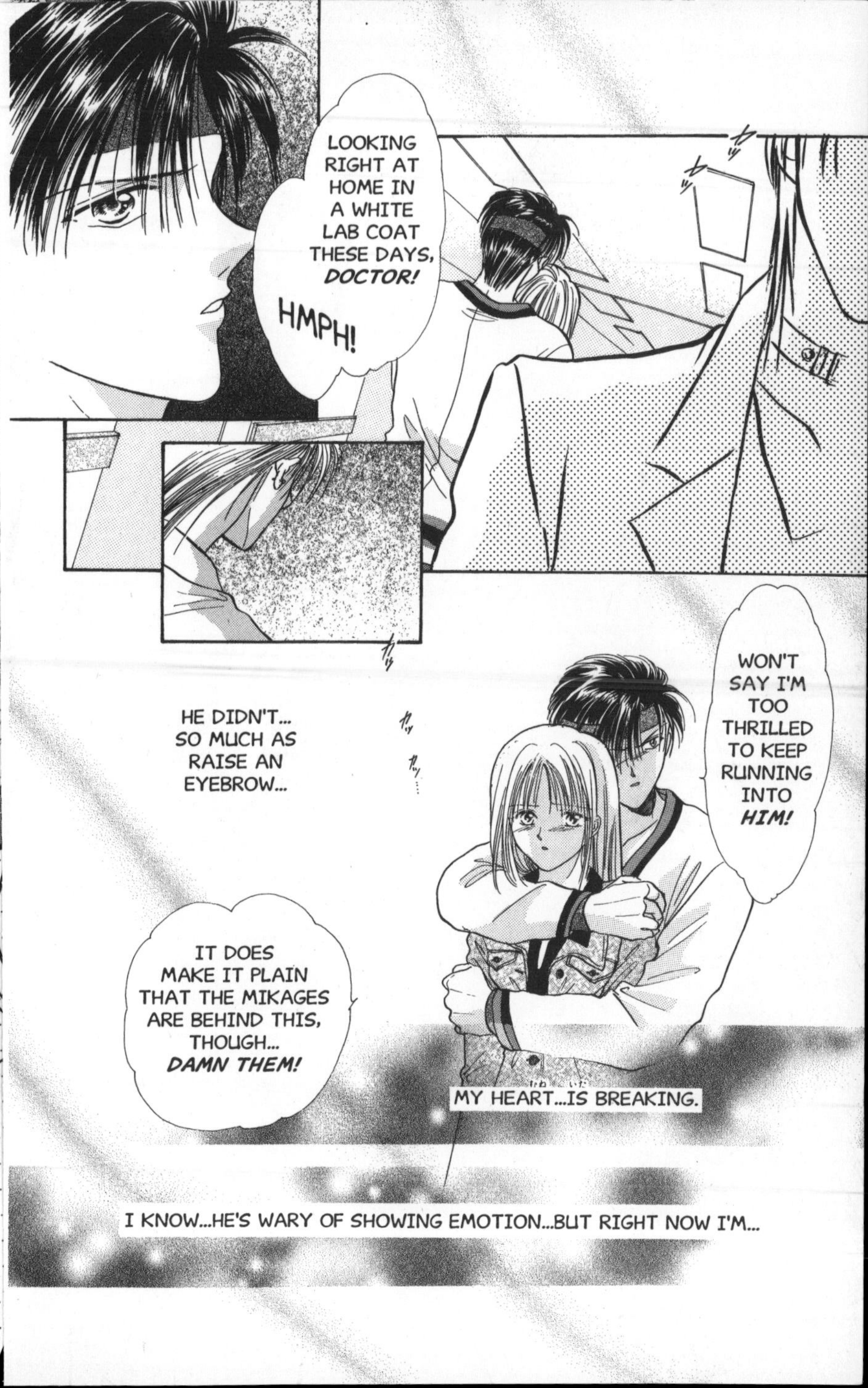
LOOKING RIGHT AT HOME IN A WHITE LAB COAT THESE DAYS, DOCTOR!
HMPH!
WON'T SAY I'M TOO THRILLED TO KEEP RUNNING INTO HIM!
HE DIDN'T... SO MUCH AS RAISE AN EYEBROW...
IT DOES MAKE IT PLAIN THAT THE MIKAGES ARE BEHIND THIS, THOUGH... DAMN THEM!
MY HEART...IS BREAKING.
I KNOW...HE'S WARY OF SHOWING EMOTION...BUT RIGHT NOW I'M...
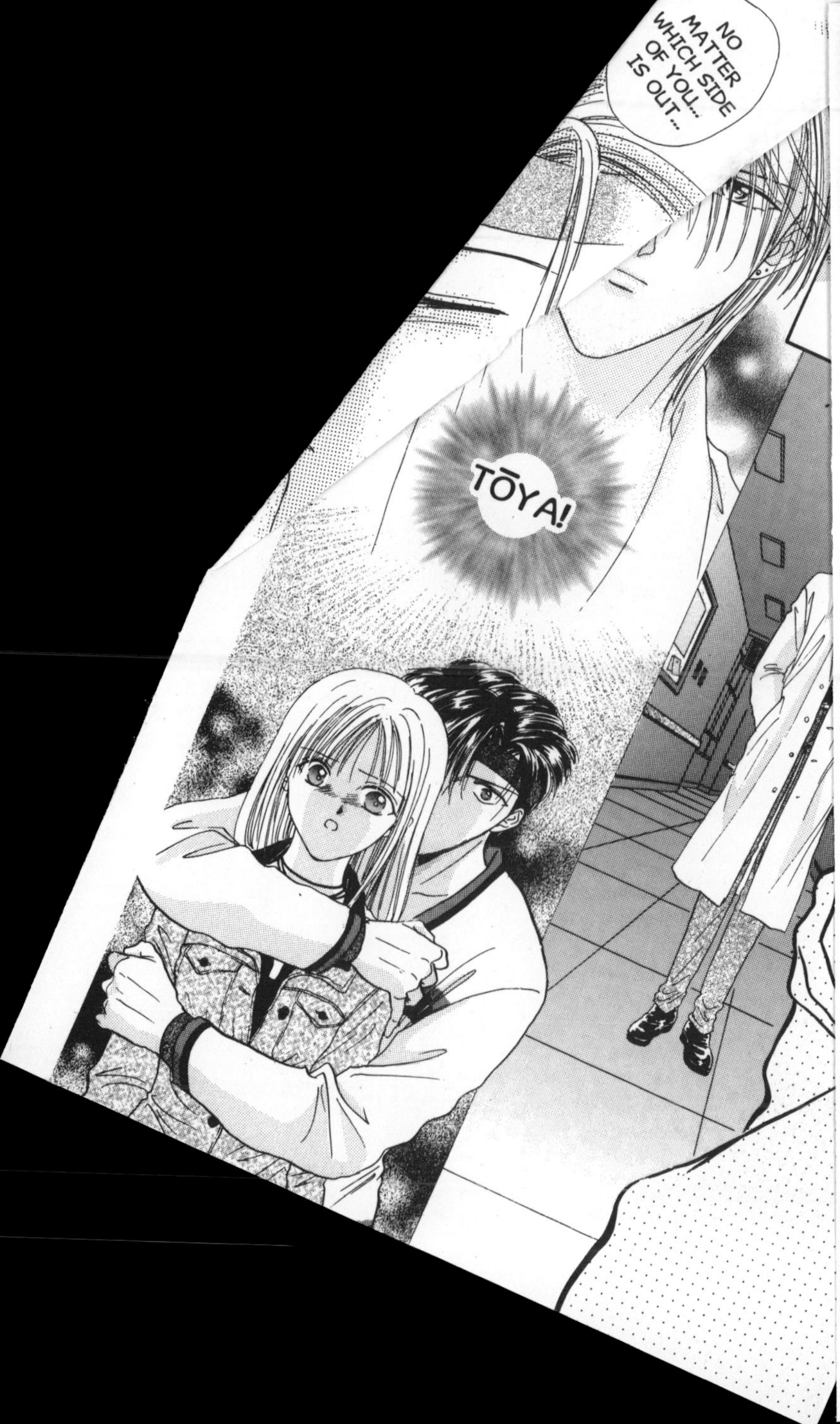
NO MATTER WHICH SIDE OF YOU... IS OUT...
TŌYA!

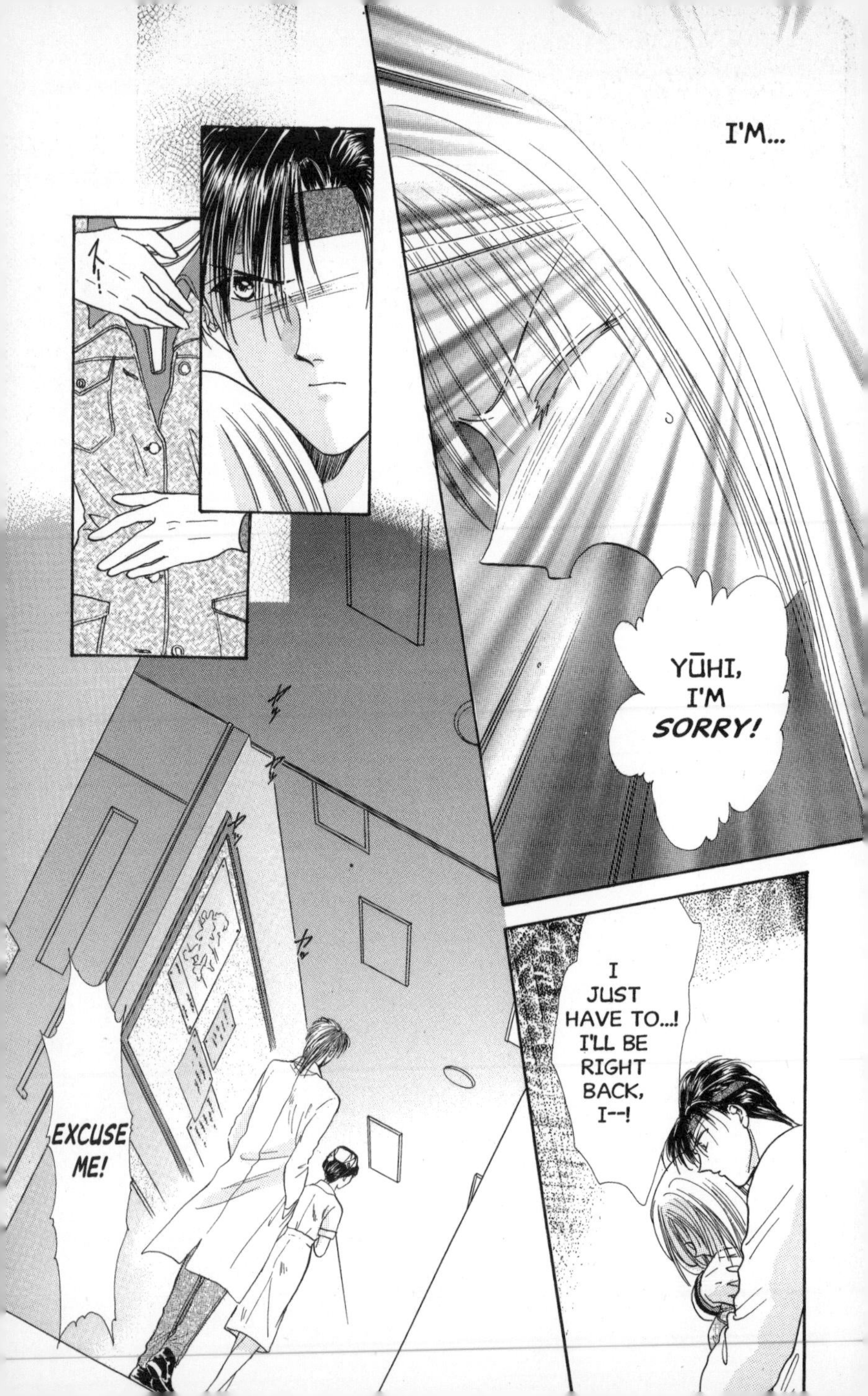
I'M...
YŪHI, I'M *SORRY!*
I JUST HAVE TO...! I'LL BE RIGHT BACK, I--!
EXCUSE ME!

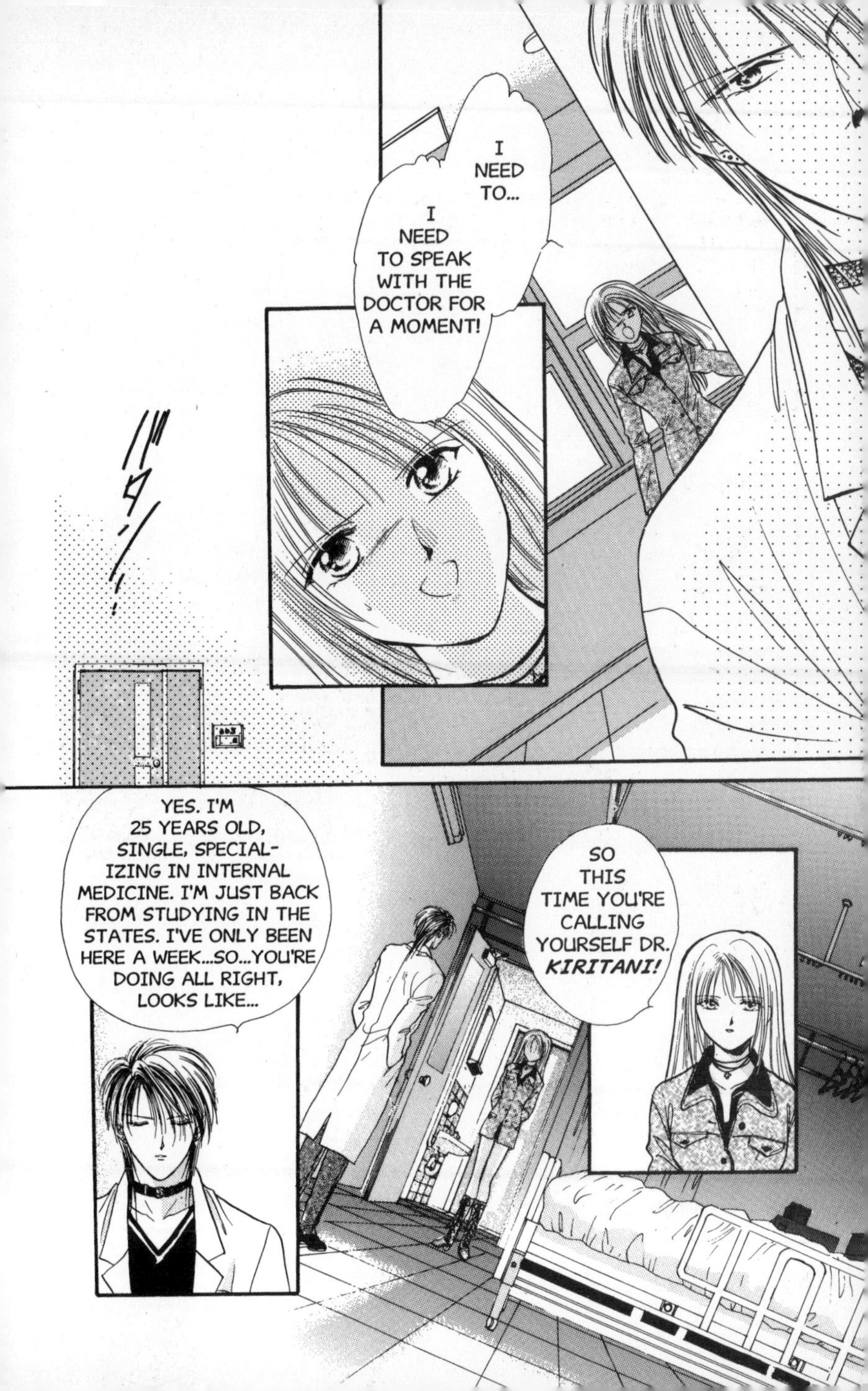
I NEED TO...
I NEED TO SPEAK WITH THE DOCTOR FOR A MOMENT!
SO THIS TIME YOU'RE CALLING YOURSELF DR. *KIRITANI!*
YES. I'M 25 YEARS OLD, SINGLE, SPECIAL-IZING IN INTERNAL MEDICINE. I'M JUST BACK FROM STUDYING IN THE STATES. I'VE ONLY BEEN HERE A WEEK...SO...YOU'RE DOING ALL RIGHT, LOOKS LIKE...

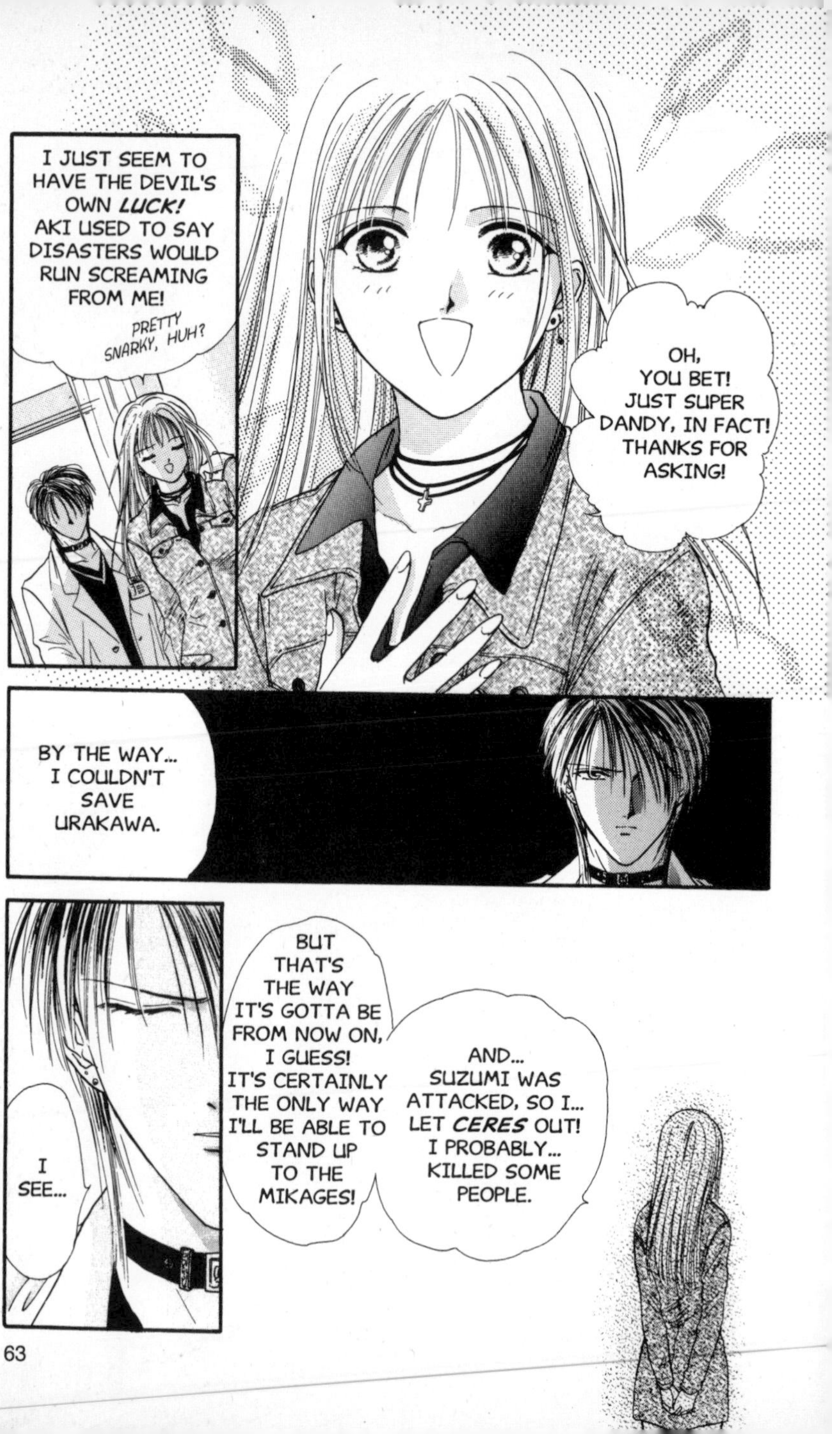
OH, YOU BET! JUST SUPER DANDY, IN FACT! THANKS FOR ASKING!
I JUST SEEM TO HAVE THE DEVIL'S OWN *LUCK!* AKI USED TO SAY DISASTERS WOULD RUN SCREAMING FROM ME!
PRETTY SNARKY, HUH?
BY THE WAY... I COULDN'T SAVE URAKAWA.
AND... SUZUMI WAS ATTACKED, SO I... LET *CERES* OUT! I PROBABLY... KILLED SOME PEOPLE.
BUT THAT'S THE WAY IT'S GOTTA BE FROM NOW ON, I GUESS! IT'S CERTAINLY THE ONLY WAY I'LL BE ABLE TO STAND UP TO THE MIKAGES!
I SEE...

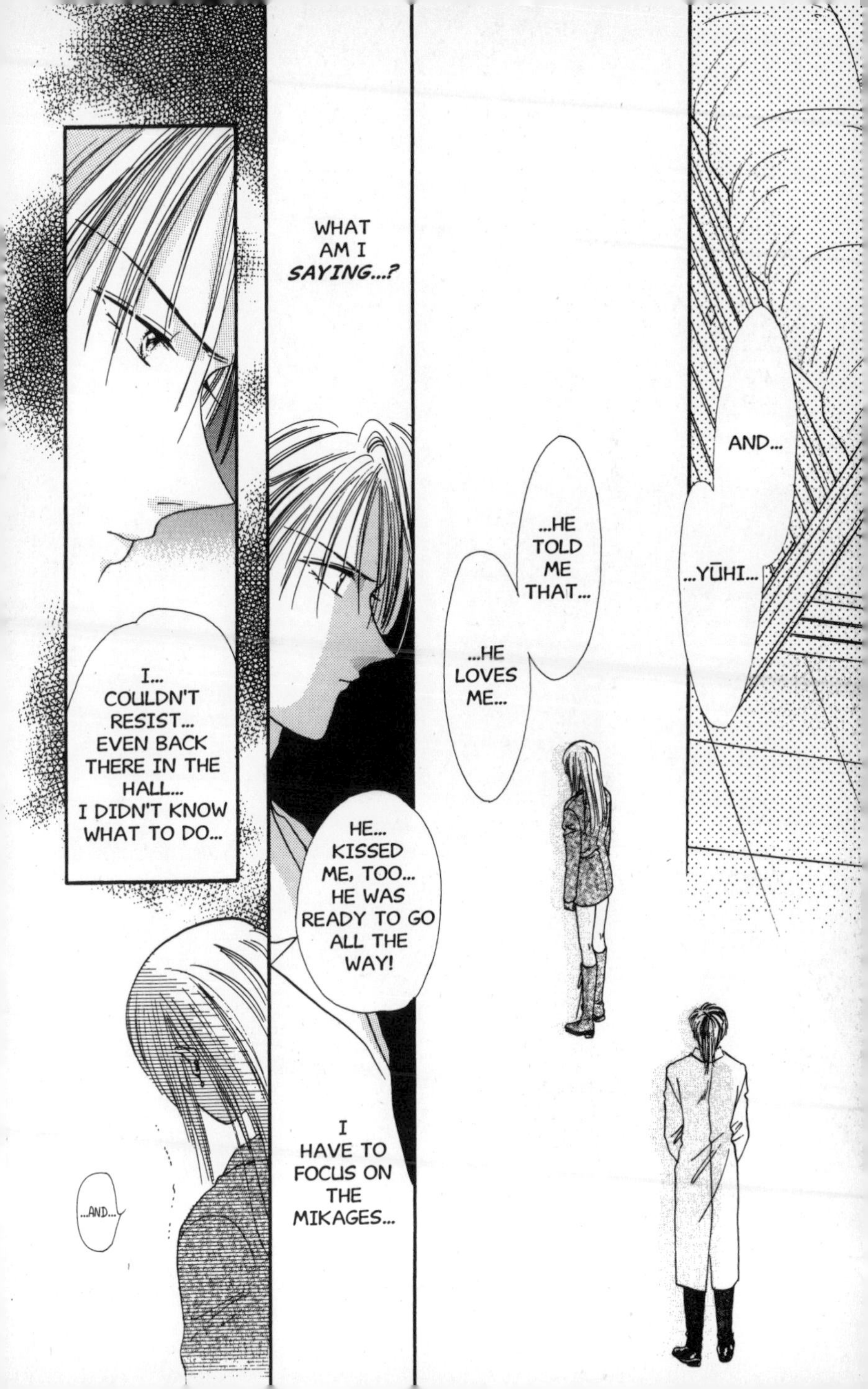
AND...
...YŪHI...
...HE TOLD ME THAT...
...HE LOVES ME...
WHAT AM I *SAYING...?*
HE... KISSED ME, TOO... HE WAS READY TO GO ALL THE WAY!
I HAVE TO FOCUS ON THE MIKAGES...
I... COULDN'T RESIST... EVEN BACK THERE IN THE HALL... I DIDN'T KNOW WHAT TO DO...
...AND...

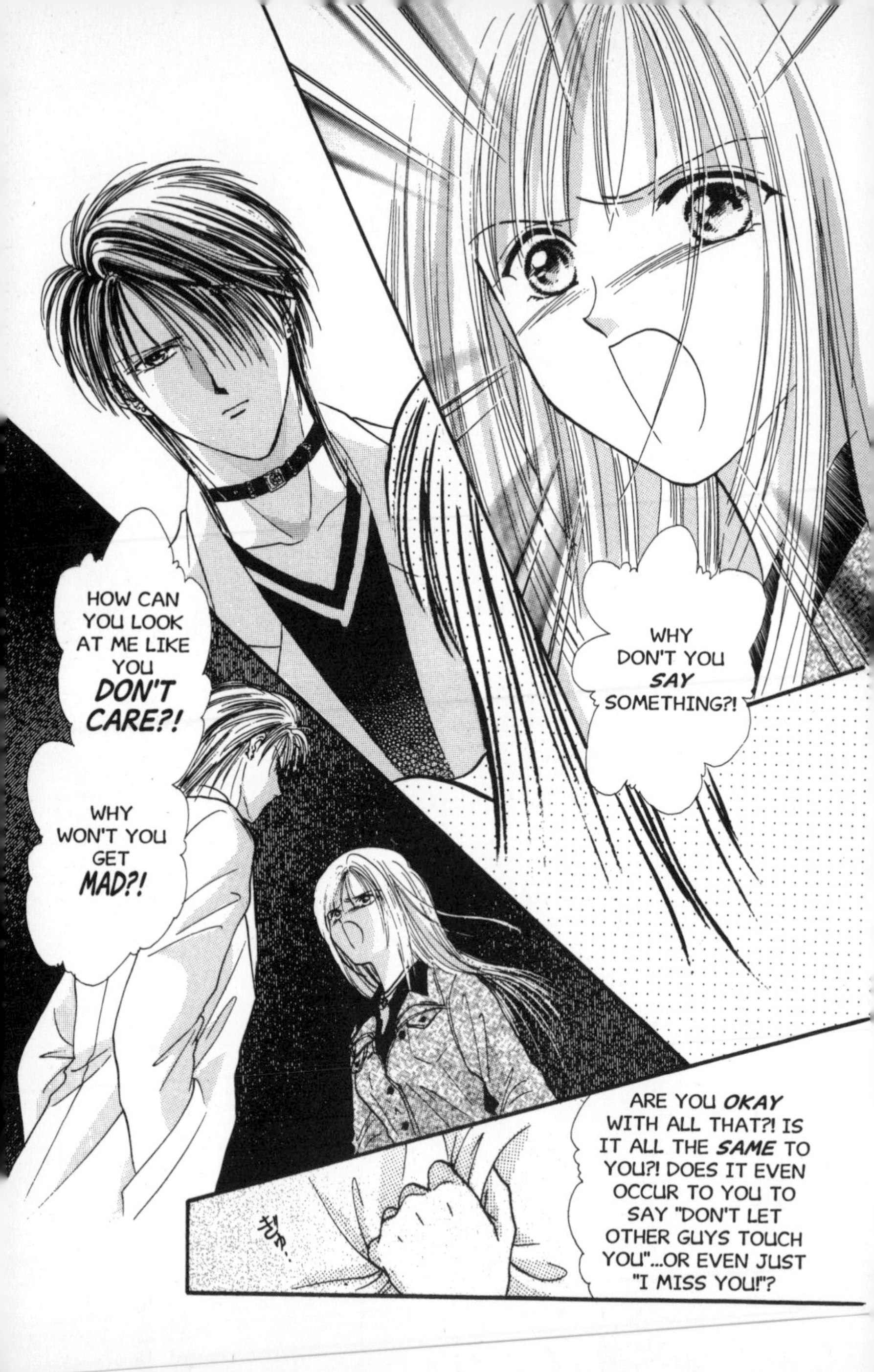
WHY DON'T YOU *SAY* SOMETHING?!
HOW CAN YOU LOOK AT ME LIKE YOU ***DON'T CARE?!***
WHY WON'T YOU GET ***MAD?!***
ARE YOU ***OKAY*** WITH ALL THAT?! IS IT ALL THE ***SAME*** TO YOU?! DOES IT EVEN OCCUR TO YOU TO SAY "DON'T LET OTHER GUYS TOUCH YOU"...OR EVEN JUST "I MISS YOU!"?

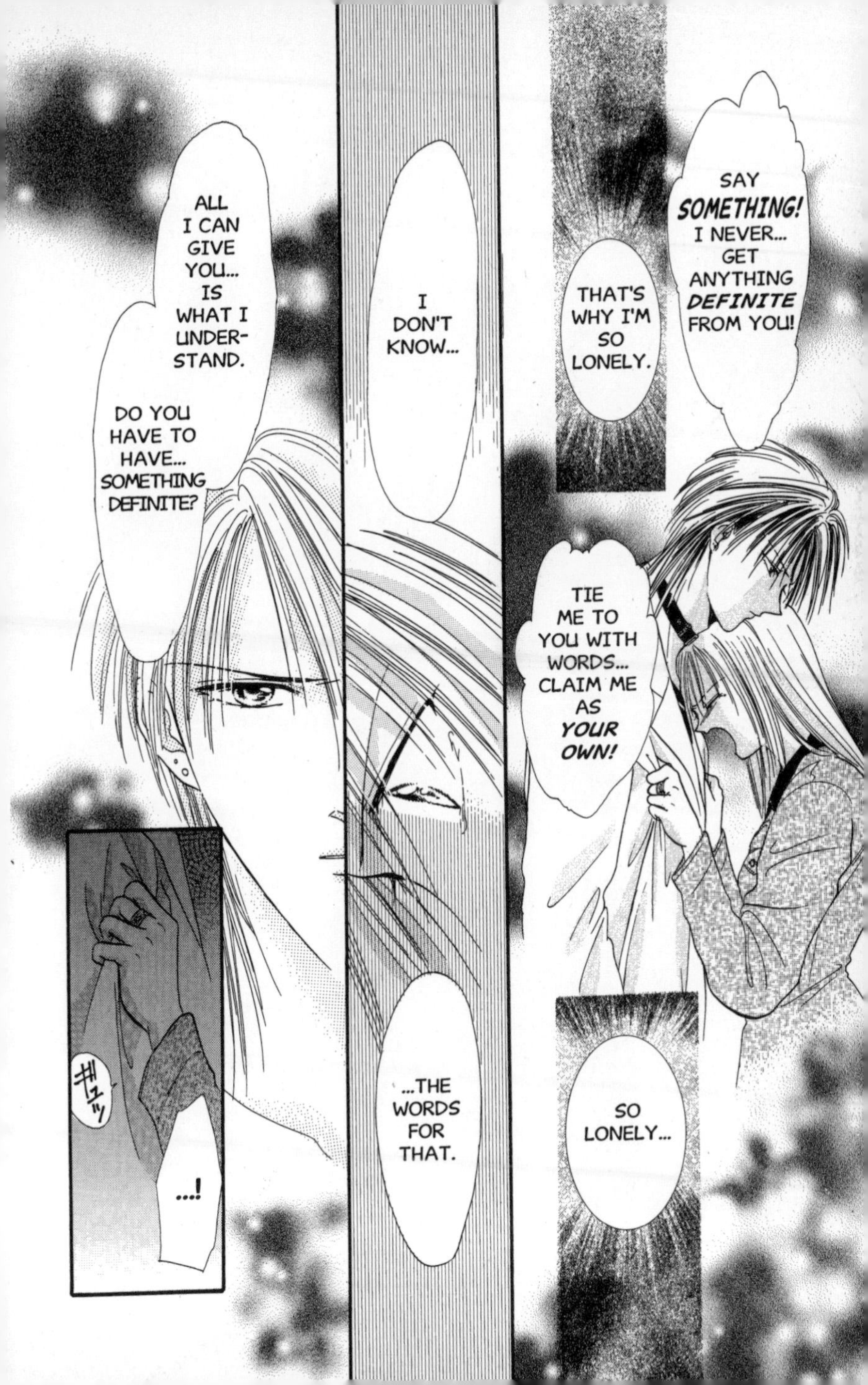
SAY SOMETHING! I NEVER... GET ANYTHING DEFINITE FROM YOU!
THAT'S WHY I'M SO LONELY.
TIE ME TO YOU WITH WORDS... CLAIM ME AS YOUR OWN!
SO LONELY...
I DON'T KNOW...
...THE WORDS FOR THAT.
ALL I CAN GIVE YOU... IS WHAT I UNDERSTAND.
DO YOU HAVE TO HAVE... SOMETHING DEFINITE?
ギュッ
...!

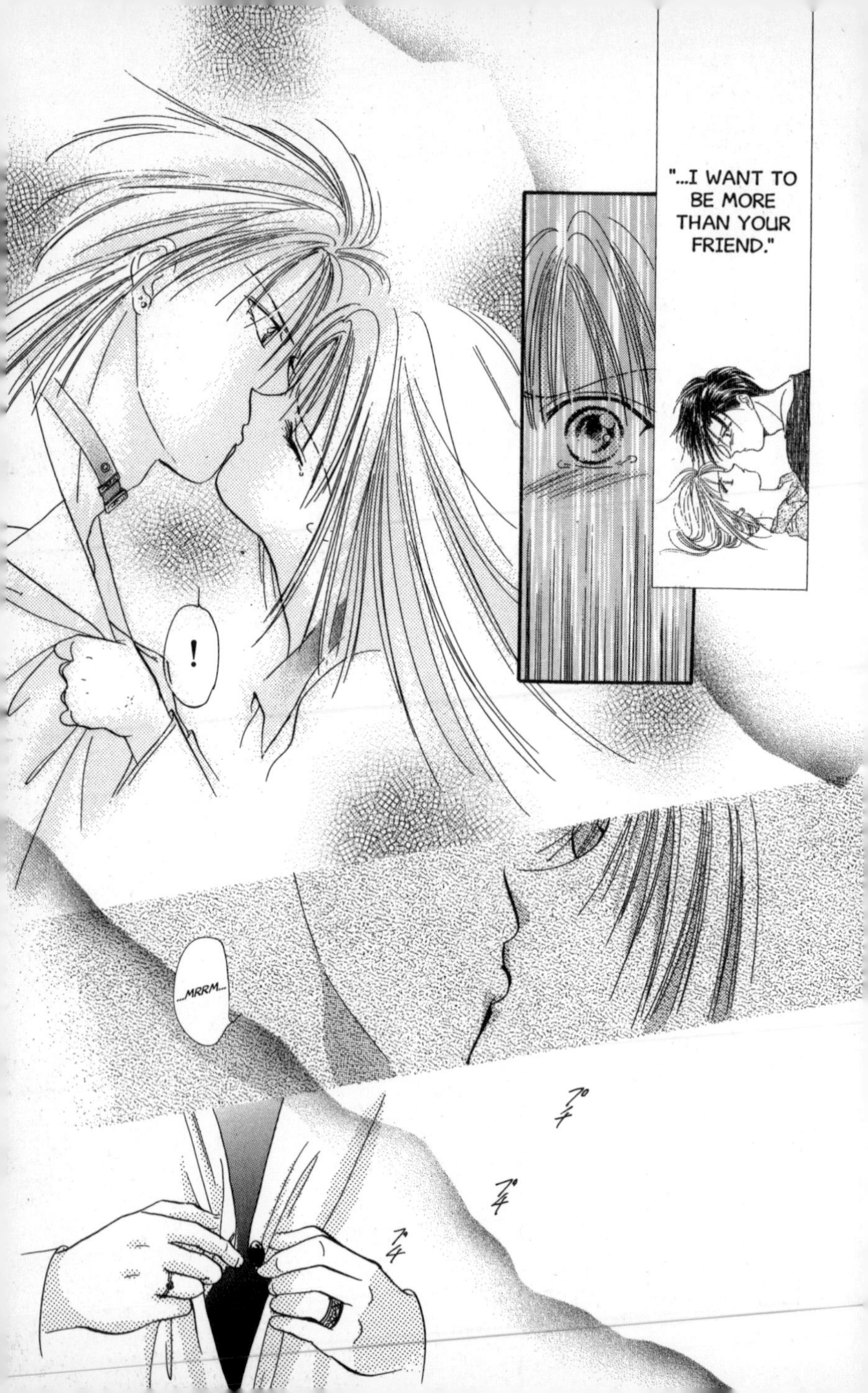
"...I WANT TO BE MORE THAN YOUR FRIEND."
!
...MRRM...
プチ
プチ
プチ

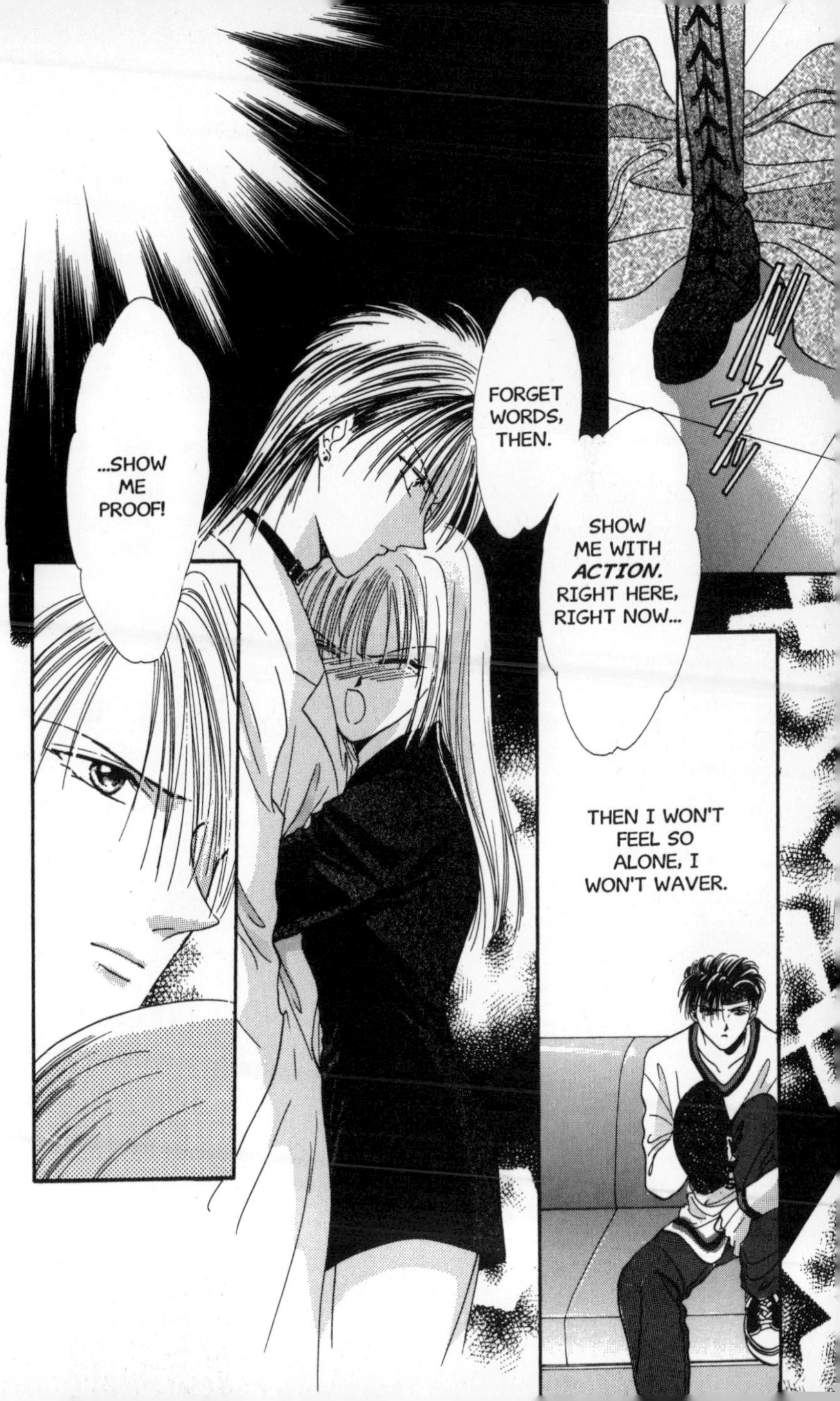
FORGET WORDS, THEN.
SHOW ME WITH *ACTION.* RIGHT HERE, RIGHT NOW...
...SHOW ME PROOF!
THEN I WON'T FEEL SO ALONE, I WON'T WAVER.

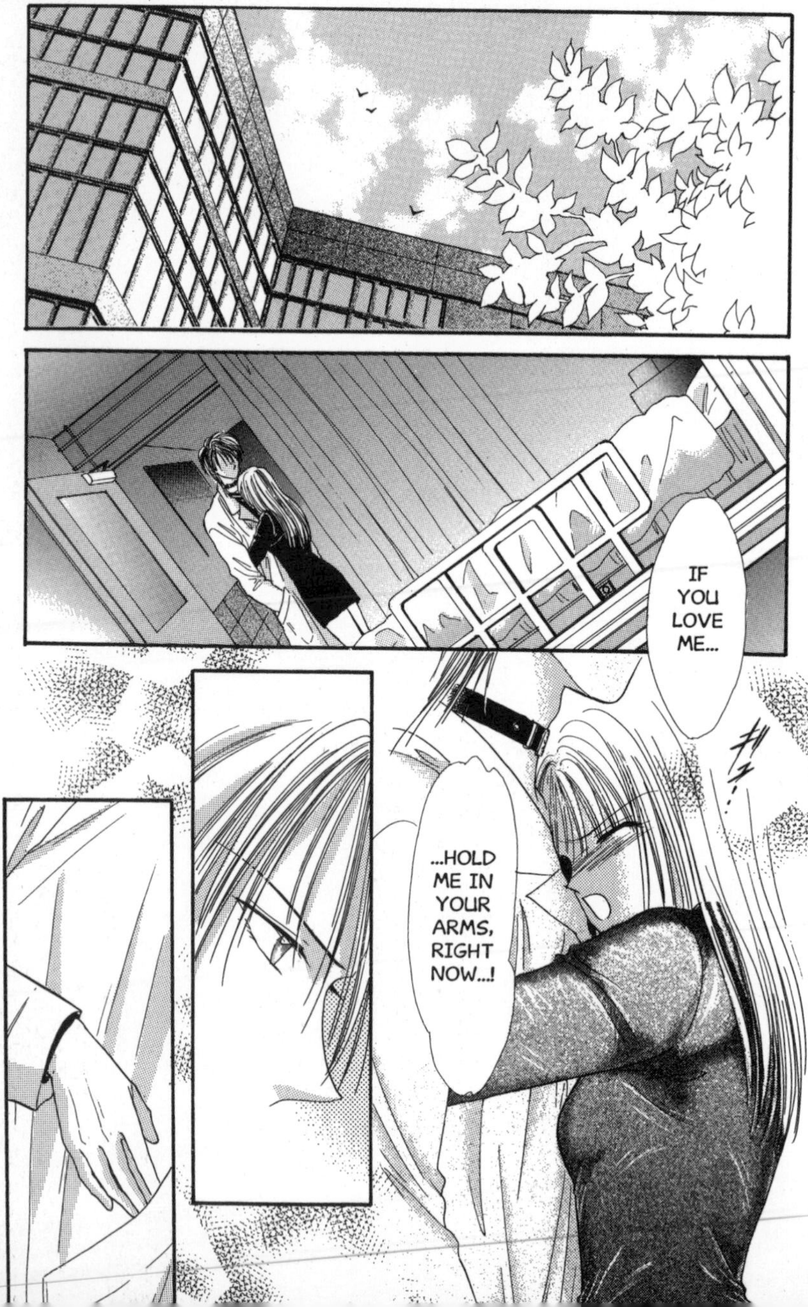
IF YOU LOVE ME...
...HOLD ME IN YOUR ARMS, RIGHT NOW...!

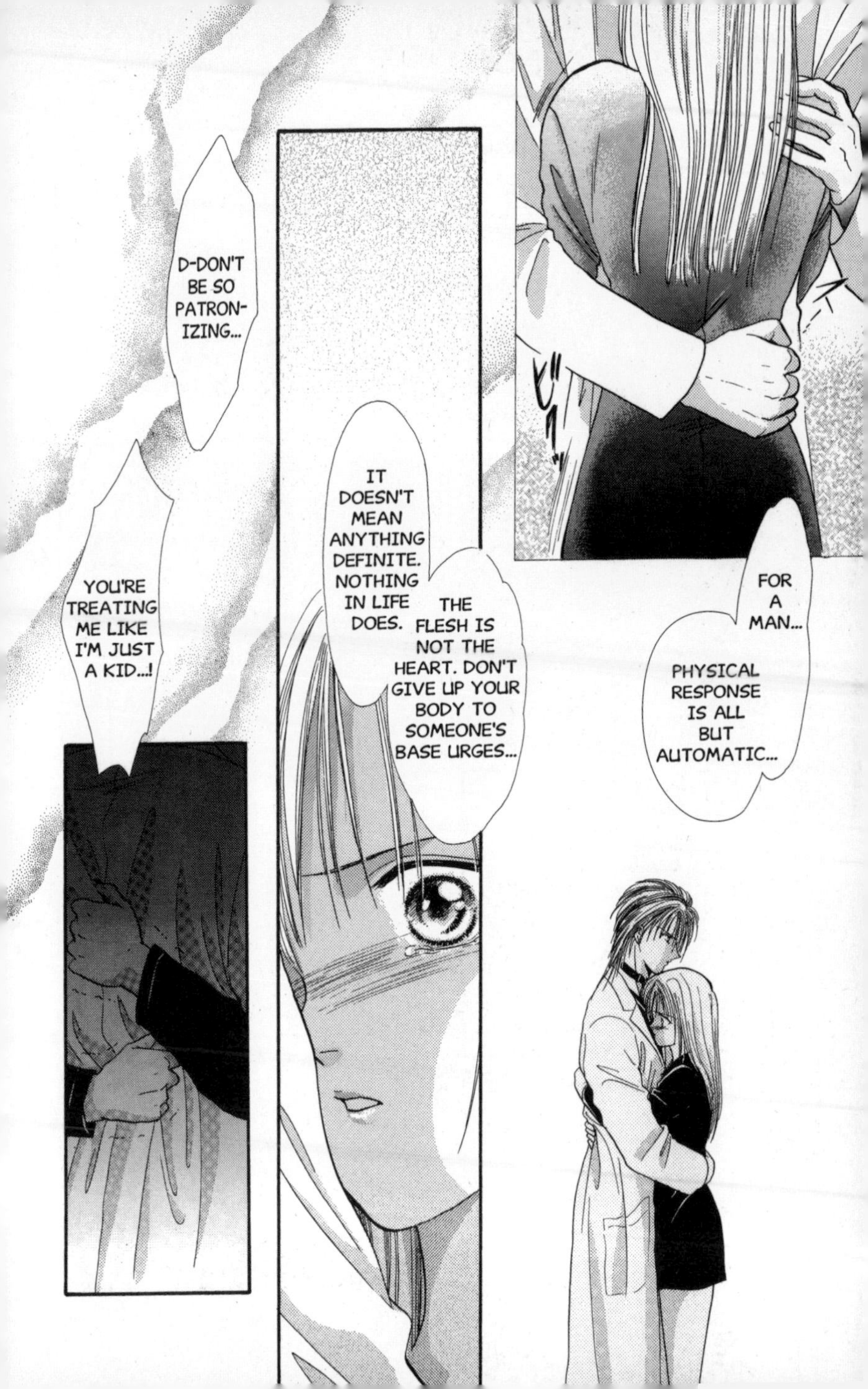
FOR A MAN...
PHYSICAL RESPONSE IS ALL BUT AUTOMATIC...
IT DOESN'T MEAN ANYTHING DEFINITE. NOTHING IN LIFE DOES.
THE FLESH IS NOT THE HEART. DON'T GIVE UP YOUR BODY TO SOMEONE'S BASE URGES...
D-DON'T BE SO PATRON-IZING...
YOU'RE TREATING ME LIKE I'M JUST A KID...!

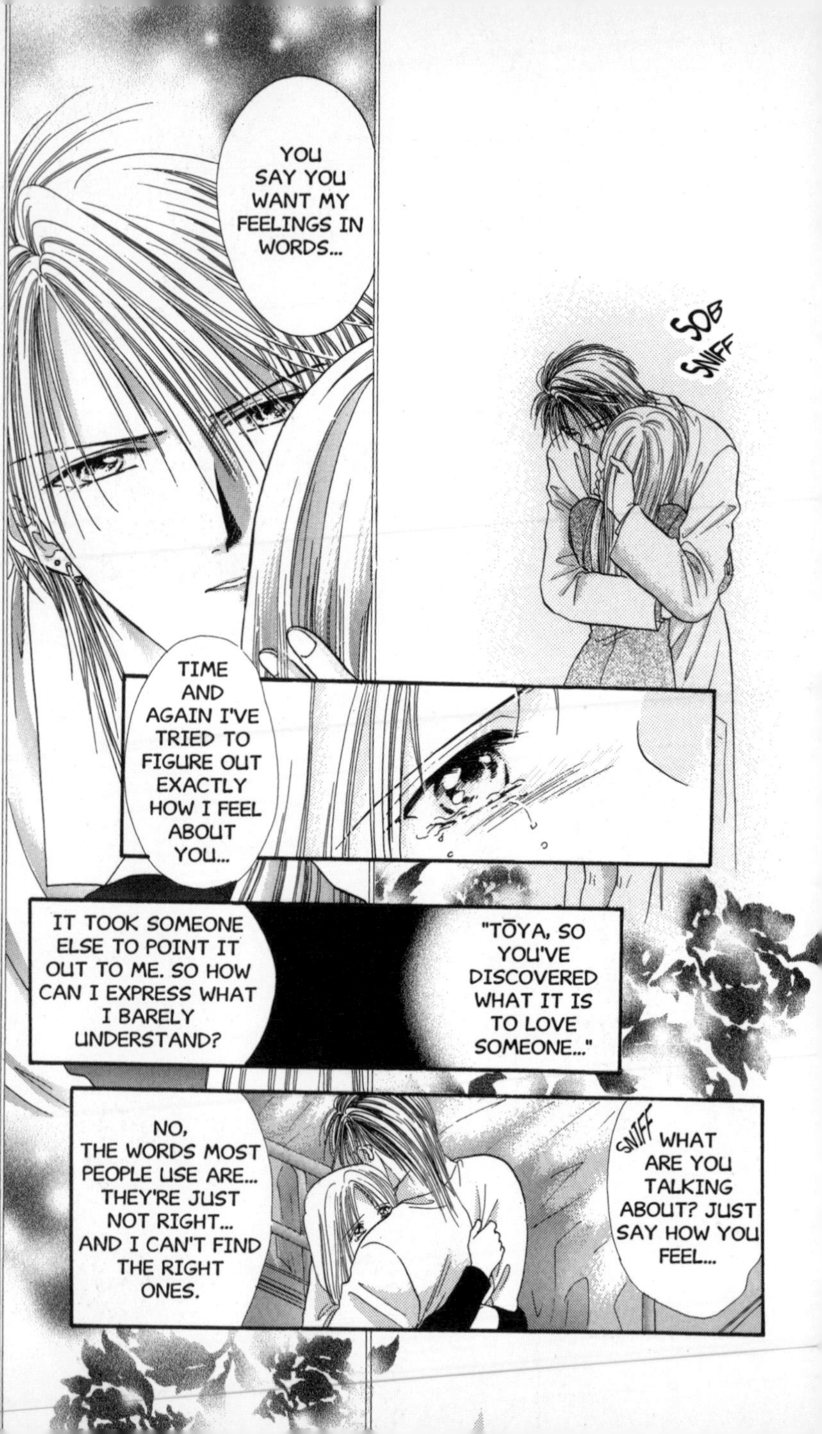
SOB
SNIFF
YOU SAY YOU WANT MY FEELINGS IN WORDS...
TIME AND AGAIN I'VE TRIED TO FIGURE OUT EXACTLY HOW I FEEL ABOUT YOU...
"TŌYA, SO YOU'VE DISCOVERED WHAT IT IS TO LOVE SOMEONE..."
IT TOOK SOMEONE ELSE TO POINT IT OUT TO ME. SO HOW CAN I EXPRESS WHAT I BARELY UNDERSTAND?
SNIFF
WHAT ARE YOU TALKING ABOUT? JUST SAY HOW YOU FEEL...
NO, THE WORDS MOST PEOPLE USE ARE... THEY'RE JUST NOT RIGHT... AND I CAN'T FIND THE RIGHT ONES.

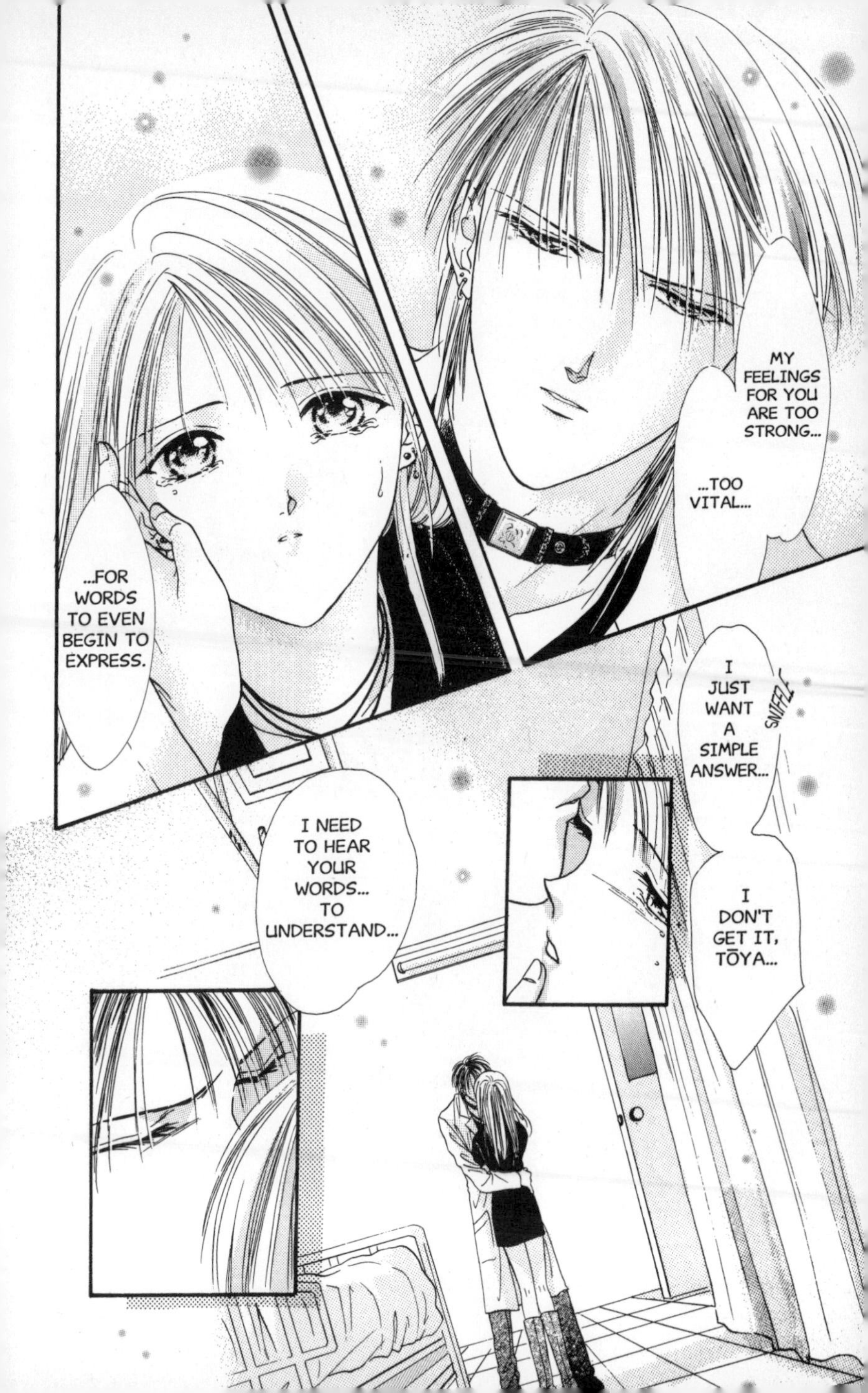
MY FEELINGS FOR YOU ARE TOO STRONG...
...TOO VITAL...
...FOR WORDS TO EVEN BEGIN TO EXPRESS.
I JUST WANT A SIMPLE ANSWER...
SNIFFL
I DON'T GET IT, TŌYA...
I NEED TO HEAR YOUR WORDS... TO UNDERSTAND...

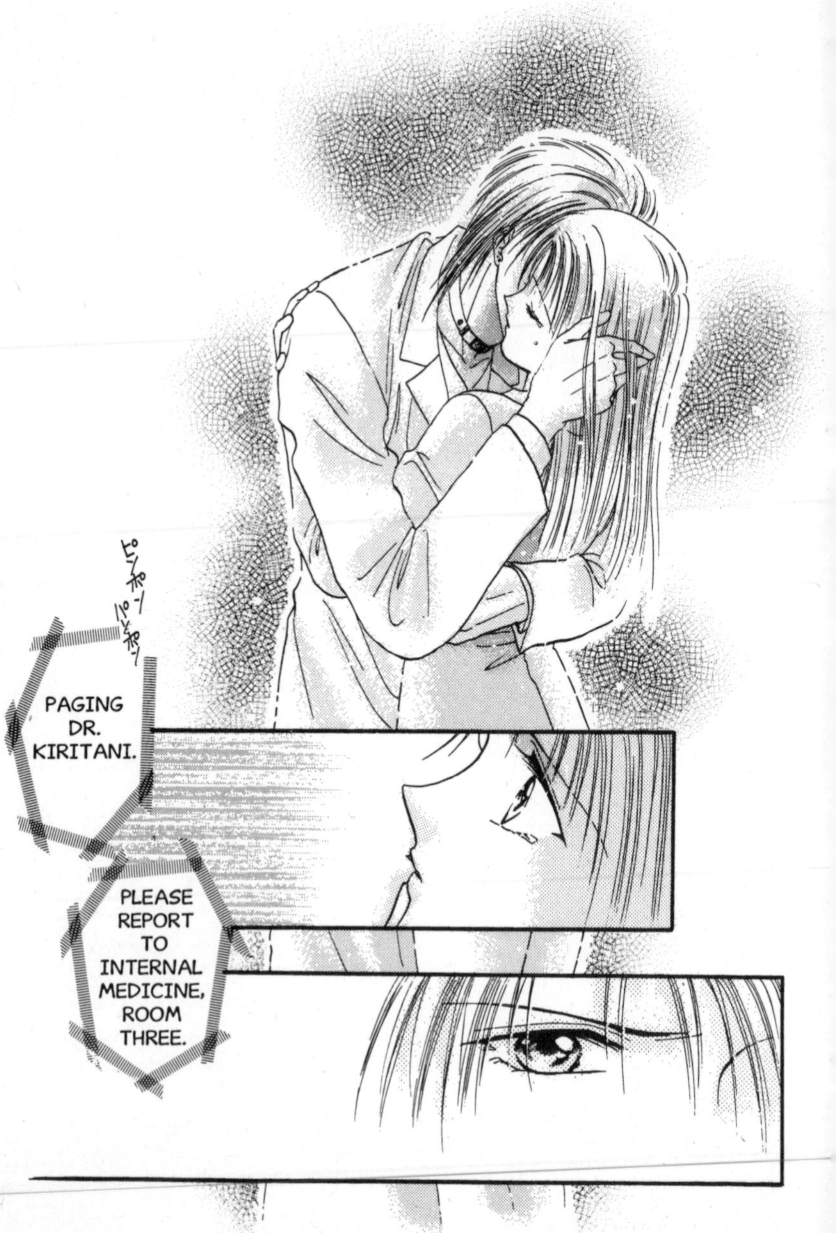
ピンポーン
PAGING DR. KIRITANI.
PLEASE REPORT TO INTERNAL MEDICINE, ROOM THREE.

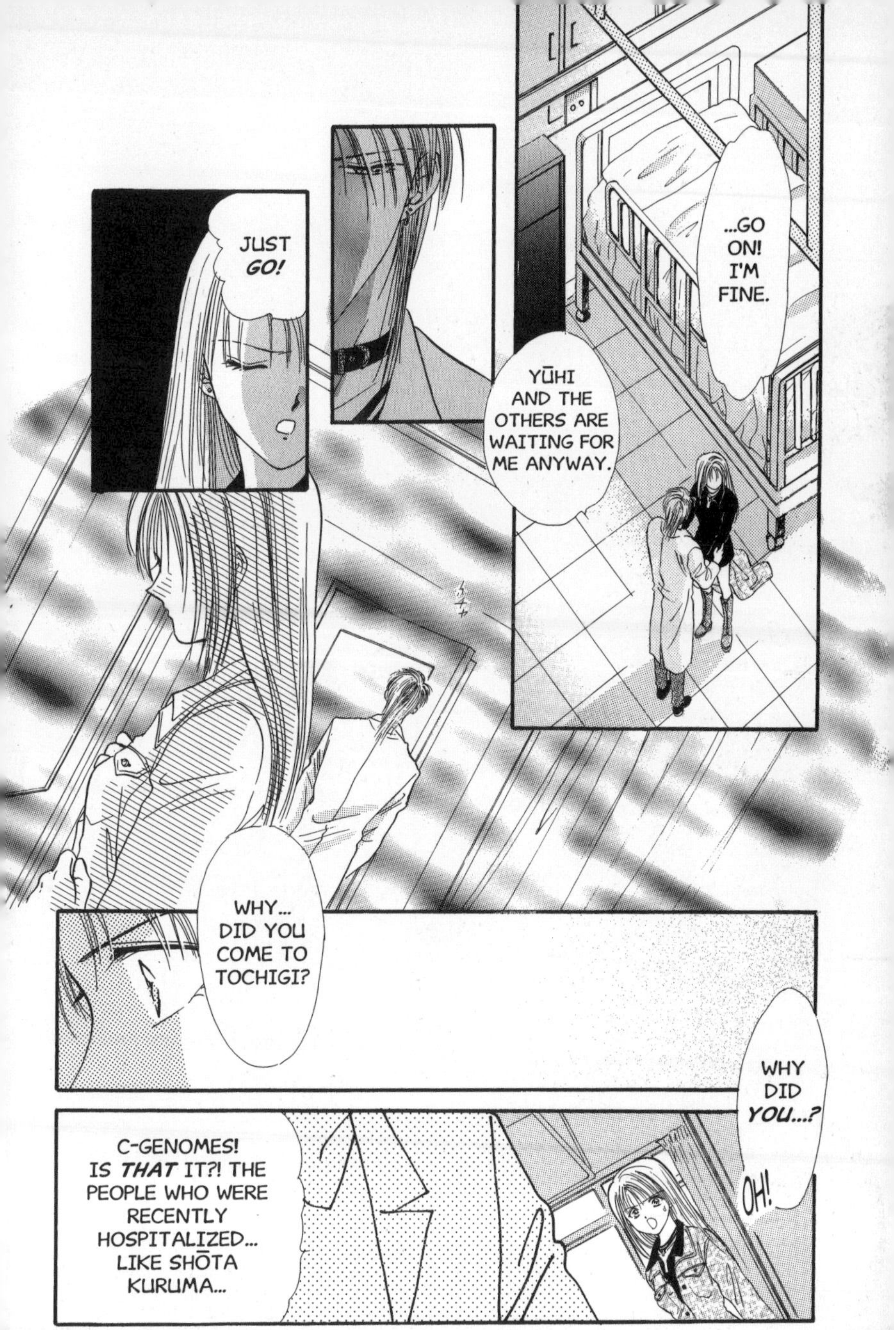
...GO ON! I'M FINE.
YŪHI AND THE OTHERS ARE WAITING FOR ME ANYWAY.
JUST *GO!*
WHY... DID YOU COME TO TOCHIGI?
WHY DID *YOU...?*
OH!
C-GENOMES! IS *THAT* IT?! THE PEOPLE WHO WERE RECENTLY HOSPITALIZED... LIKE SHŌTA KURUMA...

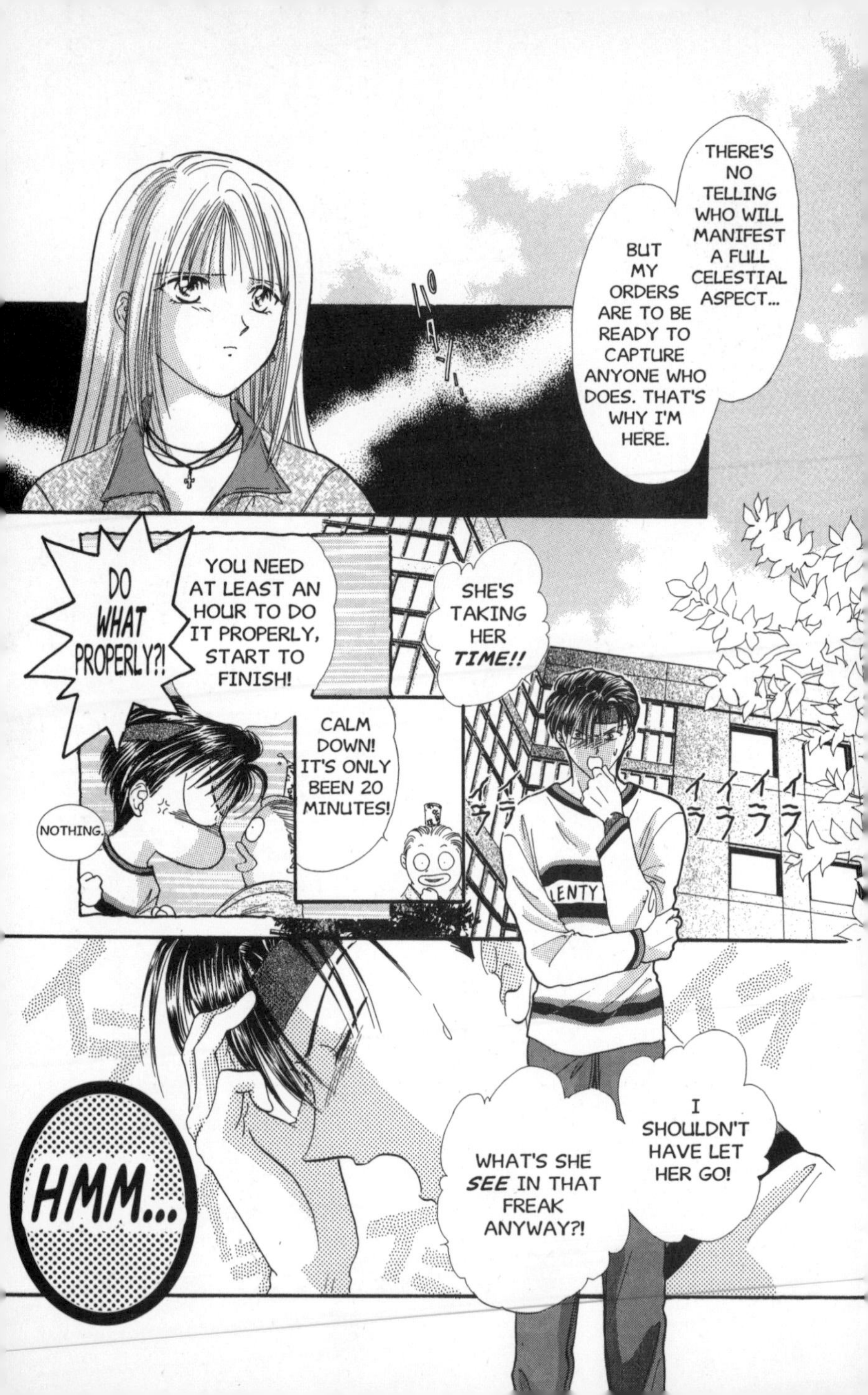
THERE'S NO TELLING WHO WILL MANIFEST A FULL CELESTIAL ASPECT...
BUT MY ORDERS ARE TO BE READY TO CAPTURE ANYONE WHO DOES. THAT'S WHY I'M HERE.
SHE'S TAKING HER *TIME!!*
YOU NEED AT LEAST AN HOUR TO DO IT PROPERLY, START TO FINISH!
DO *WHAT* PROPERLY?!
CALM DOWN! IT'S ONLY BEEN 20 MINUTES!
NOTHING.
I SHOULDN'T HAVE LET HER GO!
WHAT'S SHE *SEE* IN THAT FREAK ANYWAY?!
HMM...

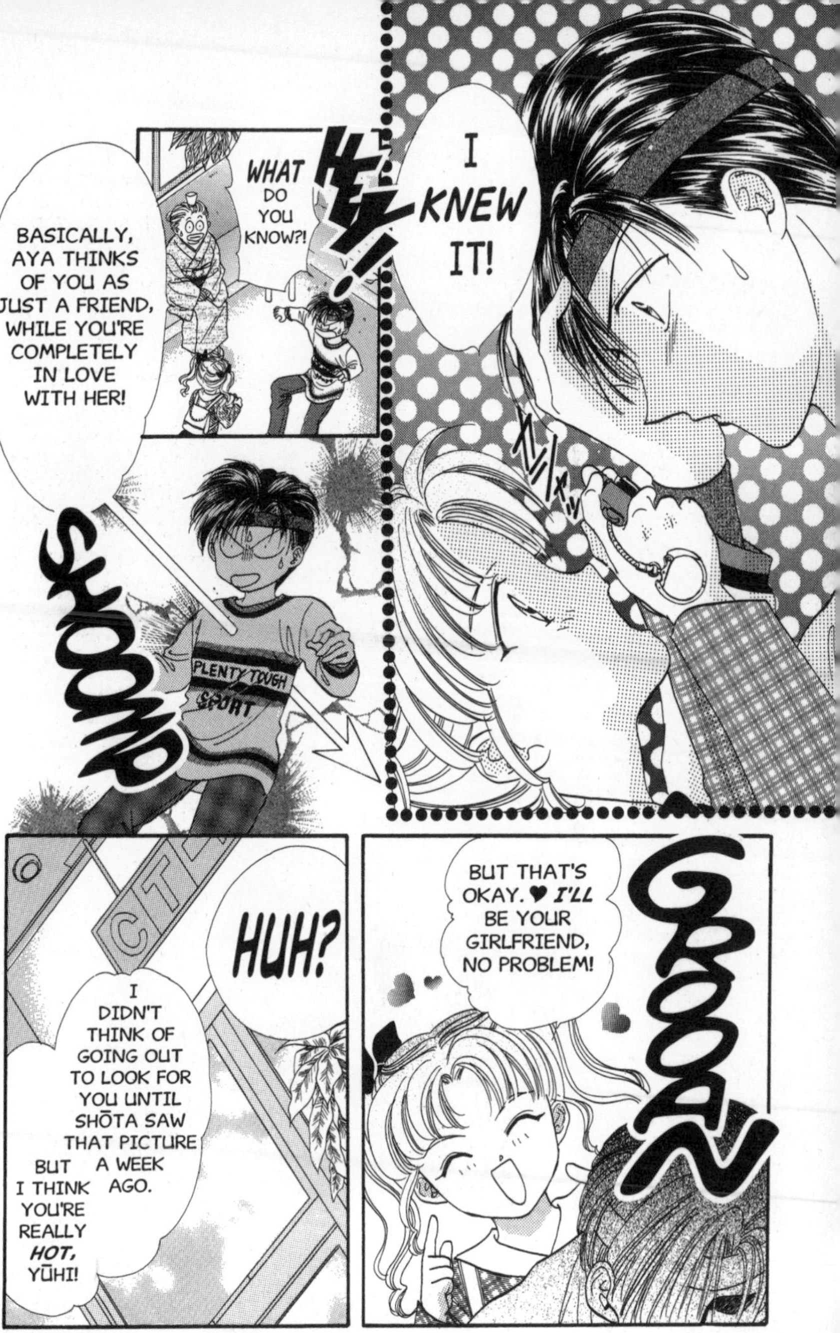
I KNEW IT!
HEY!
WHAT DO YOU KNOW?!
BASICALLY, AYA THINKS OF YOU AS JUST A FRIEND, WHILE YOU'RE COMPLETELY IN LOVE WITH HER!
SHOOMP
GROAN
BUT THAT'S OKAY. ♥ I'LL BE YOUR GIRLFRIEND, NO PROBLEM!
HUH?
I DIDN'T THINK OF GOING OUT TO LOOK FOR YOU UNTIL SHŌTA SAW THAT PICTURE A WEEK AGO.
BUT I THINK YOU'RE REALLY HOT, YŪHI!
PLENTY TOUGH SPORT

...By the way!
I've finally gotten hooked on Final Fantasy VII. ◡̈ When I was in bed with a cold and a high fever around New Year's, I got brainwashed (?) by all those commercials on TV, so I pre-ordered F.F. VII. I got it, but I hadn't touched it in six months... What? Why didn't I play it right away? I was busy with work, I moved, I just didn't have the time...and besides, I'd never played an RPG game before! Seriously! I owned F.F. III for the Super Nintendo, but back then, those games were so slow and boring, and I hated all the fighting and item management you had to do all the time. So even if though I gave it a try, I gave up on it right away. But this time, I was curious to see the graphics from the point of view of an artist—I thought I could learn something from it. I started playing F.F. VII and... "Hey, this is pretty cool. Ooh...This is interesting, what happens next? ...Geez, I'm totally hooked!"
It was all because I fell in love with Cloud. One of my friends also started playing, and we're both gaga over him. "Could you draw Cloud for me?" "Sure!" ~~...Do I really have the time for that?!~~ Come to think of it, my editors (and my readers) think I'm a hard-core gamer because I've written about video games in my past columns. Sorry - I own very few games, and I don't play much. I have the SNES, PlayStation, and the Sega Saturn (my editor at the time got it for me for my birthday ♥). But I have fewer than 10 games in all. They were just collecting dust. There was a time when I was hooked on Street Fighter II (when it first came out), but I quickly lost interest. (I stopped playing fighting games because they hurt my drawing hand.) I play less than the average person. However, now I have awoken to their splendor! But I have so much work to do! Wh-what should I do...?
So now I just listen to the F.F. soundtrack...

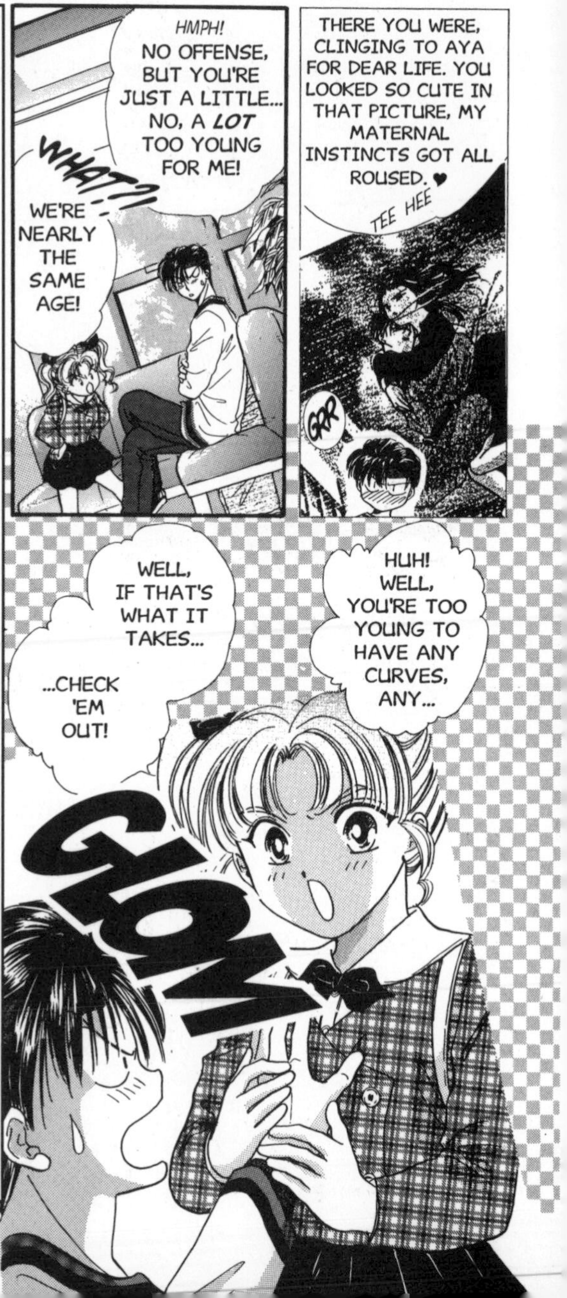
THERE YOU WERE, CLINGING TO AYA FOR DEAR LIFE. YOU LOOKED SO CUTE IN THAT PICTURE, MY MATERNAL INSTINCTS GOT ALL ROUSED. ♥
TEE HEE
GRR
HMPH!
NO OFFENSE, BUT YOU'RE JUST A LITTLE... NO, A *LOT* TOO YOUNG FOR ME!
WHAT?!
WE'RE NEARLY THE SAME AGE!
HUH! WELL, YOU'RE TOO YOUNG TO HAVE ANY CURVES, ANY...
WELL, IF THAT'S WHAT IT TAKES...
...CHECK 'EM OUT!
GLOW

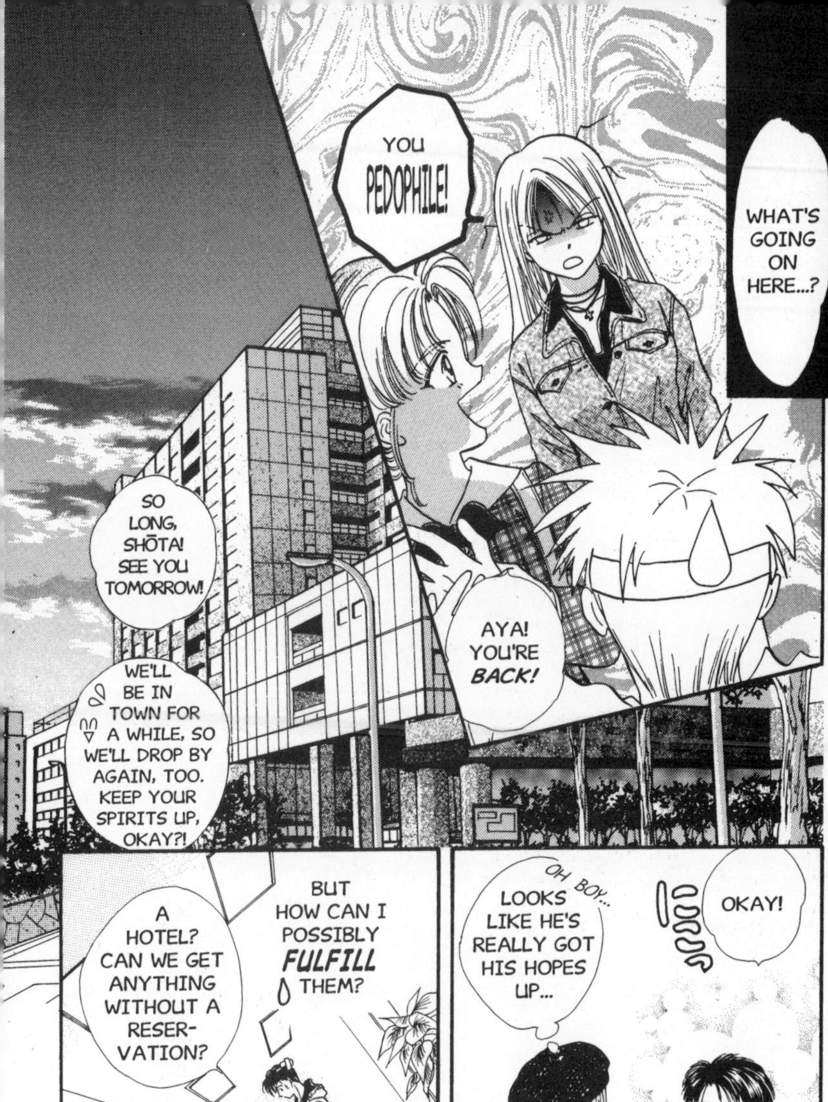
WHAT'S GOING ON HERE...?
YOU PEDOPHILE!
AYA! YOU'RE *BACK!*
SO LONG, SHŌTA! SEE YOU TOMORROW!
WE'LL BE IN TOWN FOR A WHILE, SO WE'LL DROP BY AGAIN, TOO. KEEP YOUR SPIRITS UP, OKAY?!
OKAY!
LOOKS LIKE HE'S REALLY GOT HIS HOPES UP...
OH BOY...
BUT HOW CAN I POSSIBLY *FULFILL* THEM?
A HOTEL? CAN WE GET ANYTHING WITHOUT A RESERVATION?
ALL WE HAVE TO DO IS FLASH THE AOGIRI BUSINESS CARD. THE NAME CARRIES A LOT OF WEIGHT!

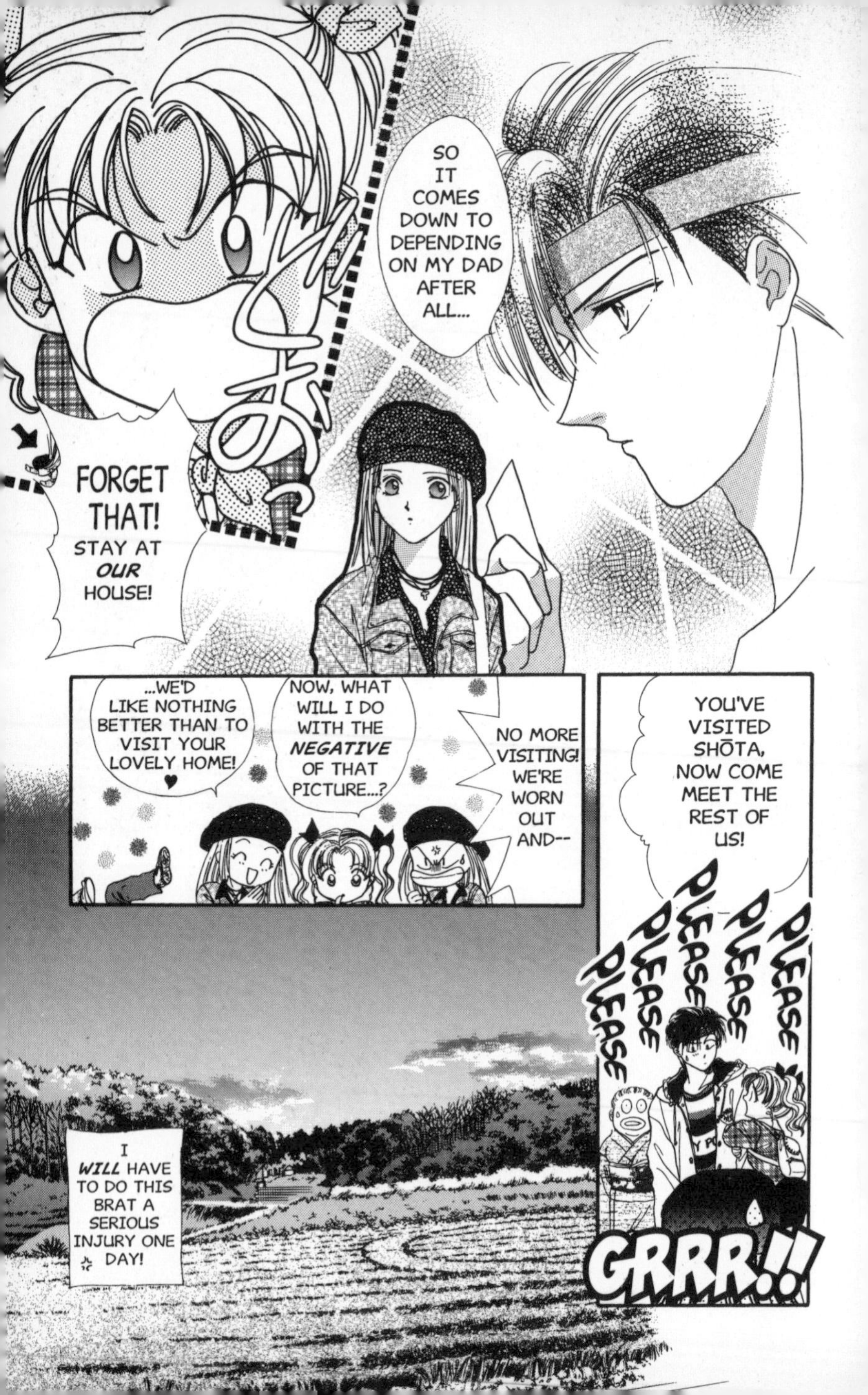
SO IT COMES DOWN TO DEPENDING ON MY DAD AFTER ALL...
FORGET THAT! STAY AT *OUR* HOUSE!
YOU'VE VISITED SHŌTA, NOW COME MEET THE REST OF US!
PLEASE PLEASE PLEASE PLEASE PLEASE
GRRR!!
NO MORE VISITING! WE'RE WORN OUT AND--
NOW, WHAT WILL I DO WITH THE *NEGATIVE* OF THAT PICTURE...?
...WE'D LIKE NOTHING BETTER THAN TO VISIT YOUR LOVELY HOME! ♥
I *WILL* HAVE TO DO THIS BRAT A SERIOUS INJURY ONE DAY!

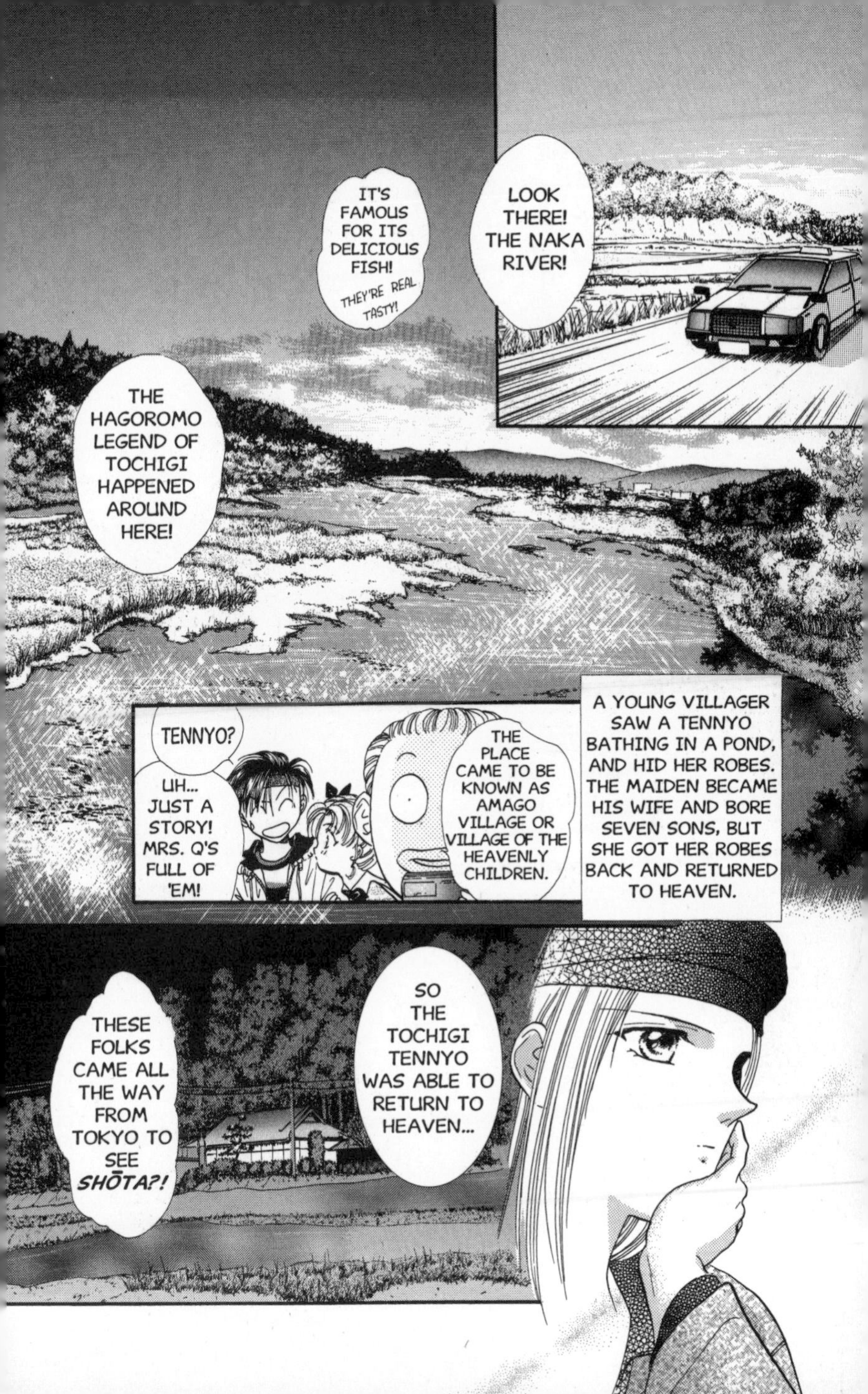
LOOK THERE! THE NAKA RIVER!
IT'S FAMOUS FOR ITS DELICIOUS FISH!
THEY'RE REAL TASTY!
THE HAGOROMO LEGEND OF TOCHIGI HAPPENED AROUND HERE!
A YOUNG VILLAGER SAW A TENNYO BATHING IN A POND, AND HID HER ROBES. THE MAIDEN BECAME HIS WIFE AND BORE SEVEN SONS, BUT SHE GOT HER ROBES BACK AND RETURNED TO HEAVEN.
THE PLACE CAME TO BE KNOWN AS AMAGO VILLAGE OR VILLAGE OF THE HEAVENLY CHILDREN.
TENNYO?
UH... JUST A STORY! MRS. Q'S FULL OF 'EM!
SO THE TOCHIGI TENNYO WAS ABLE TO RETURN TO HEAVEN...
THESE FOLKS CAME ALL THE WAY FROM TOKYO TO SEE *SHŌTA?!*

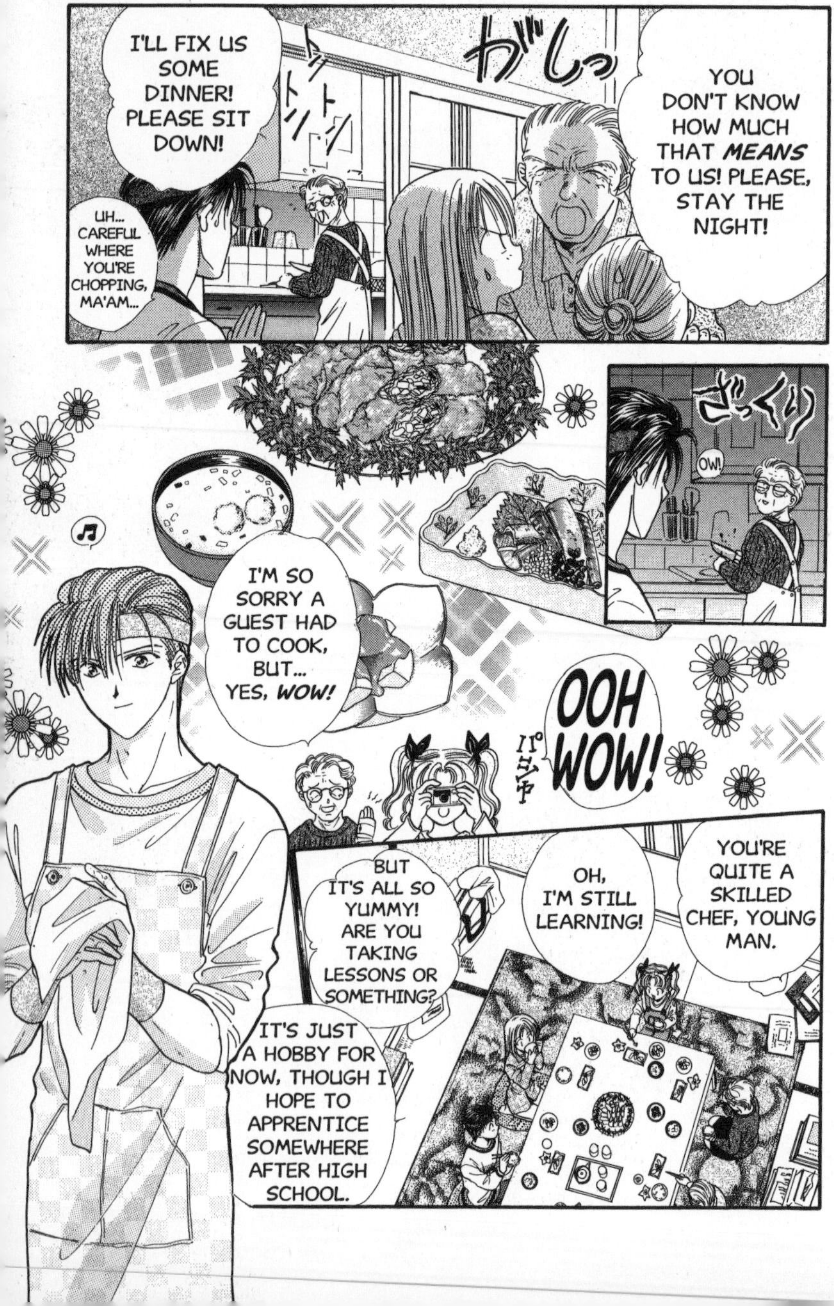
がしっ
YOU DON'T KNOW HOW MUCH THAT ***MEANS*** TO US! PLEASE, STAY THE NIGHT!
I'LL FIX US SOME DINNER! PLEASE SIT DOWN!
UH... CAREFUL WHERE YOU'RE CHOPPING, MA'AM...
ざっくり
OW!
I'M SO SORRY A GUEST HAD TO COOK, BUT... YES, ***WOW!***
パシャ
OOH WOW!
YOU'RE QUITE A SKILLED CHEF, YOUNG MAN.
OH, I'M STILL LEARNING!
BUT IT'S ALL SO YUMMY! ARE YOU TAKING LESSONS OR SOMETHING?
IT'S JUST A HOBBY FOR NOW, THOUGH I HOPE TO APPRENTICE SOMEWHERE AFTER HIGH SCHOOL.

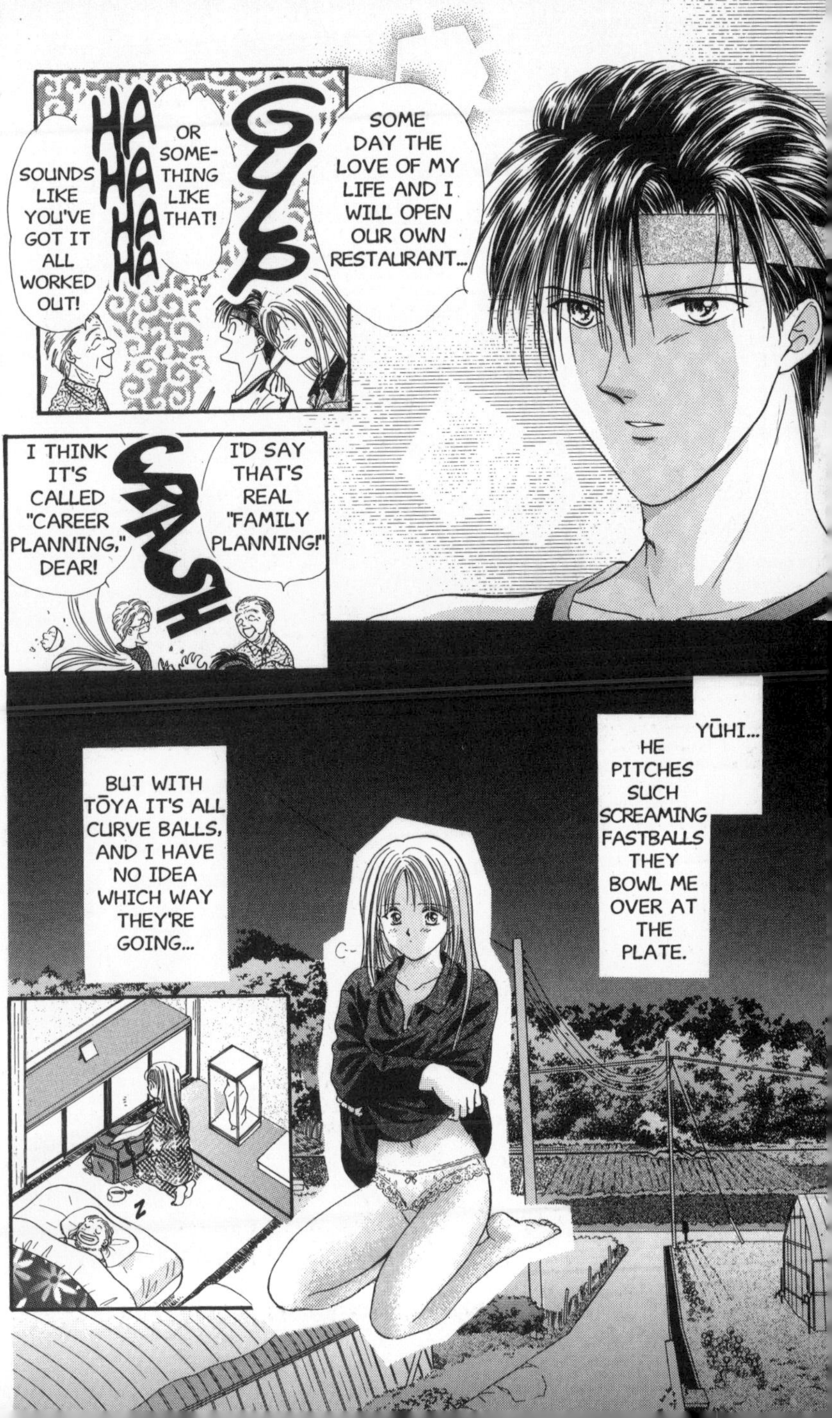
SOME DAY THE LOVE OF MY LIFE AND I WILL OPEN OUR OWN RESTAURANT...
GULP
OR SOMETHING LIKE THAT!
HA HA HA HA HA
SOUNDS LIKE YOU'VE GOT IT ALL WORKED OUT!
I'D SAY THAT'S REAL "FAMILY PLANNING!"
CRASH
I THINK IT'S CALLED "CAREER PLANNING," DEAR!
YŪHI...
HE PITCHES SUCH SCREAMING FASTBALLS THEY BOWL ME OVER AT THE PLATE.
BUT WITH TŌYA IT'S ALL CURVE BALLS, AND I HAVE NO IDEA WHICH WAY THEY'RE GOING...
Z

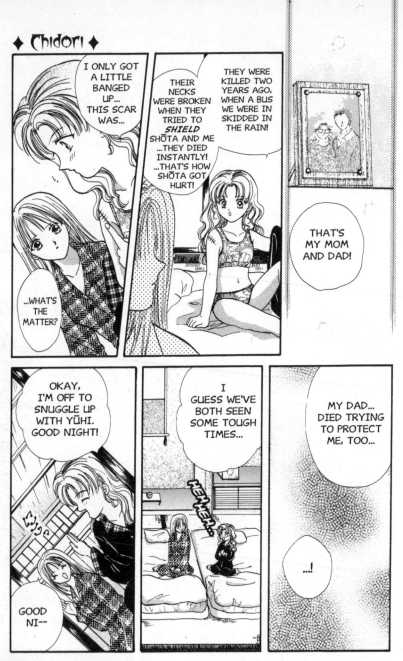

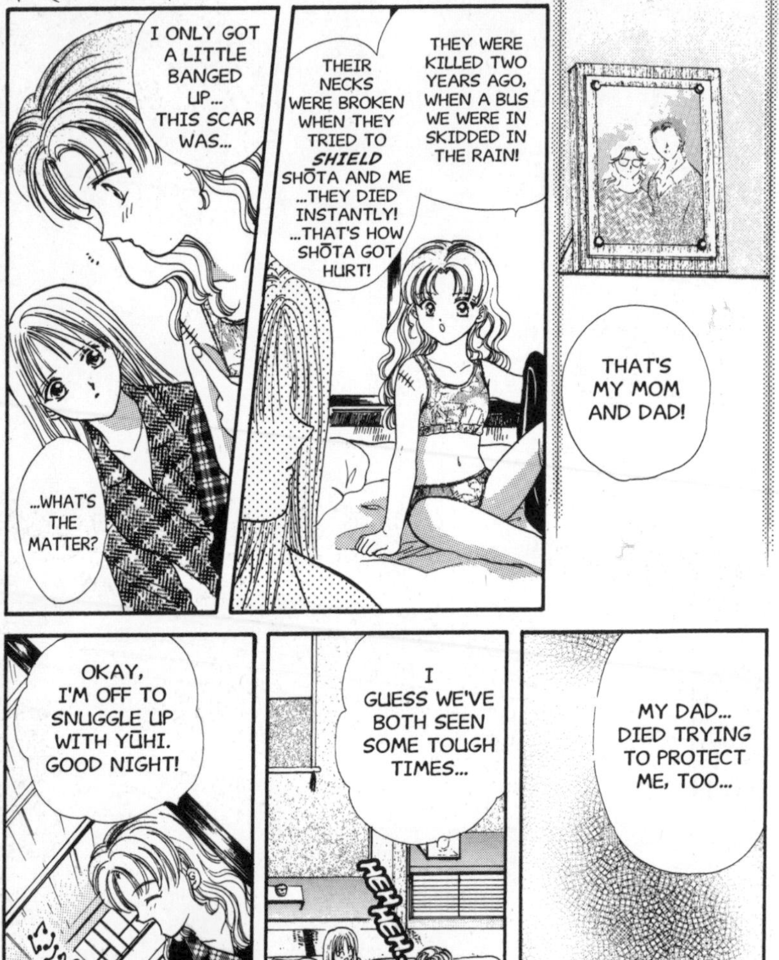
THAT'S MY MOM AND DAD!
THEY WERE KILLED TWO YEARS AGO, WHEN A BUS WE WERE IN SKIDDED IN THE RAIN!
THEIR NECKS WERE BROKEN WHEN THEY TRIED TO SHIELD SHŌTA AND ME ...THEY DIED INSTANTLY! ...THAT'S HOW SHŌTA GOT HURT!
I ONLY GOT A LITTLE BANGED UP... THIS SCAR WAS...
...WHAT'S THE MATTER?
MY DAD... DIED TRYING TO PROTECT ME, TOO...
...!
I GUESS WE'VE BOTH SEEN SOME TOUGH TIMES...
HEH HEH...
OKAY, I'M OFF TO SNUGGLE UP WITH YŪHI. GOOD NIGHT!
GOOD NI--

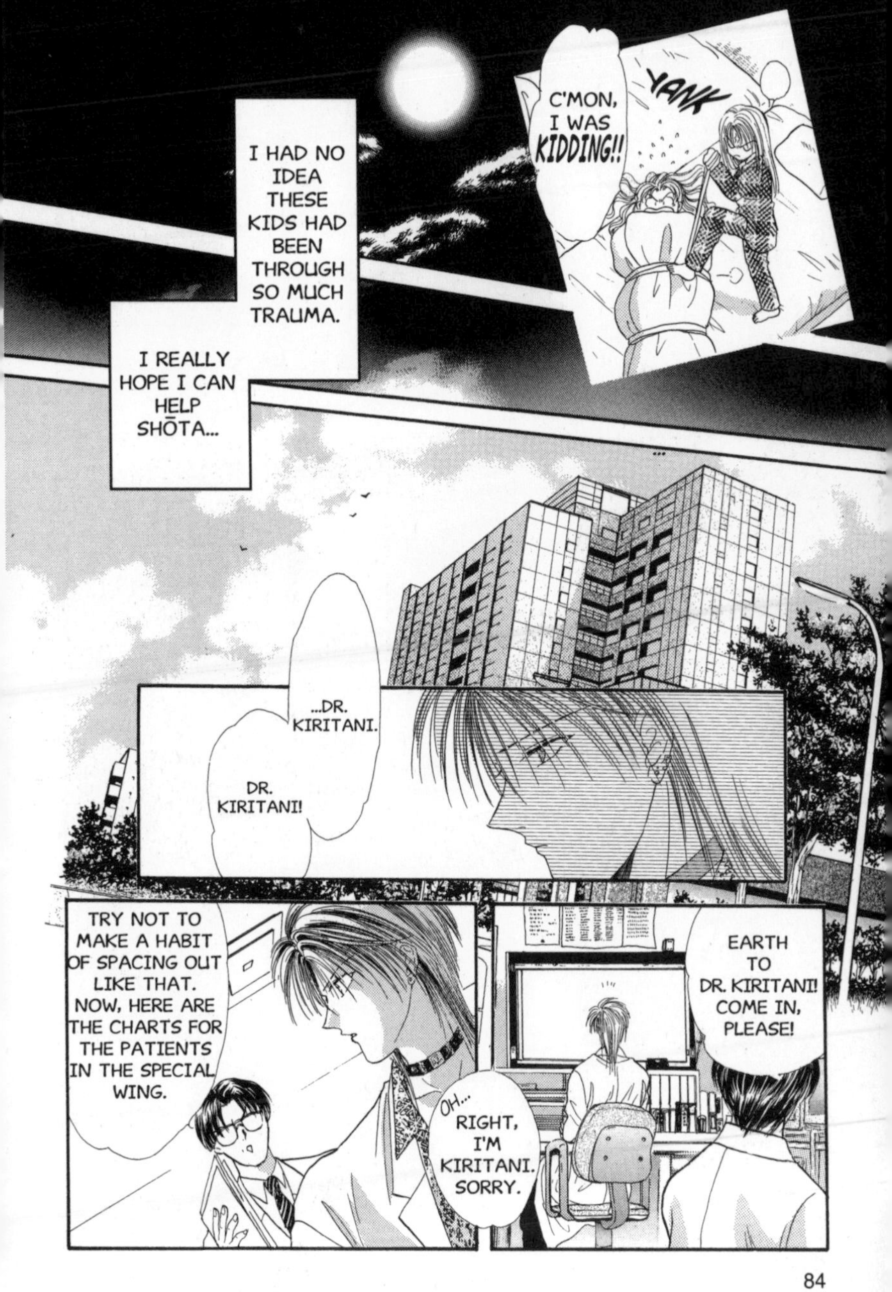
YANK
C'MON, I WAS KIDDING!!
I HAD NO IDEA THESE KIDS HAD BEEN THROUGH SO MUCH TRAUMA.
I REALLY HOPE I CAN HELP SHŌTA...
...
...DR. KIRITANI.
DR. KIRITANI!
EARTH TO DR. KIRITANI! COME IN, PLEASE!
OH... RIGHT, I'M KIRITANI. SORRY.
TRY NOT TO MAKE A HABIT OF SPACING OUT LIKE THAT. NOW, HERE ARE THE CHARTS FOR THE PATIENTS IN THE SPECIAL WING.

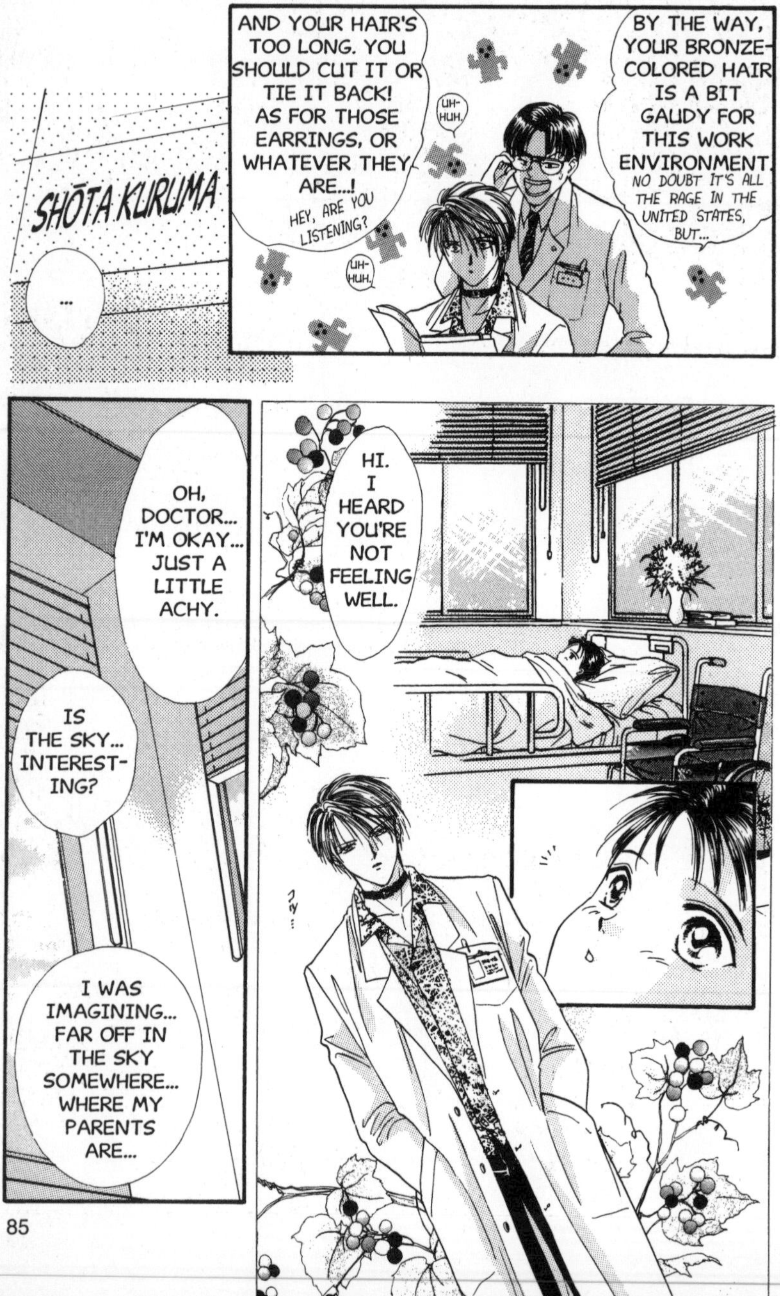

BY THE WAY, YOUR BRONZE-COLORED HAIR IS A BIT GAUDY FOR THIS WORK ENVIRONMENT.
NO DOUBT IT'S ALL THE RAGE IN THE UNITED STATES, BUT...
UH-HUH.
AND YOUR HAIR'S TOO LONG. YOU SHOULD CUT IT OR TIE IT BACK! AS FOR THOSE EARRINGS, OR WHATEVER THEY ARE...!
HEY, ARE YOU LISTENING?
UH-HUH.
SHŌTA KURUMA
...
HI. I HEARD YOU'RE NOT FEELING WELL.
OH, DOCTOR... I'M OKAY... JUST A LITTLE ACHY.
IS THE SKY... INTERESTING?
I WAS IMAGINING... FAR OFF IN THE SKY SOMEWHERE... WHERE MY PARENTS ARE...

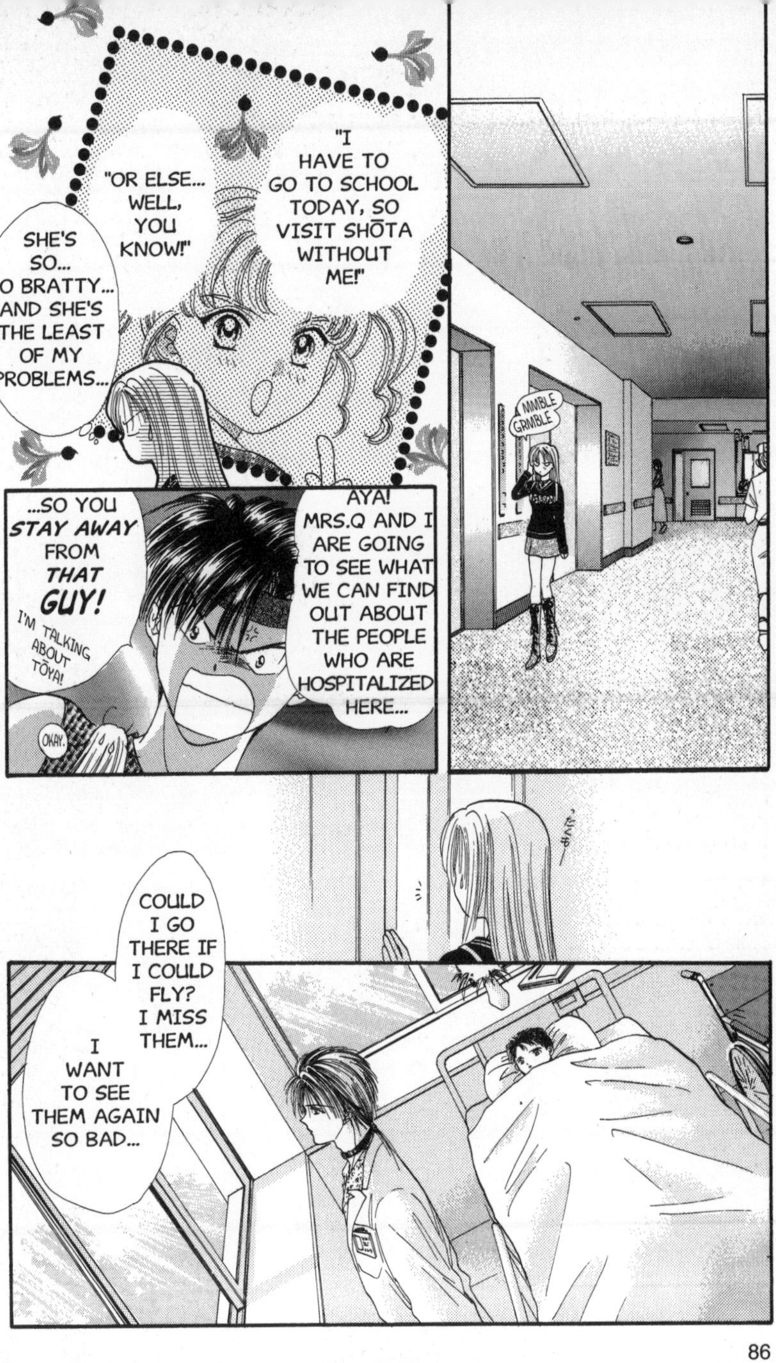
MMBLE GRMBLE
"I HAVE TO GO TO SCHOOL TODAY, SO VISIT SHŌTA WITHOUT ME!"
"OR ELSE... WELL, YOU KNOW!"
SHE'S SO... SO BRATTY... AND SHE'S THE LEAST OF MY PROBLEMS...
AYA! MRS.Q AND I ARE GOING TO SEE WHAT WE CAN FIND OUT ABOUT THE PEOPLE WHO ARE HOSPITALIZED HERE...
...SO YOU STAY AWAY FROM THAT GUY!
I'M TALKING ABOUT TŌYA!
OKAY.
COULD I GO THERE IF I COULD FLY? I MISS THEM...
I WANT TO SEE THEM AGAIN SO BAD...

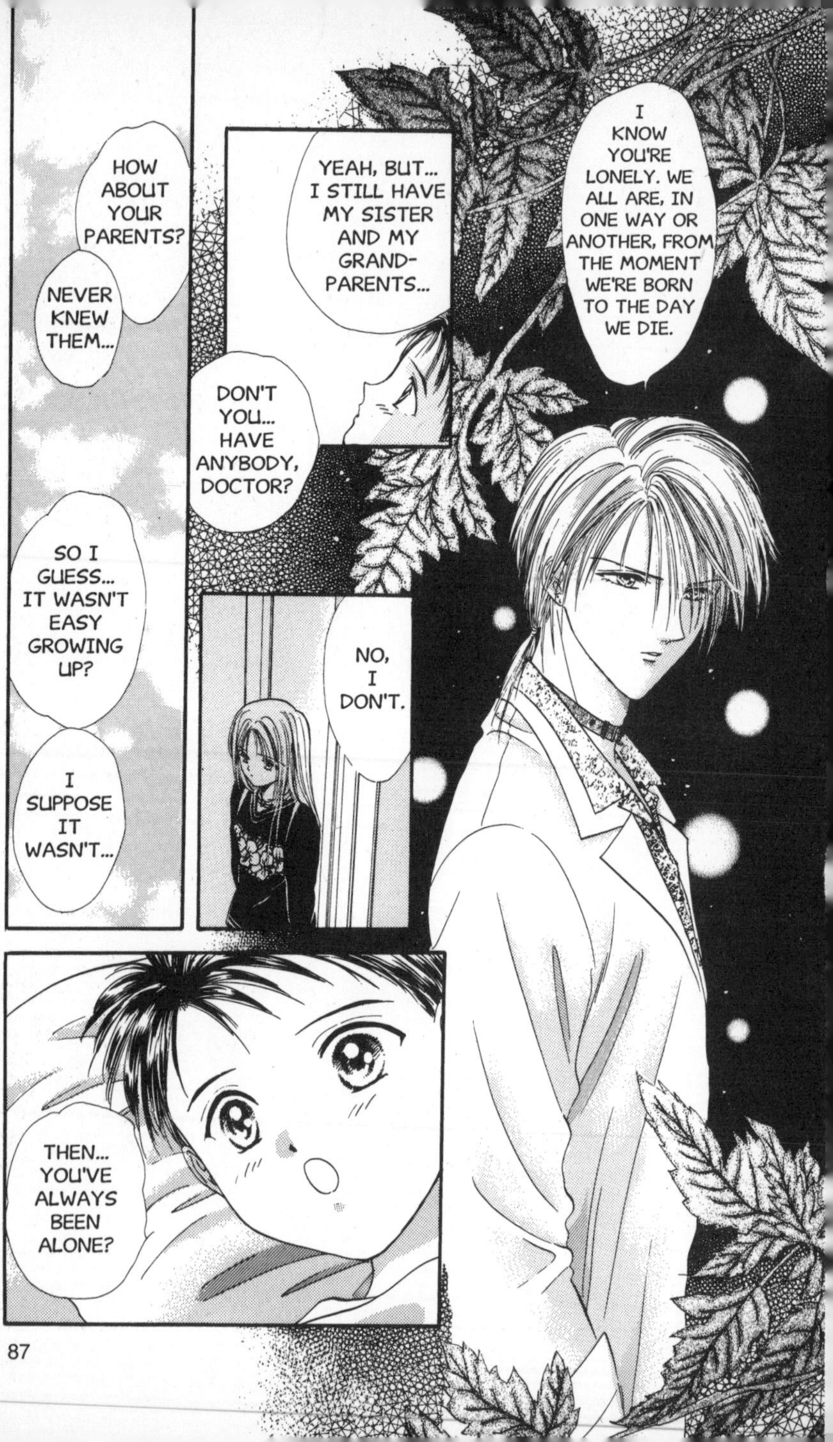
HOW ABOUT YOUR PARENTS?
NEVER KNEW THEM...
SO I GUESS... IT WASN'T EASY GROWING UP?
I SUPPOSE IT WASN'T...
THEN... YOU'VE ALWAYS BEEN ALONE?
YEAH, BUT... I STILL HAVE MY SISTER AND MY GRAND-PARENTS...
DON'T YOU... HAVE ANYBODY, DOCTOR?
NO, I DON'T.
I KNOW YOU'RE LONELY. WE ALL ARE, IN ONE WAY OR ANOTHER, FROM THE MOMENT WE'RE BORN TO THE DAY WE DIE.

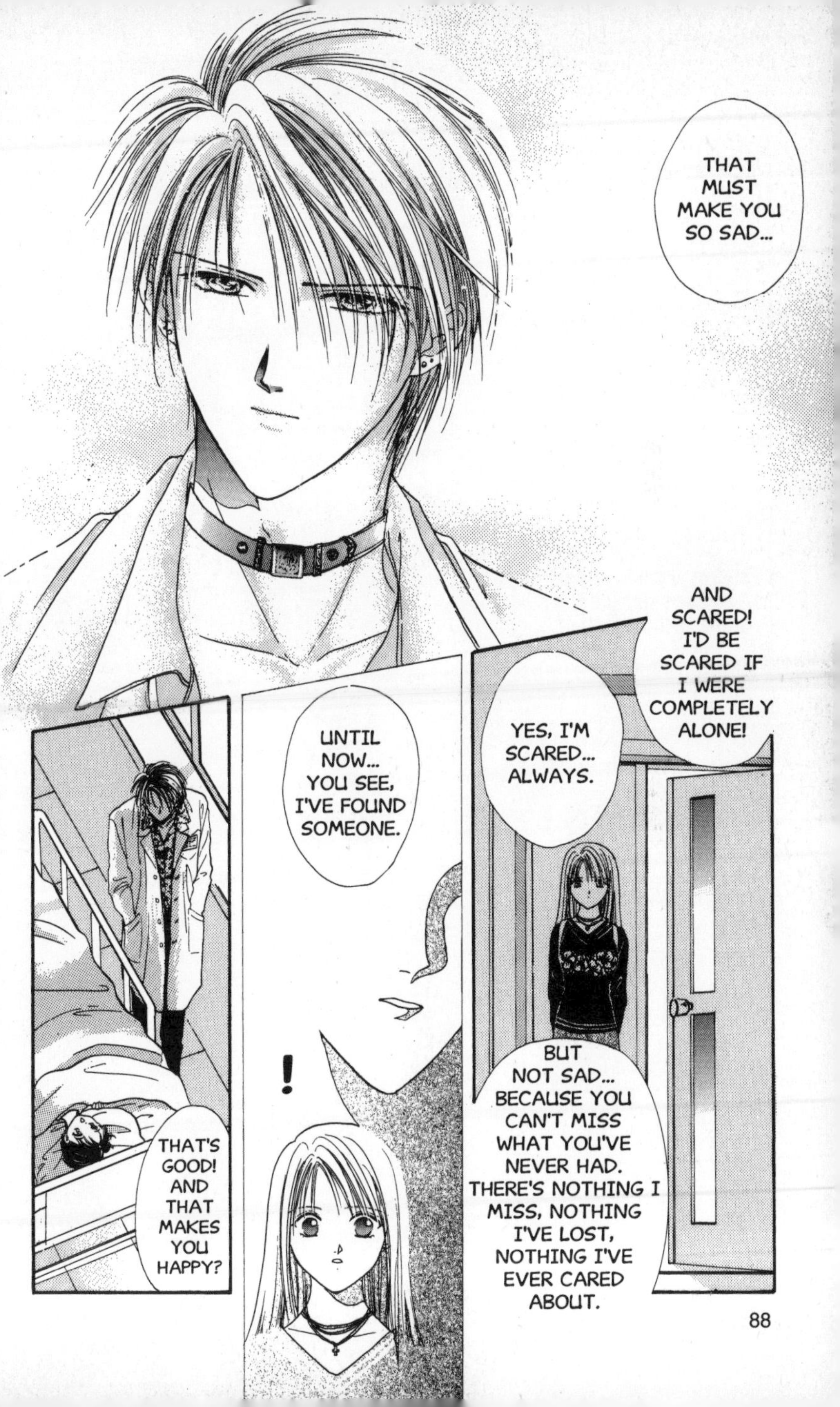
THAT MUST MAKE YOU SO SAD...
AND SCARED! I'D BE SCARED IF I WERE COMPLETELY ALONE!
YES, I'M SCARED... ALWAYS.
BUT NOT SAD... BECAUSE YOU CAN'T MISS WHAT YOU'VE NEVER HAD. THERE'S NOTHING I MISS, NOTHING I'VE LOST, NOTHING I'VE EVER CARED ABOUT.
UNTIL NOW... YOU SEE, I'VE FOUND SOMEONE.
!
THAT'S GOOD! AND THAT MAKES YOU HAPPY?

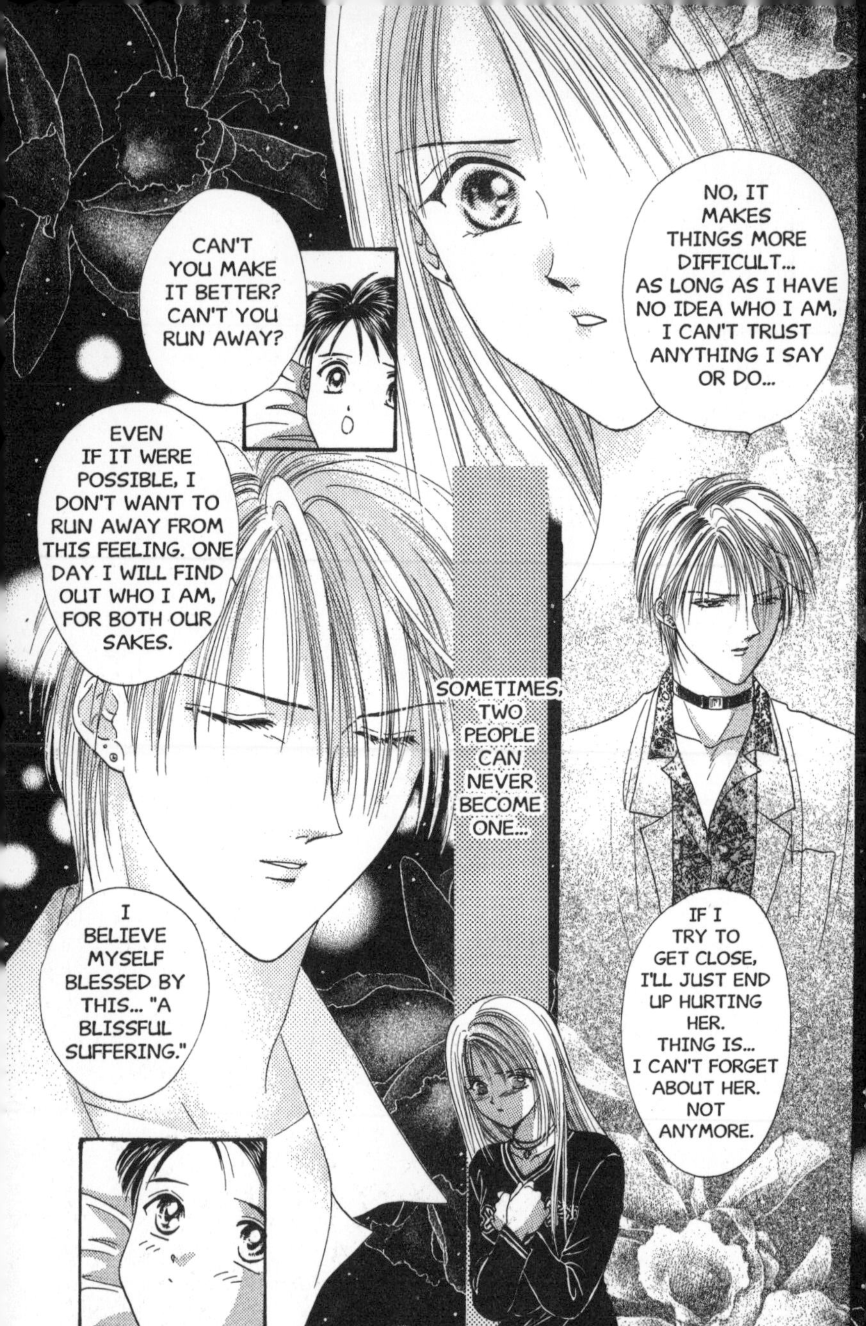
NO, IT MAKES THINGS MORE DIFFICULT... AS LONG AS I HAVE NO IDEA WHO I AM, I CAN'T TRUST ANYTHING I SAY OR DO...
CAN'T YOU MAKE IT BETTER? CAN'T YOU RUN AWAY?
EVEN IF IT WERE POSSIBLE, I DON'T WANT TO RUN AWAY FROM THIS FEELING. ONE DAY I WILL FIND OUT WHO I AM, FOR BOTH OUR SAKES.
SOMETIMES, TWO PEOPLE CAN NEVER BECOME ONE...
IF I TRY TO GET CLOSE, I'LL JUST END UP HURTING HER. THING IS... I CAN'T FORGET ABOUT HER. NOT ANYMORE.
I BELIEVE MYSELF BLESSED BY THIS... "A BLISSFUL SUFFERING."

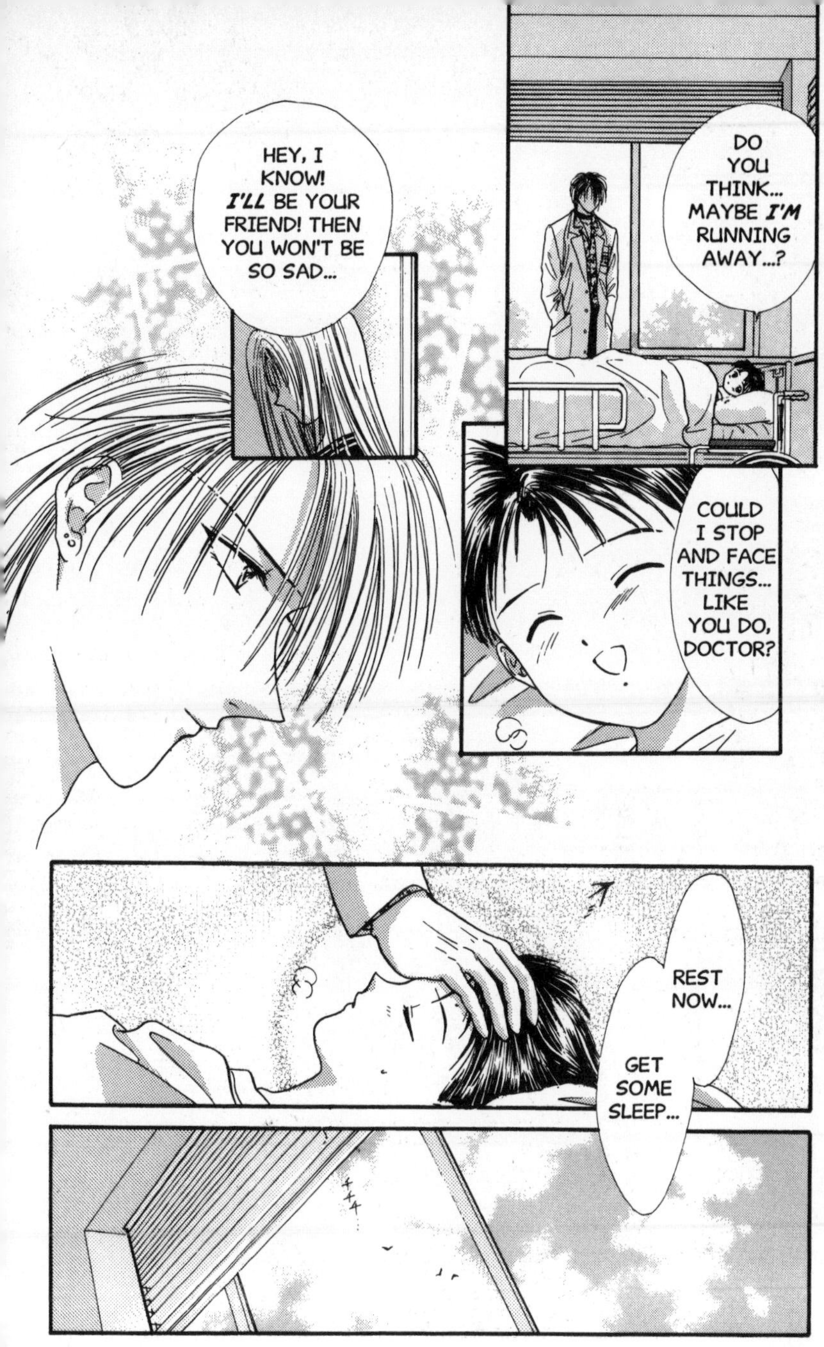

DO YOU THINK... MAYBE I'M RUNNING AWAY...?
COULD I STOP AND FACE THINGS... LIKE YOU DO, DOCTOR?
HEY, I KNOW! I'LL BE YOUR FRIEND! THEN YOU WON'T BE SO SAD...
REST NOW...
GET SOME SLEEP...

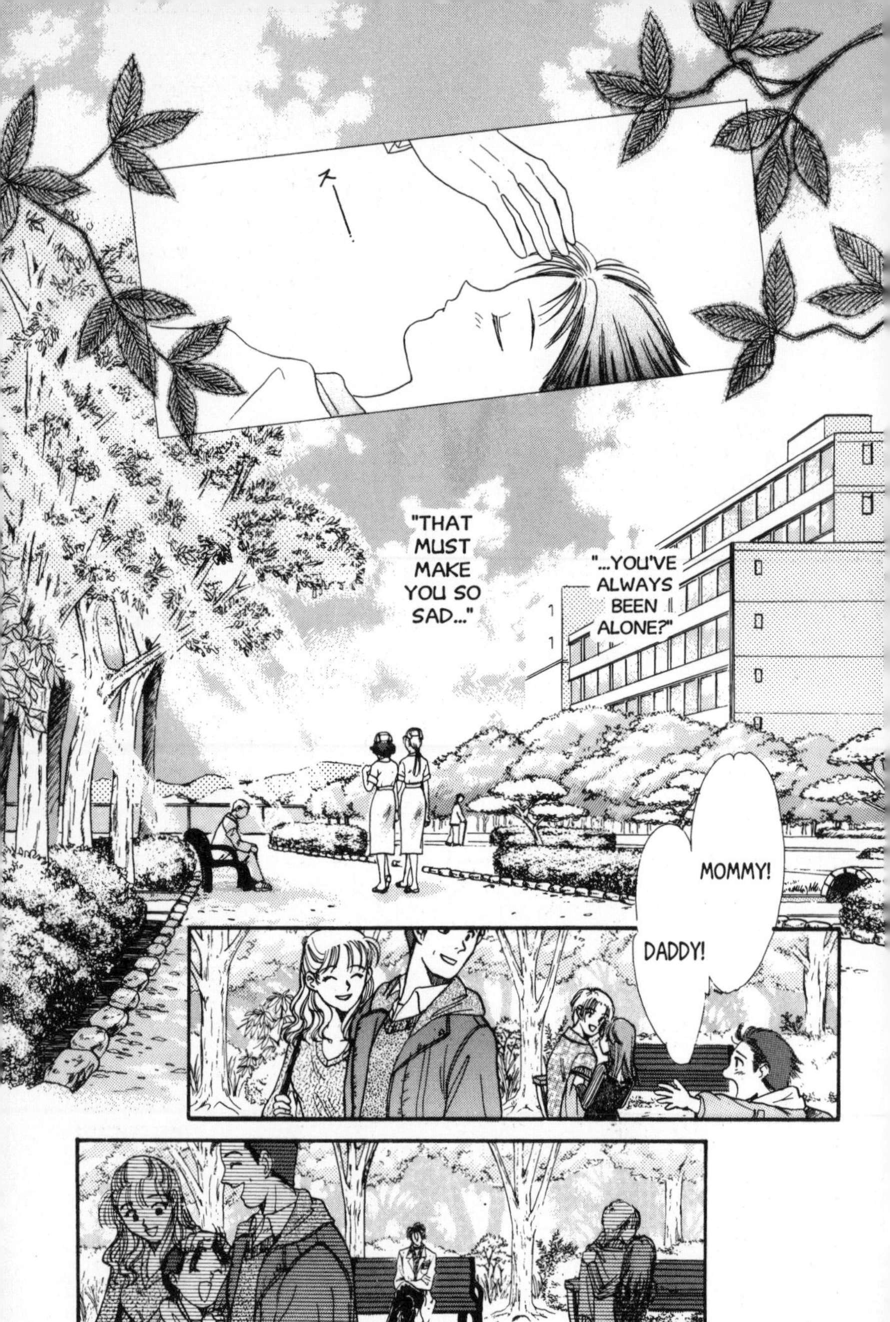
"...YOU'VE ALWAYS BEEN ALONE?"
"THAT MUST MAKE YOU SO SAD..."
MOMMY!
DADDY!

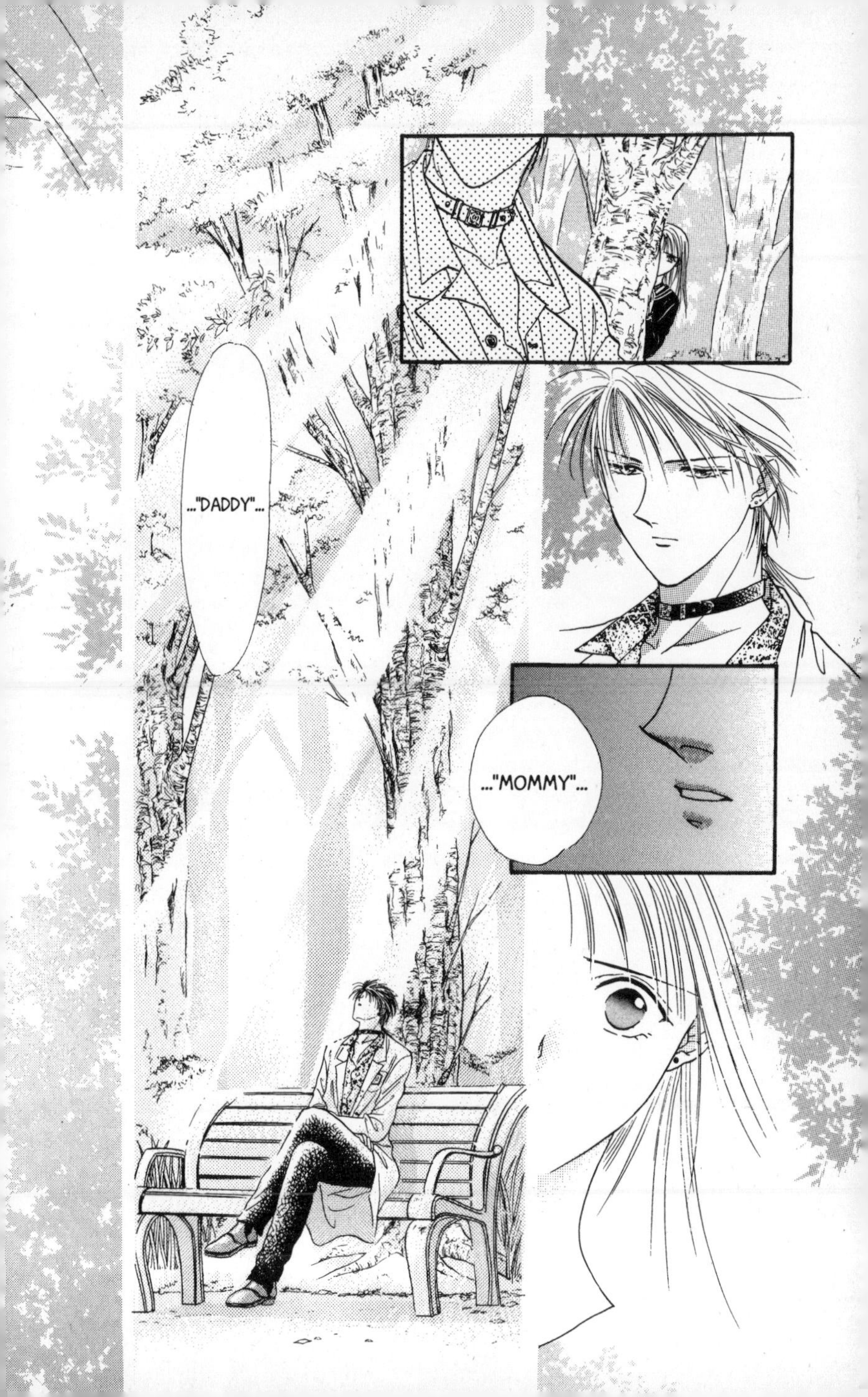
..."MOMMY"...
..."DADDY"...

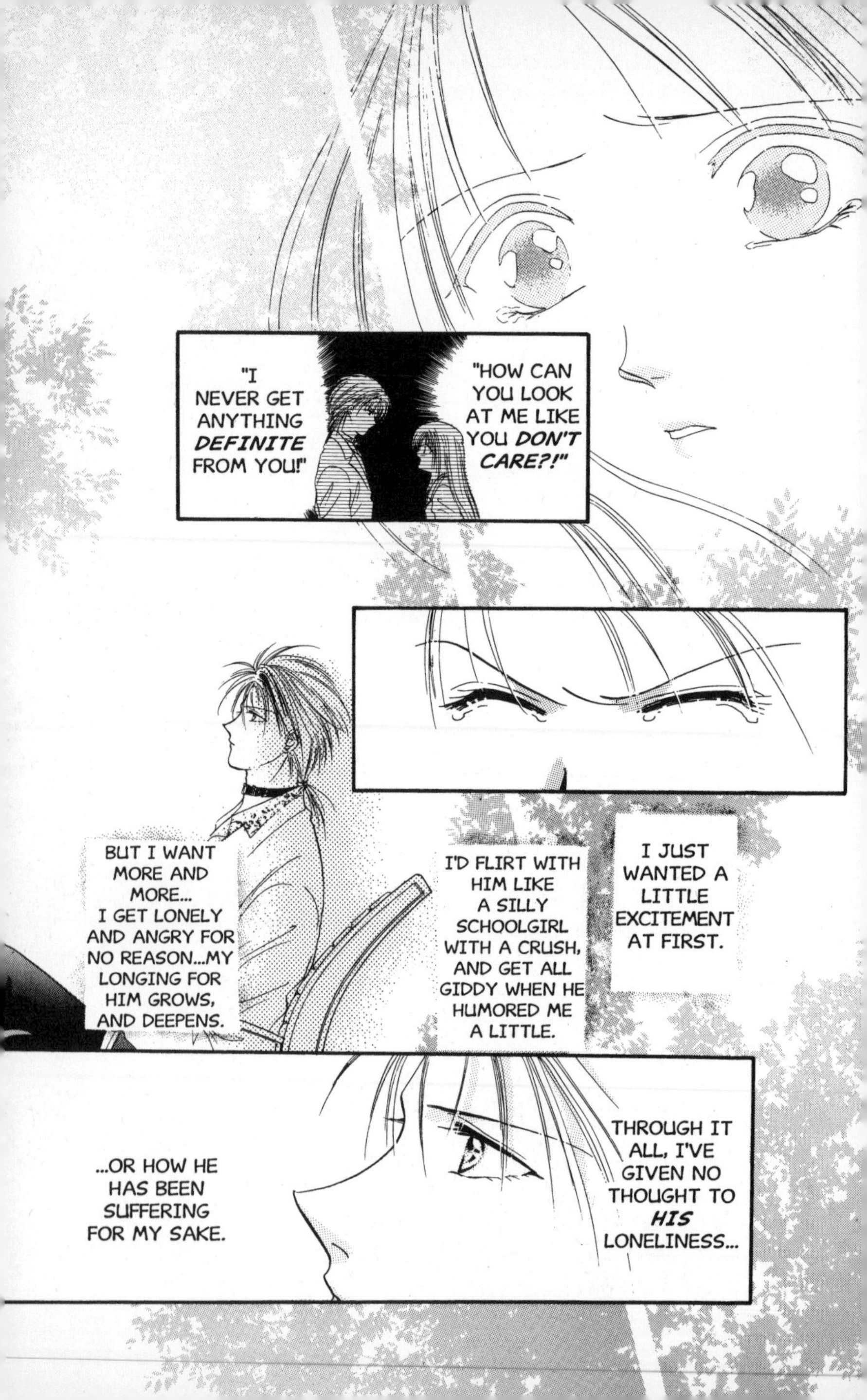
"HOW CAN YOU LOOK AT ME LIKE YOU *DON'T CARE?!*"
"I NEVER GET ANYTHING *DEFINITE* FROM YOU!"
I JUST WANTED A LITTLE EXCITEMENT AT FIRST.
I'D FLIRT WITH HIM LIKE A SILLY SCHOOLGIRL WITH A CRUSH, AND GET ALL GIDDY WHEN HE HUMORED ME A LITTLE.
BUT I WANT MORE AND MORE... I GET LONELY AND ANGRY FOR NO REASON...MY LONGING FOR HIM GROWS, AND DEEPENS.
THROUGH IT ALL, I'VE GIVEN NO THOUGHT TO *HIS* LONELINESS...
...OR HOW HE HAS BEEN SUFFERING FOR MY SAKE.

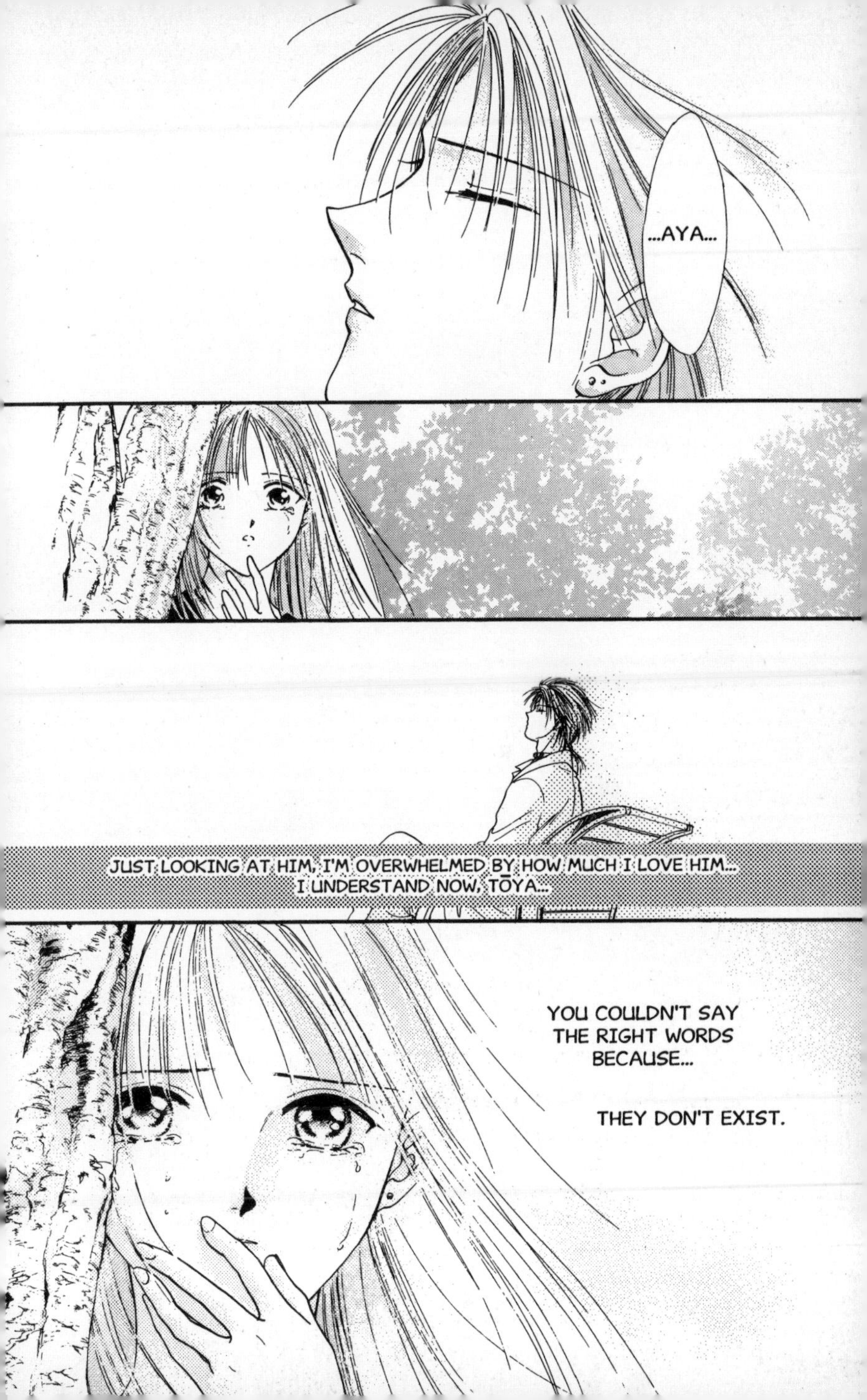
...AYA...
JUST LOOKING AT HIM, I'M OVERWHELMED BY HOW MUCH I LOVE HIM...
I UNDERSTAND NOW, TŌYA...
YOU COULDN'T SAY THE RIGHT WORDS BECAUSE...
THEY DON'T EXIST.

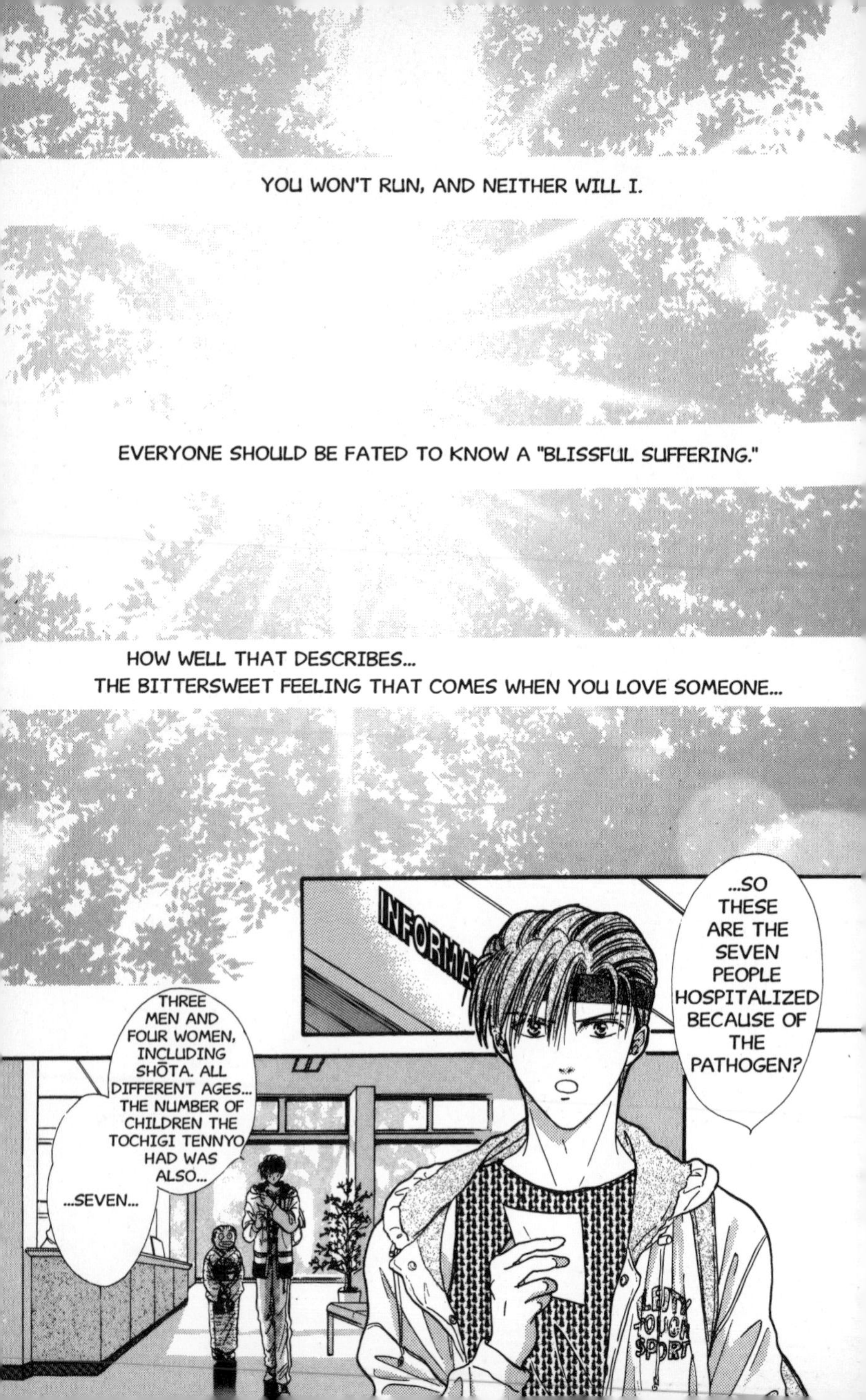
YOU WON'T RUN, AND NEITHER WILL I.
EVERYONE SHOULD BE FATED TO KNOW A "BLISSFUL SUFFERING."
HOW WELL THAT DESCRIBES... THE BITTERSWEET FEELING THAT COMES WHEN YOU LOVE SOMEONE...
...SO THESE ARE THE SEVEN PEOPLE HOSPITALIZED BECAUSE OF THE PATHOGEN?
THREE MEN AND FOUR WOMEN, INCLUDING SHŌTA. ALL DIFFERENT AGES... THE NUMBER OF CHILDREN THE TOCHIGI TENNYO HAD WAS ALSO...
...SEVEN...

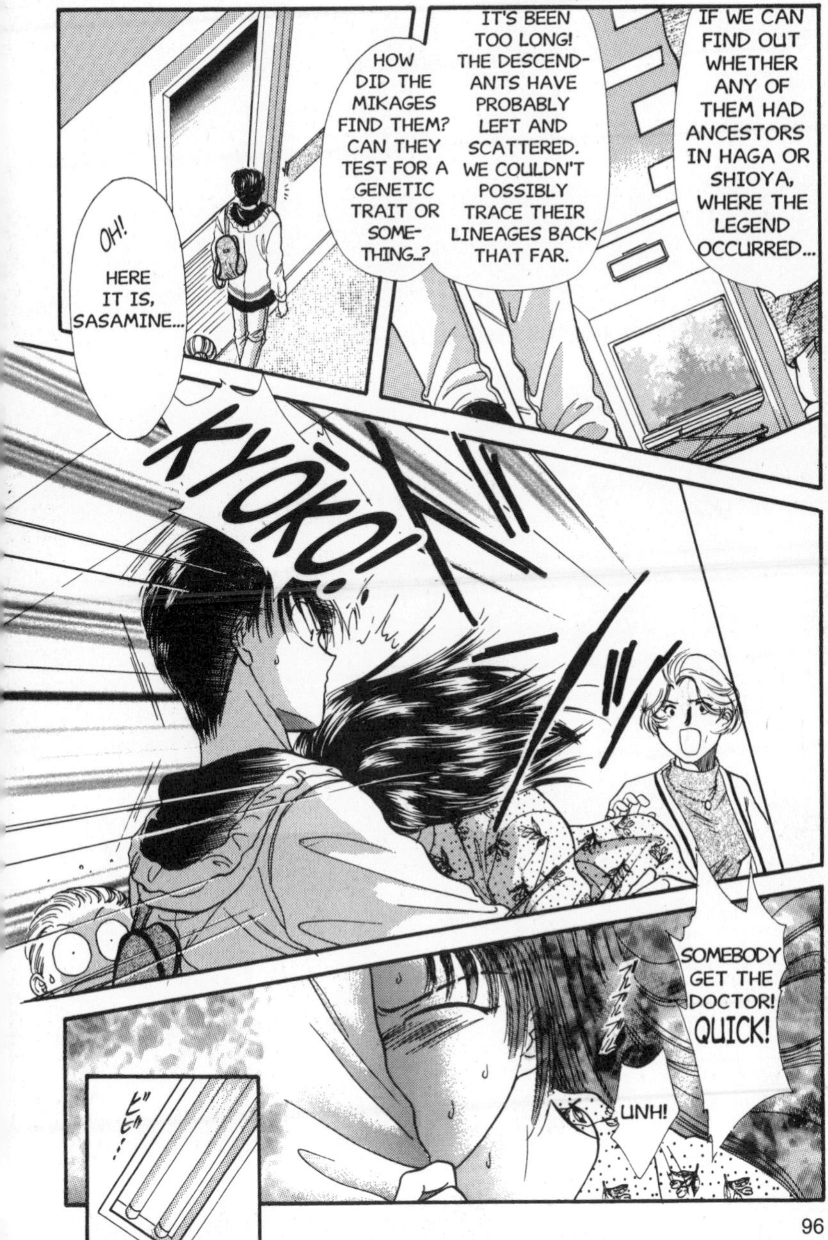
IF WE CAN FIND OUT WHETHER ANY OF THEM HAD ANCESTORS IN HAGA OR SHIOYA, WHERE THE LEGEND OCCURRED...
IT'S BEEN TOO LONG! THE DESCEND-ANTS HAVE PROBABLY LEFT AND SCATTERED. WE COULDN'T POSSIBLY TRACE THEIR LINEAGES BACK THAT FAR.
HOW DID THE MIKAGES FIND THEM? CAN THEY TEST FOR A GENETIC TRAIT OR SOME-THING...?
OH!
HERE IT IS, SASAMINE...
KYOKO!
SOMEBODY GET THE DOCTOR! QUICK!
UNH!

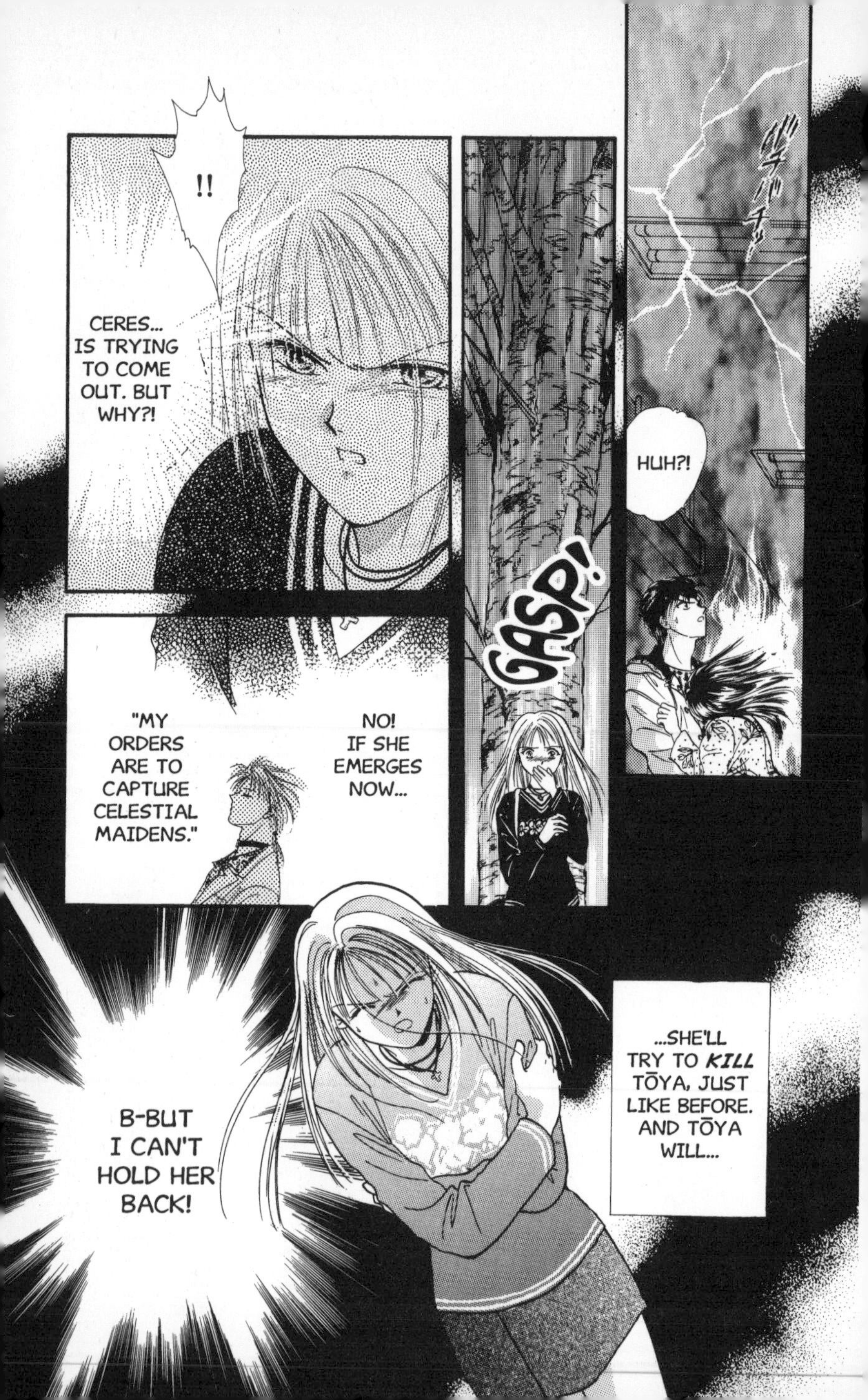
HUH?!
GASP!
!!
CERES... IS TRYING TO COME OUT. BUT WHY?!
NO! IF SHE EMERGES NOW...
"MY ORDERS ARE TO CAPTURE CELESTIAL MAIDENS."
...SHE'LL TRY TO *KILL* TŌYA, JUST LIKE BEFORE. AND TŌYA WILL...
B-BUT I CAN'T HOLD HER BACK!

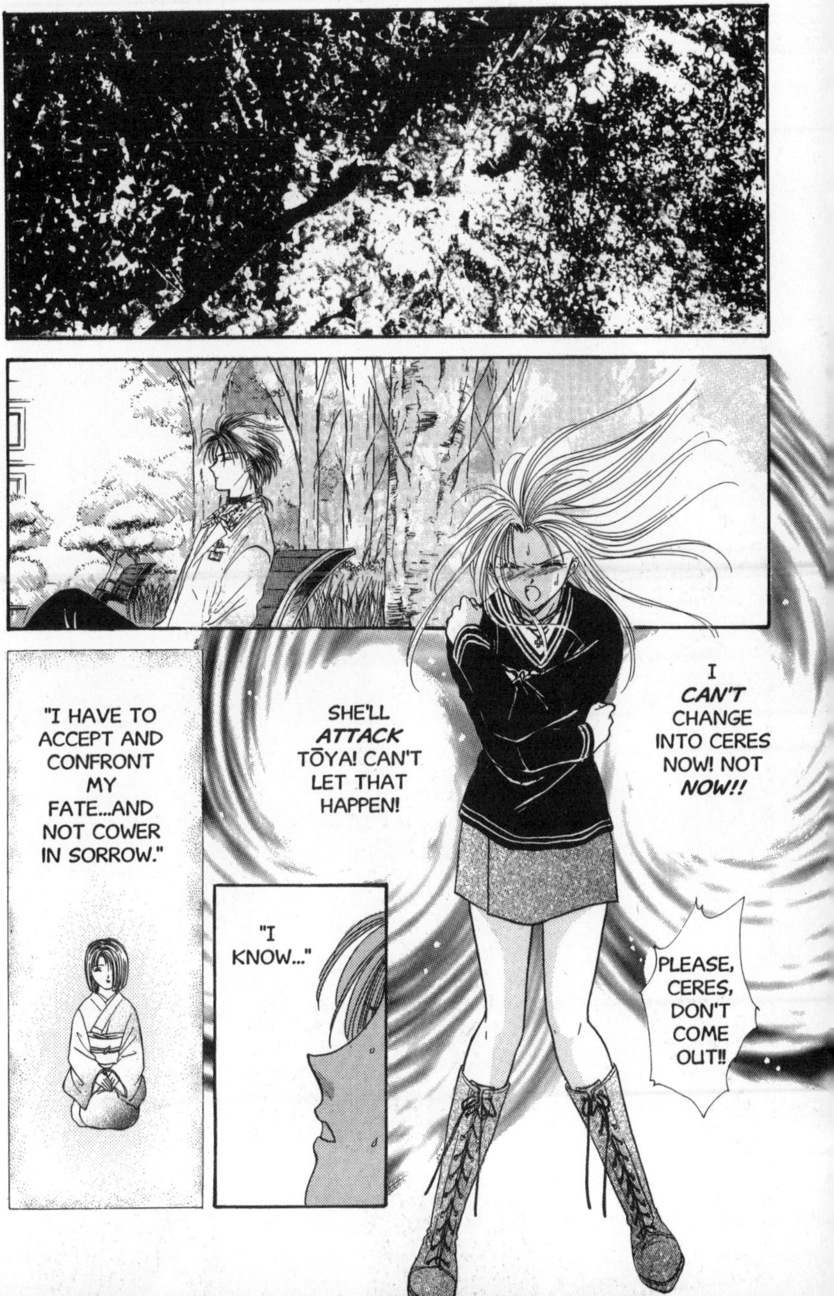
I *CAN'T* CHANGE INTO CERES NOW! NOT *NOW!!*
SHE'LL *ATTACK* TŌYA! CAN'T LET THAT HAPPEN!
PLEASE, CERES, DON'T COME OUT!!
"I HAVE TO ACCEPT AND CONFRONT MY FATE...AND NOT COWER IN SORROW."
"I KNOW..."

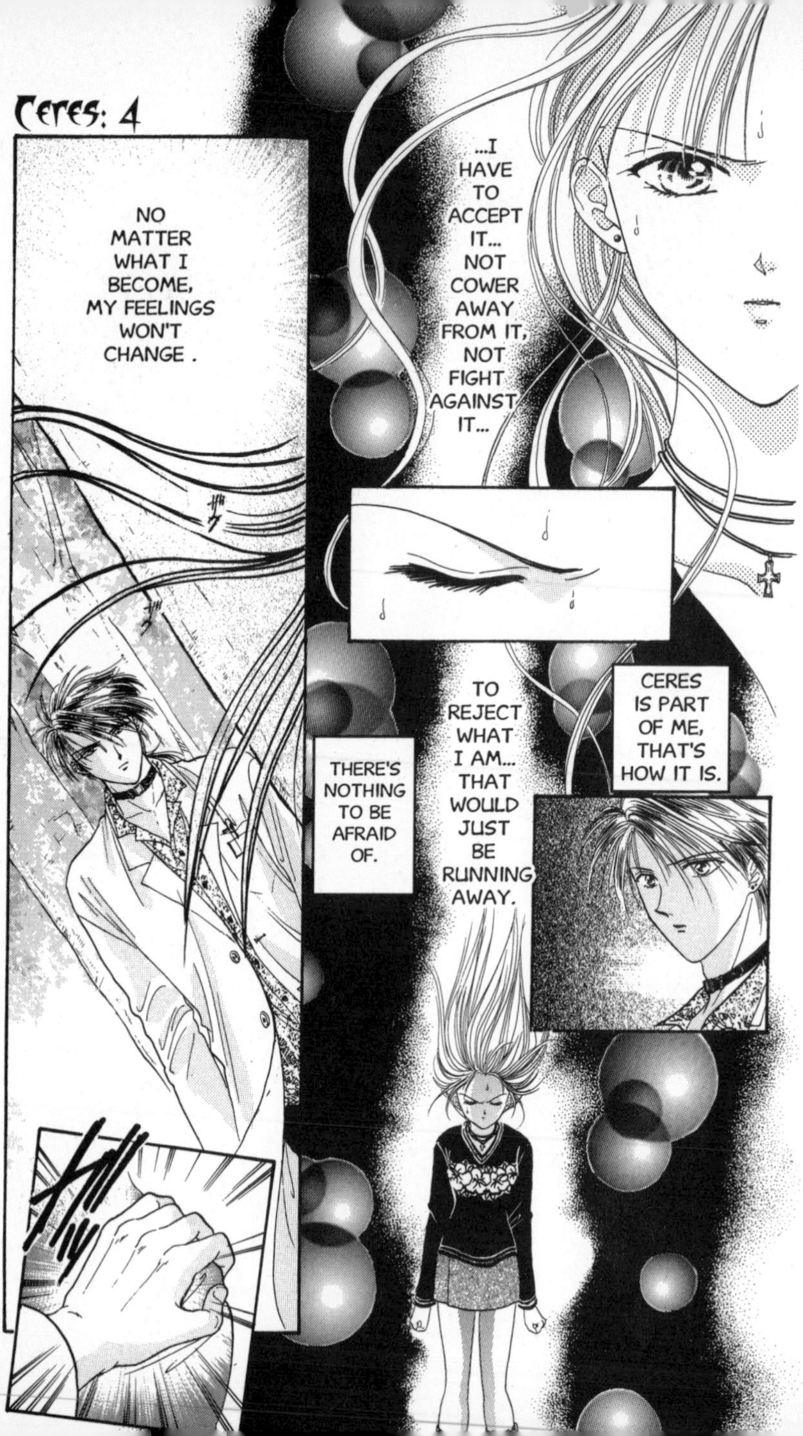
...I HAVE TO ACCEPT IT... NOT COWER AWAY FROM IT, NOT FIGHT AGAINST IT...
CERES IS PART OF ME, THAT'S HOW IT IS.
TO REJECT WHAT I AM... THAT WOULD JUST BE RUNNING AWAY.
THERE'S NOTHING TO BE AFRAID OF.
NO MATTER WHAT I BECOME, MY FEELINGS WON'T CHANGE .

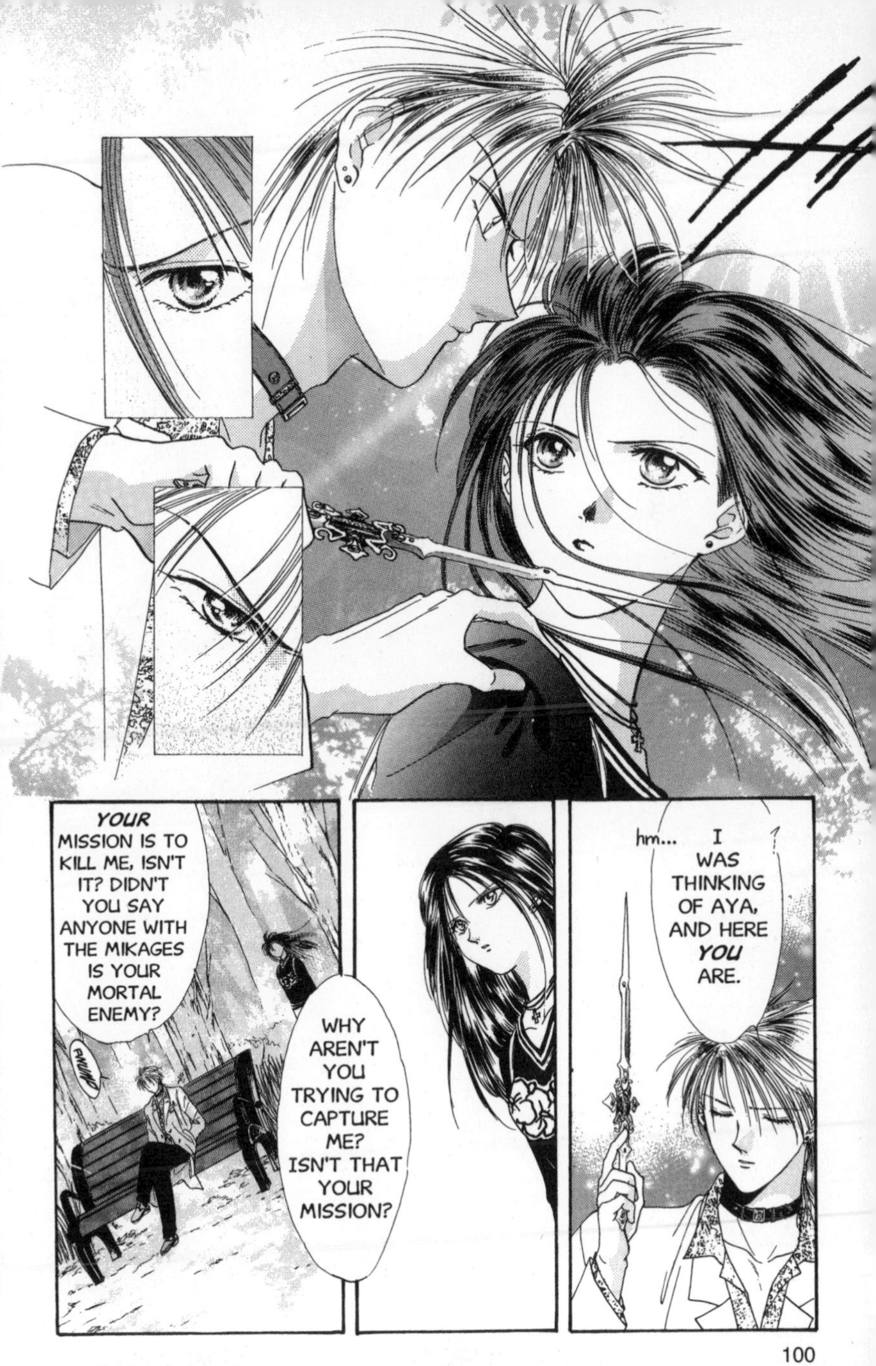
hm... I WAS THINKING OF AYA, AND HERE *YOU* ARE.
WHY AREN'T YOU TRYING TO CAPTURE ME? ISN'T THAT YOUR MISSION?
YOUR MISSION IS TO KILL ME, ISN'T IT? DIDN'T YOU SAY ANYONE WITH THE MIKAGES IS YOUR MORTAL ENEMY?
FWUMP

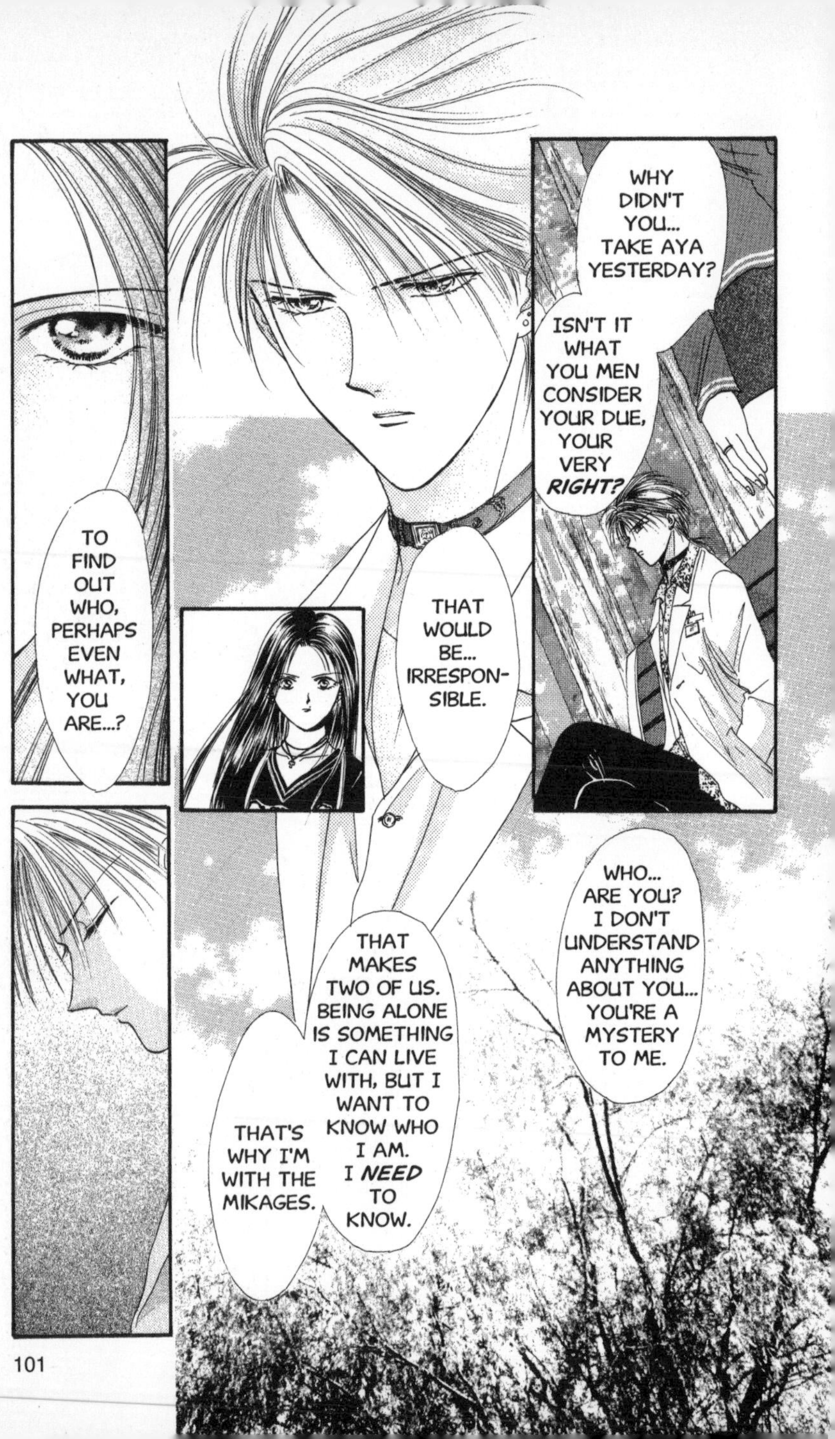
WHY DIDN'T YOU... TAKE AYA YESTERDAY?
ISN'T IT WHAT YOU MEN CONSIDER YOUR DUE, YOUR VERY *RIGHT?*
THAT WOULD BE... IRRESPON-SIBLE.
TO FIND OUT WHO, PERHAPS EVEN WHAT, YOU ARE...?
WHO... ARE YOU? I DON'T UNDERSTAND ANYTHING ABOUT YOU... YOU'RE A MYSTERY TO ME.
THAT MAKES TWO OF US. BEING ALONE IS SOMETHING I CAN LIVE WITH, BUT I WANT TO KNOW WHO I AM. I *NEED* TO KNOW.
THAT'S WHY I'M WITH THE MIKAGES.

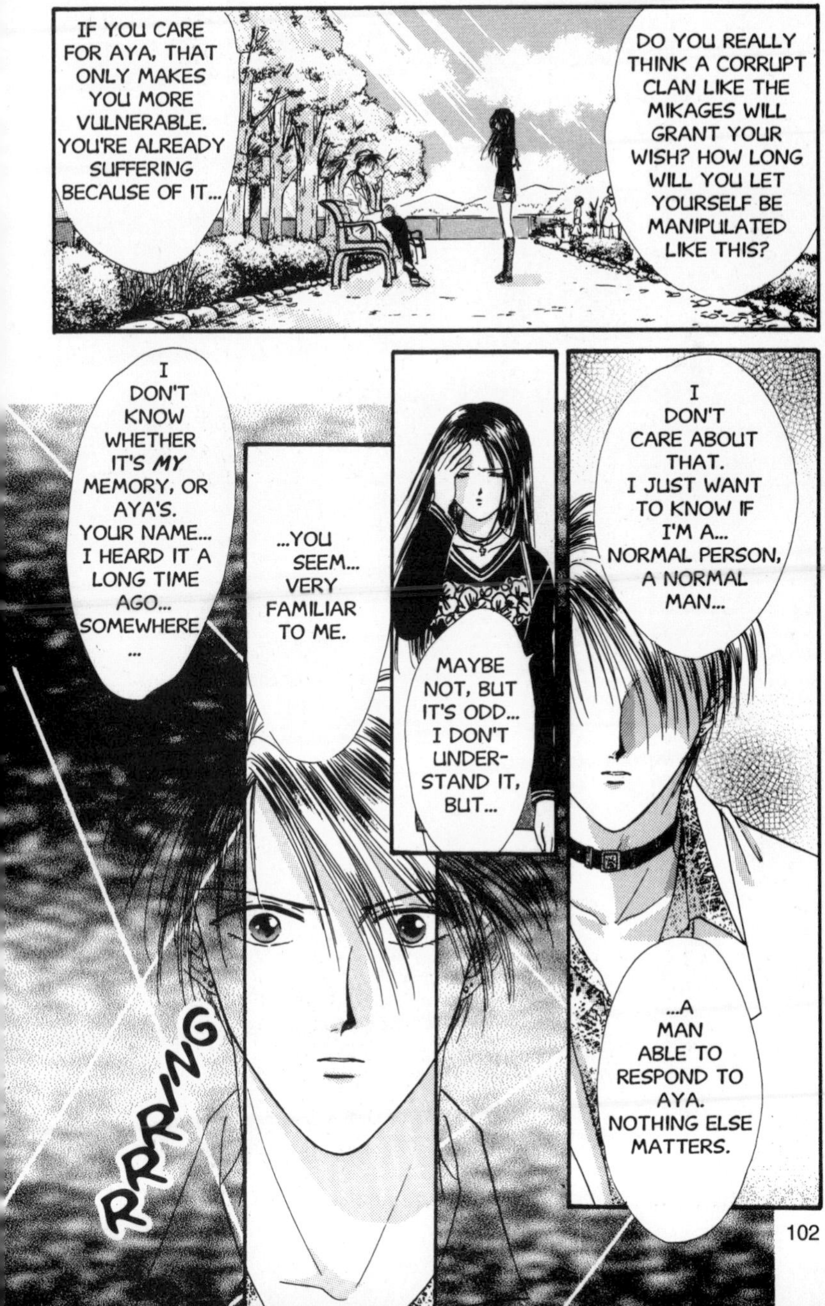
DO YOU REALLY THINK A CORRUPT CLAN LIKE THE MIKAGES WILL GRANT YOUR WISH? HOW LONG WILL YOU LET YOURSELF BE MANIPULATED LIKE THIS?
IF YOU CARE FOR AYA, THAT ONLY MAKES YOU MORE VULNERABLE. YOU'RE ALREADY SUFFERING BECAUSE OF IT...
I DON'T CARE ABOUT THAT. I JUST WANT TO KNOW IF I'M A... NORMAL PERSON, A NORMAL MAN...
...A MAN ABLE TO RESPOND TO AYA. NOTHING ELSE MATTERS.
MAYBE NOT, BUT IT'S ODD... I DON'T UNDER-STAND IT, BUT...
...YOU SEEM... VERY FAMILIAR TO ME.
I DON'T KNOW WHETHER IT'S *MY* MEMORY, OR AYA'S. YOUR NAME... I HEARD IT A LONG TIME AGO... SOMEWHERE...
RRRING

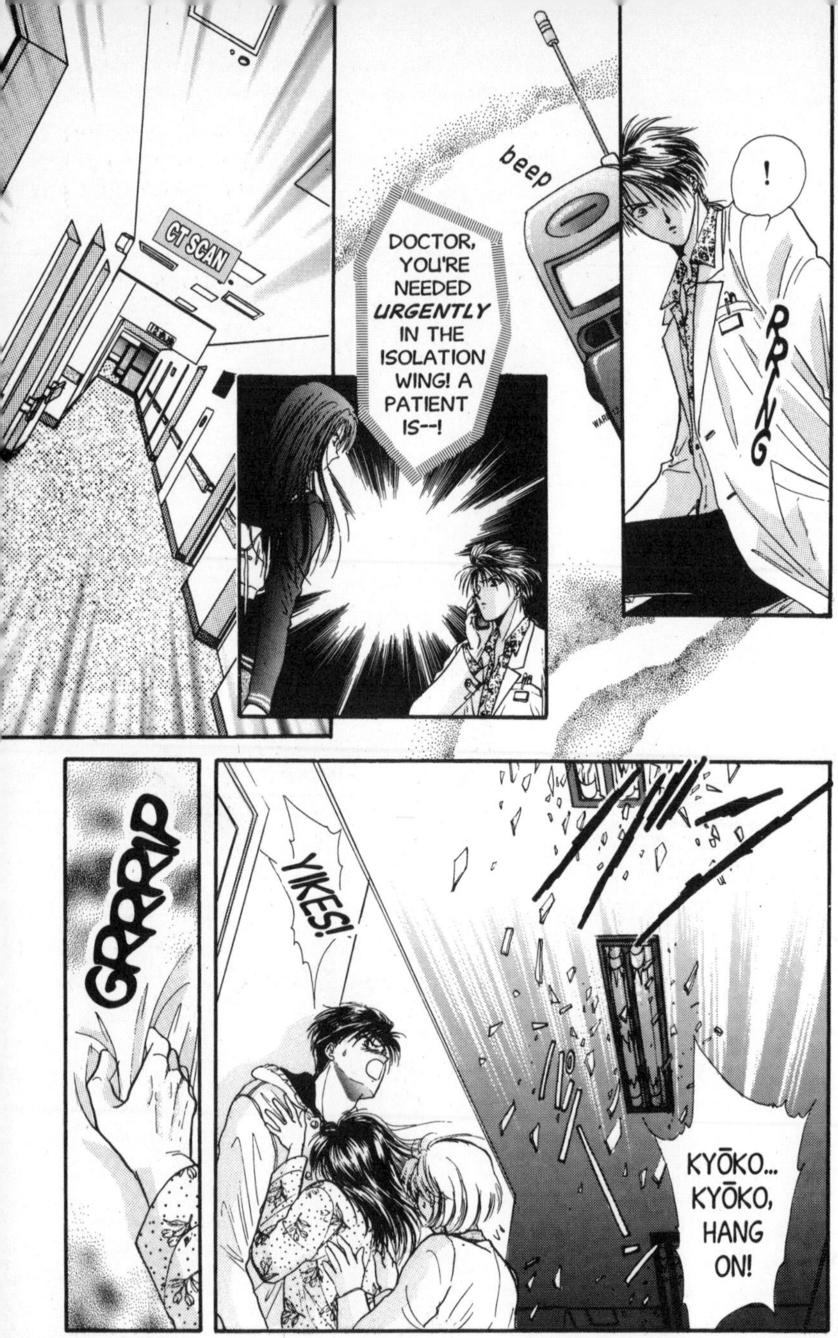

!
beep
RRRING
DOCTOR, YOU'RE NEEDED **URGENTLY** IN THE ISOLATION WING! A PATIENT IS--!
CT SCAN
YIKES!
KYŌKO... KYŌKO, HANG ON!
GRRRIP

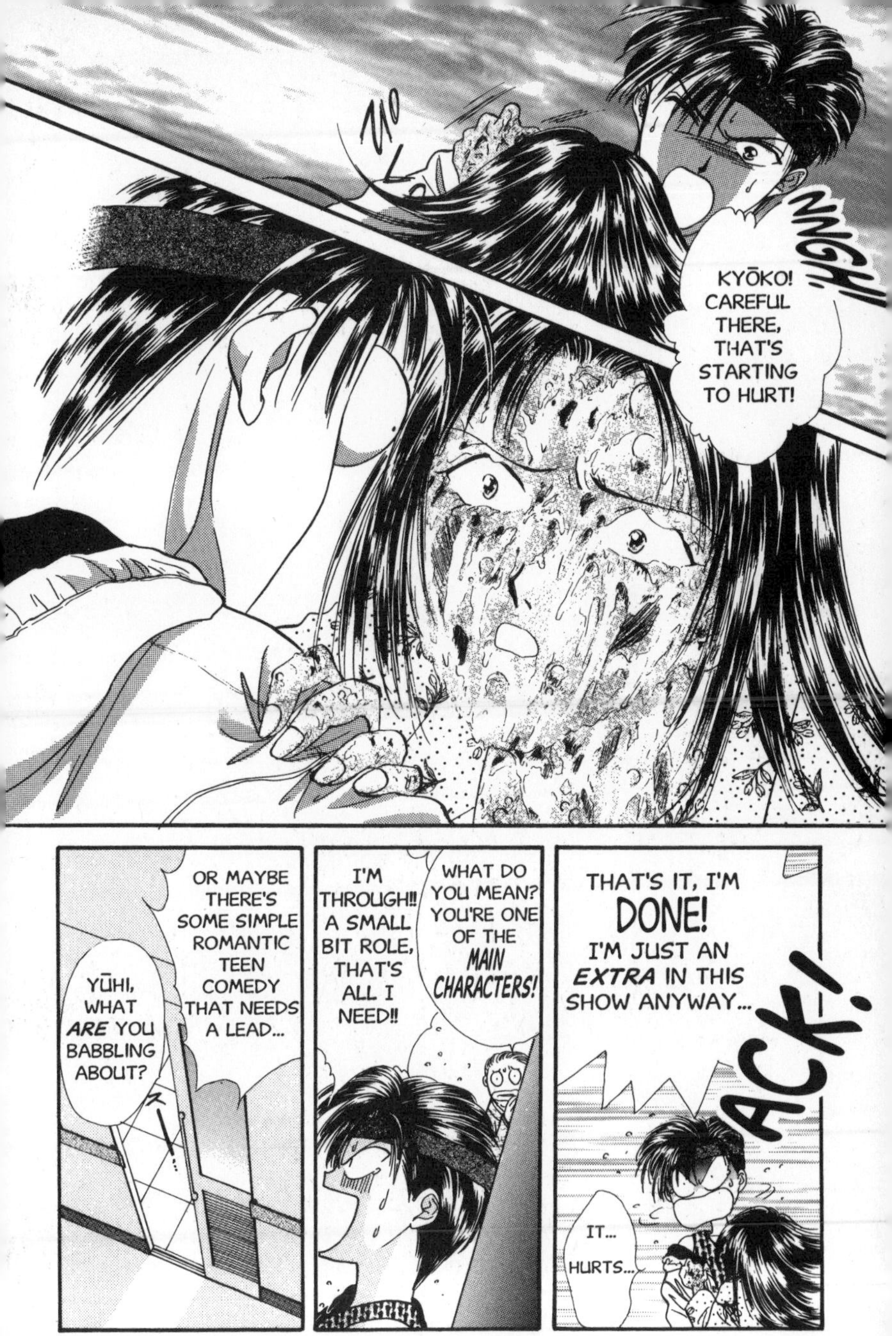
NNGH!!
KYŌKO! CAREFUL THERE, THAT'S STARTING TO HURT!
THAT'S IT, I'M DONE! I'M JUST AN EXTRA IN THIS SHOW ANYWAY...
ACK!
IT... HURTS...
WHAT DO YOU MEAN? YOU'RE ONE OF THE MAIN CHARACTERS!
I'M THROUGH!! A SMALL BIT ROLE, THAT'S ALL I NEED!!
OR MAYBE THERE'S SOME SIMPLE ROMANTIC TEEN COMEDY THAT NEEDS A LEAD...
YŪHI, WHAT ARE YOU BABBLING ABOUT?

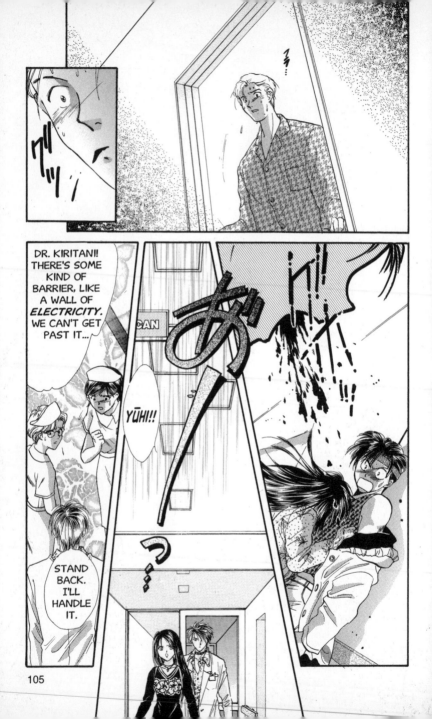

DR. KIRITANI! THERE'S SOME KIND OF BARRIER, LIKE A WALL OF *ELECTRICITY*. WE CAN'T GET PAST IT...

YŪHI!!

STAND BACK. I'LL HANDLE IT.

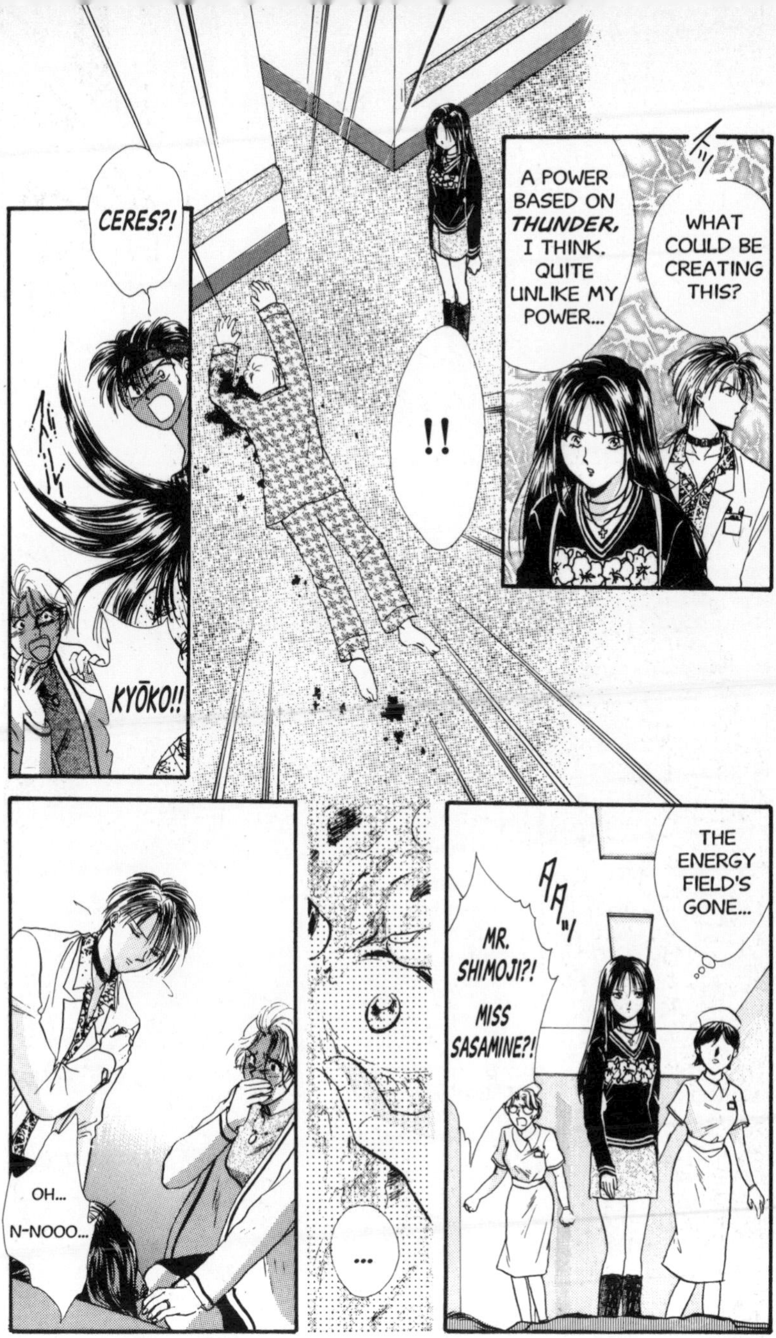
WHAT COULD BE CREATING THIS?
A POWER BASED ON THUNDER, I THINK. QUITE UNLIKE MY POWER...
!!
CERES?!
KYŌKO!!
THE ENERGY FIELD'S GONE...
AA!
MR. SHIMOJI?! MISS SASAMINE?!
...
OH... N-NOOO...

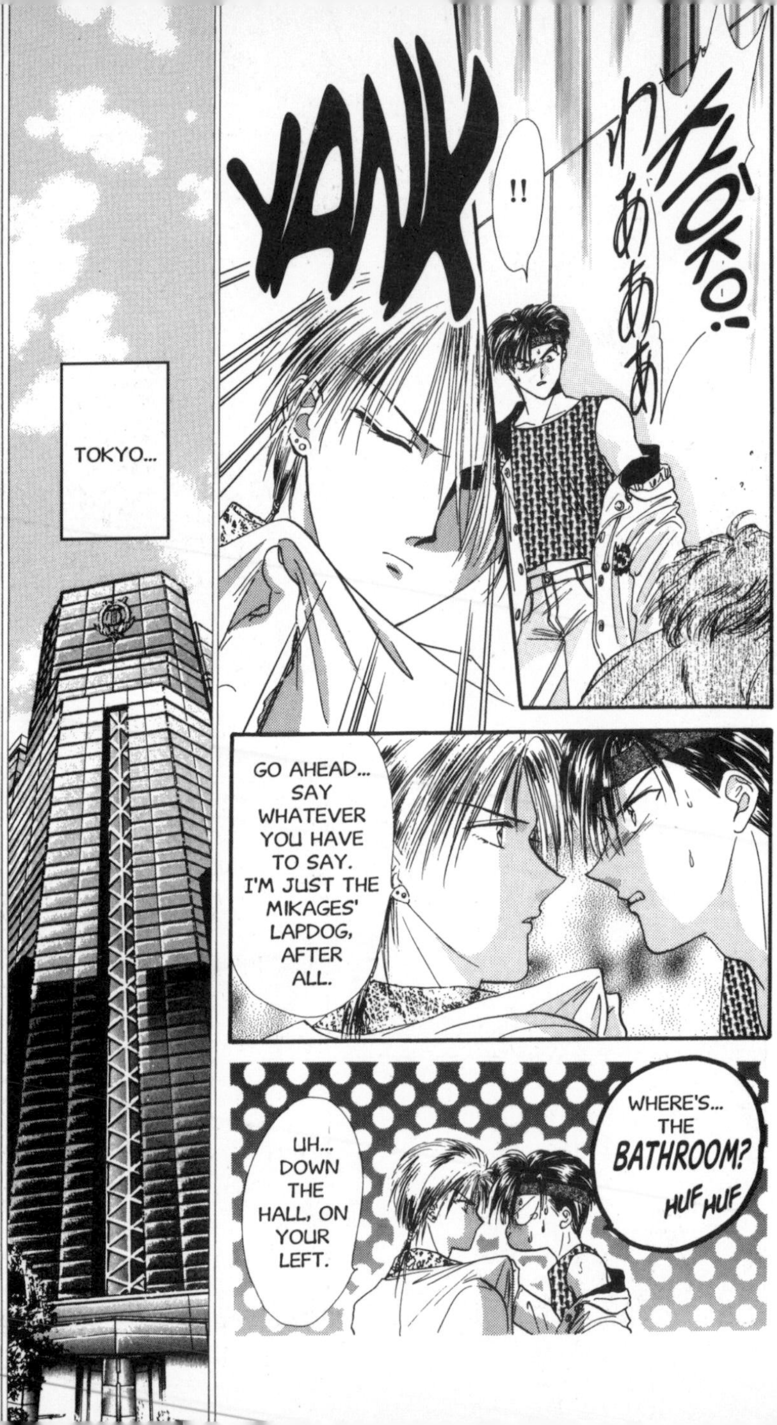
KYOKO!
わあああ
!!
YANK
GO AHEAD... SAY WHATEVER YOU HAVE TO SAY. I'M JUST THE MIKAGES' LAPDOG, AFTER ALL.
WHERE'S... THE BATHROOM?
HUF HUF
UH... DOWN THE HALL, ON YOUR LEFT.
TOKYO...

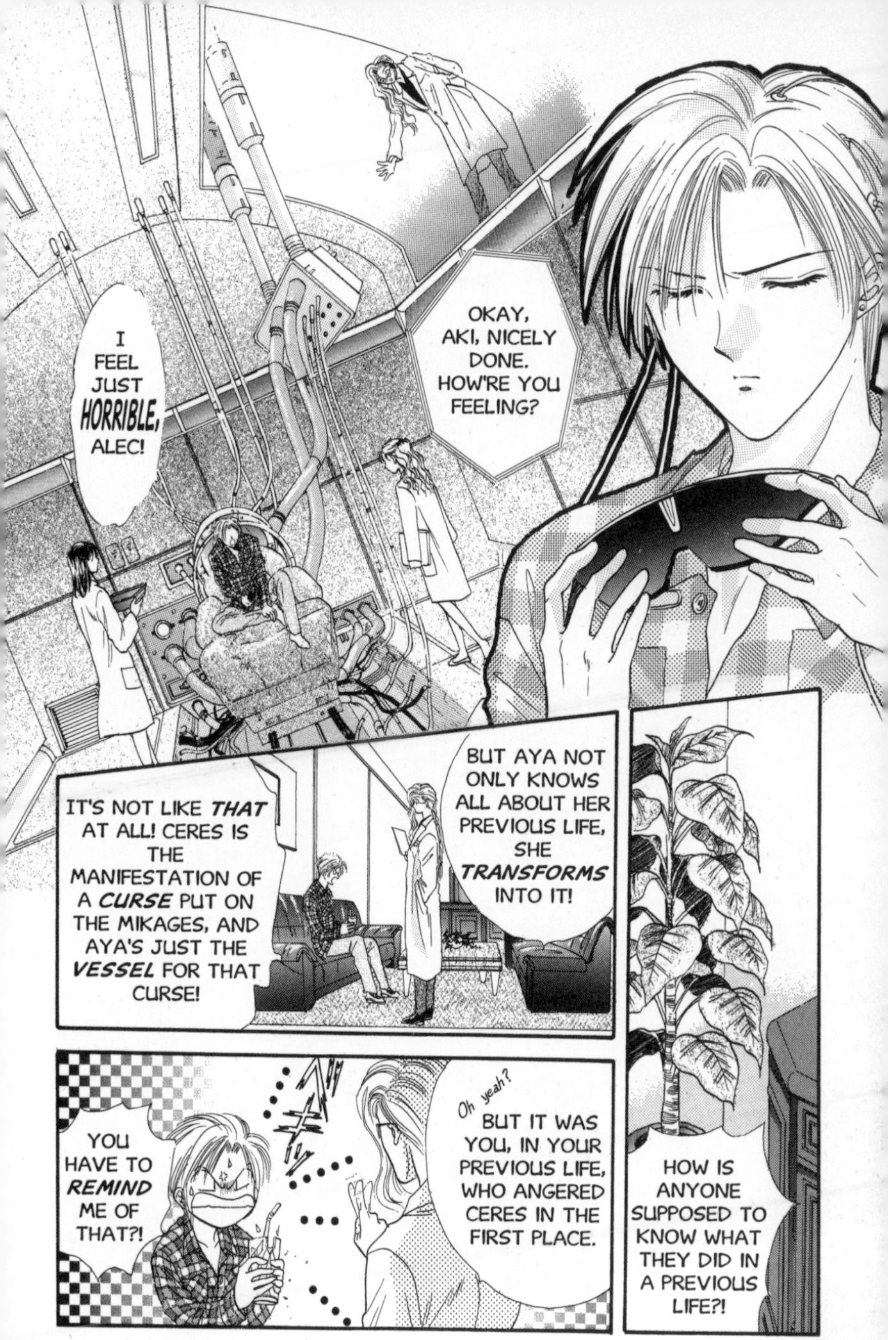
OKAY, AKI, NICELY DONE. HOW'RE YOU FEELING?
I FEEL JUST HORRIBLE, ALEC!
BUT AYA NOT ONLY KNOWS ALL ABOUT HER PREVIOUS LIFE, SHE TRANSFORMS INTO IT!
IT'S NOT LIKE THAT AT ALL! CERES IS THE MANIFESTATION OF A CURSE PUT ON THE MIKAGES, AND AYA'S JUST THE VESSEL FOR THAT CURSE!
Oh yeah?
BUT IT WAS YOU, IN YOUR PREVIOUS LIFE, WHO ANGERED CERES IN THE FIRST PLACE.
YOU HAVE TO REMIND ME OF THAT?!
HOW IS ANYONE SUPPOSED TO KNOW WHAT THEY DID IN A PREVIOUS LIFE?!

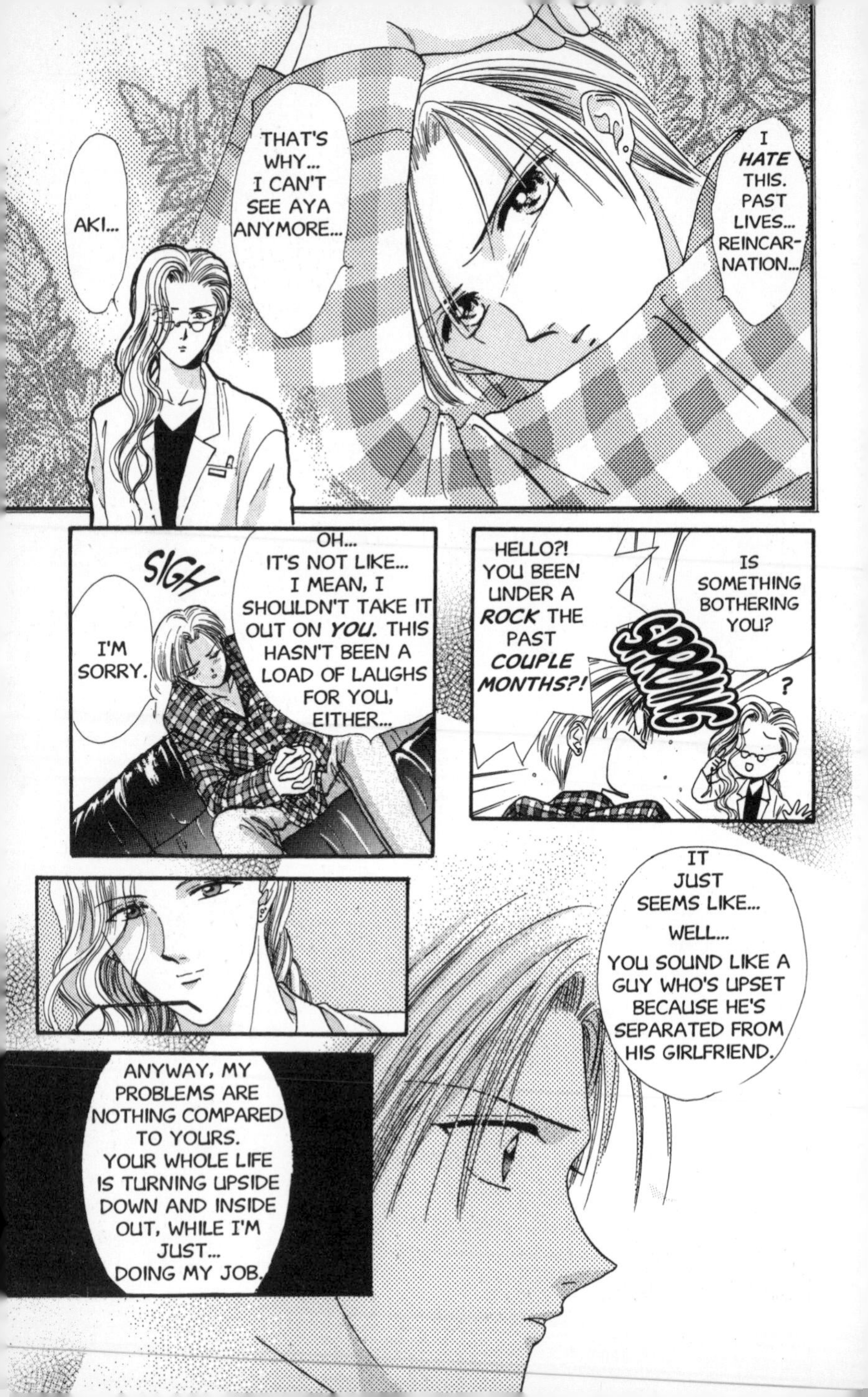
I HATE THIS. PAST LIVES... REINCARNATION...
THAT'S WHY... I CAN'T SEE AYA ANYMORE...
AKI...
IS SOMETHING BOTHERING YOU?
?
HELLO?! YOU BEEN UNDER A ROCK THE PAST COUPLE MONTHS?!
OH... IT'S NOT LIKE... I MEAN, I SHOULDN'T TAKE IT OUT ON YOU. THIS HASN'T BEEN A LOAD OF LAUGHS FOR YOU, EITHER...
SIGH
I'M SORRY.
IT JUST SEEMS LIKE... WELL... YOU SOUND LIKE A GUY WHO'S UPSET BECAUSE HE'S SEPARATED FROM HIS GIRLFRIEND.
ANYWAY, MY PROBLEMS ARE NOTHING COMPARED TO YOURS. YOUR WHOLE LIFE IS TURNING UPSIDE DOWN AND INSIDE OUT, WHILE I'M JUST... DOING MY JOB.

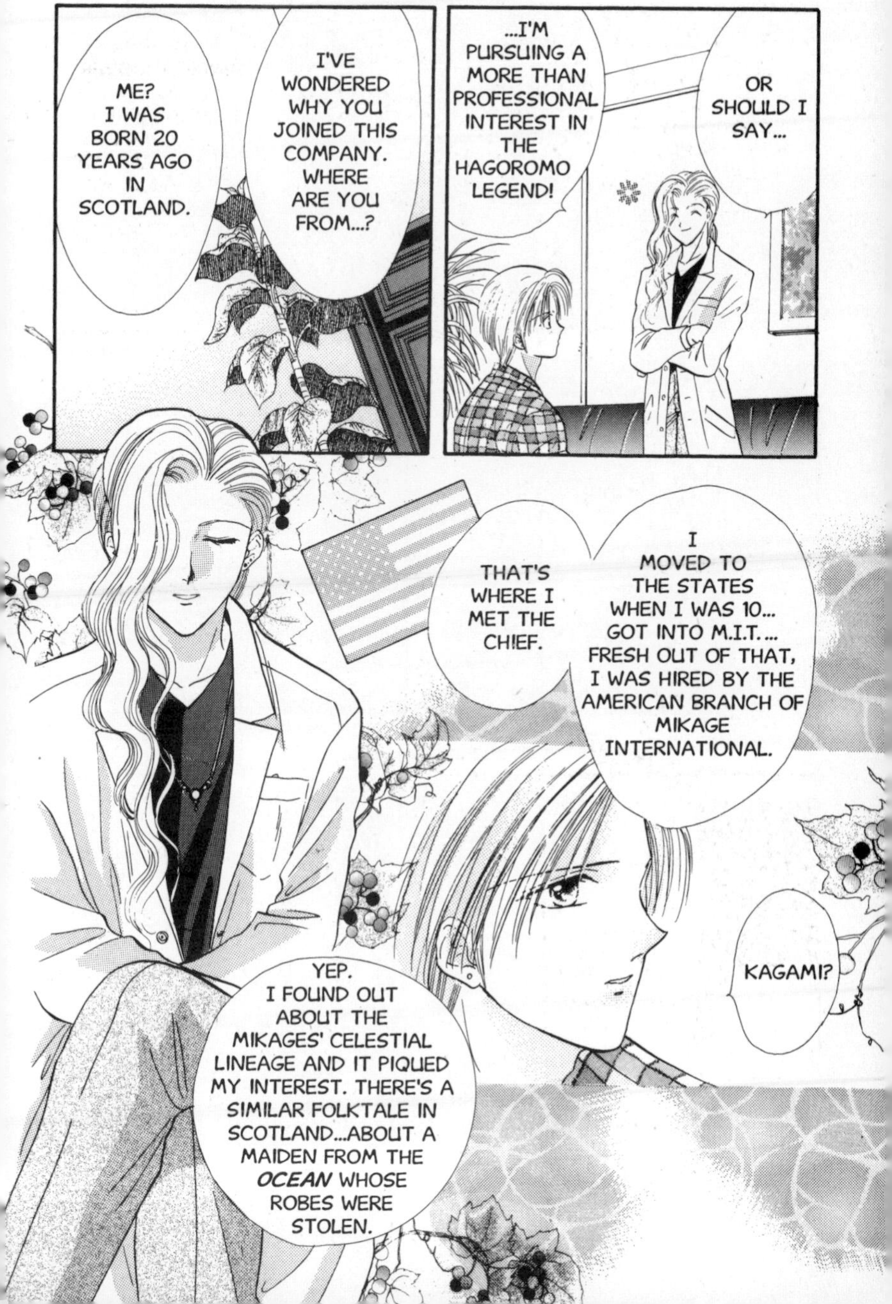
OR SHOULD I SAY...
...I'M PURSUING A MORE THAN PROFESSIONAL INTEREST IN THE HAGOROMO LEGEND!
I'VE WONDERED WHY YOU JOINED THIS COMPANY. WHERE ARE YOU FROM...?
ME? I WAS BORN 20 YEARS AGO IN SCOTLAND.
I MOVED TO THE STATES WHEN I WAS 10... GOT INTO M.I.T.... FRESH OUT OF THAT, I WAS HIRED BY THE AMERICAN BRANCH OF MIKAGE INTERNATIONAL.
THAT'S WHERE I MET THE CHIEF.
KAGAMI?
YEP. I FOUND OUT ABOUT THE MIKAGES' CELESTIAL LINEAGE AND IT PIQUED MY INTEREST. THERE'S A SIMILAR FOLKTALE IN SCOTLAND...ABOUT A MAIDEN FROM THE *OCEAN* WHOSE ROBES WERE STOLEN.

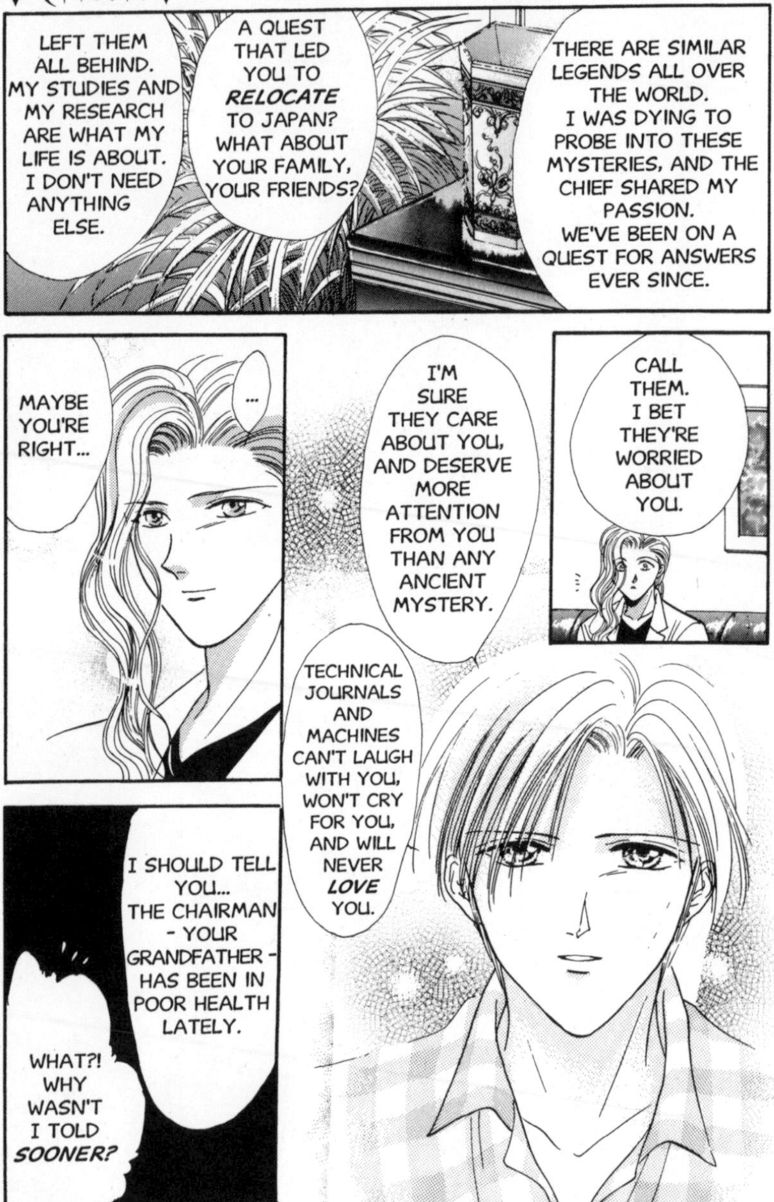
THERE ARE SIMILAR LEGENDS ALL OVER THE WORLD. I WAS DYING TO PROBE INTO THESE MYSTERIES, AND THE CHIEF SHARED MY PASSION. WE'VE BEEN ON A QUEST FOR ANSWERS EVER SINCE.
A QUEST THAT LED YOU TO *RELOCATE* TO JAPAN? WHAT ABOUT YOUR FAMILY, YOUR FRIENDS?
LEFT THEM ALL BEHIND. MY STUDIES AND MY RESEARCH ARE WHAT MY LIFE IS ABOUT. I DON'T NEED ANYTHING ELSE.
CALL THEM. I BET THEY'RE WORRIED ABOUT YOU.
I'M SURE THEY CARE ABOUT YOU, AND DESERVE MORE ATTENTION FROM YOU THAN ANY ANCIENT MYSTERY.
TECHNICAL JOURNALS AND MACHINES CAN'T LAUGH WITH YOU, WON'T CRY FOR YOU, AND WILL NEVER *LOVE* YOU.
...
MAYBE YOU'RE RIGHT...
I SHOULD TELL YOU... THE CHAIRMAN - YOUR GRANDFATHER - HAS BEEN IN POOR HEALTH LATELY.
WHAT?! WHY WASN'T I TOLD *SOONER?*

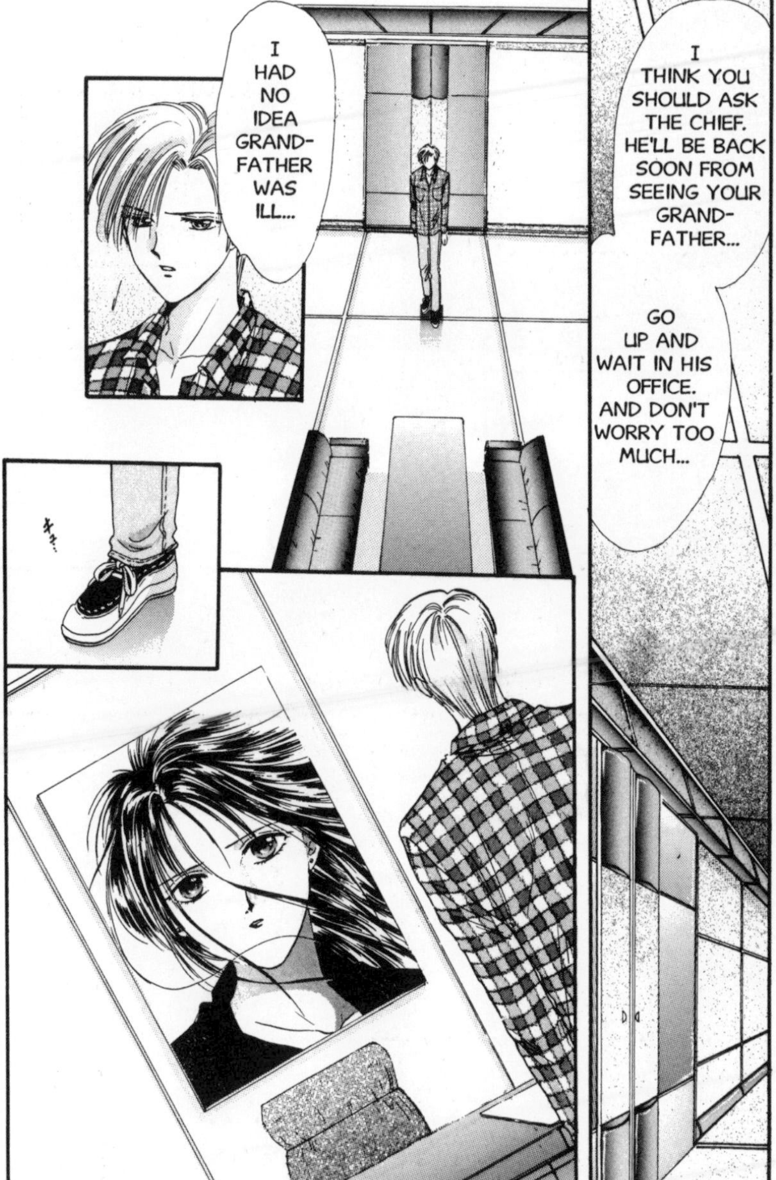
I THINK YOU SHOULD ASK THE CHIEF. HE'LL BE BACK SOON FROM SEEING YOUR GRAND-FATHER...
GO UP AND WAIT IN HIS OFFICE. AND DON'T WORRY TOO MUCH...
I HAD NO IDEA GRAND-FATHER WAS ILL...

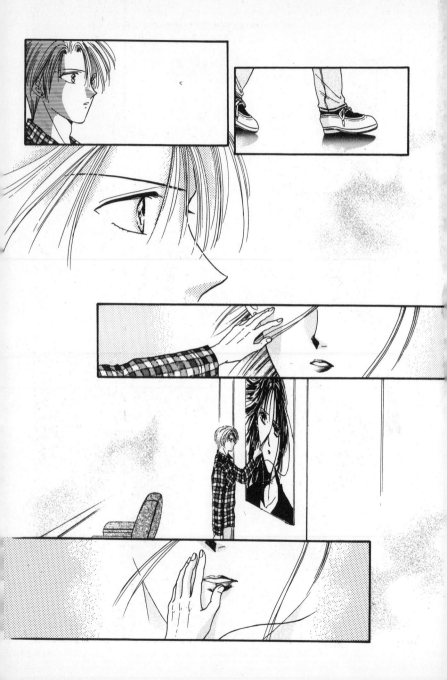

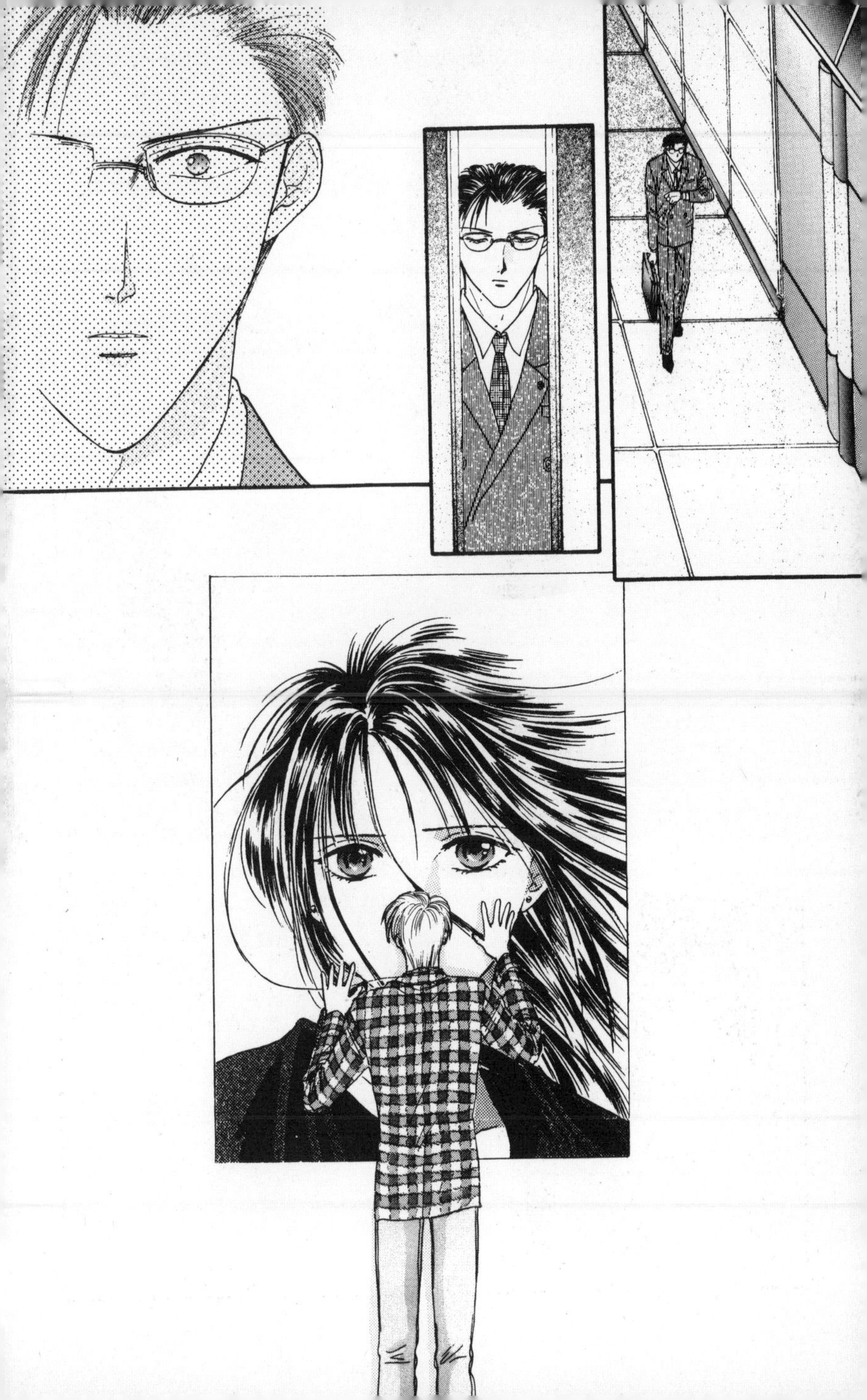

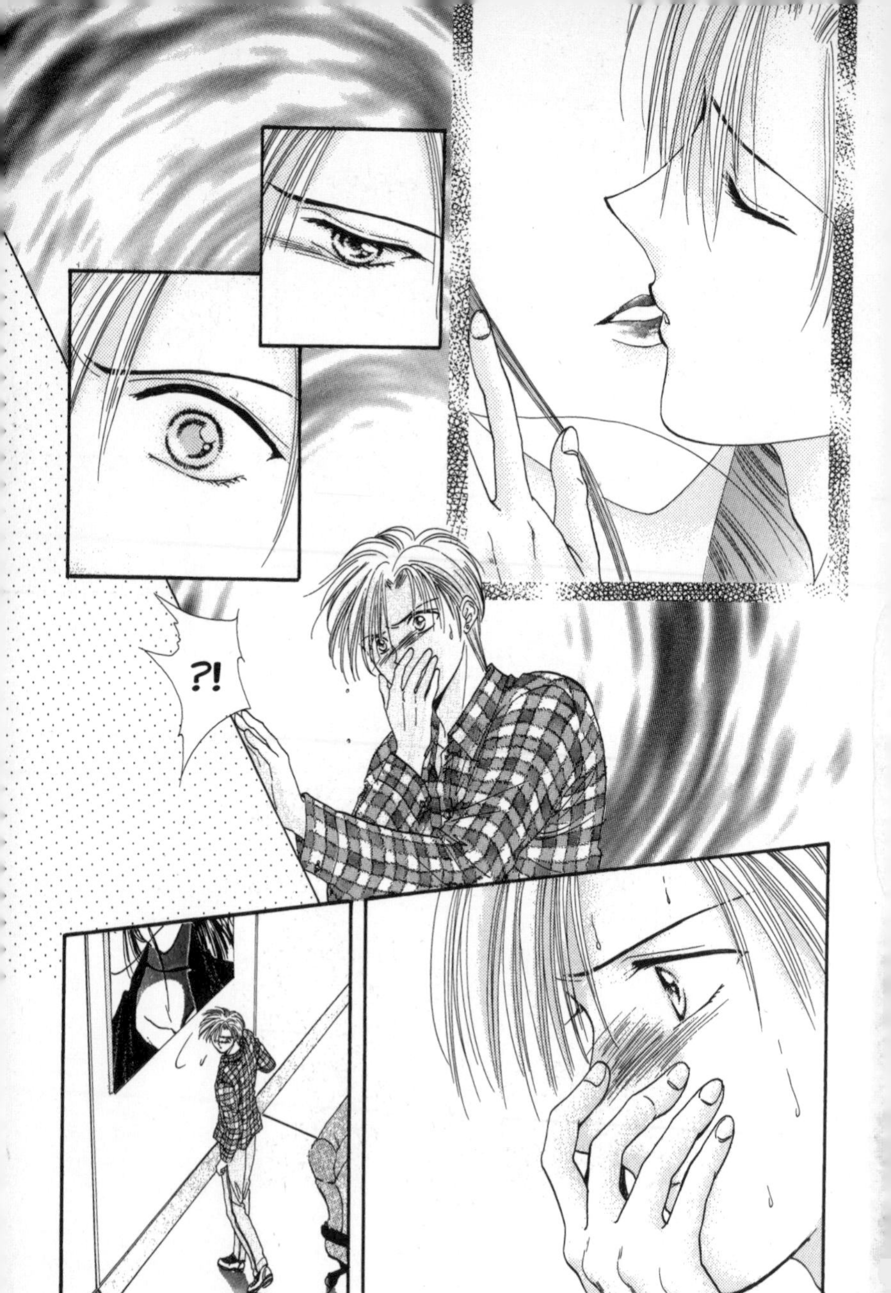
?!

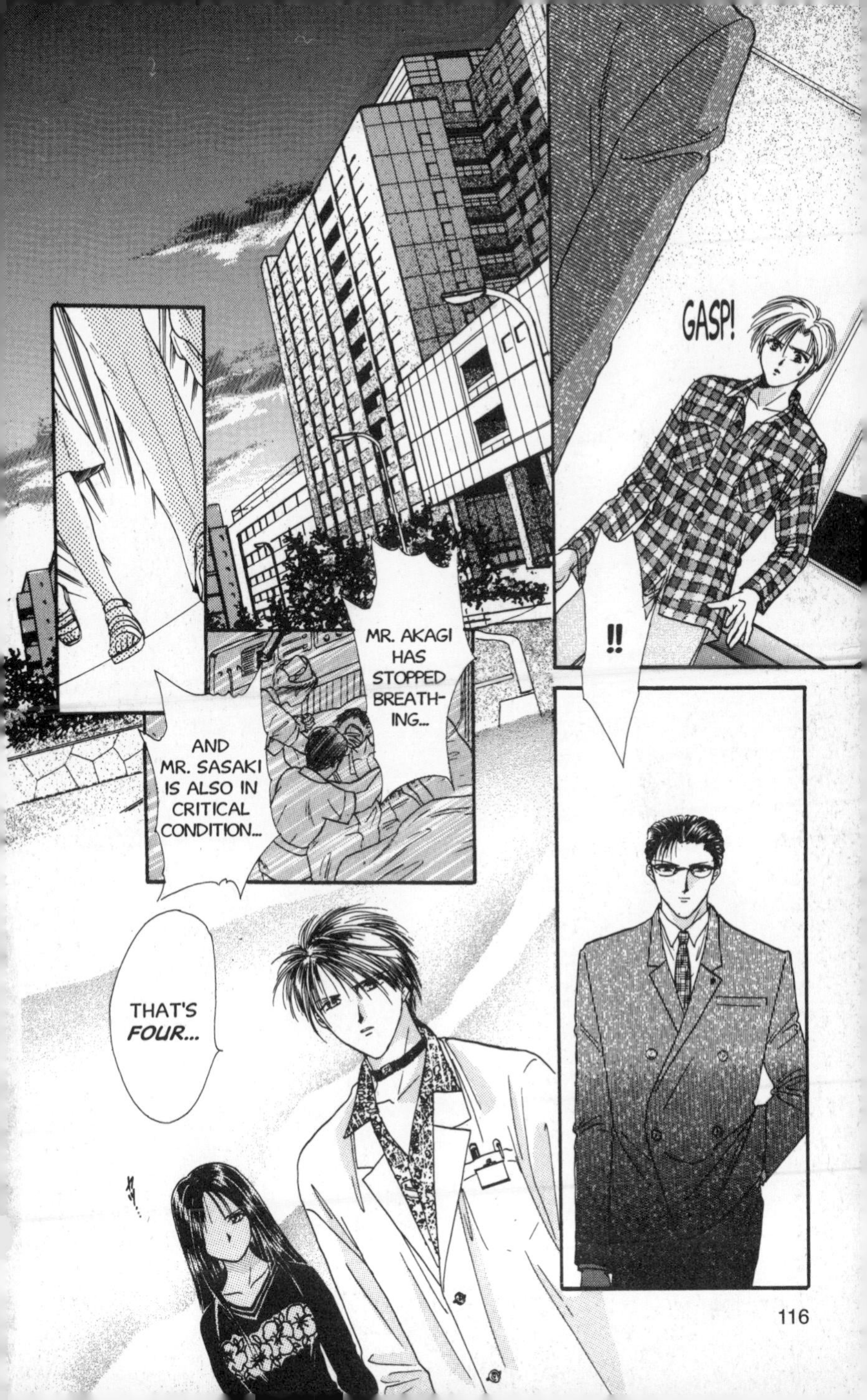
GASP!
!!
MR. AKAGI HAS STOPPED BREATH-ING...
AND MR. SASAKI IS ALSO IN CRITICAL CONDITION...
THAT'S *FOUR*...

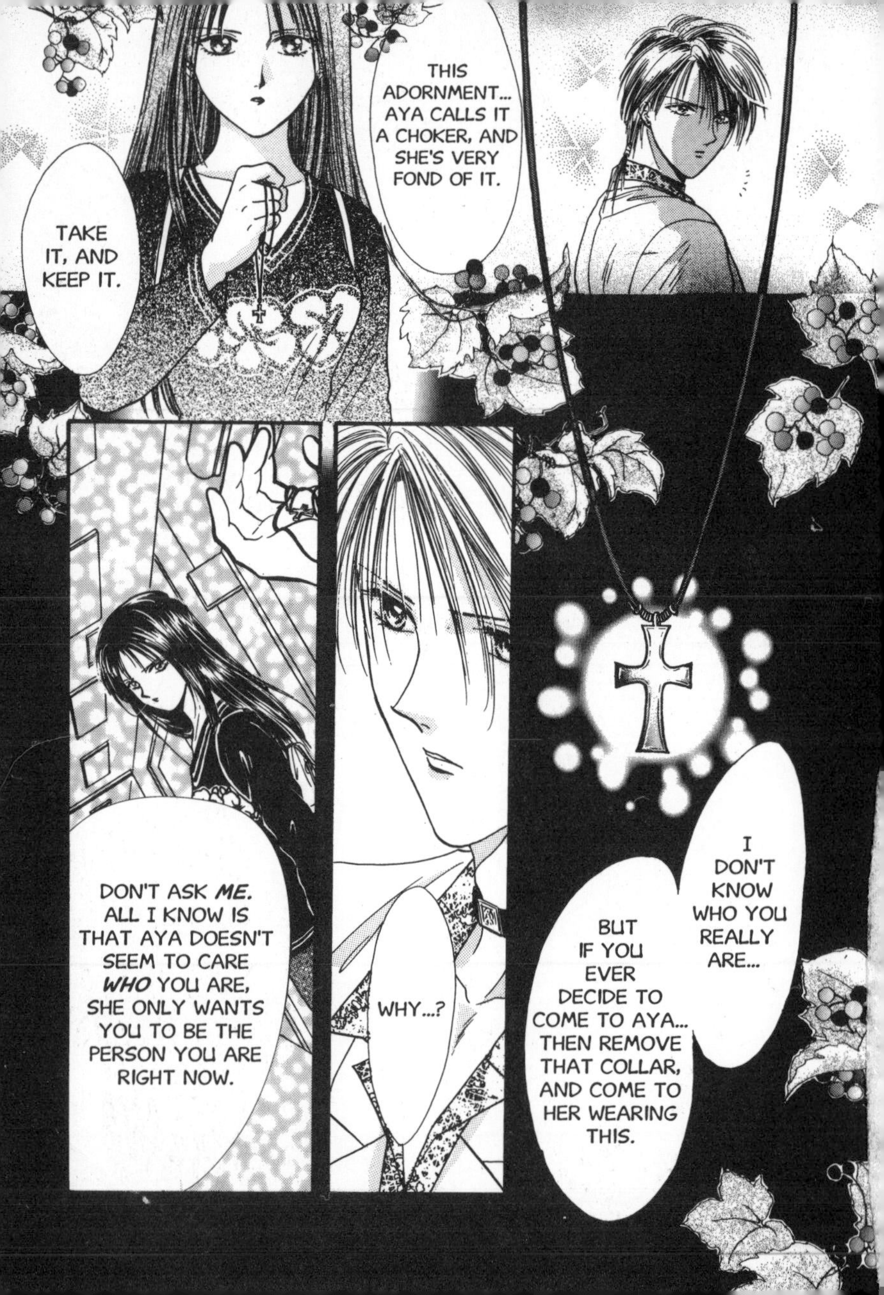
THIS ADORNMENT... AYA CALLS IT A CHOKER, AND SHE'S VERY FOND OF IT.
TAKE IT, AND KEEP IT.
I DON'T KNOW WHO YOU REALLY ARE...
BUT IF YOU EVER DECIDE TO COME TO AYA... THEN REMOVE THAT COLLAR, AND COME TO HER WEARING THIS.
WHY...?
DON'T ASK *ME.* ALL I KNOW IS THAT AYA DOESN'T SEEM TO CARE *WHO* YOU ARE, SHE ONLY WANTS YOU TO BE THE PERSON YOU ARE RIGHT NOW.

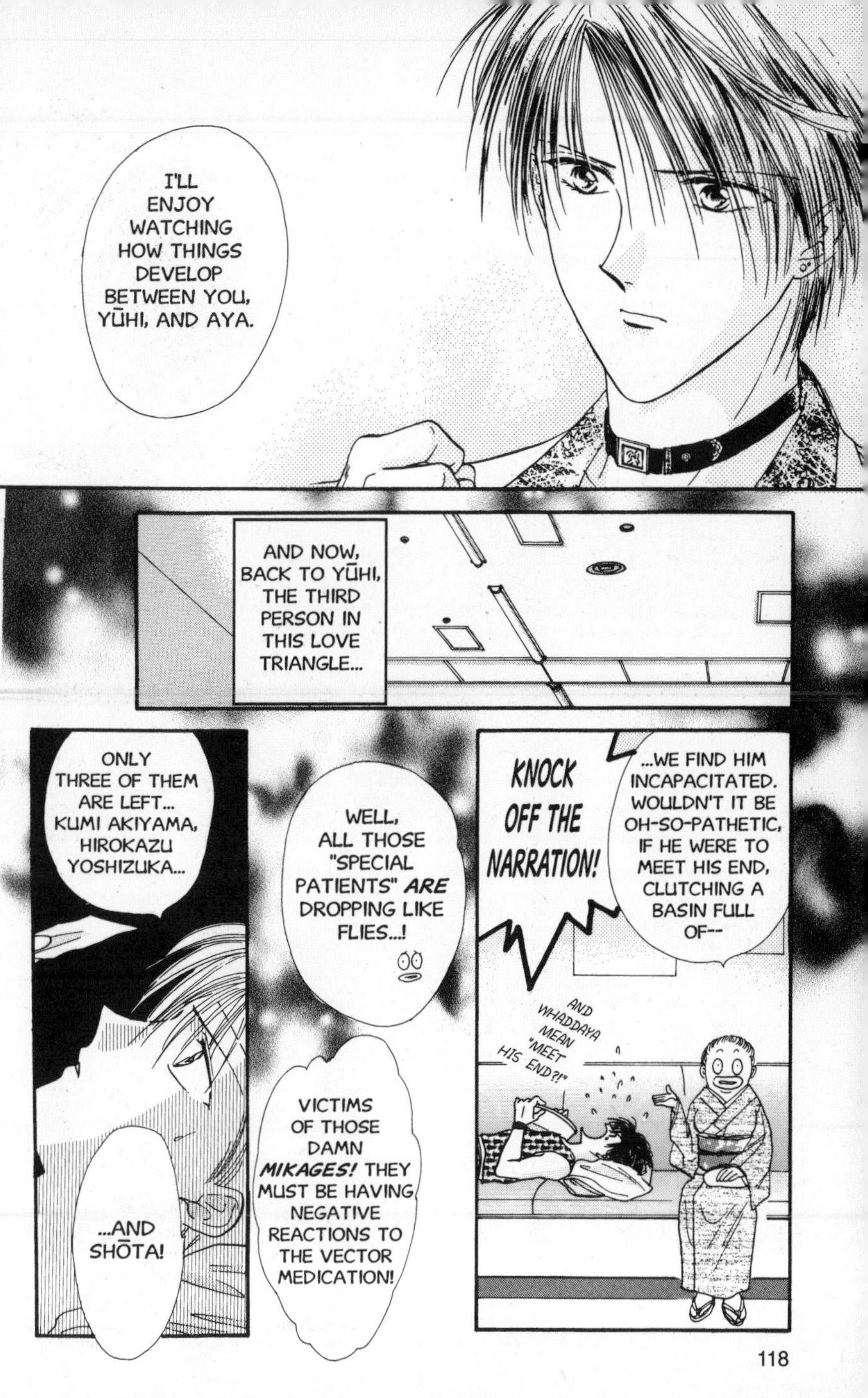
I'LL ENJOY WATCHING HOW THINGS DEVELOP BETWEEN YOU, YŪHI, AND AYA.
AND NOW, BACK TO YŪHI, THE THIRD PERSON IN THIS LOVE TRIANGLE...
...WE FIND HIM INCAPACITATED. WOULDN'T IT BE OH-SO-PATHETIC, IF HE WERE TO MEET HIS END, CLUTCHING A BASIN FULL OF--
KNOCK OFF THE NARRATION!
AND WHADDAYA MEAN "MEET HIS END?!"
WELL, ALL THOSE "SPECIAL PATIENTS" ARE DROPPING LIKE FLIES...!
ONLY THREE OF THEM ARE LEFT... KUMI AKIYAMA, HIROKAZU YOSHIZUKA...
...AND SHŌTA!
VICTIMS OF THOSE DAMN MIKAGES! THEY MUST BE HAVING NEGATIVE REACTIONS TO THE VECTOR MEDICATION!

Ceres: 4

So I'm head over heels in love with Cloud. I seem to have a weakness for the strong silent type.
Sephiroth and Vincent too!
Well, I've talked about how I love this character or that character before, but I don't want you to misunderstand. The way a creator "loves" a character and the way a reader "loves" a character are different. As their creator, my feelings include a bit of calculation - whether they are well developed, well drawn, or easy to draw. And I hope I wouldn't be so silly as to be infatuated with my own characters so much that I would lose sleep over them. If one of my characters were to come on to me, frankly, it would feel like incest and gross me out. ◡̈ I mean, they're like my children I gave **birth** to. That's why my "love" and a reader's "love" for my characters are totally different. Come to think of it, I once received a letter that told me I was "really fickle."
I chuckled to myself and thought, "It must be because I always have a different favorite character." Well, as I stated above, don't confuse it with **real** love. ◡̈ I'm actually very faithful. (Dare I say it myself?) Once I fall in love with someone, I cease to even think of other guys as "the opposite sex." ◡̈
For some reason, two of my editors once told me, "You seem like the devoted type," and I was freaked out. Um...why?! ◡̈
It's a little sickening to imagine myself that way, so at least I won't act that way in public. I tend to be tomboyish (I firmly believe I was a guy in my previous life.) so I don't understand girls sometimes. Maybe that's why my work is rather gender-neutral. At this rate, I wonder if I'll get more and more masculine... Don't worry! At least I haven't fallen in love with a woman yet! But I like to draw nude bodies... Could it be...? hmm... Something left over from my previous life...???

But for now, I'll just settle for Cloud.
Cool men are the best!

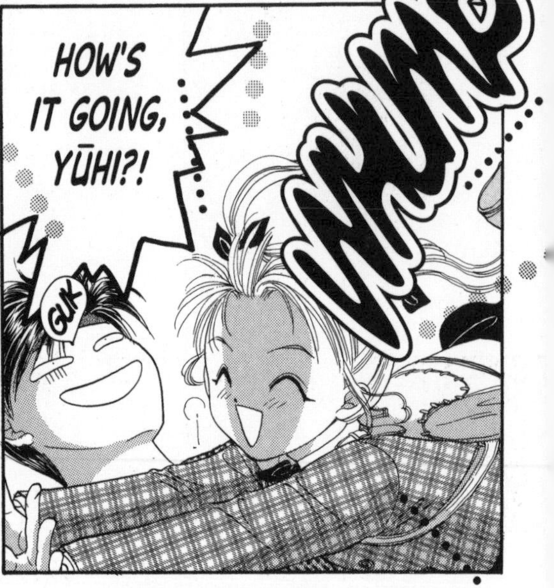
WHUMP
HOW'S IT GOING, YŪHI?!
GUK

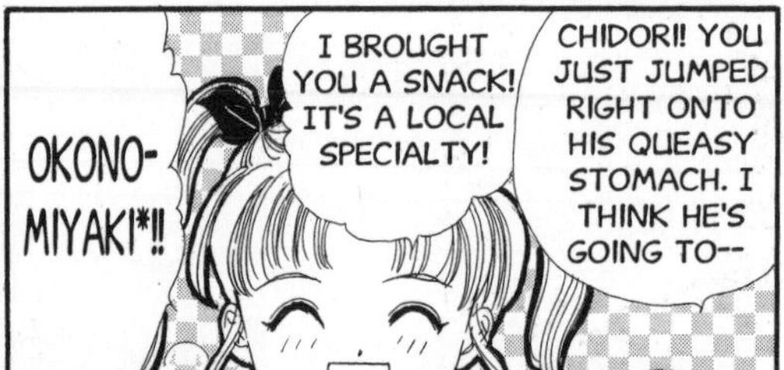
CHIDORI!! YOU JUST JUMPED RIGHT ONTO HIS QUEASY STOMACH. I THINK HE'S GOING TO--
I BROUGHT YOU A SNACK! IT'S A LOCAL SPECIALTY!
OKONO-MIYAKI*!!
TA DA

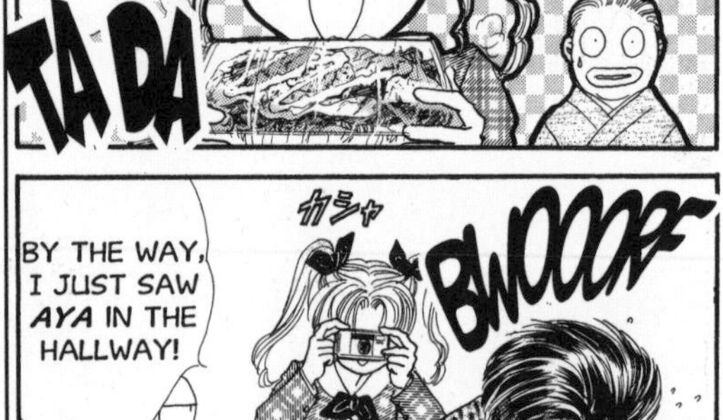
BWOOORF
カシャ
BY THE WAY, I JUST SAW *AYA* IN THE HALLWAY!

*CABBAGE PANCAKE TOPPED WITH MEAT, FISH FLAKES, SEAWEED, SPECIAL SAUCE, AND MAYONNAISE.

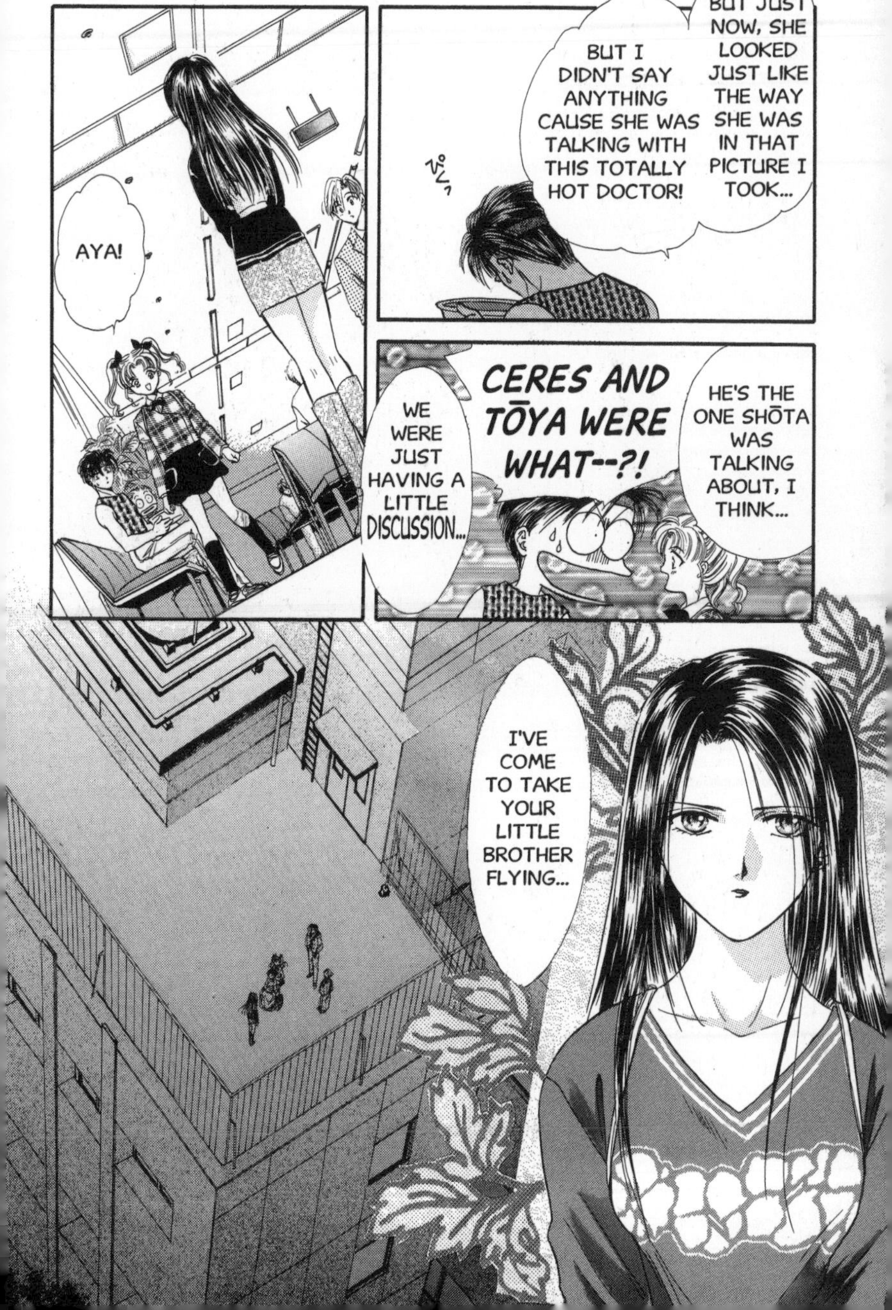
BUT JUST NOW, SHE LOOKED JUST LIKE THE WAY SHE WAS IN THAT PICTURE I TOOK...
BUT I DIDN'T SAY ANYTHING CAUSE SHE WAS TALKING WITH THIS TOTALLY HOT DOCTOR!
HE'S THE ONE SHŌTA WAS TALKING ABOUT, I THINK...
CERES AND TŌYA WERE WHAT--?!
WE WERE JUST HAVING A LITTLE DISCUSSION...
AYA!
I'VE COME TO TAKE YOUR LITTLE BROTHER FLYING...

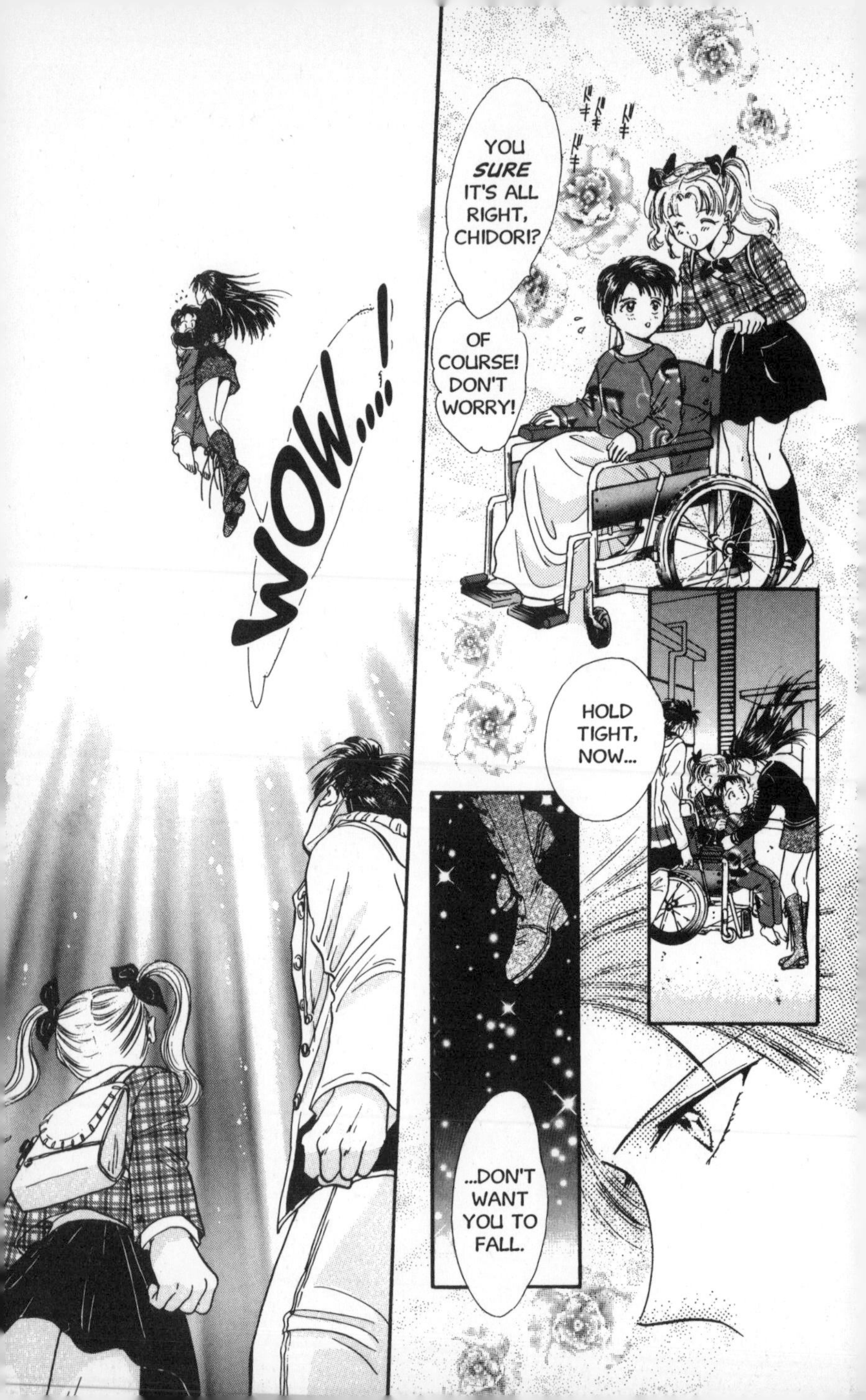
YOU *SURE* IT'S ALL RIGHT, CHIDORI?
OF COURSE! DON'T WORRY!
HOLD TIGHT, NOW...
...DON'T WANT YOU TO FALL.
WOW...!

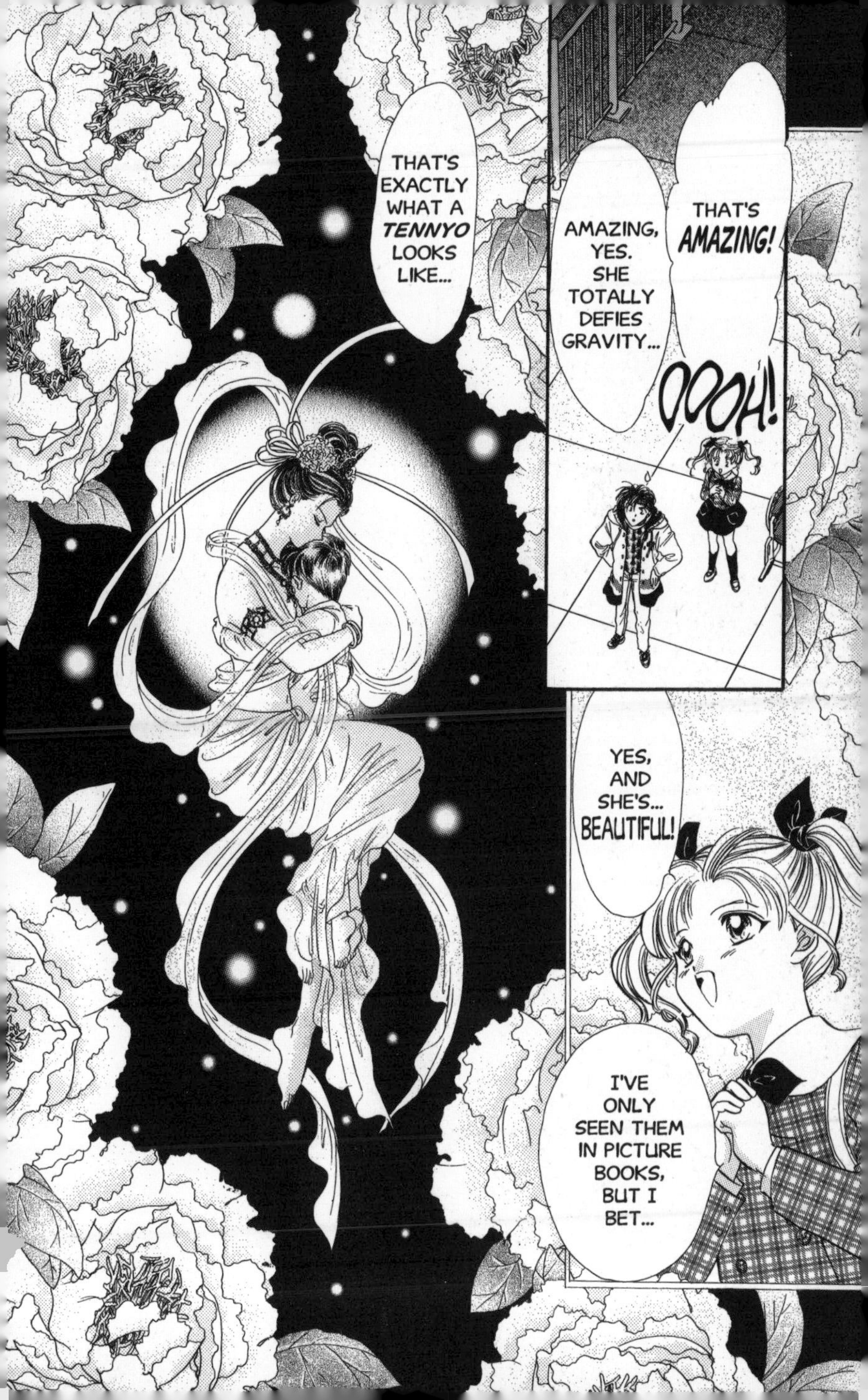

THAT'S AMAZING!
AMAZING, YES. SHE TOTALLY DEFIES GRAVITY...
OOOH!
YES, AND SHE'S... BEAUTIFUL!
I'VE ONLY SEEN THEM IN PICTURE BOOKS, BUT I BET...
THAT'S EXACTLY WHAT A *TENNYO* LOOKS LIKE...

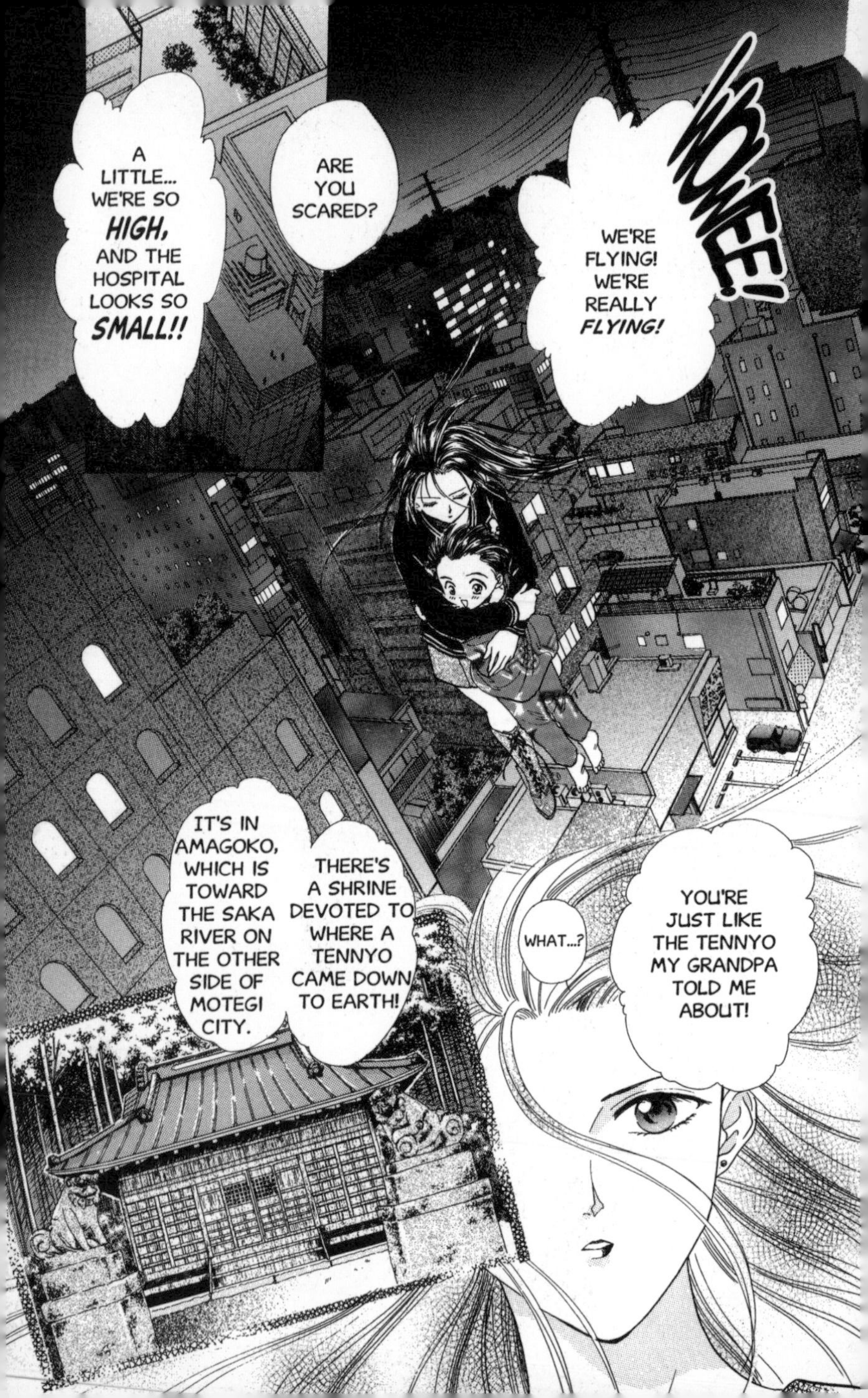
WOWEE!
WE'RE FLYING! WE'RE REALLY FLYING!
ARE YOU SCARED?
A LITTLE... WE'RE SO HIGH, AND THE HOSPITAL LOOKS SO SMALL!!
YOU'RE JUST LIKE THE TENNYO MY GRANDPA TOLD ME ABOUT!
WHAT...?
THERE'S A SHRINE DEVOTED TO WHERE A TENNYO CAME DOWN TO EARTH!
IT'S IN AMAGOKO, WHICH IS TOWARD THE SAKA RIVER ON THE OTHER SIDE OF MOTEGI CITY.

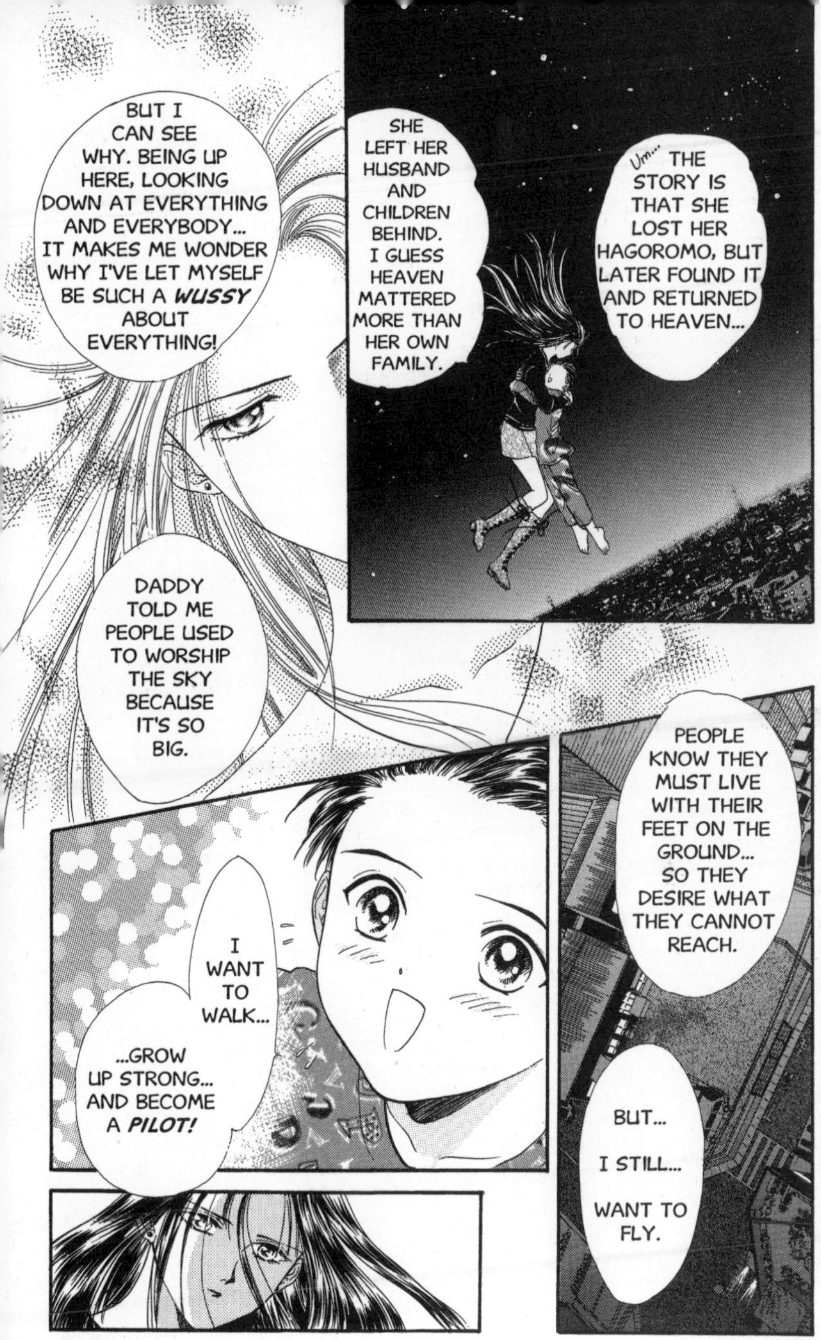
Um... THE STORY IS THAT SHE LOST HER HAGOROMO, BUT LATER FOUND IT AND RETURNED TO HEAVEN...
SHE LEFT HER HUSBAND AND CHILDREN BEHIND. I GUESS HEAVEN MATTERED MORE THAN HER OWN FAMILY.
BUT I CAN SEE WHY. BEING UP HERE, LOOKING DOWN AT EVERYTHING AND EVERYBODY... IT MAKES ME WONDER WHY I'VE LET MYSELF BE SUCH A *WUSSY* ABOUT EVERYTHING!
DADDY TOLD ME PEOPLE USED TO WORSHIP THE SKY BECAUSE IT'S SO BIG.
PEOPLE KNOW THEY MUST LIVE WITH THEIR FEET ON THE GROUND... SO THEY DESIRE WHAT THEY CANNOT REACH.
BUT... I STILL... WANT TO FLY.
I WANT TO WALK...
...GROW UP STRONG... AND BECOME A *PILOT!*

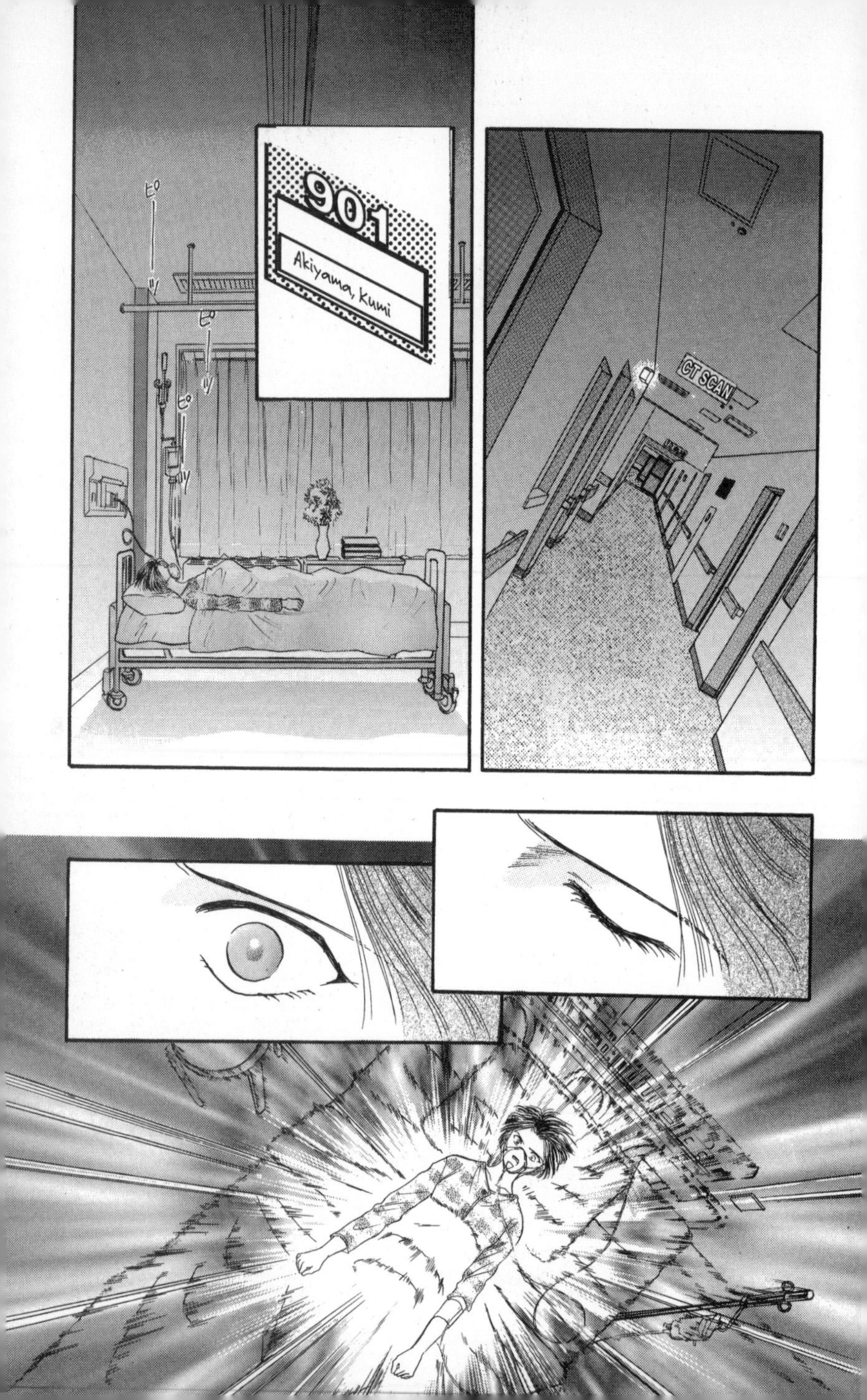
CT SCAN
901
Akiyama, Kumi
ピーーッ
ピーーッ
ピーーッ

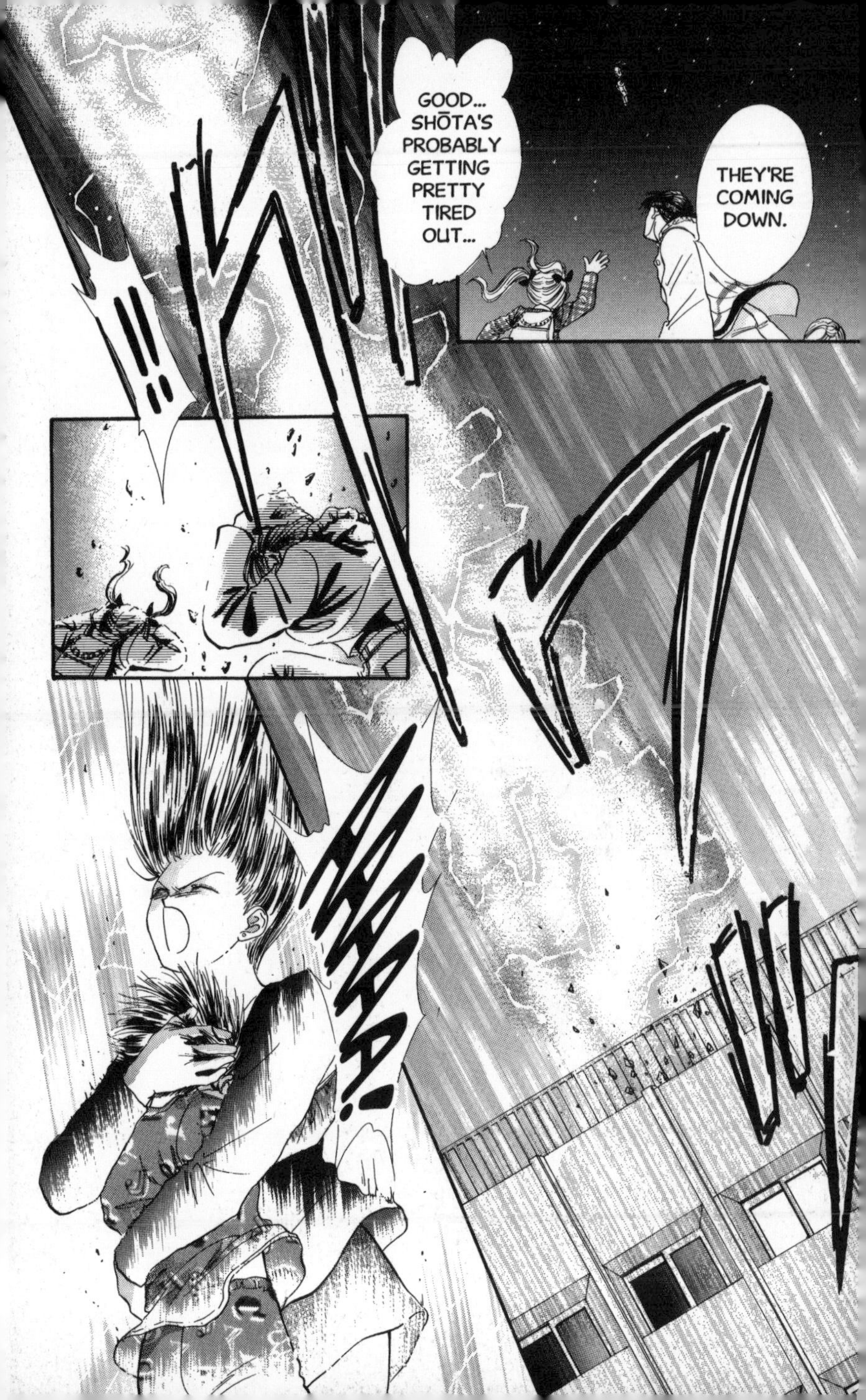
THEY'RE COMING DOWN.
GOOD... SHŌTA'S PROBABLY GETTING PRETTY TIRED OUT...

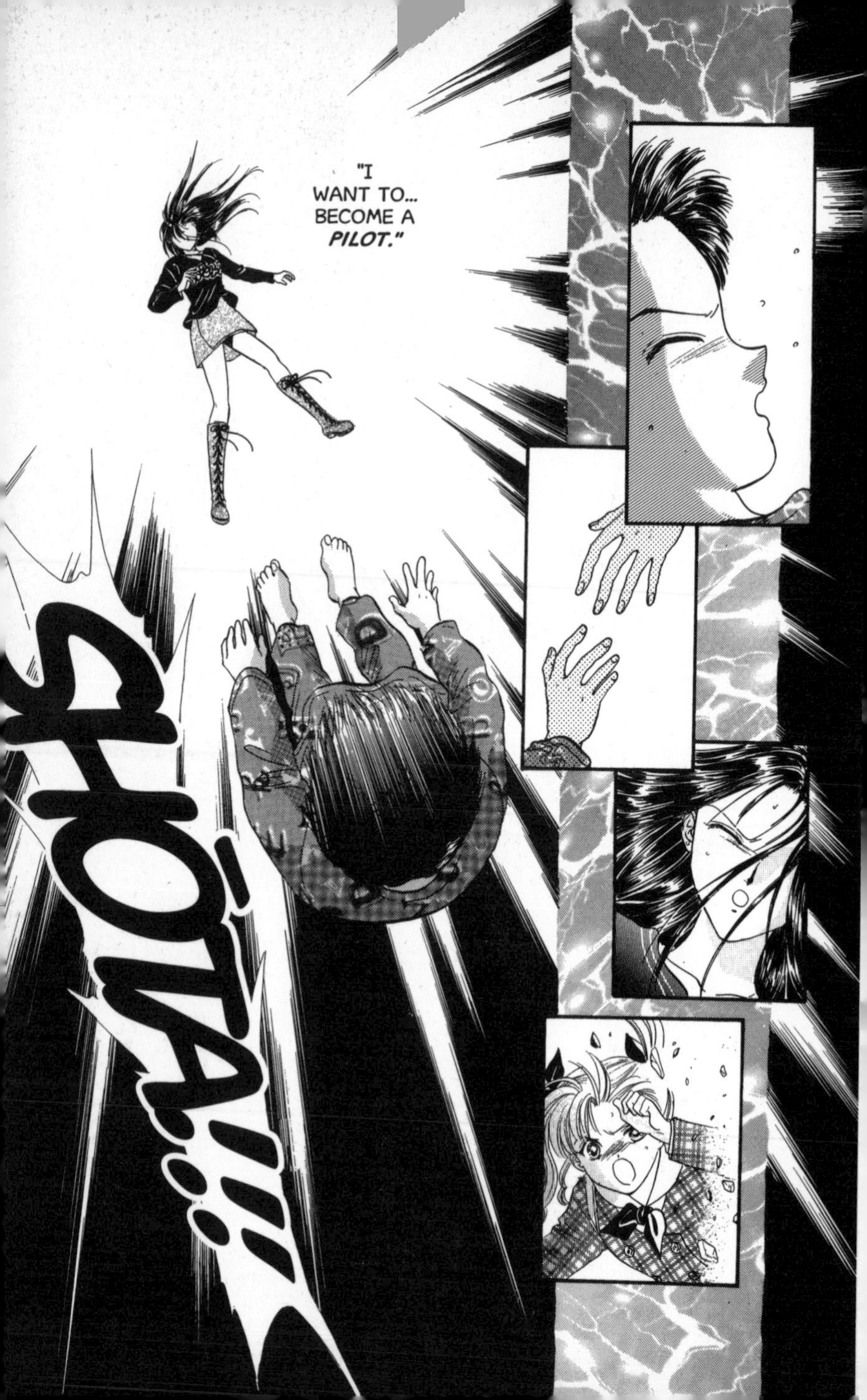
"I WANT TO... BECOME A *PILOT.*"
SHŌTA!!!

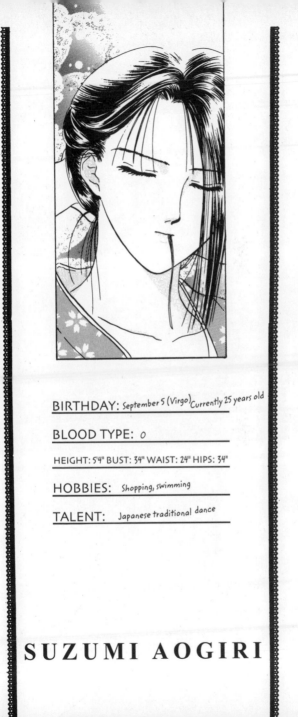

BIRTHDAY: September 5 (Virgo) Currently 25 years old

BLOOD TYPE: O

HEIGHT: 5'4" BUST: 34" WAIST: 24" HIPS: 34"

HOBBIES: Shopping, swimming

TALENT: Japanese traditional dance

SUZUMI AOGIRI

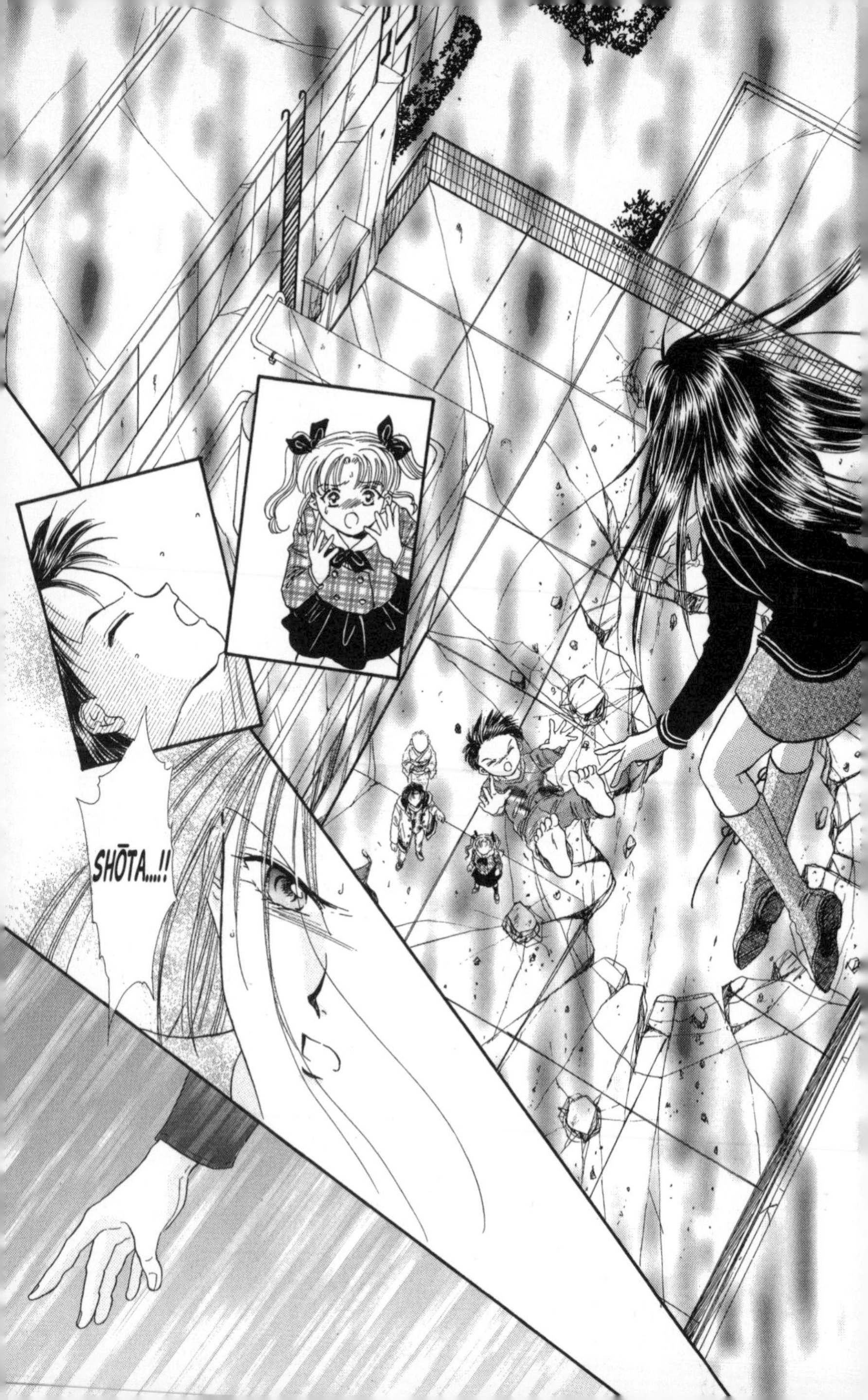
SHŌTA...!!

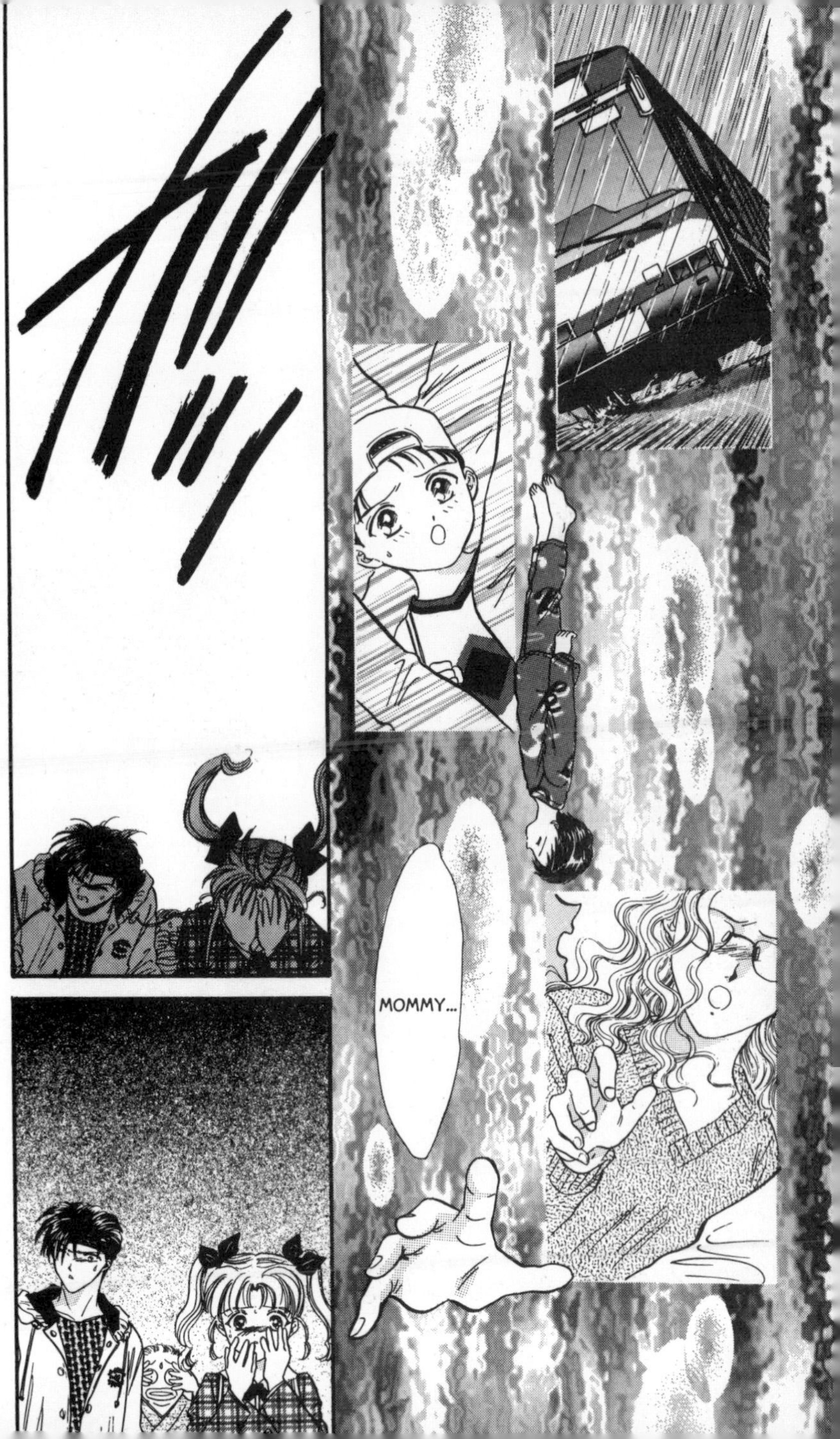
MOMMY...

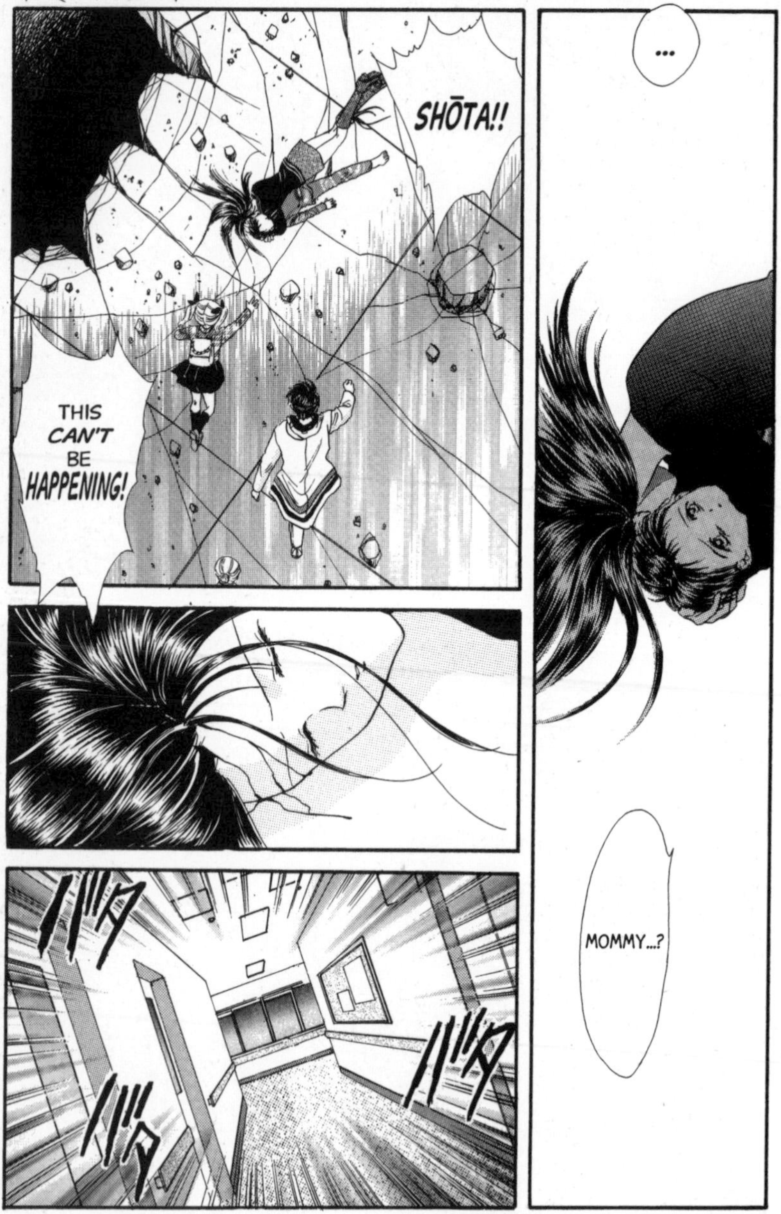
...
MOMMY...?
SHŌTA!!
THIS CAN'T BE HAPPENING!

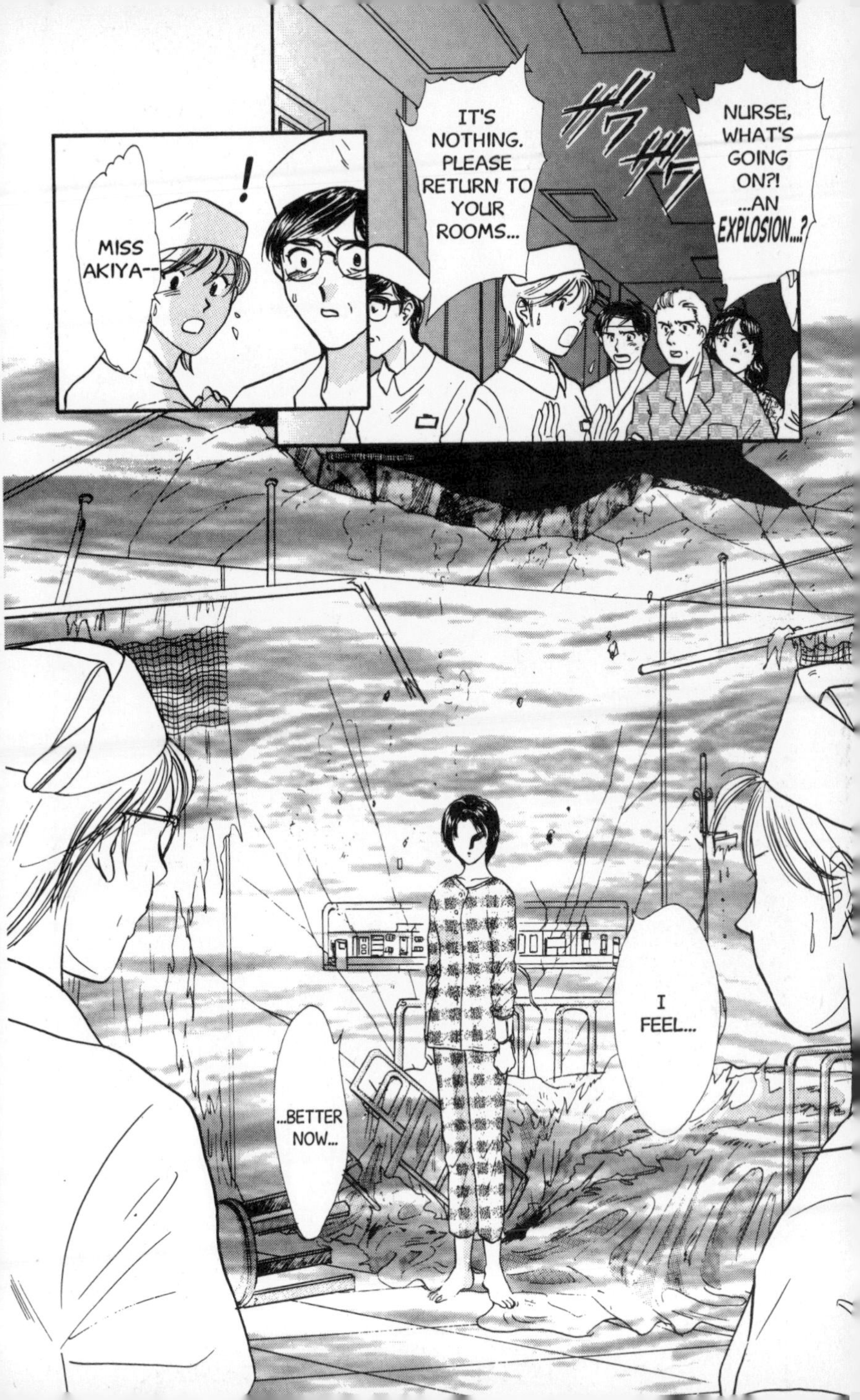
NURSE, WHAT'S GOING ON?! ...AN EXPLOSION...?
ザワ ザワ
IT'S NOTHING. PLEASE RETURN TO YOUR ROOMS...
!
MISS AKIYA--
I FEEL...
...BETTER NOW...

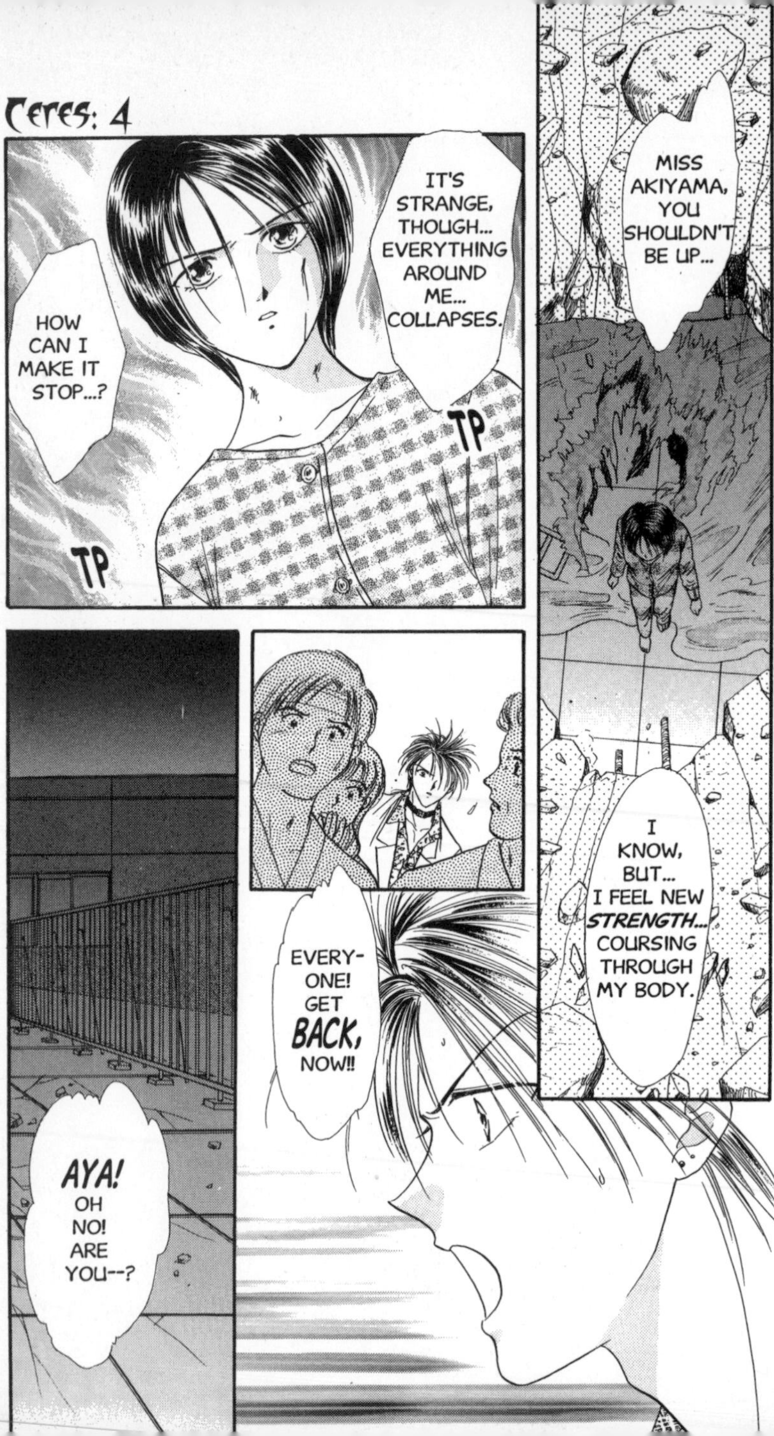
MISS AKIYAMA, YOU SHOULDN'T BE UP...
I KNOW, BUT... I FEEL NEW STRENGTH... COURSING THROUGH MY BODY.
IT'S STRANGE, THOUGH... EVERYTHING AROUND ME... COLLAPSES.
TP
TP
HOW CAN I MAKE IT STOP...?
EVERY-ONE! GET BACK, NOW!!
AYA! OH NO! ARE YOU--?

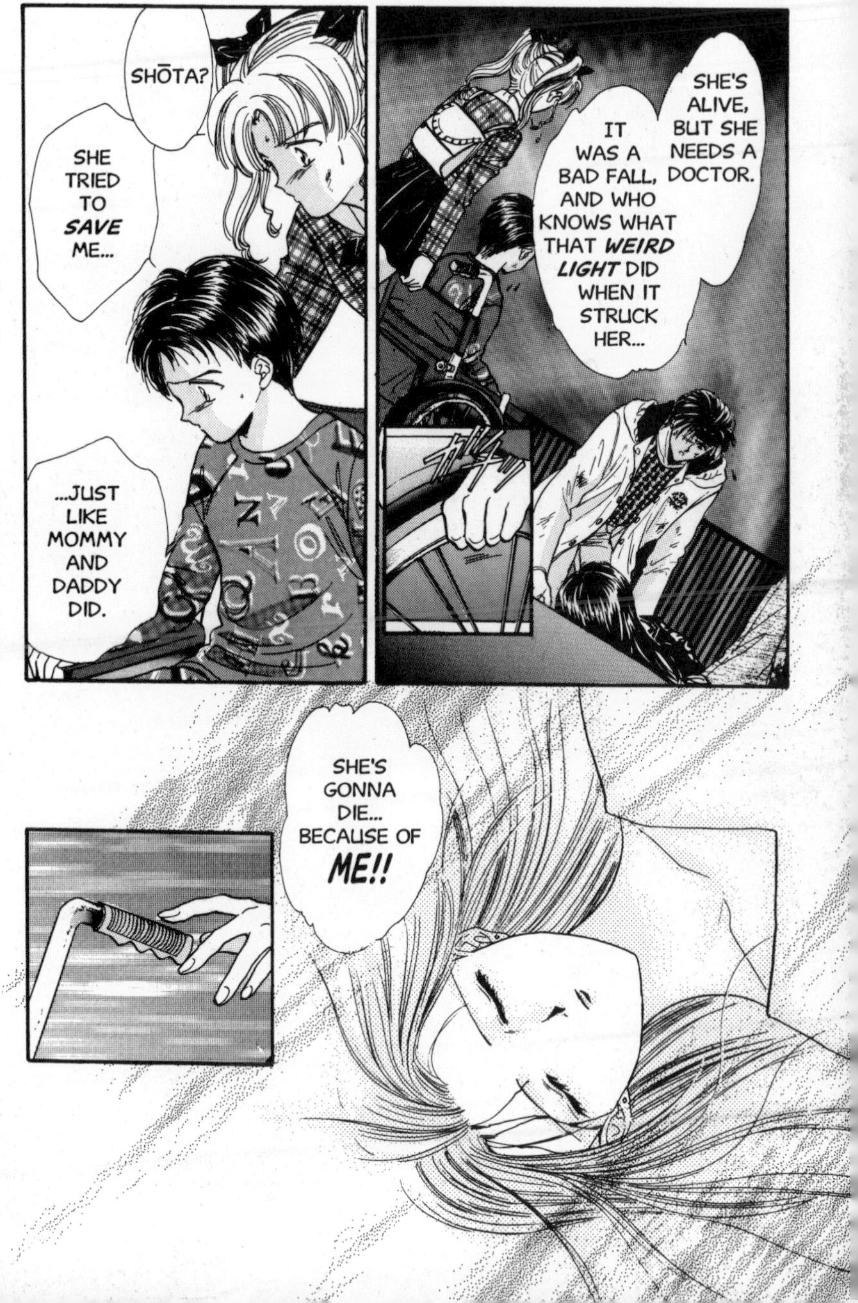
SHE'S ALIVE, BUT SHE NEEDS A DOCTOR.
IT WAS A BAD FALL, AND WHO KNOWS WHAT THAT *WEIRD LIGHT* DID WHEN IT STRUCK HER...
SHŌTA?
SHE TRIED TO *SAVE* ME...
...JUST LIKE MOMMY AND DADDY DID.
SHE'S GONNA DIE... BECAUSE OF **ME!!**

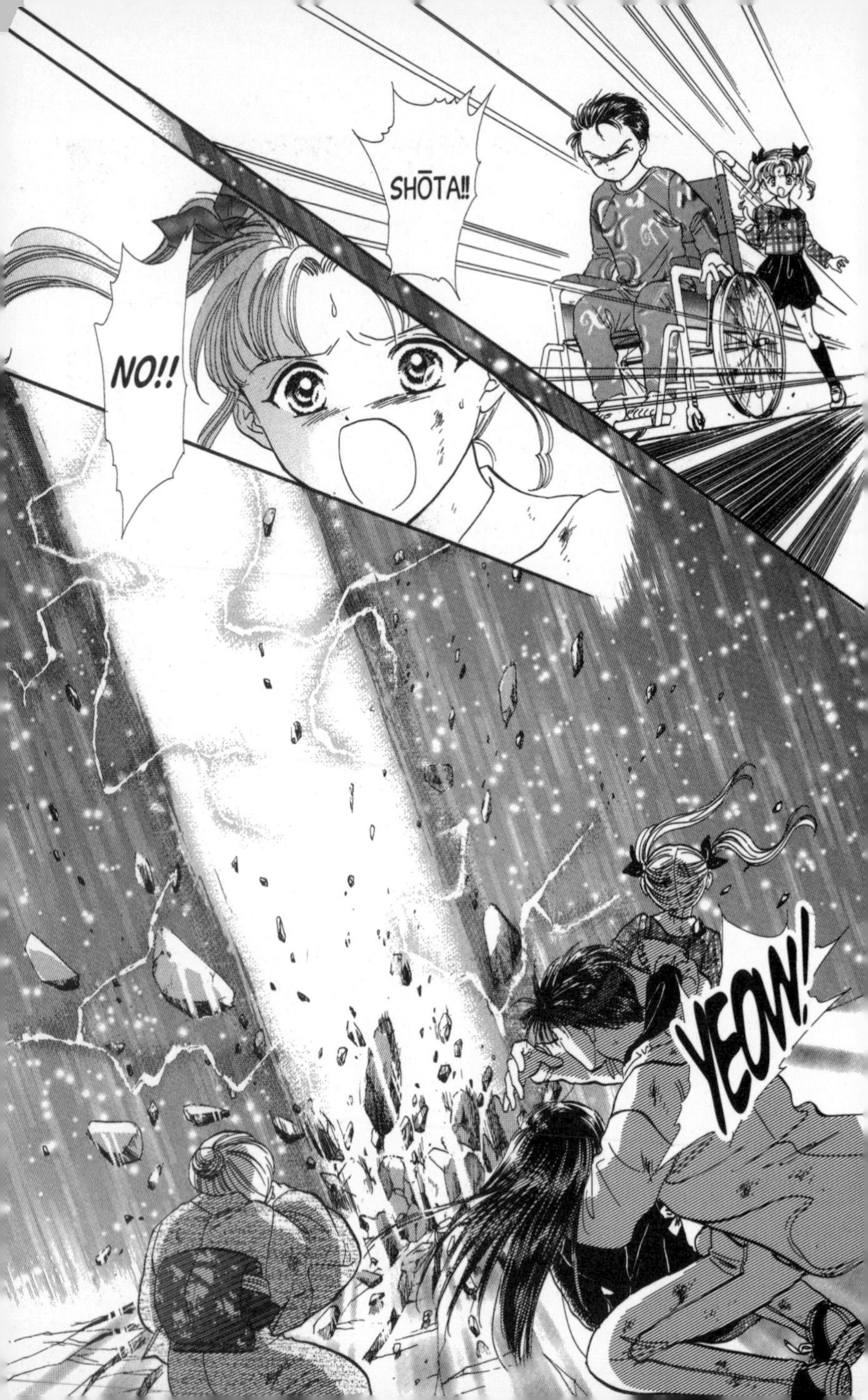
SHŌTA!!
NO!!
YEOW!

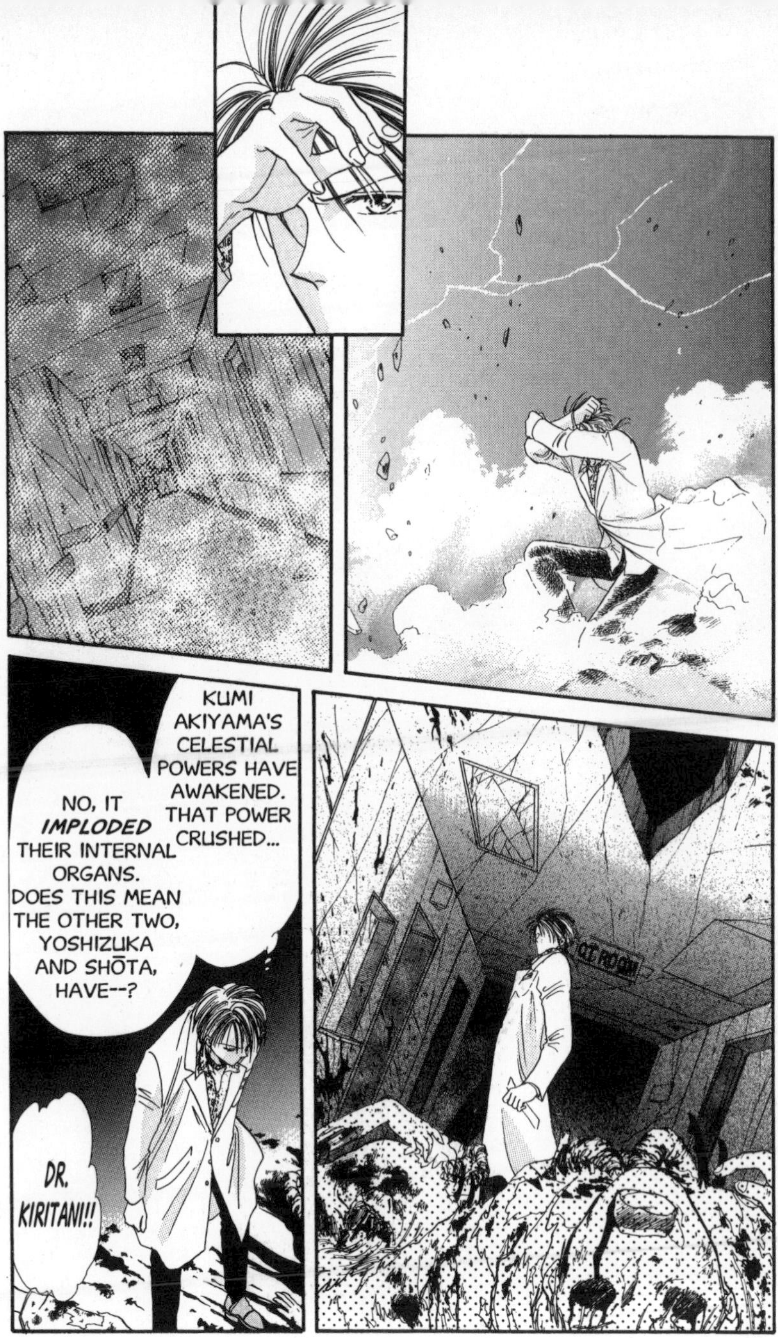
KUMI AKIYAMA'S CELESTIAL POWERS HAVE AWAKENED. THAT POWER CRUSHED...
NO, IT *IMPLODED* THEIR INTERNAL ORGANS. DOES THIS MEAN THE OTHER TWO, YOSHIZUKA AND SHŌTA, HAVE--?
DR. KIRITANI!!

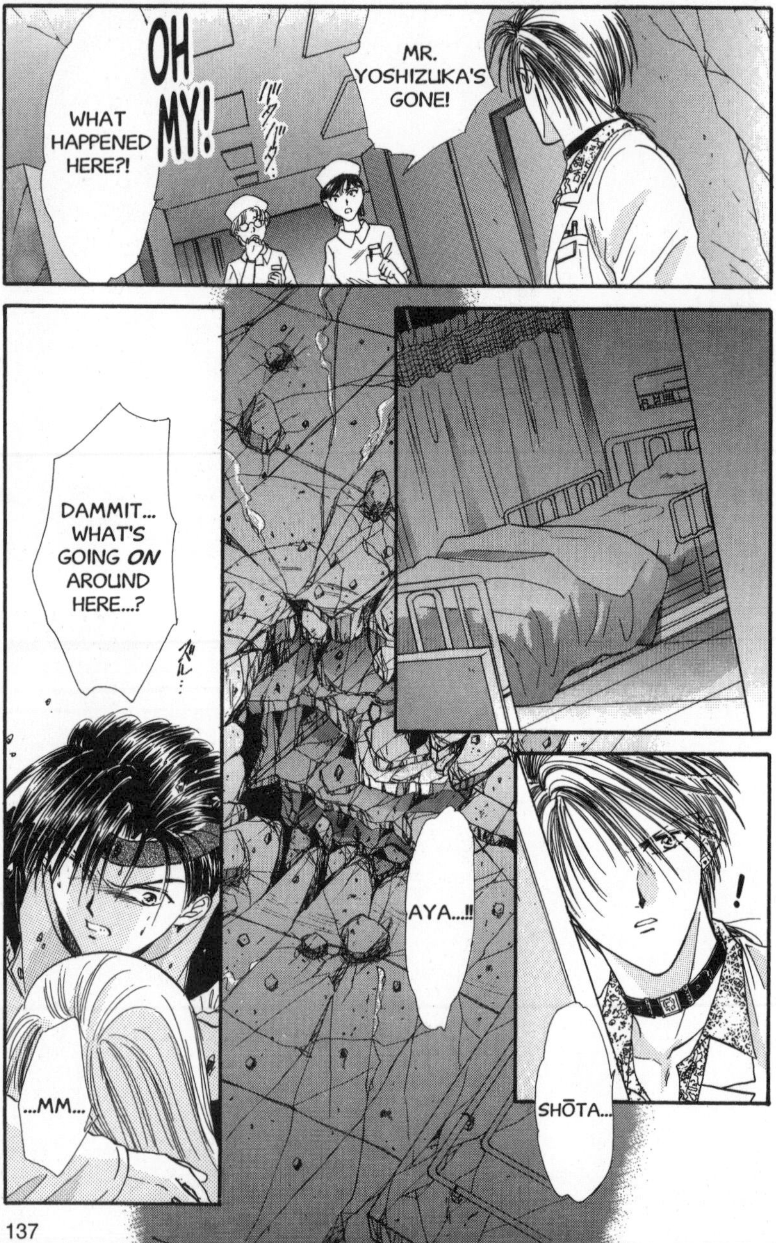
MR. YOSHIZUKA'S GONE!
OH MY!
WHAT HAPPENED HERE?!
DAMMIT... WHAT'S GOING *ON* AROUND HERE...?
!
SHŌTA...
AYA...!!
...MM...

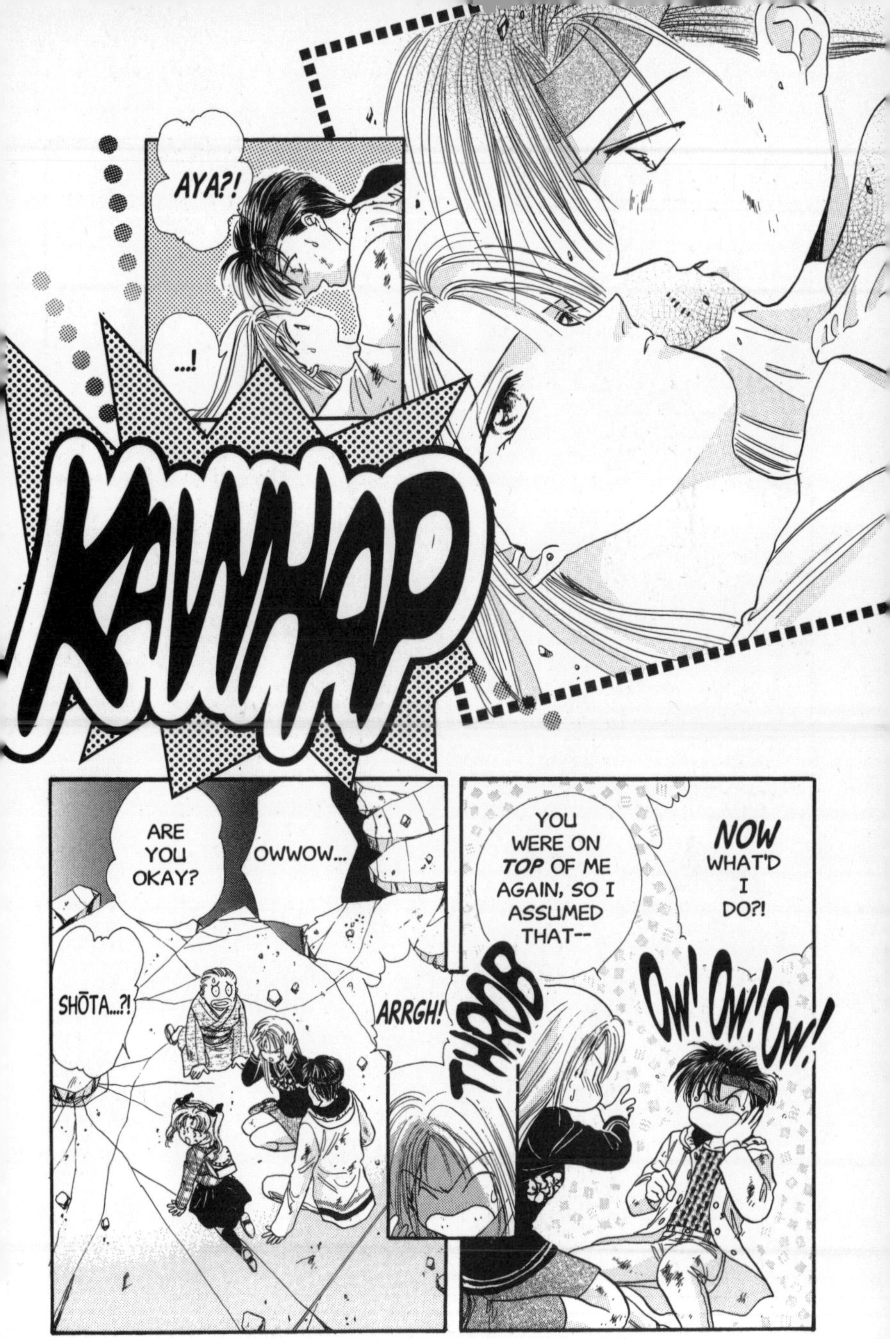
AYA?!
...!
KAWHAP
NOW WHAT'D I DO?!
YOU WERE ON TOP OF ME AGAIN, SO I ASSUMED THAT--
OW! OW! OW!
THROB
OWWOW...
ARE YOU OKAY?
ARRGH!
SHŌTA...?!

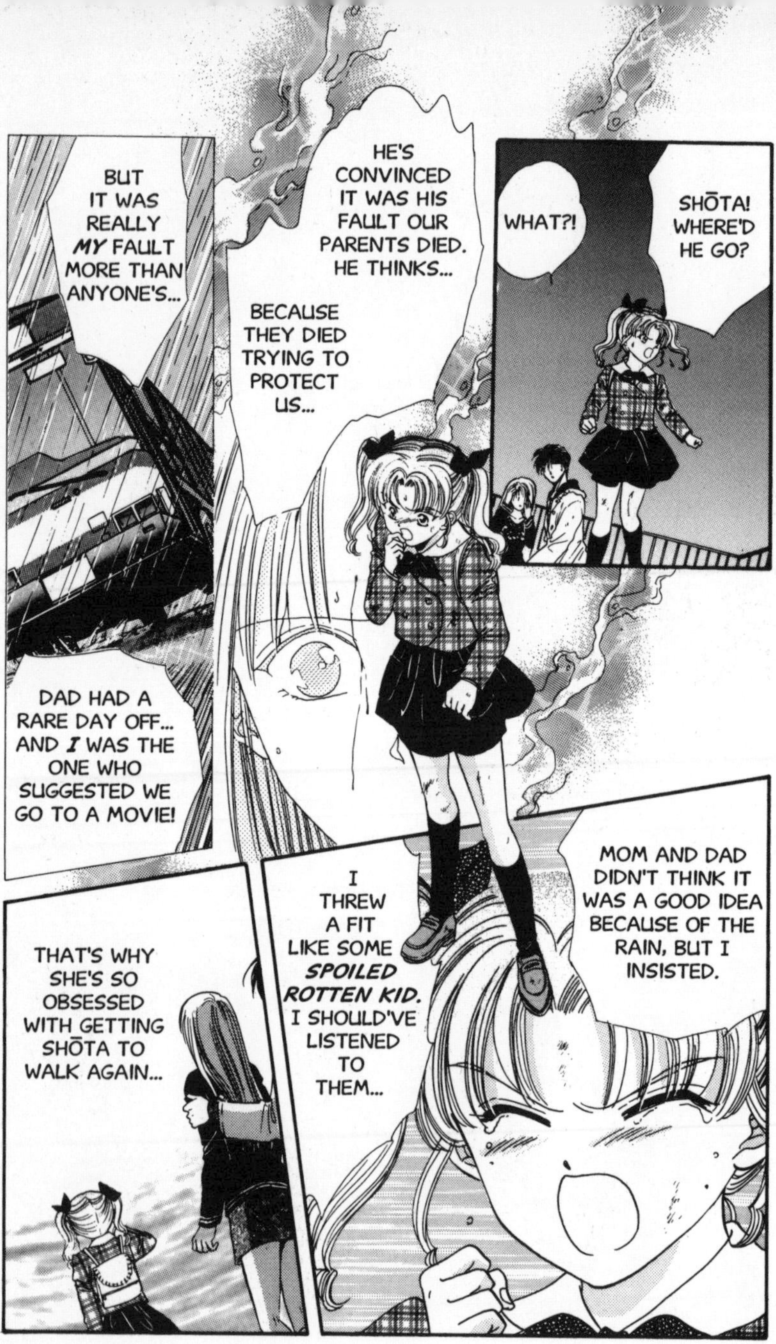
SHŌTA! WHERE'D HE GO?
WHAT?!
HE'S CONVINCED IT WAS HIS FAULT OUR PARENTS DIED. HE THINKS...
BECAUSE THEY DIED TRYING TO PROTECT US...
BUT IT WAS REALLY MY FAULT MORE THAN ANYONE'S...
DAD HAD A RARE DAY OFF... AND I WAS THE ONE WHO SUGGESTED WE GO TO A MOVIE!
MOM AND DAD DIDN'T THINK IT WAS A GOOD IDEA BECAUSE OF THE RAIN, BUT I INSISTED.
I THREW A FIT LIKE SOME SPOILED ROTTEN KID. I SHOULD'VE LISTENED TO THEM...
THAT'S WHY SHE'S SO OBSESSED WITH GETTING SHŌTA TO WALK AGAIN...

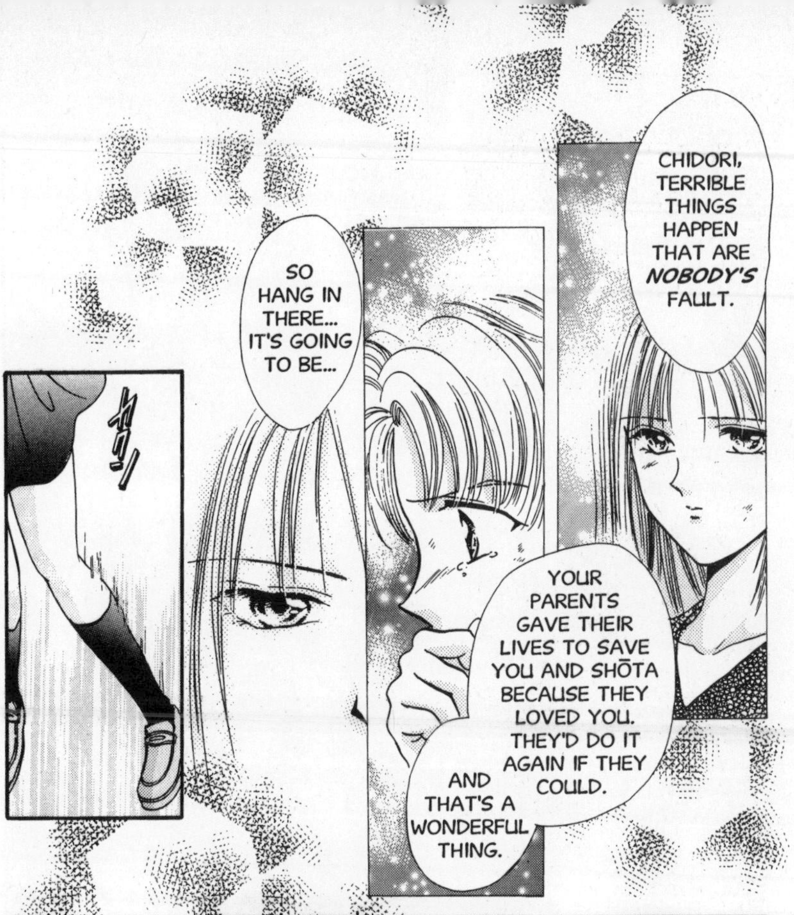
CHIDORI, TERRIBLE THINGS HAPPEN THAT ARE *NOBODY'S* FAULT.
YOUR PARENTS GAVE THEIR LIVES TO SAVE YOU AND SHŌTA BECAUSE THEY LOVED YOU. THEY'D DO IT AGAIN IF THEY COULD.
AND THAT'S A WONDERFUL THING.
SO HANG IN THERE... IT'S GOING TO BE...
CHIDORI?!
I... JUST FEEL A LITTLE NAUSEOUS...
OH MY!
IT'S SHŌTA!!

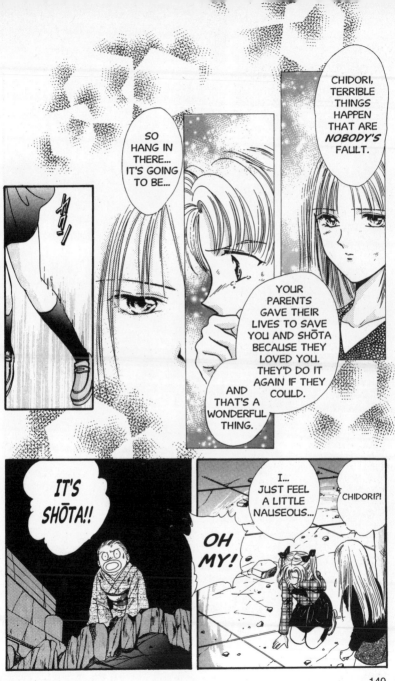

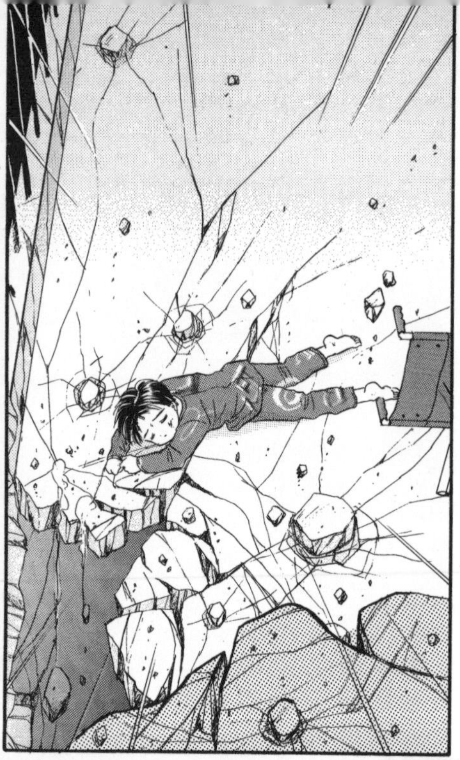

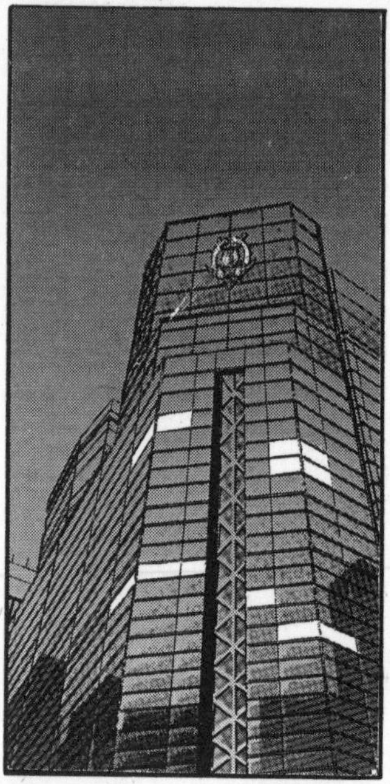

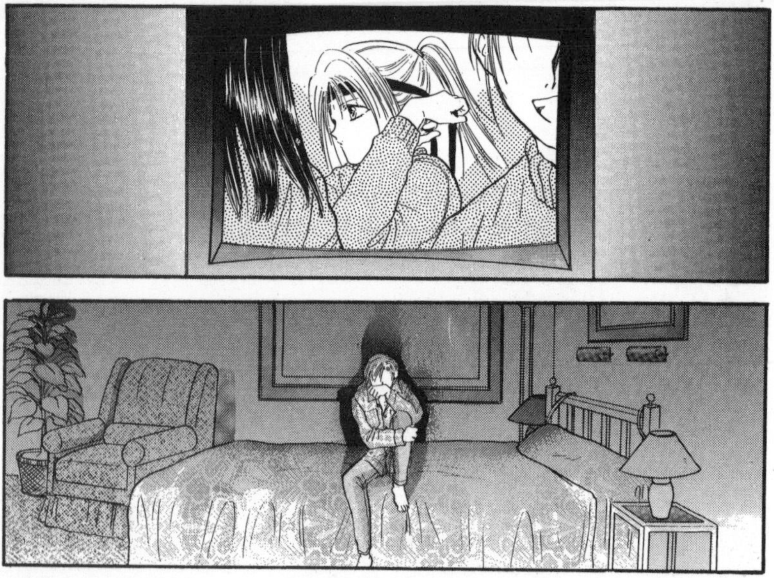

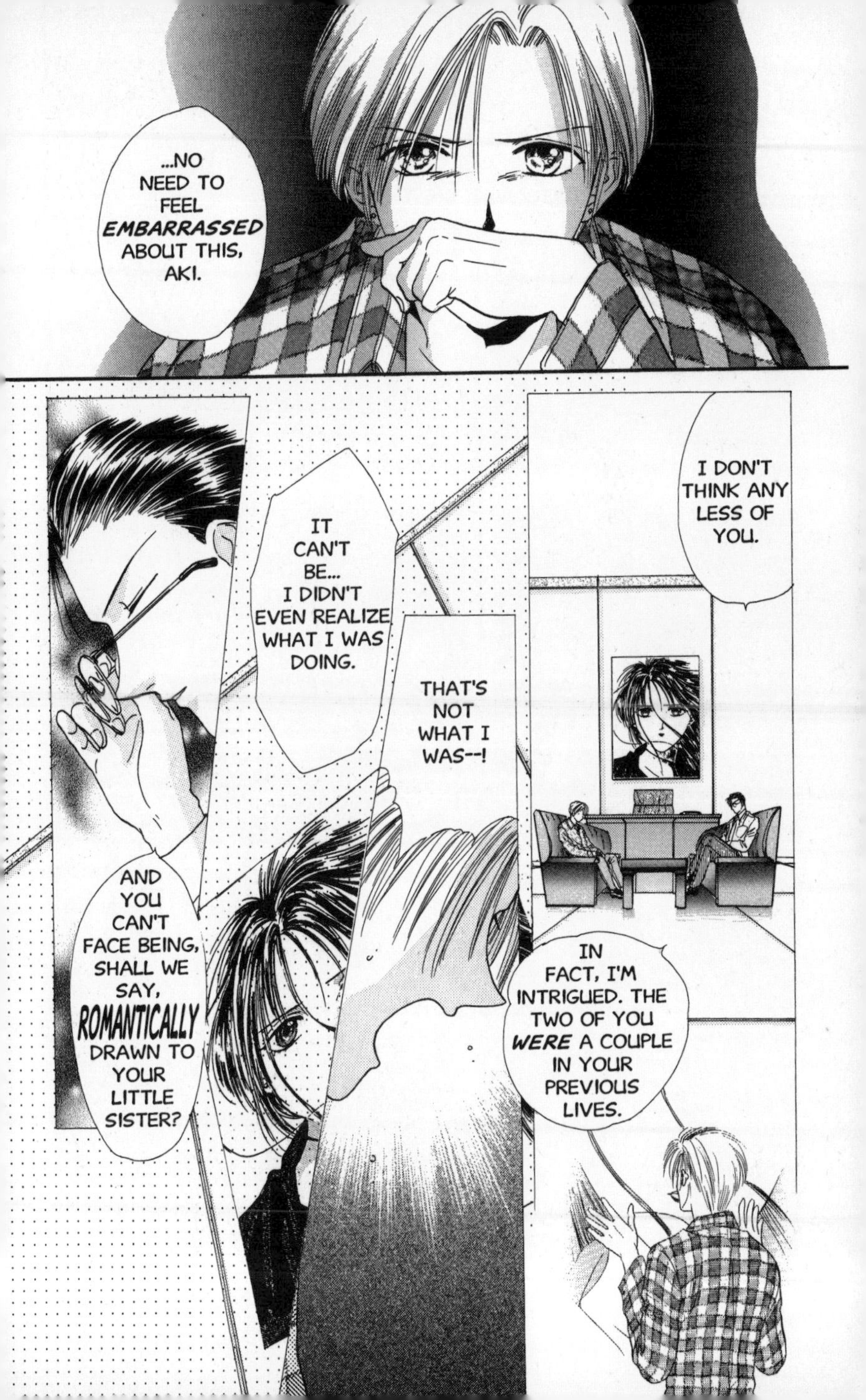
...NO NEED TO FEEL EMBARRASSED ABOUT THIS, AKI.
I DON'T THINK ANY LESS OF YOU.
IN FACT, I'M INTRIGUED. THE TWO OF YOU WERE A COUPLE IN YOUR PREVIOUS LIVES.
IT CAN'T BE... I DIDN'T EVEN REALIZE WHAT I WAS DOING.
THAT'S NOT WHAT I WAS--!
AND YOU CAN'T FACE BEING, SHALL WE SAY, ROMANTICALLY DRAWN TO YOUR LITTLE SISTER?

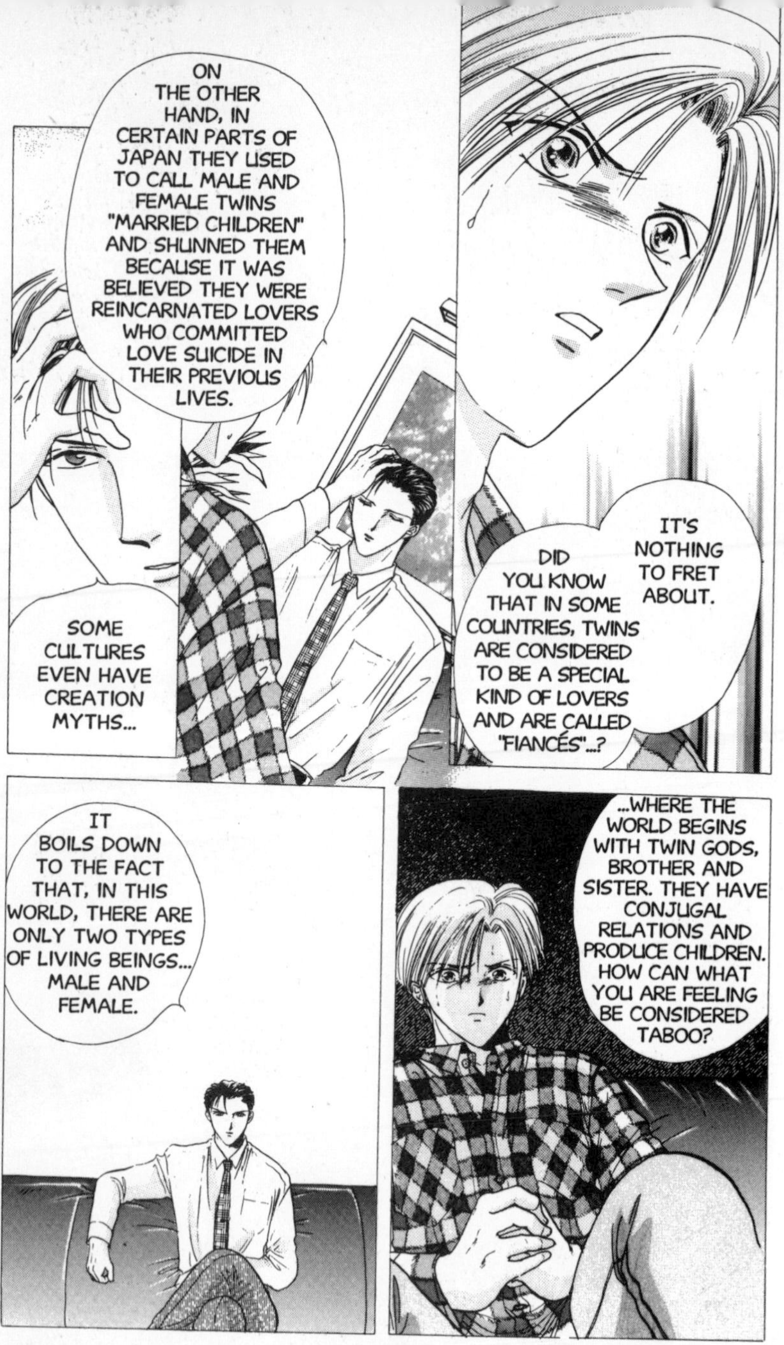
IT'S NOTHING TO FRET ABOUT.
DID YOU KNOW THAT IN SOME COUNTRIES, TWINS ARE CONSIDERED TO BE A SPECIAL KIND OF LOVERS AND ARE CALLED "FIANCÉS"...?
ON THE OTHER HAND, IN CERTAIN PARTS OF JAPAN THEY USED TO CALL MALE AND FEMALE TWINS "MARRIED CHILDREN" AND SHUNNED THEM BECAUSE IT WAS BELIEVED THEY WERE REINCARNATED LOVERS WHO COMMITTED LOVE SUICIDE IN THEIR PREVIOUS LIVES.
SOME CULTURES EVEN HAVE CREATION MYTHS...
...WHERE THE WORLD BEGINS WITH TWIN GODS, BROTHER AND SISTER. THEY HAVE CONJUGAL RELATIONS AND PRODUCE CHILDREN. HOW CAN WHAT YOU ARE FEELING BE CONSIDERED TABOO?
IT BOILS DOWN TO THE FACT THAT, IN THIS WORLD, THERE ARE ONLY TWO TYPES OF LIVING BEINGS... MALE AND FEMALE.

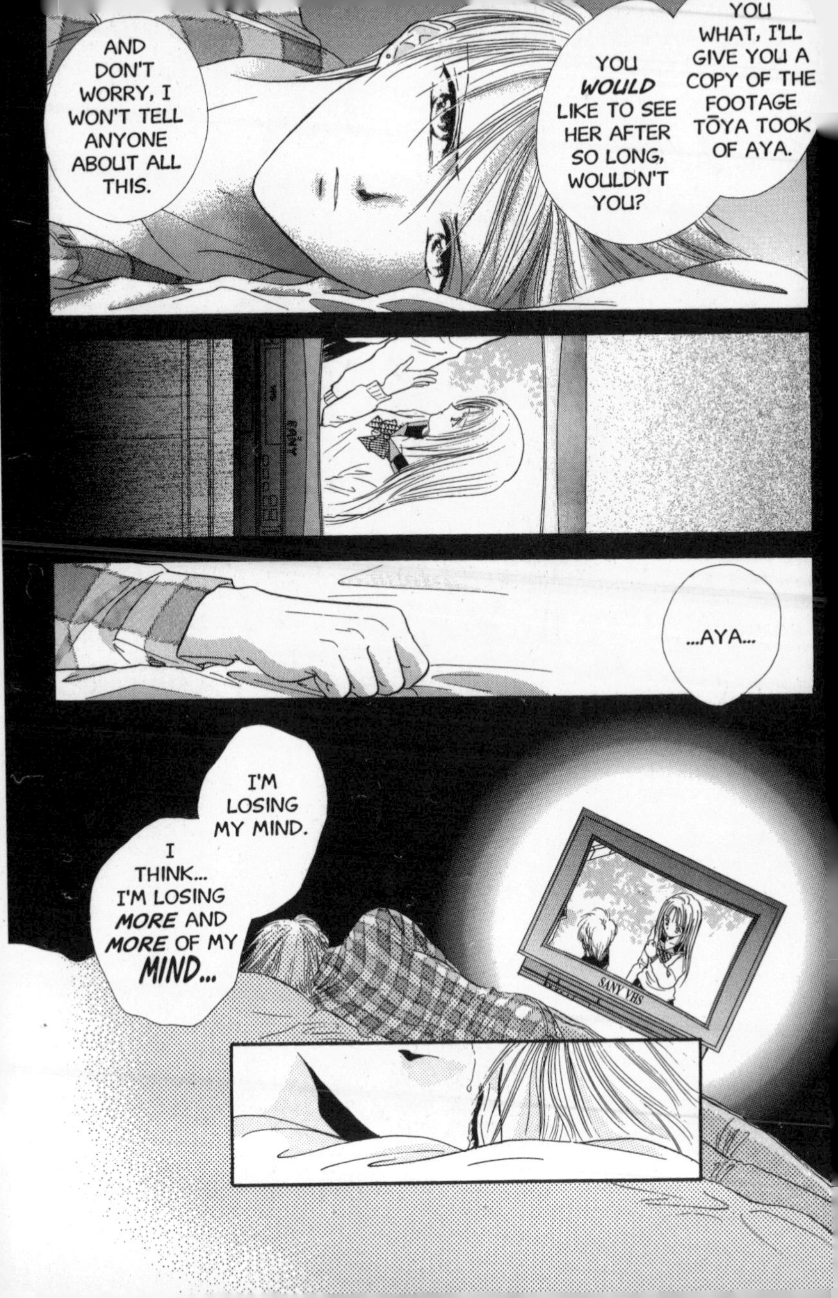
YOU WHAT, I'LL GIVE YOU A COPY OF THE FOOTAGE TŌYA TOOK OF AYA.
YOU *WOULD* LIKE TO SEE HER AFTER SO LONG, WOULDN'T YOU?
AND DON'T WORRY, I WON'T TELL ANYONE ABOUT ALL THIS.
...AYA...
I'M LOSING MY MIND.
I THINK... I'M LOSING *MORE* AND *MORE* OF MY **MIND...**
SANY VHS

◆ Chidori ◆

So... This story arc is set in Tochigi, but Amago Village actually does exist. My editor videotaped footage there for me because I was too busy with work and couldn't go myself. (I cause him a lot of trouble) There was an old lady there who claimed she was descended from a celestial maiden! My editor interviewed her, and she talked about Amago Village and how it may or may not have existed since the Jomon Period (approx. 13,000 - 300 B.C.). Wow, I guess tennyo really did exist. If we were to search all over Japan, I bet we'd find even more people of "celestial lineage." I mean, there's even a legend that Sugawara no Michizane (revered as the god of Academics) is descended from a tennyo. ... W-Wait a minute...does this mean that little old lady is a C-Genome?! Actually, I heard a story about a guy (outside of Japan) whom DNA testing found to be a direct descendant of some stone age man—Cro-Magnon Man or something like that.
These days, you can find out just about anything from DNA. But get this, his wife commented, "Now I know why my husband likes his meat rare." What a sense of humor... "HA HA HA"—Yes, that's how Americans really laugh! How can I say this? Because I just got back from vacation in Florida! It was actually supposed to be a trip to Arizona, but I thought, I might as well have some fun so I went to Disney World & Universal Studios! But the work just piled up while I was away! I'm tired, but I sure had a great time! There were rides that they don't have in Tokyo Disneyland, and they were so great! There's an alien ride called "EX" and it was **so** freaky! Things explode and water sprays on you, and you feel this warm breath on your neck... and then it's **right** behind you!! I was screaming my head off!
I wonder if it'll be coming to Japan anytime soon...

SHŌTA!
!
SHŌTA! DON'T *MOVE,* I'M COMING...
WAIT!
THE *SLIGHTEST JAR* COULD CAUSE THAT FLOOR TO COLLAPSE!

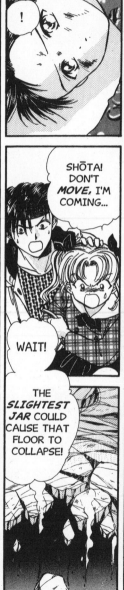

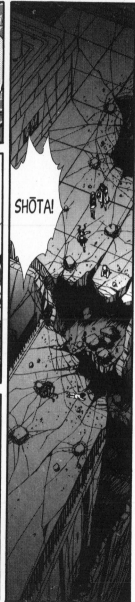

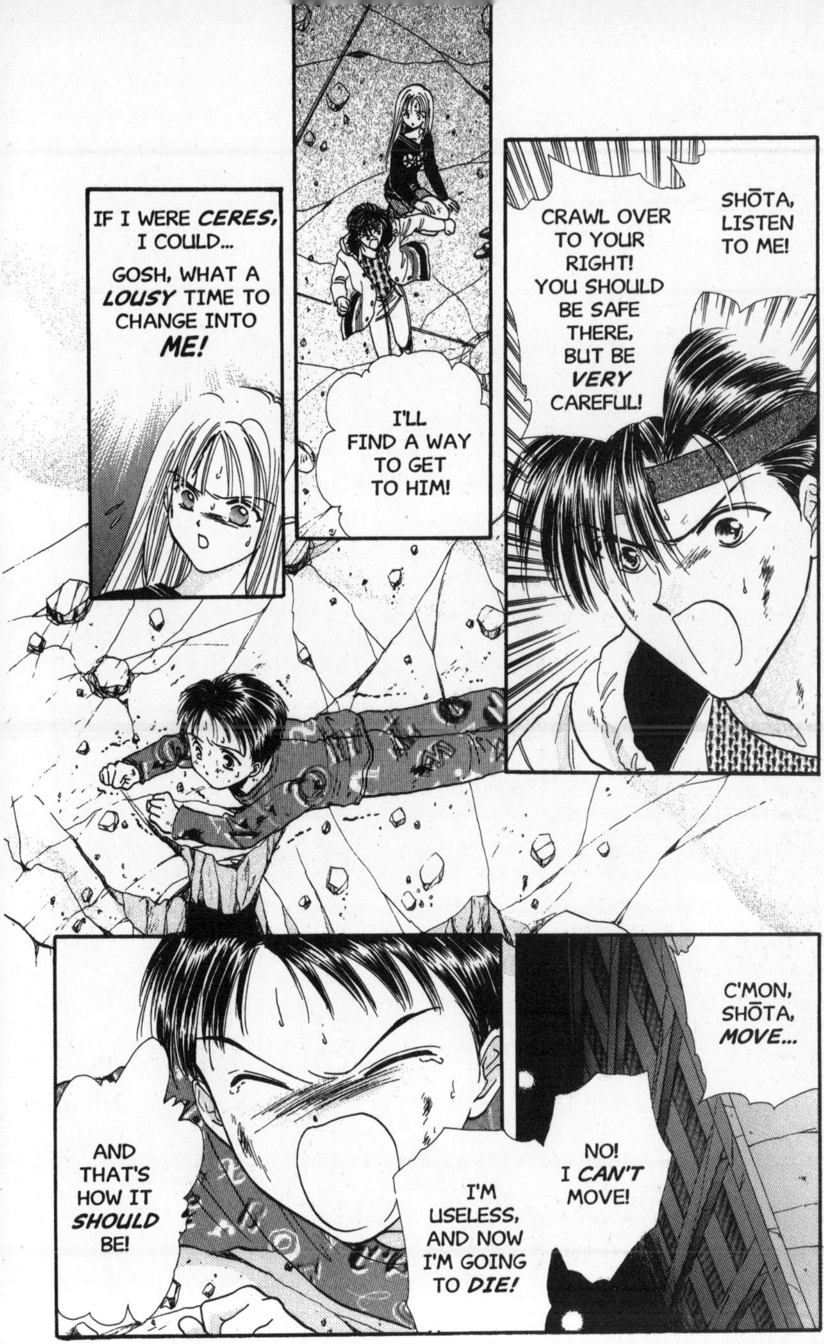

SHŌTA, LISTEN TO ME!
CRAWL OVER TO YOUR RIGHT! YOU SHOULD BE SAFE THERE, BUT BE *VERY* CAREFUL!
I'LL FIND A WAY TO GET TO HIM!
IF I WERE *CERES,* I COULD...
GOSH, WHAT A *LOUSY* TIME TO CHANGE INTO *ME!*
C'MON, SHŌTA, *MOVE...*
NO! I *CAN'T* MOVE!
I'M USELESS, AND NOW I'M GOING TO *DIE!*
AND THAT'S HOW IT *SHOULD* BE!

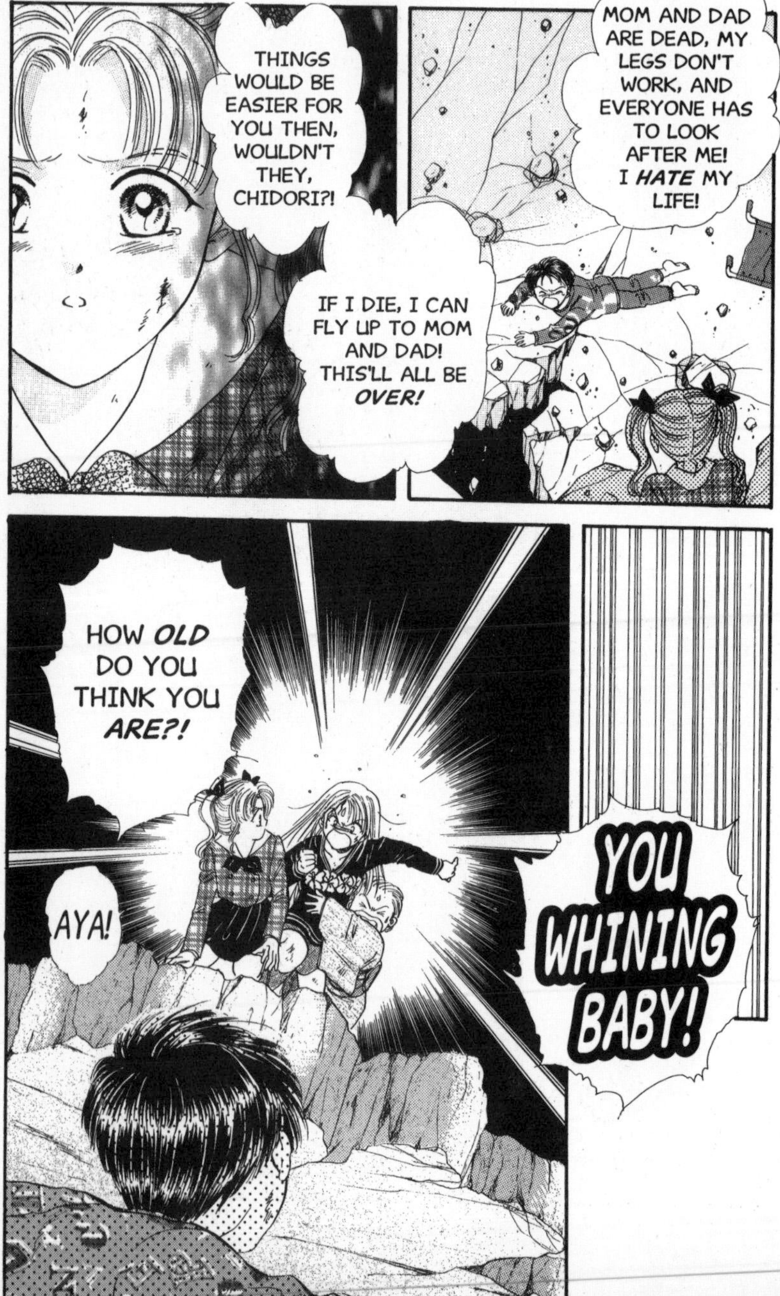
MOM AND DAD ARE DEAD, MY LEGS DON'T WORK, AND EVERYONE HAS TO LOOK AFTER ME! I *HATE* MY LIFE!
IF I DIE, I CAN FLY UP TO MOM AND DAD! THIS'LL ALL BE *OVER!*
THINGS WOULD BE EASIER FOR YOU THEN, WOULDN'T THEY, CHIDORI?!
YOU WHINING BABY!
HOW *OLD* DO YOU THINK YOU *ARE?!*
AYA!

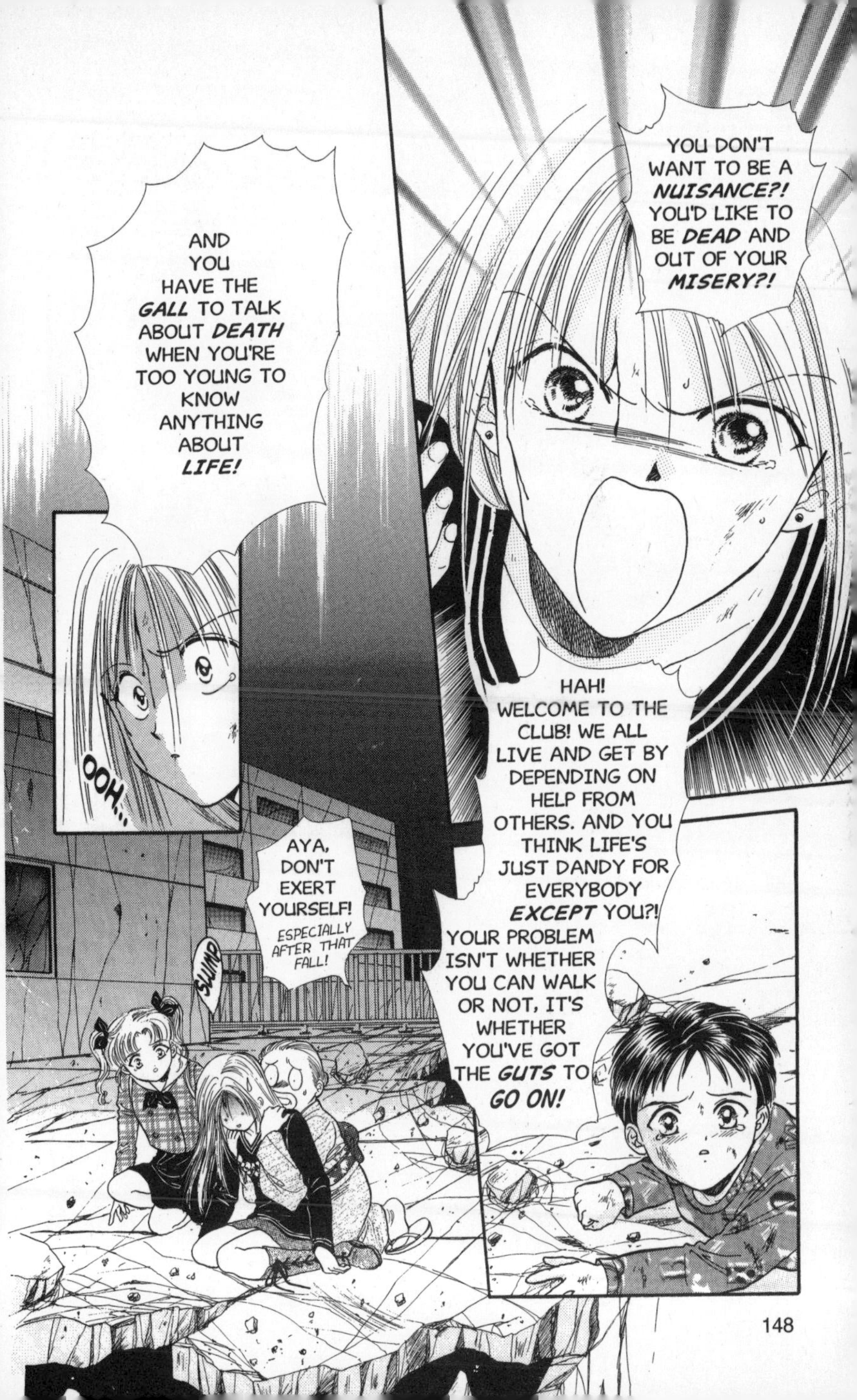
YOU DON'T WANT TO BE A *NUISANCE?!* YOU'D LIKE TO BE *DEAD* AND OUT OF YOUR *MISERY?!*
HAH! WELCOME TO THE CLUB! WE ALL LIVE AND GET BY DEPENDING ON HELP FROM OTHERS. AND YOU THINK LIFE'S JUST DANDY FOR EVERYBODY *EXCEPT* YOU?!
YOUR PROBLEM ISN'T WHETHER YOU CAN WALK OR NOT, IT'S WHETHER YOU'VE GOT THE *GUTS* TO *GO ON!*
AND YOU HAVE THE *GALL* TO TALK ABOUT *DEATH* WHEN YOU'RE TOO YOUNG TO KNOW ANYTHING ABOUT *LIFE!*
OOH...
AYA, DON'T EXERT YOURSELF!
ESPECIALLY AFTER THAT FALL!
SLUMP

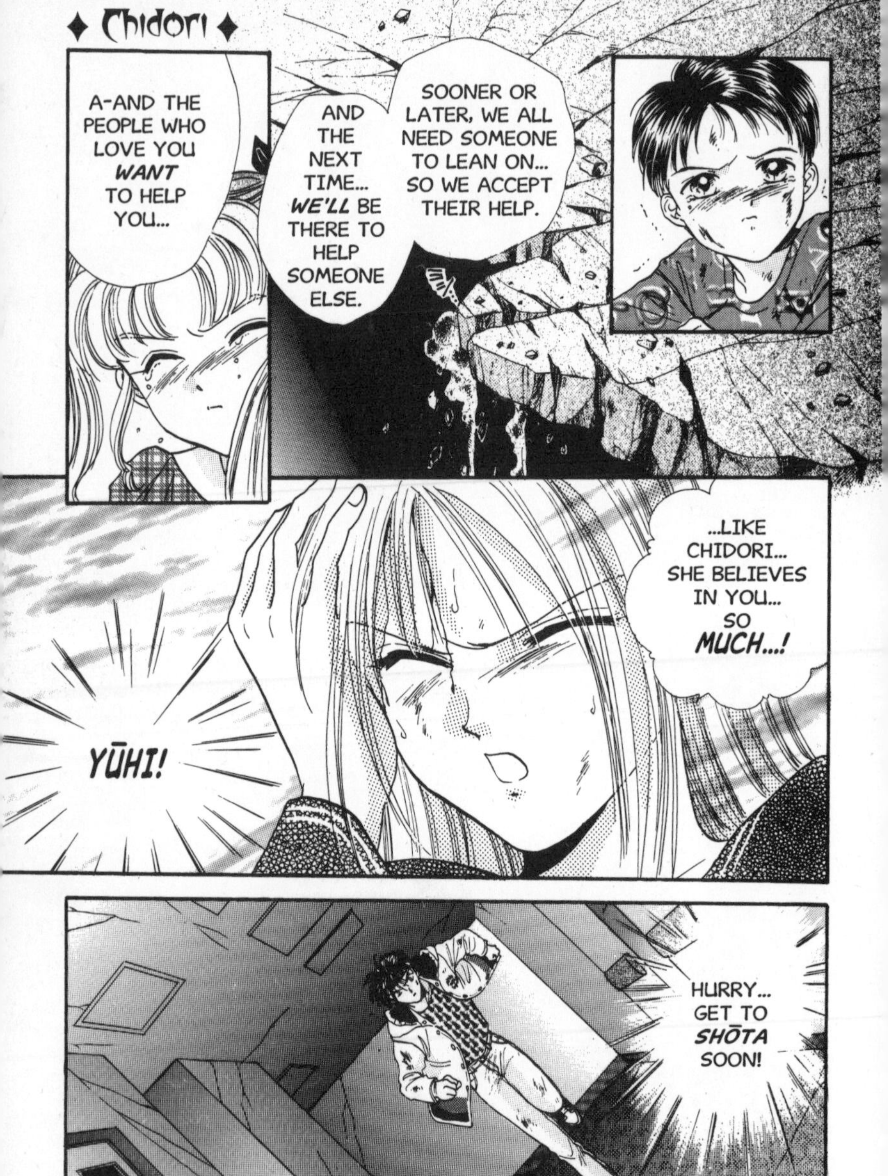
SOONER OR LATER, WE ALL NEED SOMEONE TO LEAN ON... SO WE ACCEPT THEIR HELP.
AND THE NEXT TIME... WE'LL BE THERE TO HELP SOMEONE ELSE.
A-AND THE PEOPLE WHO LOVE YOU WANT TO HELP YOU...
...LIKE CHIDORI... SHE BELIEVES IN YOU... SO MUCH...!
YŪHI!
HURRY... GET TO SHŌTA SOON!

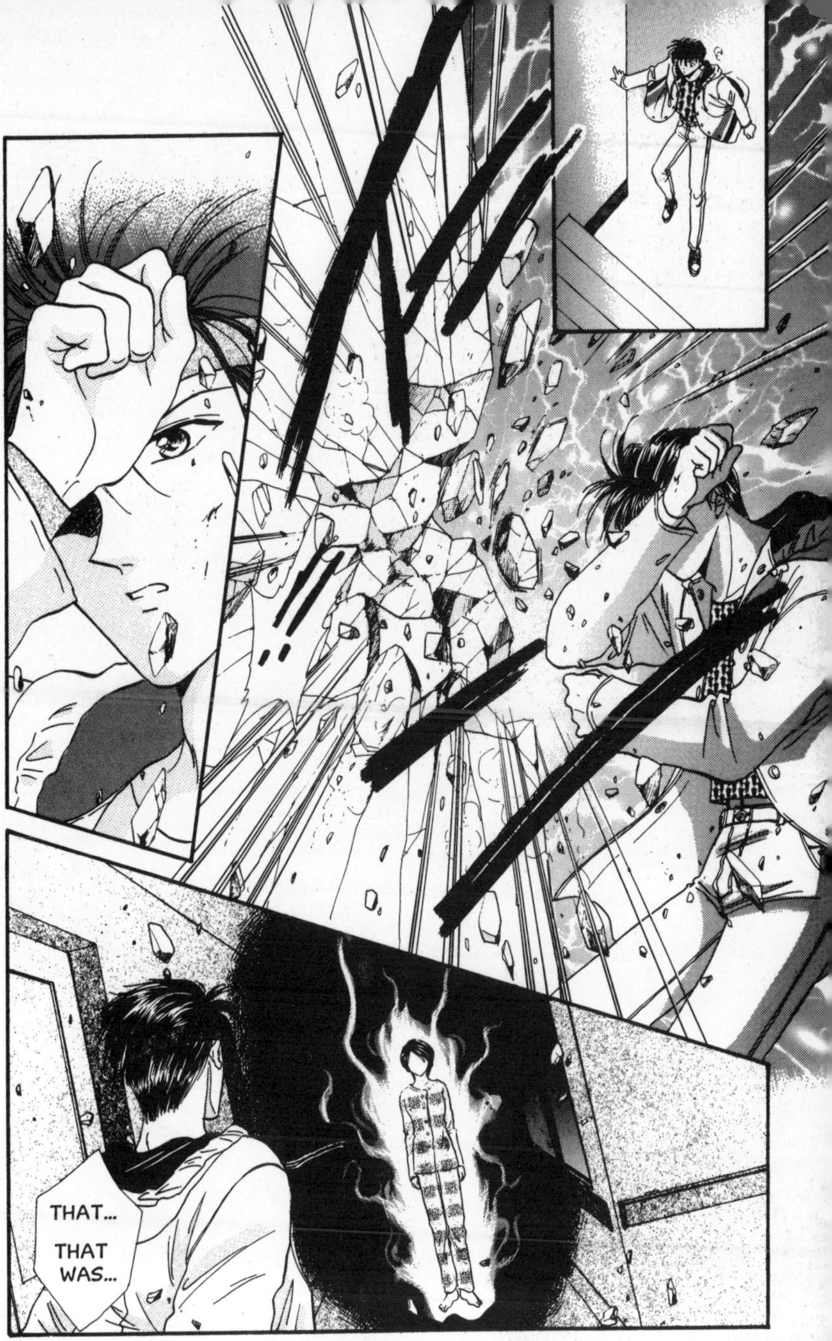
THAT...
THAT WAS...

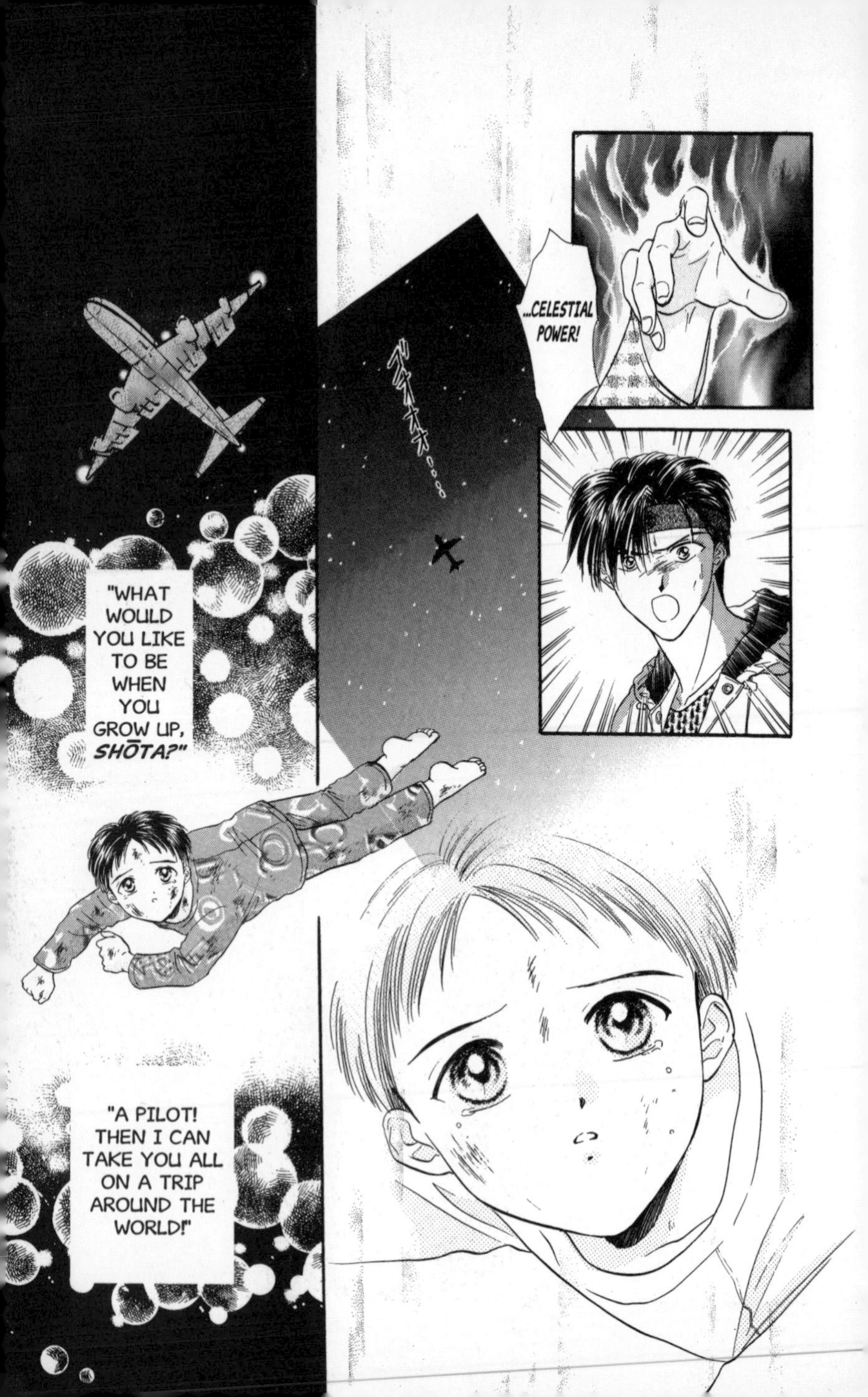
...CELESTIAL POWER!
"WHAT WOULD YOU LIKE TO BE WHEN YOU GROW UP, SHŌTA?"
"A PILOT! THEN I CAN TAKE YOU ALL ON A TRIP AROUND THE WORLD!"

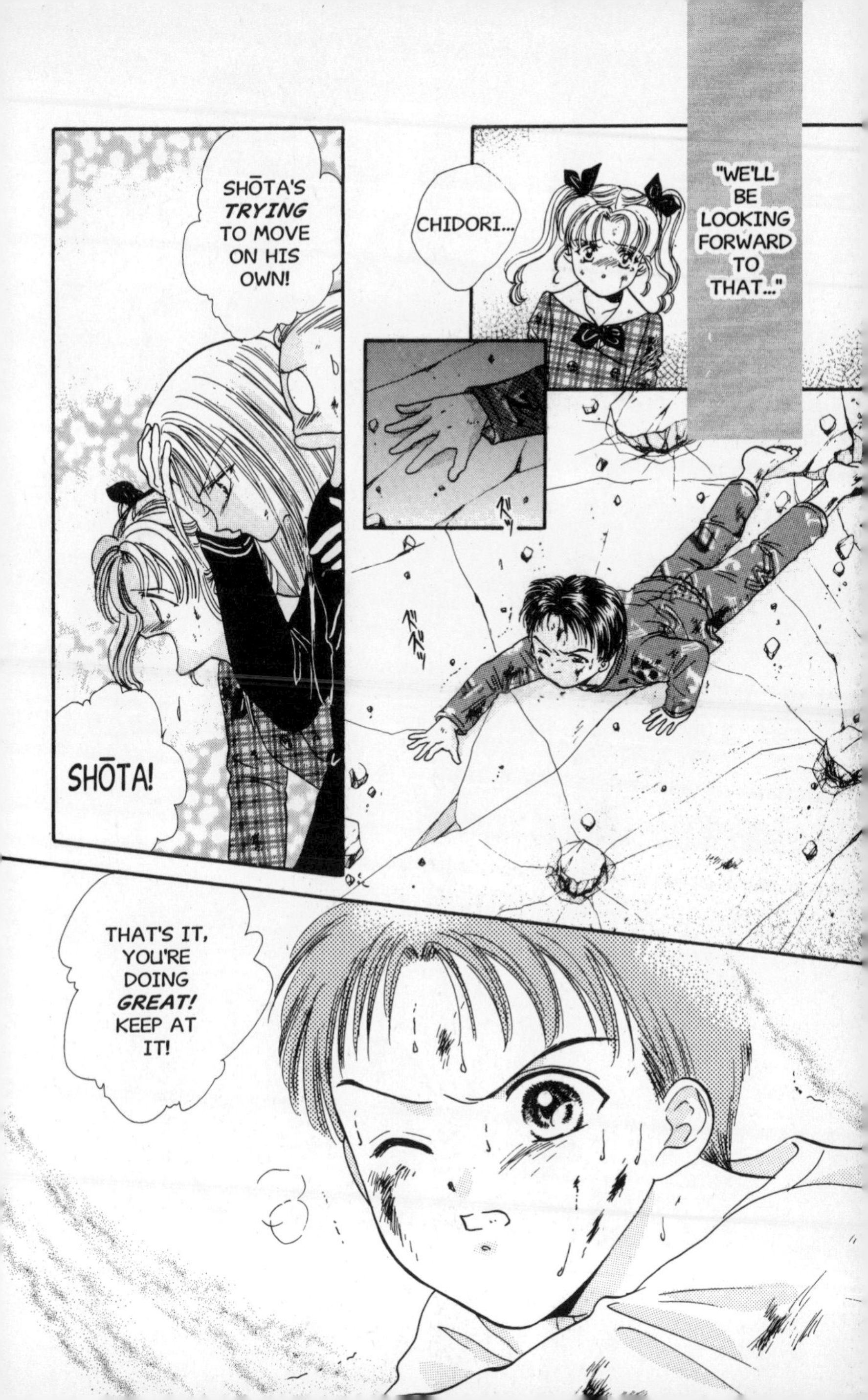
"WE'LL BE LOOKING FORWARD TO THAT..."
CHIDORI...
SHŌTA'S *TRYING* TO MOVE ON HIS OWN!
SHŌTA!
THAT'S IT, YOU'RE DOING *GREAT!* KEEP AT IT!

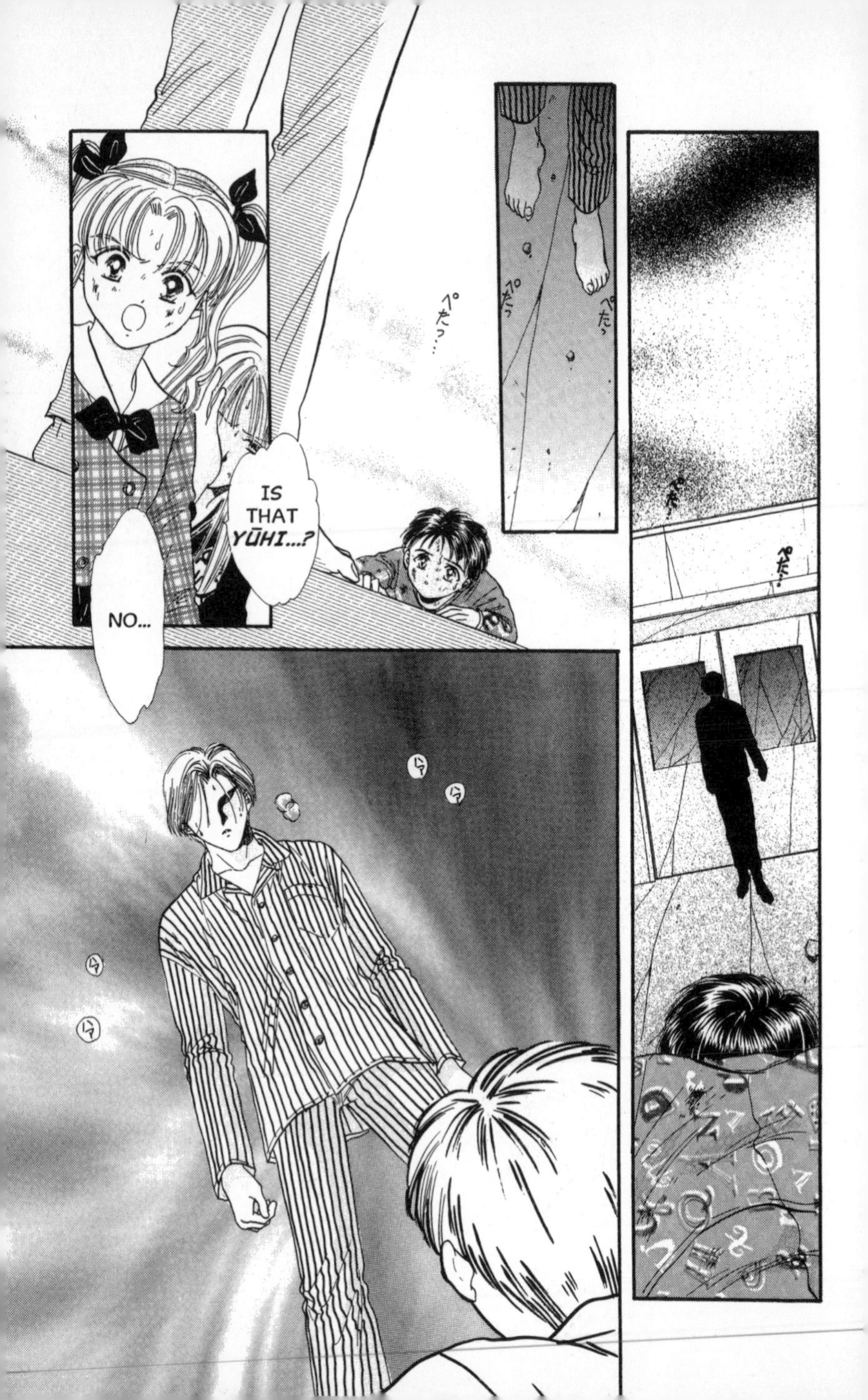
ぺたっ…
IS THAT YŪHI...?
NO...

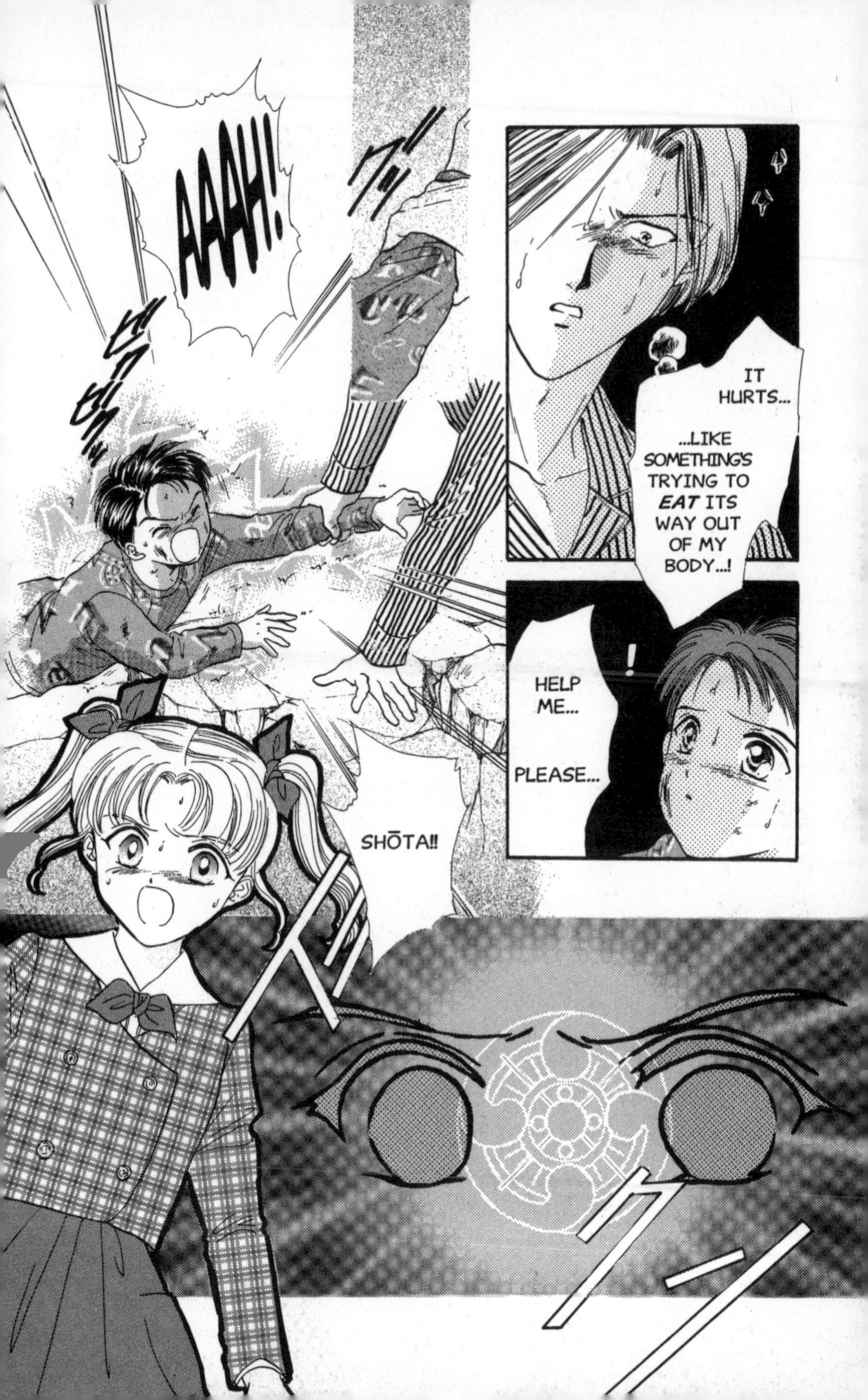
IT HURTS...
...LIKE SOMETHING'S TRYING TO ***EAT*** ITS WAY OUT OF MY BODY...!
!
HELP ME...
PLEASE...
AAAH!
SHŌTA!!

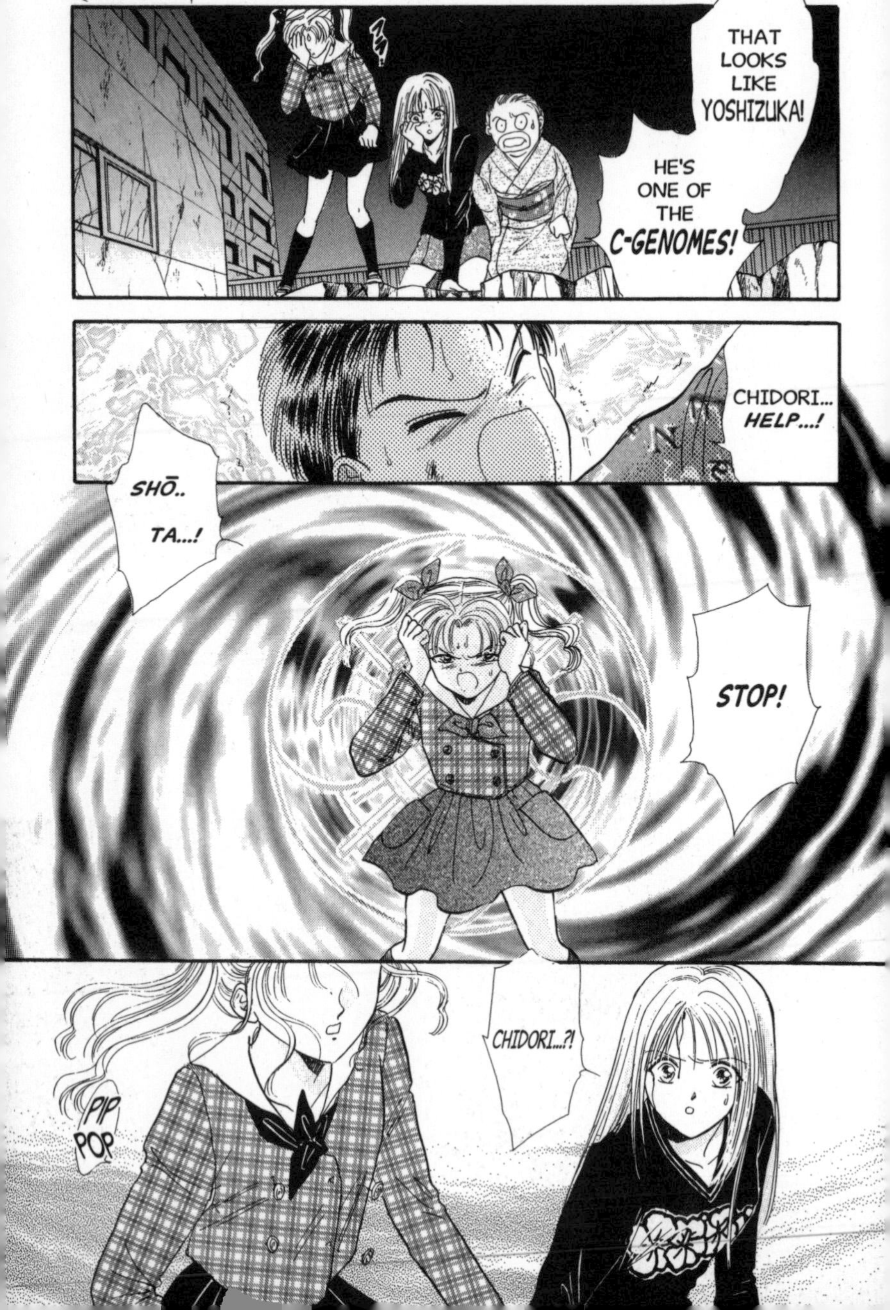
THAT LOOKS LIKE YOSHIZUKA!
HE'S ONE OF THE C-GENOMES!
CHIDORI... HELP...!
SHŌ.. TA...!
STOP!
CHIDORI...?!
PIP POP

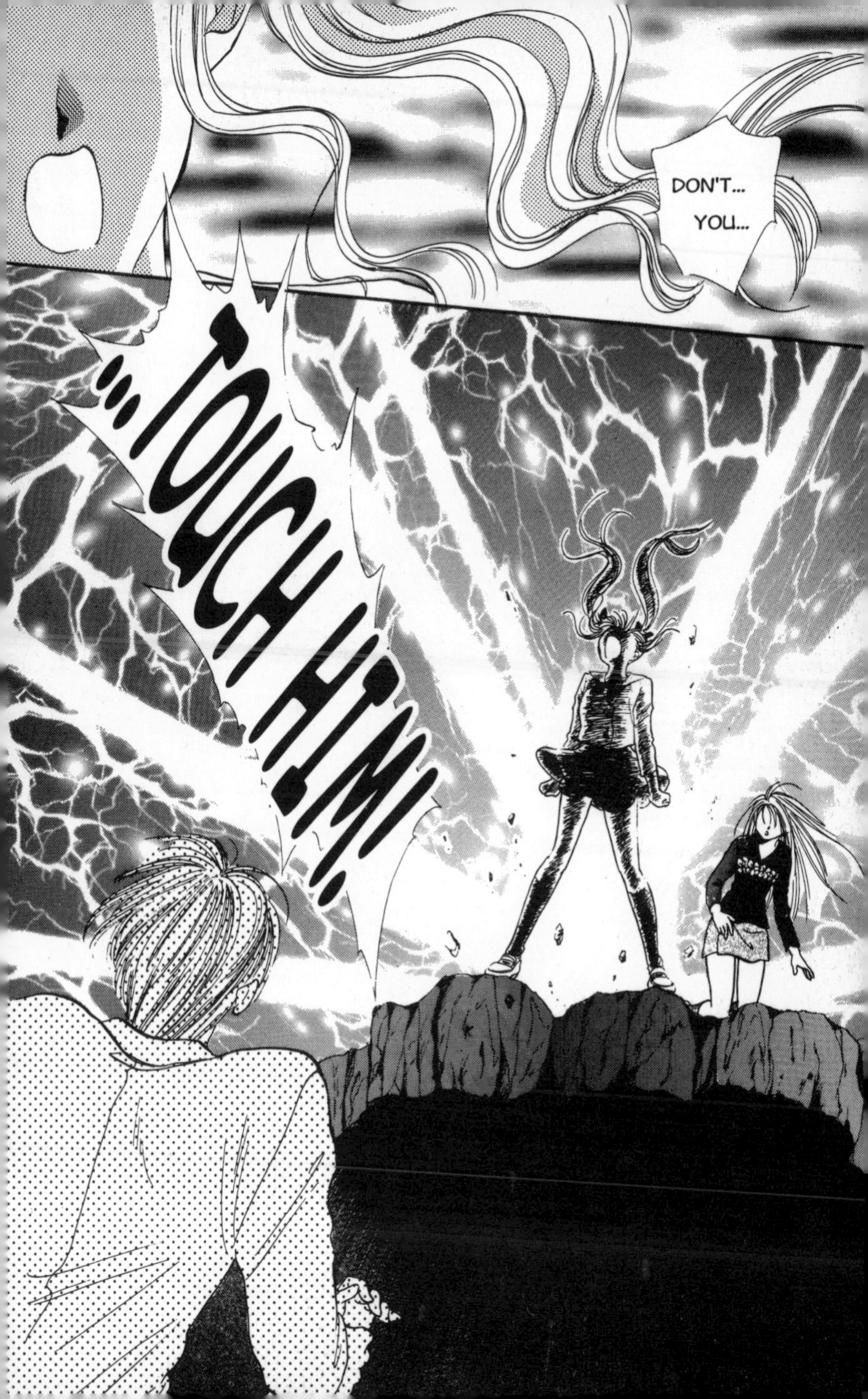
DON'T...
YOU...
...TOUCH HIM!!

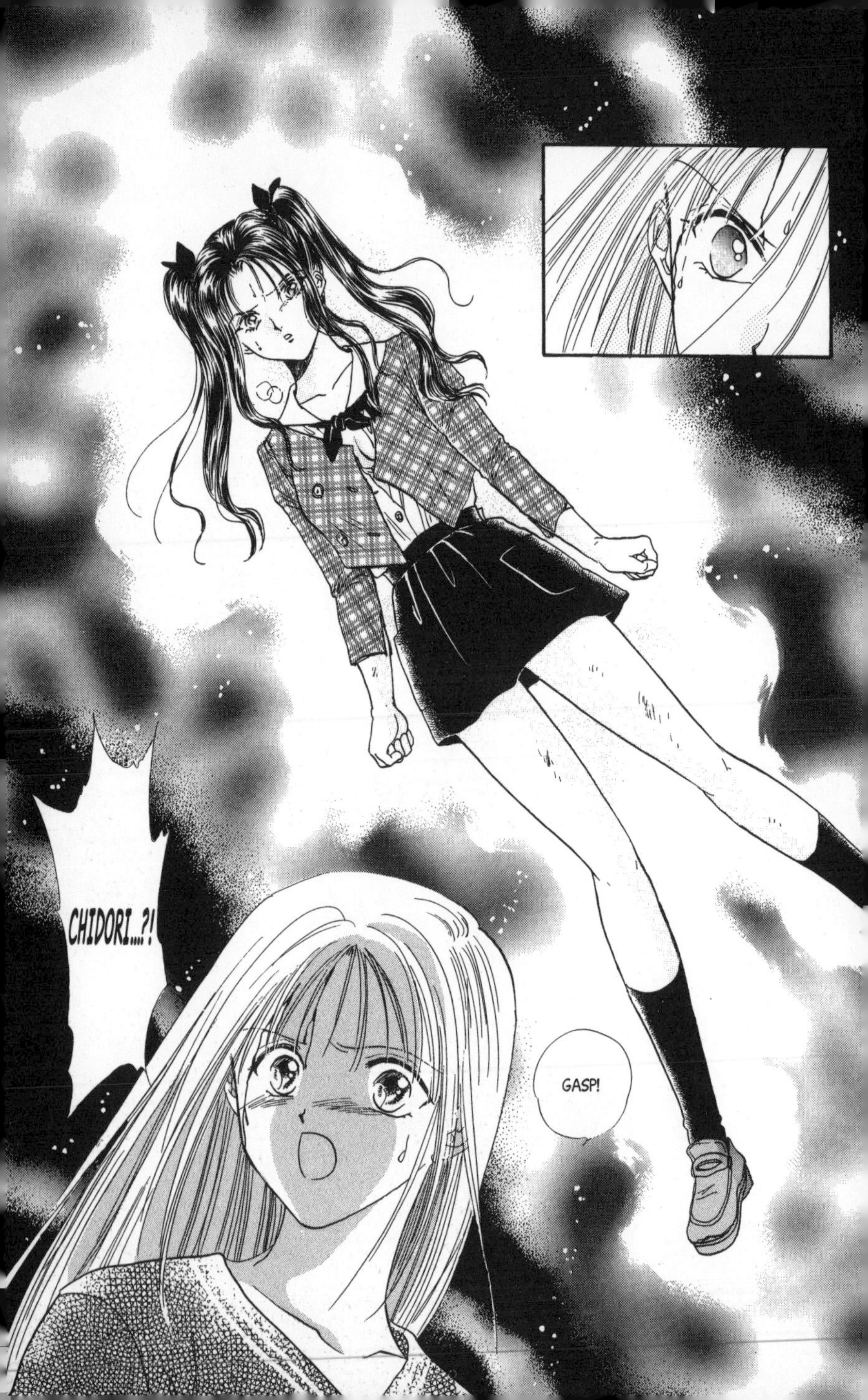
GASP!
CHIDORI...?!

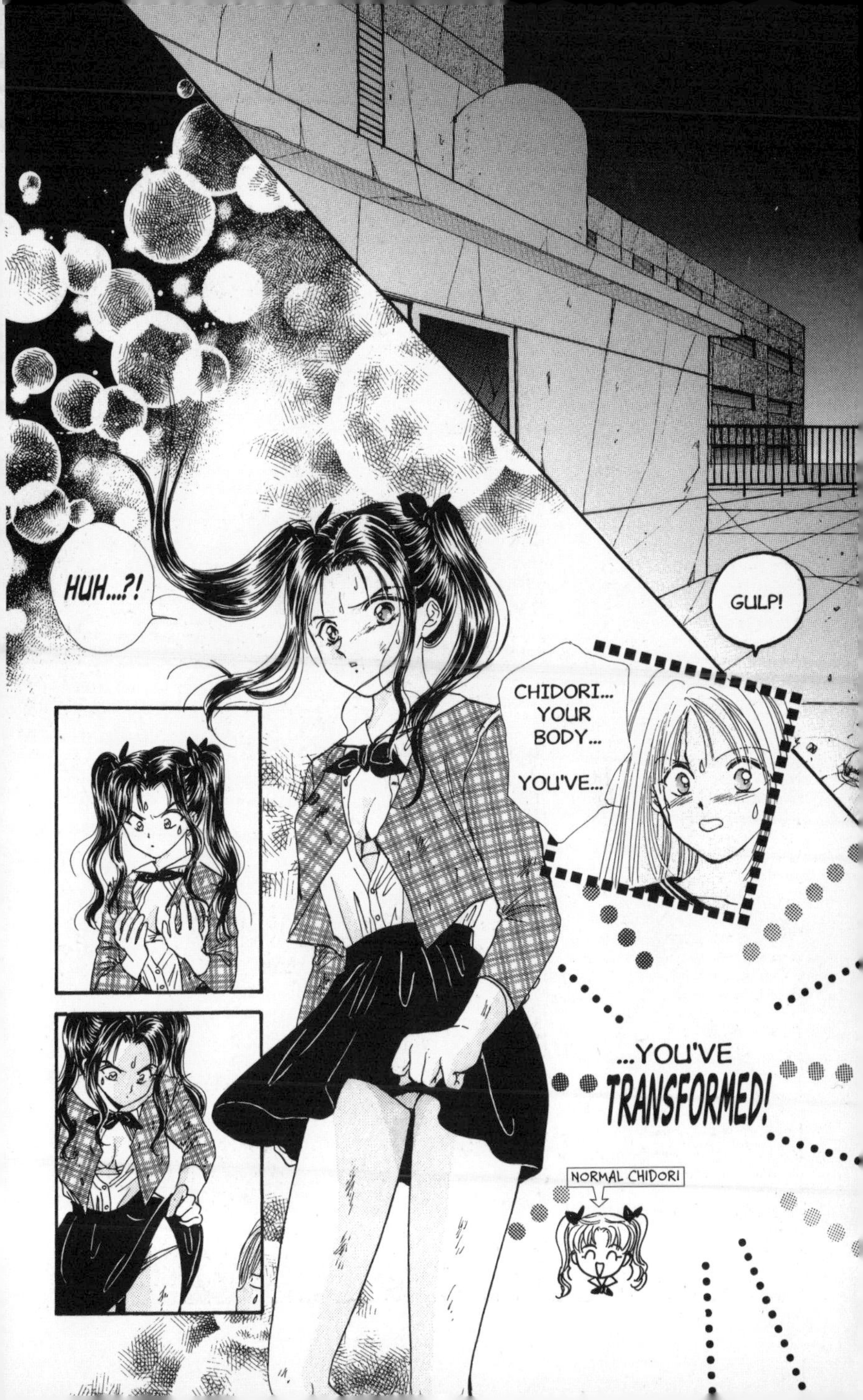
HUH...?!
GULP!
CHIDORI... YOUR BODY... YOU'VE...
...YOU'VE TRANSFORMED!
NORMAL CHIDORI

♦ Chidori ♦

In Disney World, I went to Magic Kingdom, MGM, and Epcot, and they were all great in different ways. But at Universal Studios, the big attraction was "Terminator 2 - 3D"!!!!
It was incredible! We thought all the other rides were great, but they just paled in comparison. :)
If you ever go, it's definitely a must-see!
You'll get goose bumps (I did!). When it was all over, everyone cheered and clapped! It was awesome. They built a Universal Studios in Osaka, and I wanted T2 to come to Japan, but the feature ride here is "Back to the Future"...
For certain reasons, I couldn't go on this ride, but my friend who **did** ride it said that after T2, it was "kinda lame." Well, I'll talk more about that next time...
Hmm, I talked about some serious stuff in the beginning of this volume, but it did relate to the manga. I had Chidori's character created even before serialization of **Ceres** started, and I have a lot of other characters lined up too.
I've visualized the story up to the end, but it continues to change a little bit all the time, so I don't really know what'll happen. And regarding Chidori, my assistant says Chidori is "yummy"...(?)
There are a lot of girl characters, unlike my previous title. But actually, the Mikages' side is mostly men. The structure of the story is men vs. women. There'll be a lot of significant developments in the next volume.
Maybe you'll even be shocked and surprised. (Although it's already been printed in serialized format.) We'll be getting into the crux of the story, so please don't miss it.
...But Tōya will still remain as mysterious as ever.
See you next time!

"Princess Mononoke" soundtrack plaing in the background... 8/19/97

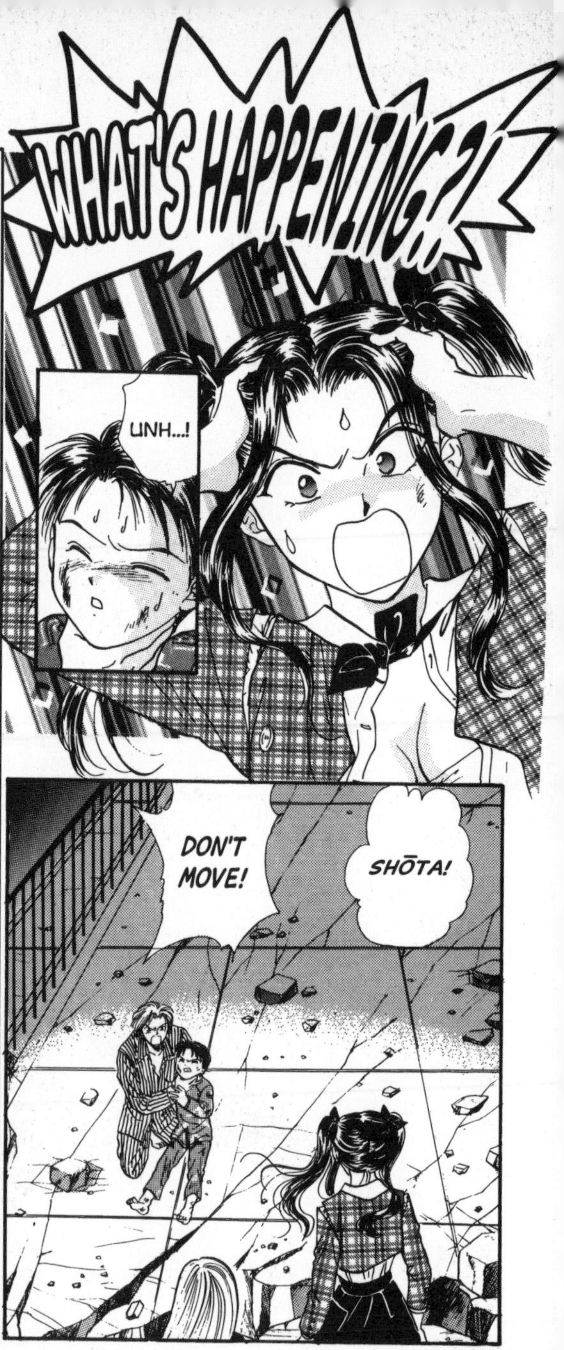
WHAT'S HAPPENING?!
UNH...!
SHŌTA!
DON'T MOVE!

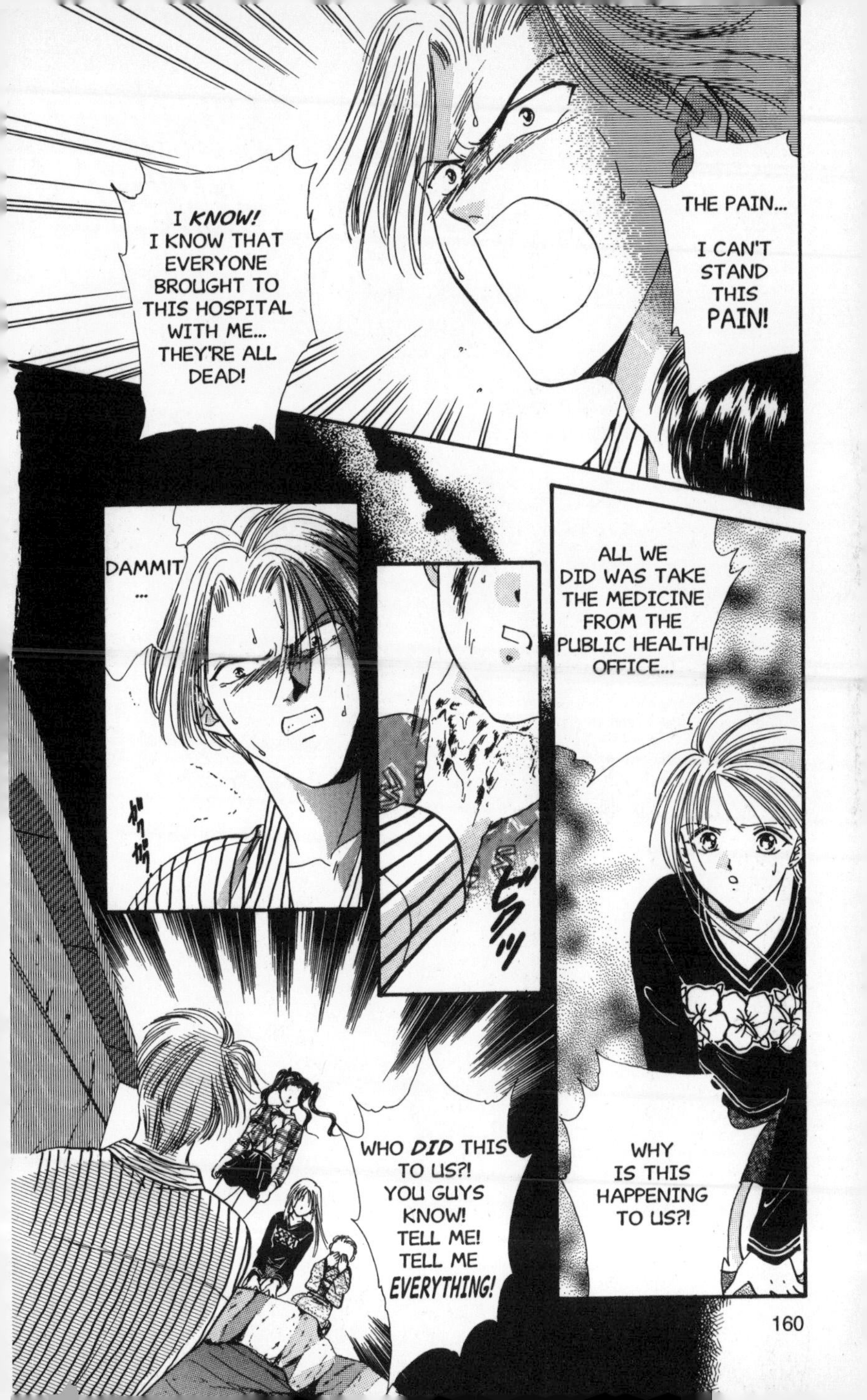
THE PAIN...
I CAN'T STAND THIS PAIN!
I *KNOW!* I KNOW THAT EVERYONE BROUGHT TO THIS HOSPITAL WITH ME... THEY'RE ALL DEAD!
ALL WE DID WAS TAKE THE MEDICINE FROM THE PUBLIC HEALTH OFFICE...
WHY IS THIS HAPPENING TO US?!
DAMMIT...
WHO *DID* THIS TO US?! YOU GUYS KNOW! TELL ME! TELL ME *EVERYTHING!*

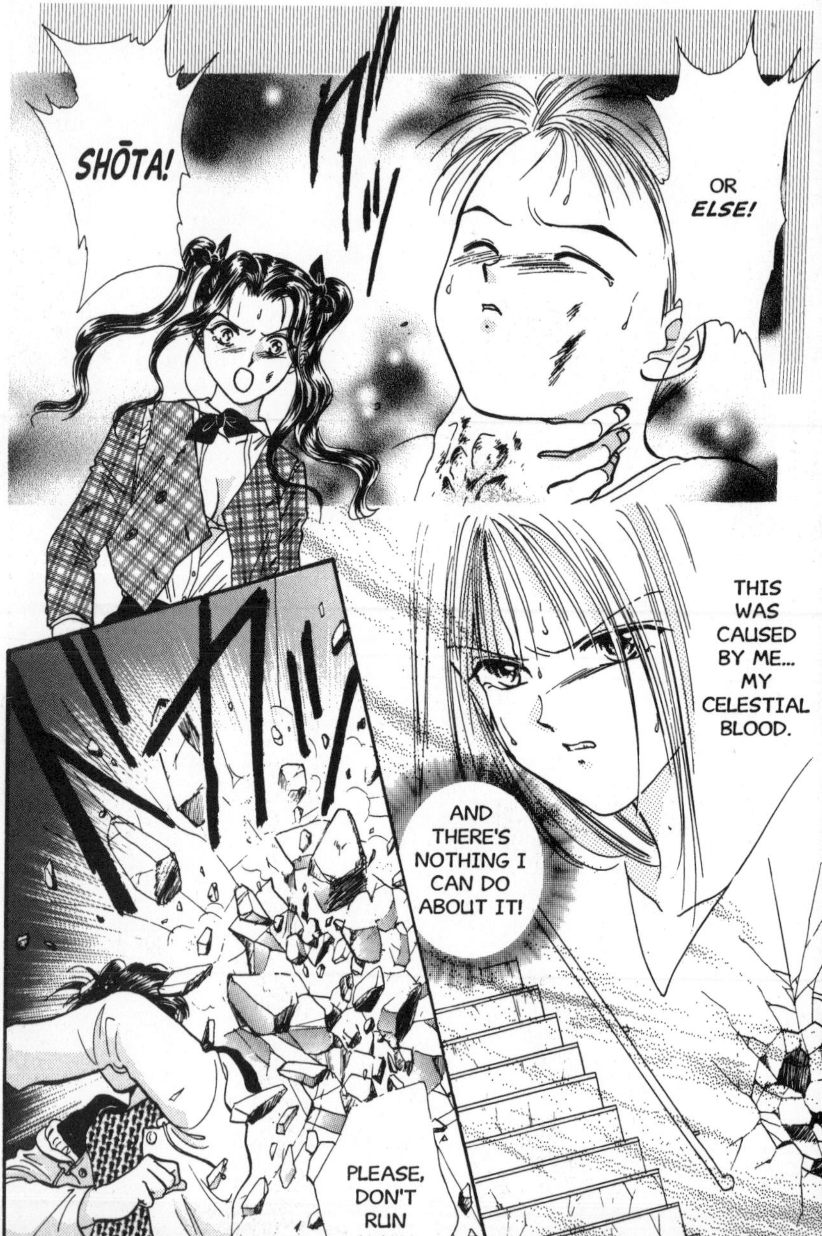
OR ELSE!
SHŌTA!
THIS WAS CAUSED BY ME... MY CELESTIAL BLOOD.
AND THERE'S NOTHING I CAN DO ABOUT IT!
PLEASE, DON'T RUN AWAY.

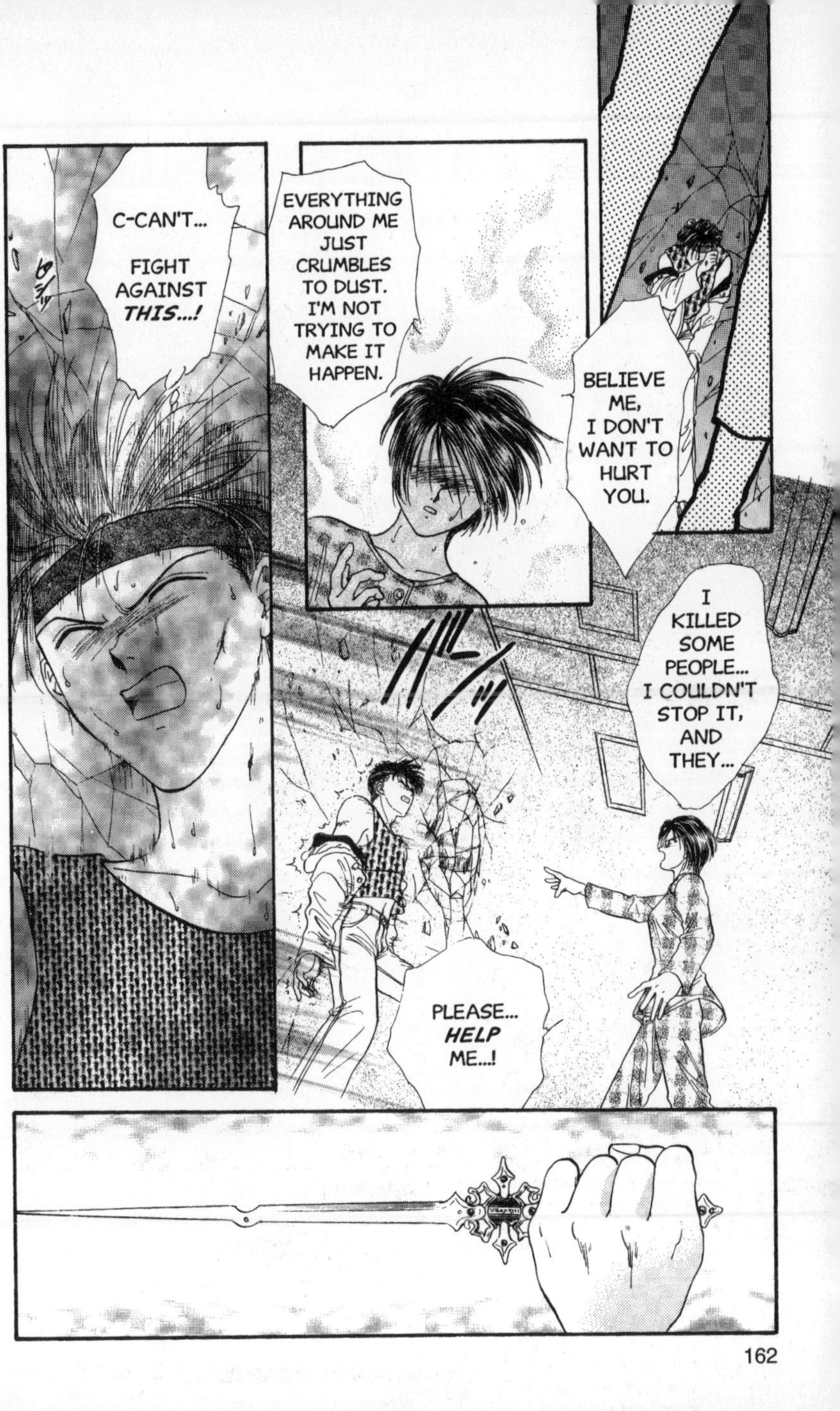
BELIEVE ME, I DON'T WANT TO HURT YOU.
EVERYTHING AROUND ME JUST CRUMBLES TO DUST. I'M NOT TRYING TO MAKE IT HAPPEN.
I KILLED SOME PEOPLE... I COULDN'T STOP IT, AND THEY...
PLEASE... *HELP* ME...!
C-CAN'T... FIGHT AGAINST *THIS*...!

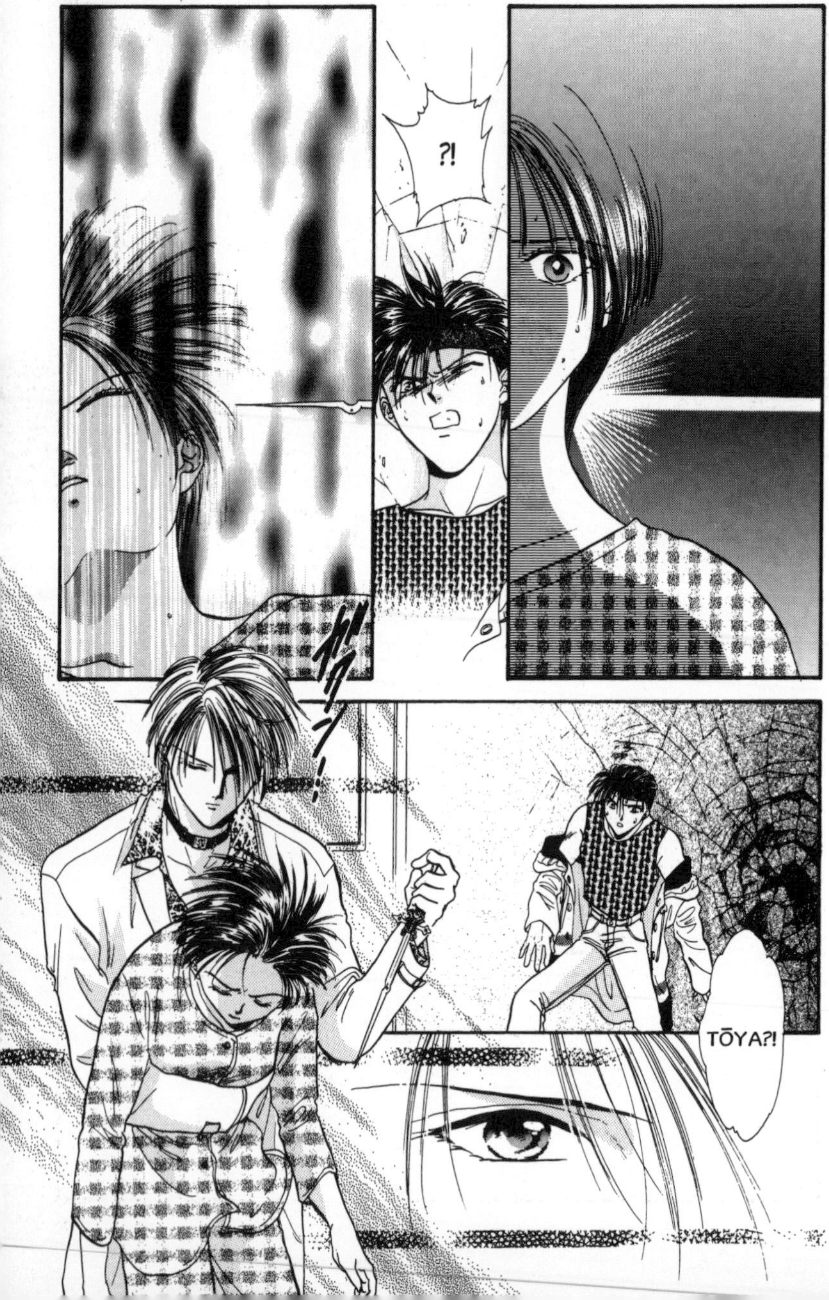
?!
TŌYA?!

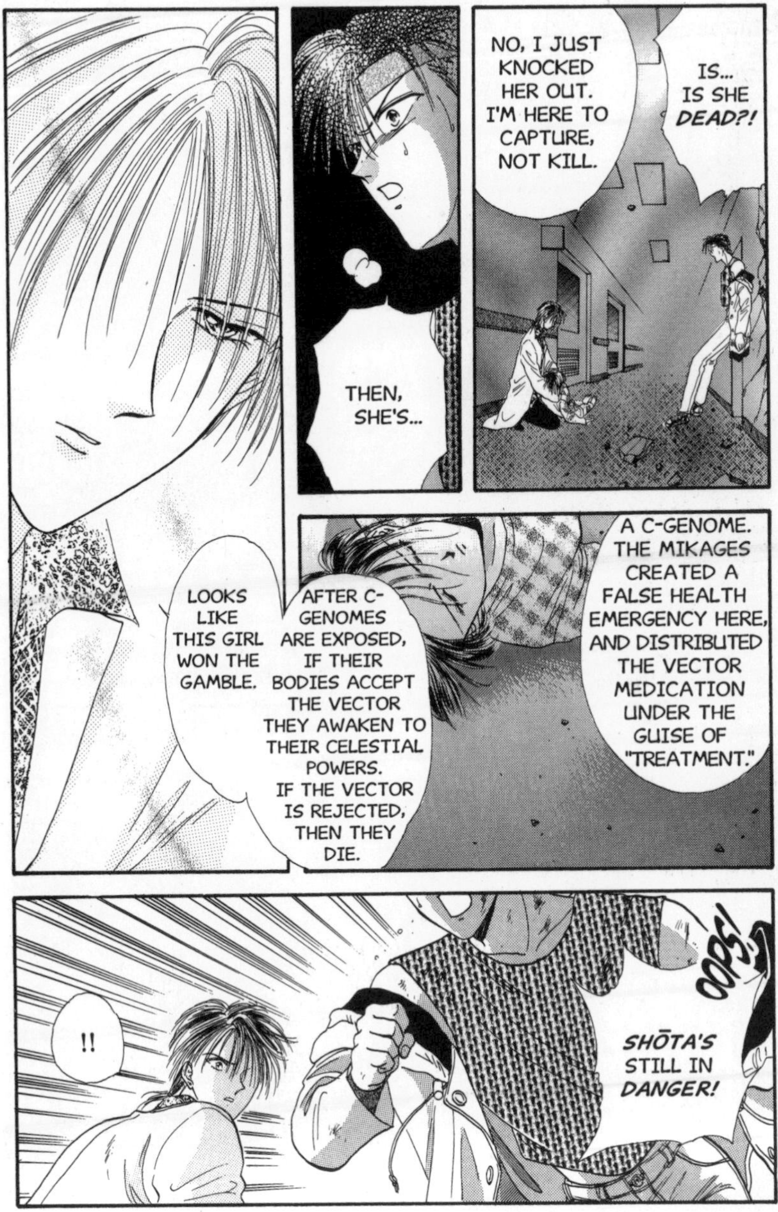

IS... IS SHE *DEAD?!*
NO, I JUST KNOCKED HER OUT. I'M HERE TO CAPTURE, NOT KILL.
THEN, SHE'S...
A C-GENOME. THE MIKAGES CREATED A FALSE HEALTH EMERGENCY HERE, AND DISTRIBUTED THE VECTOR MEDICATION UNDER THE GUISE OF "TREATMENT."
AFTER C-GENOMES ARE EXPOSED, IF THEIR BODIES ACCEPT THE VECTOR THEY AWAKEN TO THEIR CELESTIAL POWERS. IF THE VECTOR IS REJECTED, THEN THEY DIE.
LOOKS LIKE THIS GIRL WON THE GAMBLE.
OOPS!
SHŌTA'S STILL IN *DANGER!*
!!

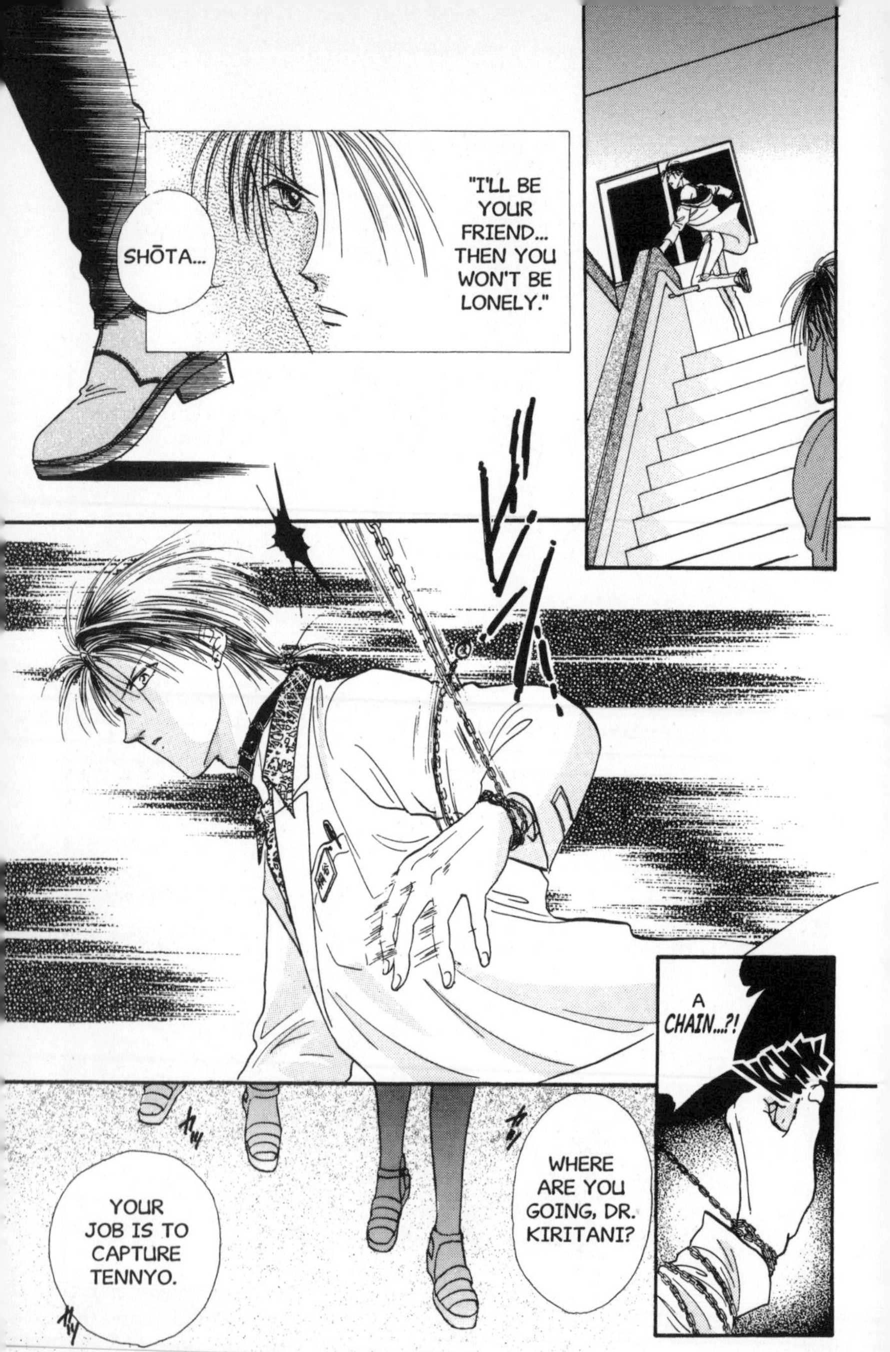
"I'LL BE YOUR FRIEND... THEN YOU WON'T BE LONELY."
SHŌTA...
A CHAIN...?!
WHERE ARE YOU GOING, DR. KIRITANI?
YOUR JOB IS TO CAPTURE TENNYO.

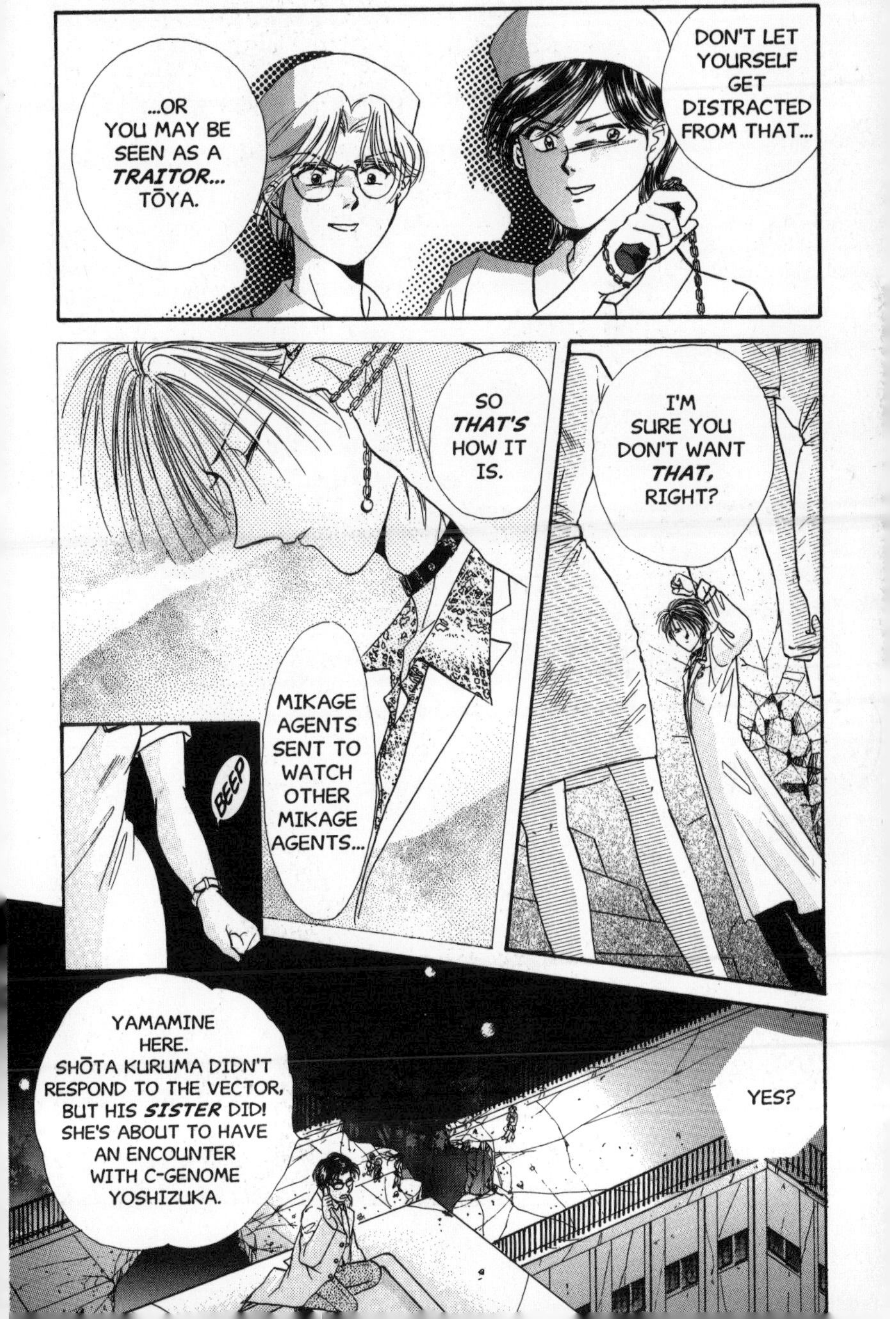
DON'T LET YOURSELF GET DISTRACTED FROM THAT...
...OR YOU MAY BE SEEN AS A *TRAITOR...* TŌYA.
I'M SURE YOU DON'T WANT *THAT,* RIGHT?
SO *THAT'S* HOW IT IS.
MIKAGE AGENTS SENT TO WATCH OTHER MIKAGE AGENTS...
BEEP
YES?
YAMAMINE HERE. SHŌTA KURUMA DIDN'T RESPOND TO THE VECTOR, BUT HIS *SISTER* DID! SHE'S ABOUT TO HAVE AN ENCOUNTER WITH C-GENOME YOSHIZUKA.

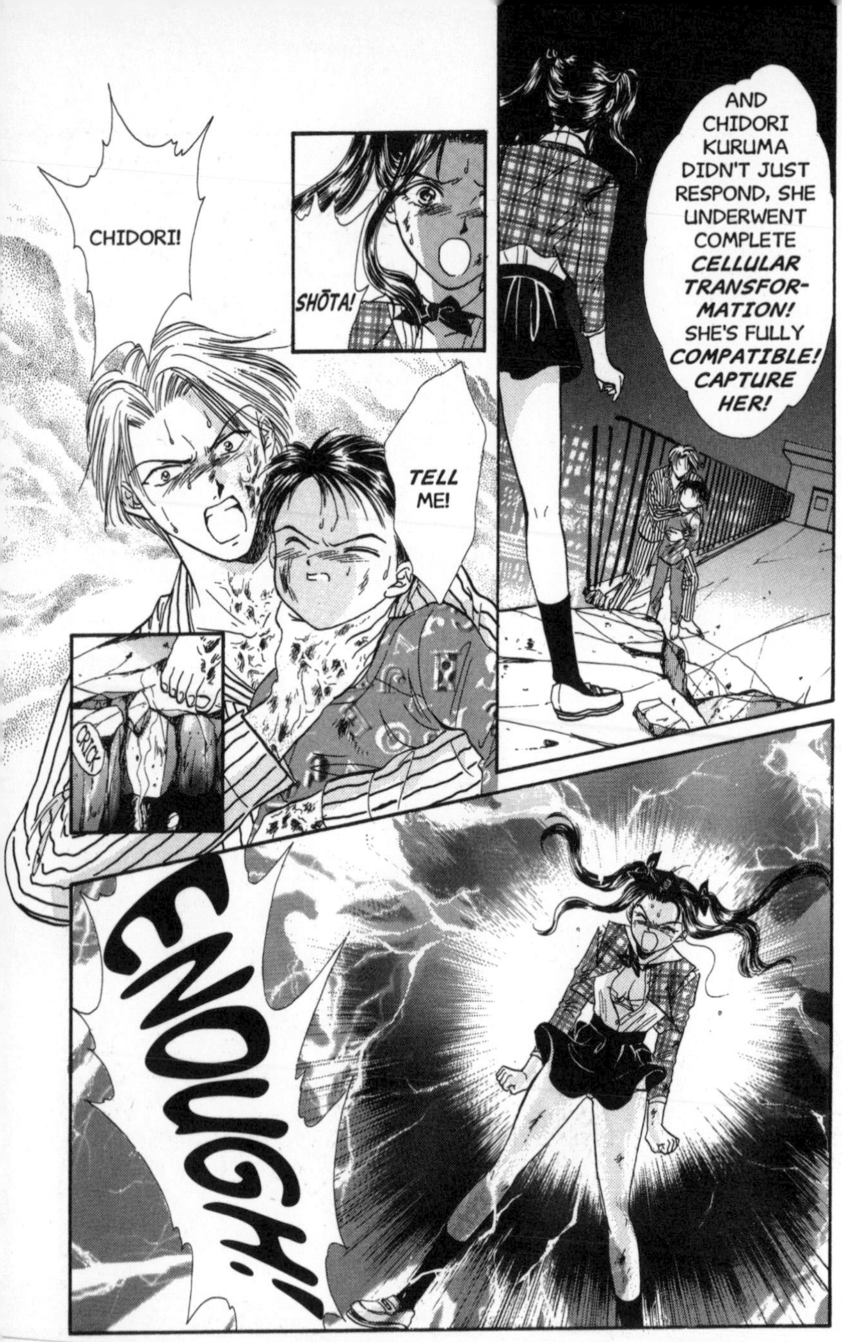
AND CHIDORI KURUMA DIDN'T JUST RESPOND, SHE UNDERWENT COMPLETE CELLULAR TRANSFORMATION! SHE'S FULLY COMPATIBLE! CAPTURE HER!
SHŌTA!
CHIDORI!
TELL ME!
CRICK
ENOUGH!

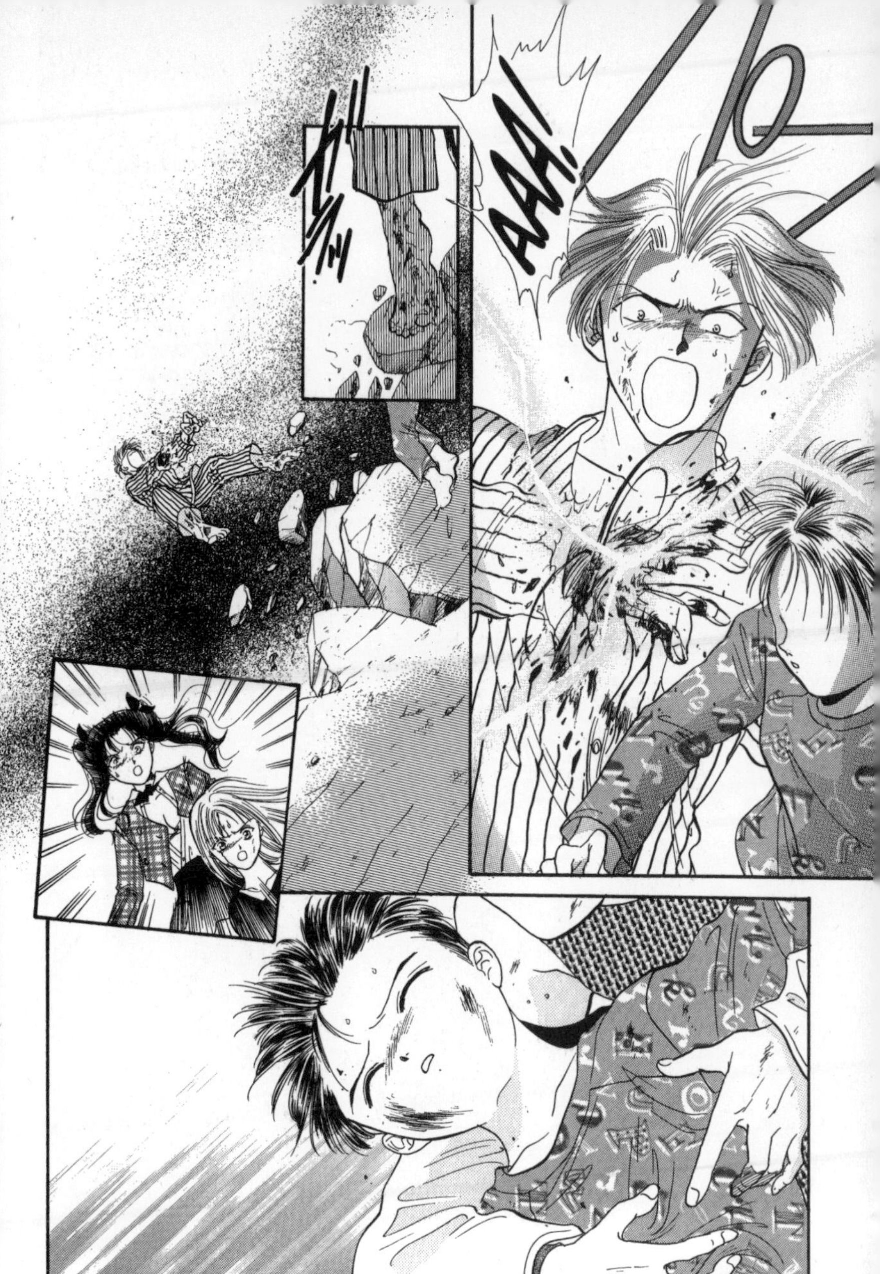
AAA!!

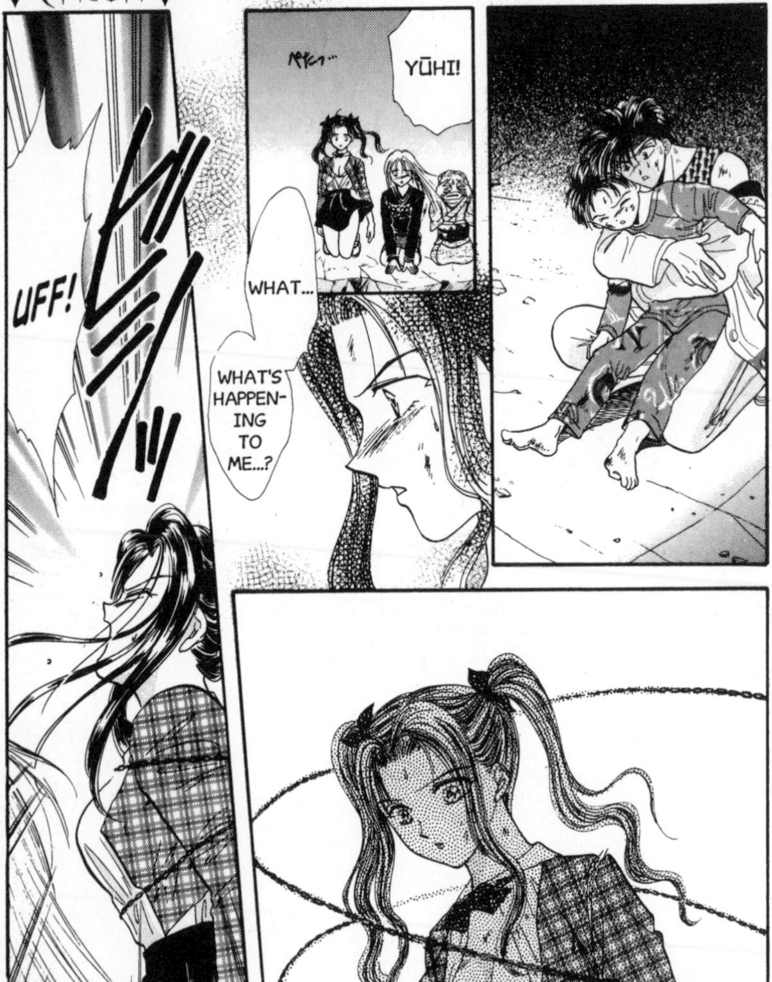
YŪHI!
WHAT...
WHAT'S HAPPEN-ING TO ME...?
UFF!

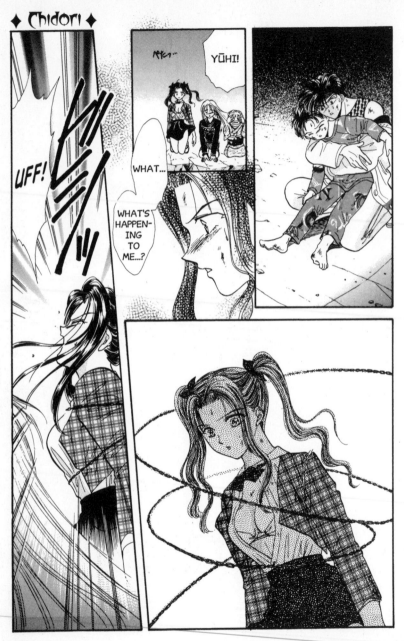

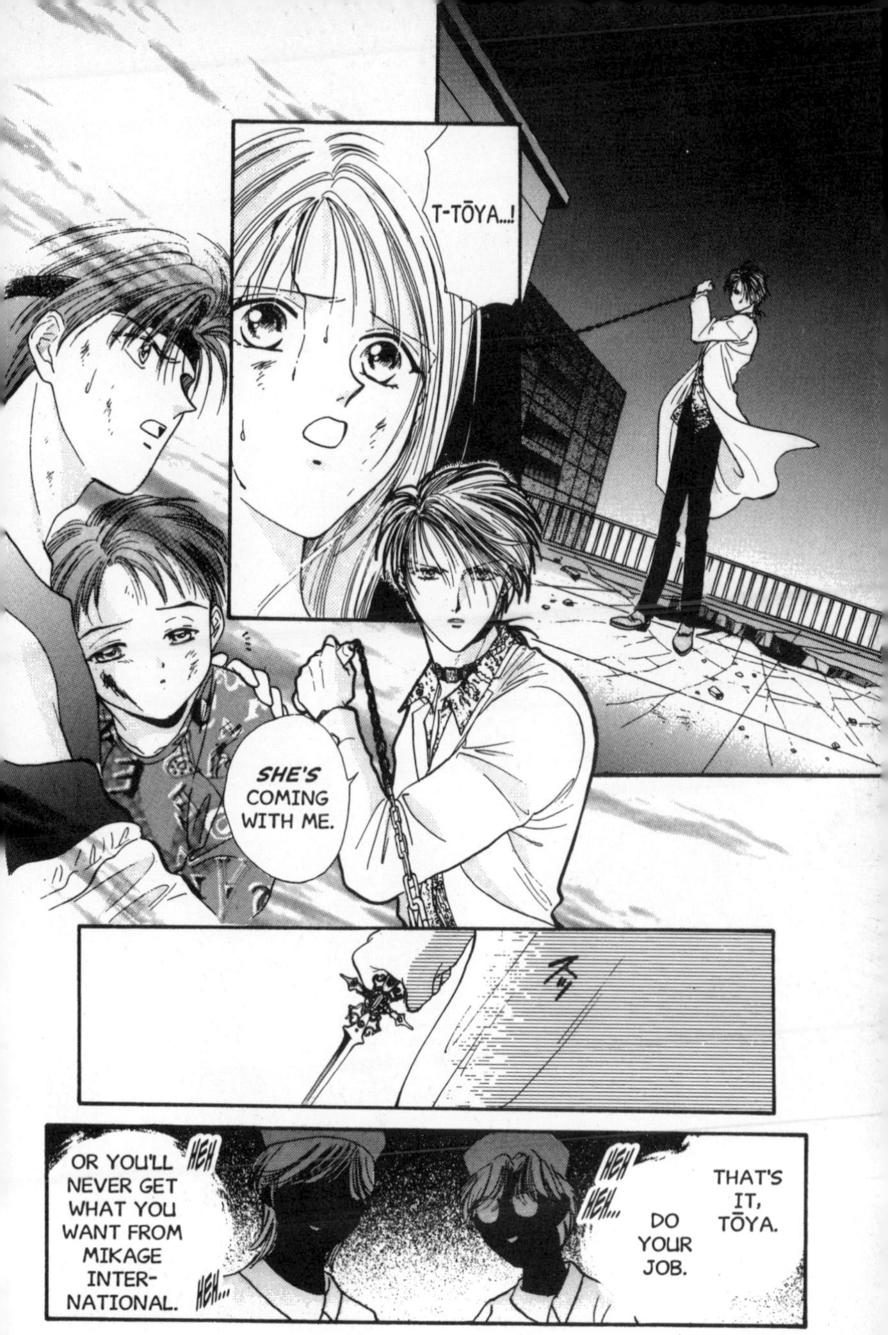
T-TŌYA...!
SHE'S COMING WITH ME.
ズッ
THAT'S IT, TŌYA.
DO YOUR JOB.
HEH HEH...
HEH
OR YOU'LL NEVER GET WHAT YOU WANT FROM MIKAGE INTER-NATIONAL.
HEH...

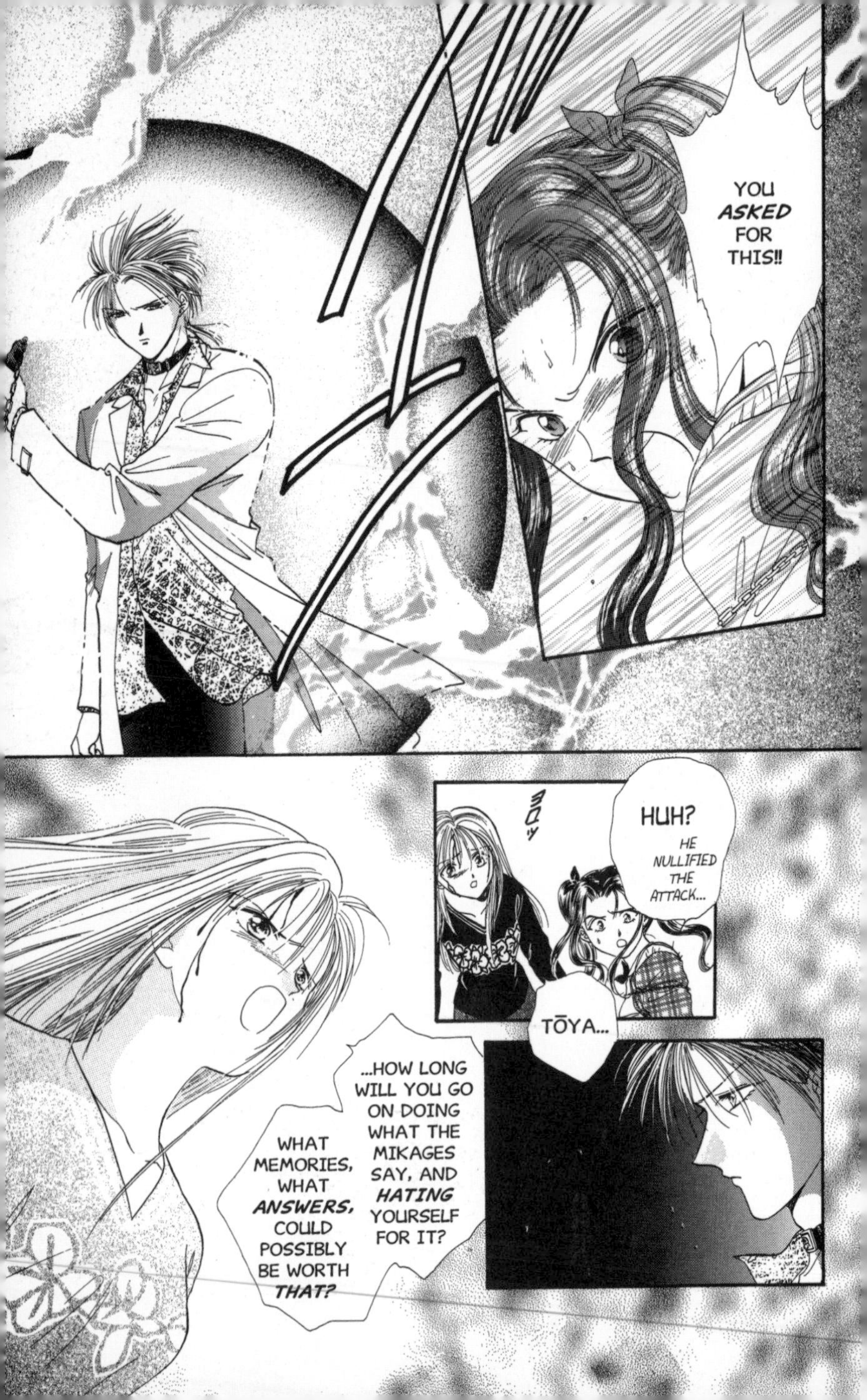
YOU ASKED FOR THIS!!
HUH?
HE NULLIFIED THE ATTACK...
TŌYA...
...HOW LONG WILL YOU GO ON DOING WHAT THE MIKAGES SAY, AND HATING YOURSELF FOR IT?
WHAT MEMORIES, WHAT ANSWERS, COULD POSSIBLY BE WORTH THAT?

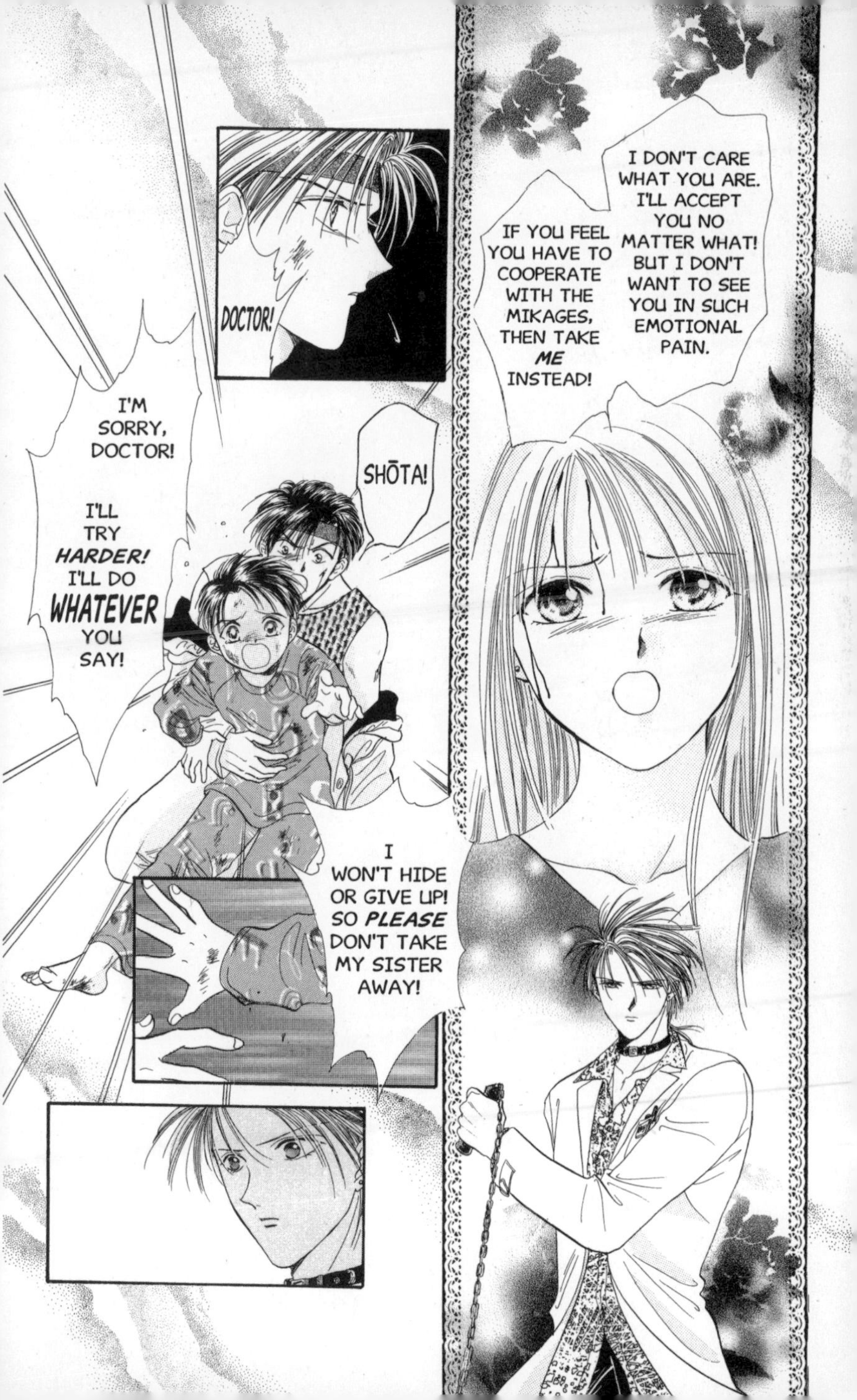
I DON'T CARE WHAT YOU ARE. I'LL ACCEPT YOU NO MATTER WHAT! BUT I DON'T WANT TO SEE YOU IN SUCH EMOTIONAL PAIN.
IF YOU FEEL YOU HAVE TO COOPERATE WITH THE MIKAGES, THEN TAKE *ME* INSTEAD!
DOCTOR!
SHŌTA!
I'M SORRY, DOCTOR!
I'LL TRY *HARDER!* I'LL DO **WHATEVER** YOU SAY!
I WON'T HIDE OR GIVE UP! SO *PLEASE* DON'T TAKE MY SISTER AWAY!

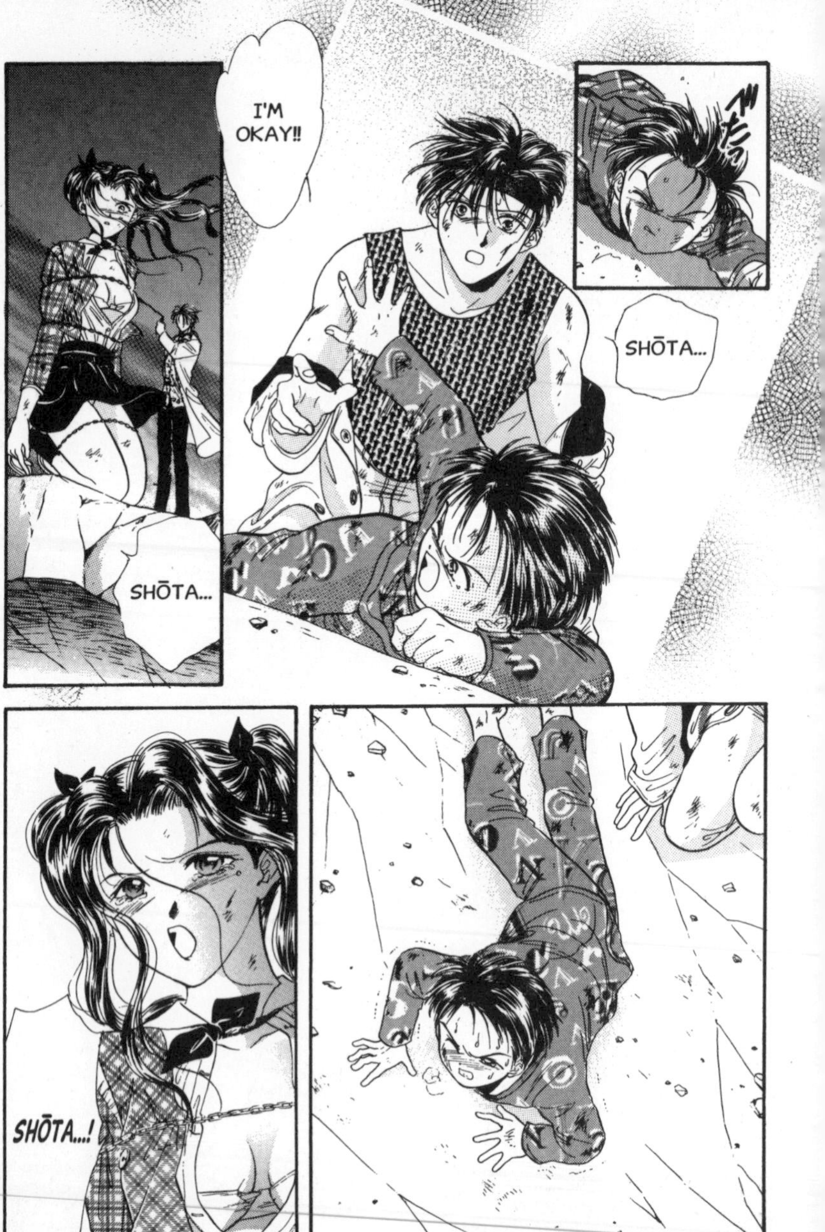

I'M OKAY!!
SHŌTA...
SHŌTA...
SHŌTA...!

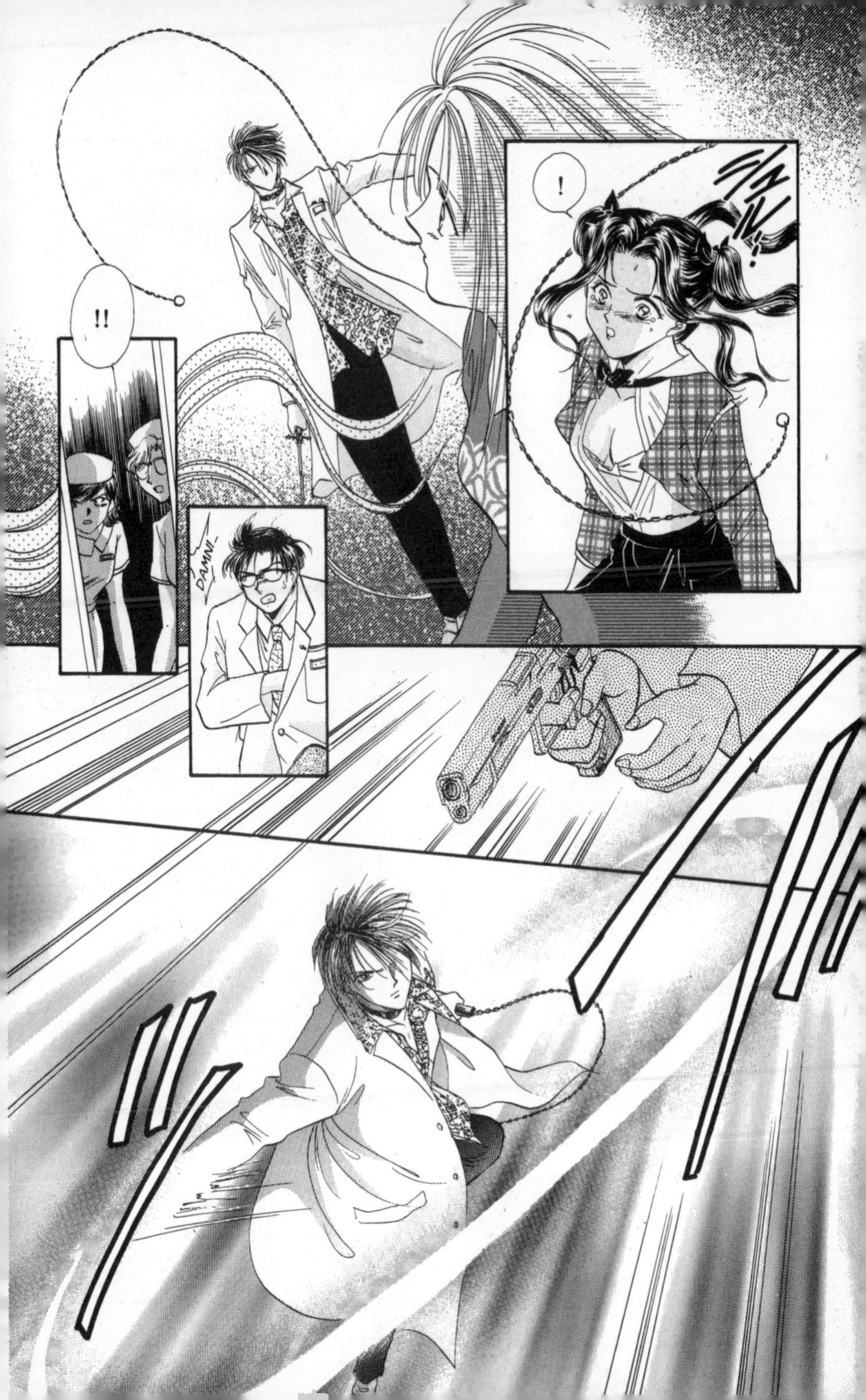
シュル!!
!
!!
DAMN!

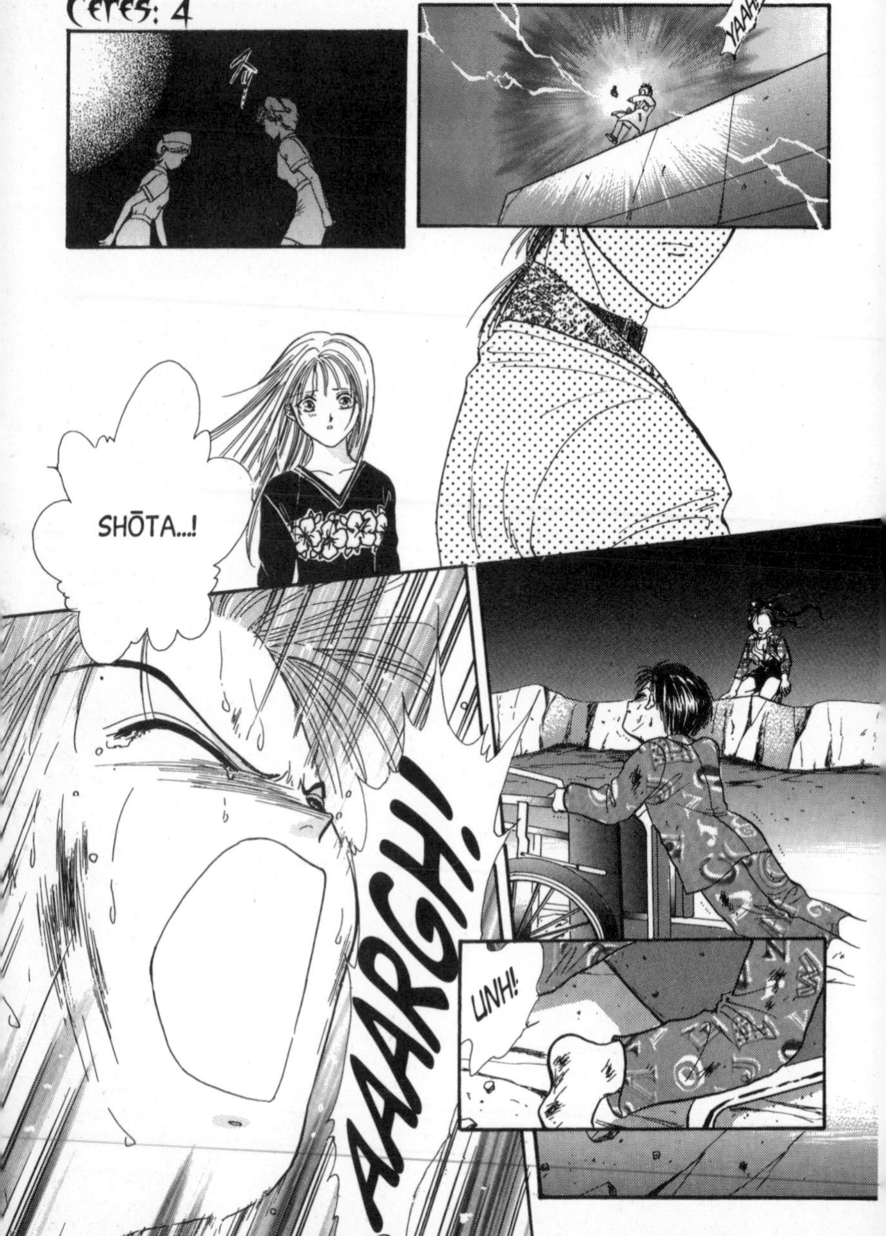
YAAH!
SHŌTA...!
UNH!
AARGH!!

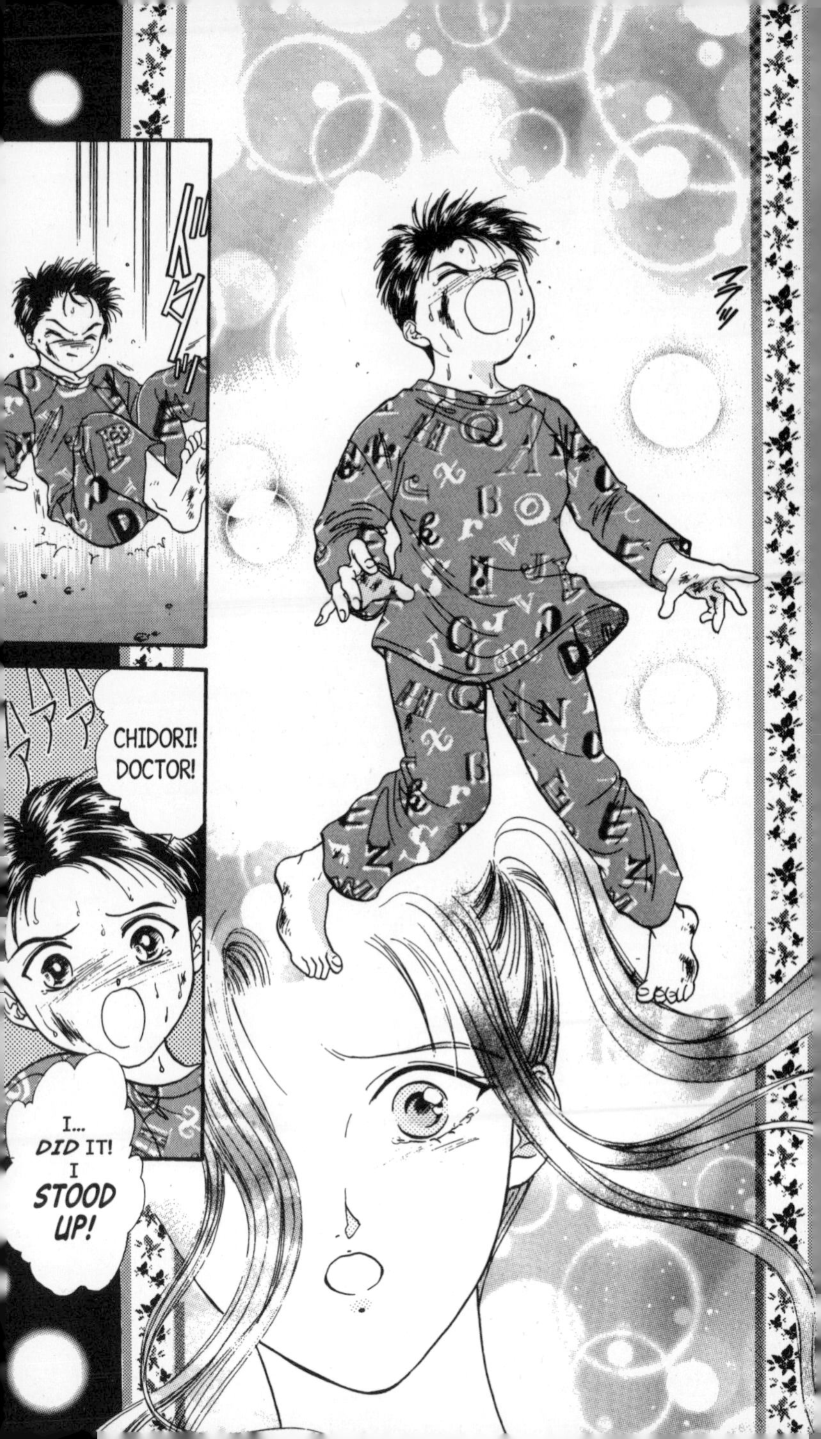
CHIDORI! DOCTOR!
I... DID IT! I STOOD UP!

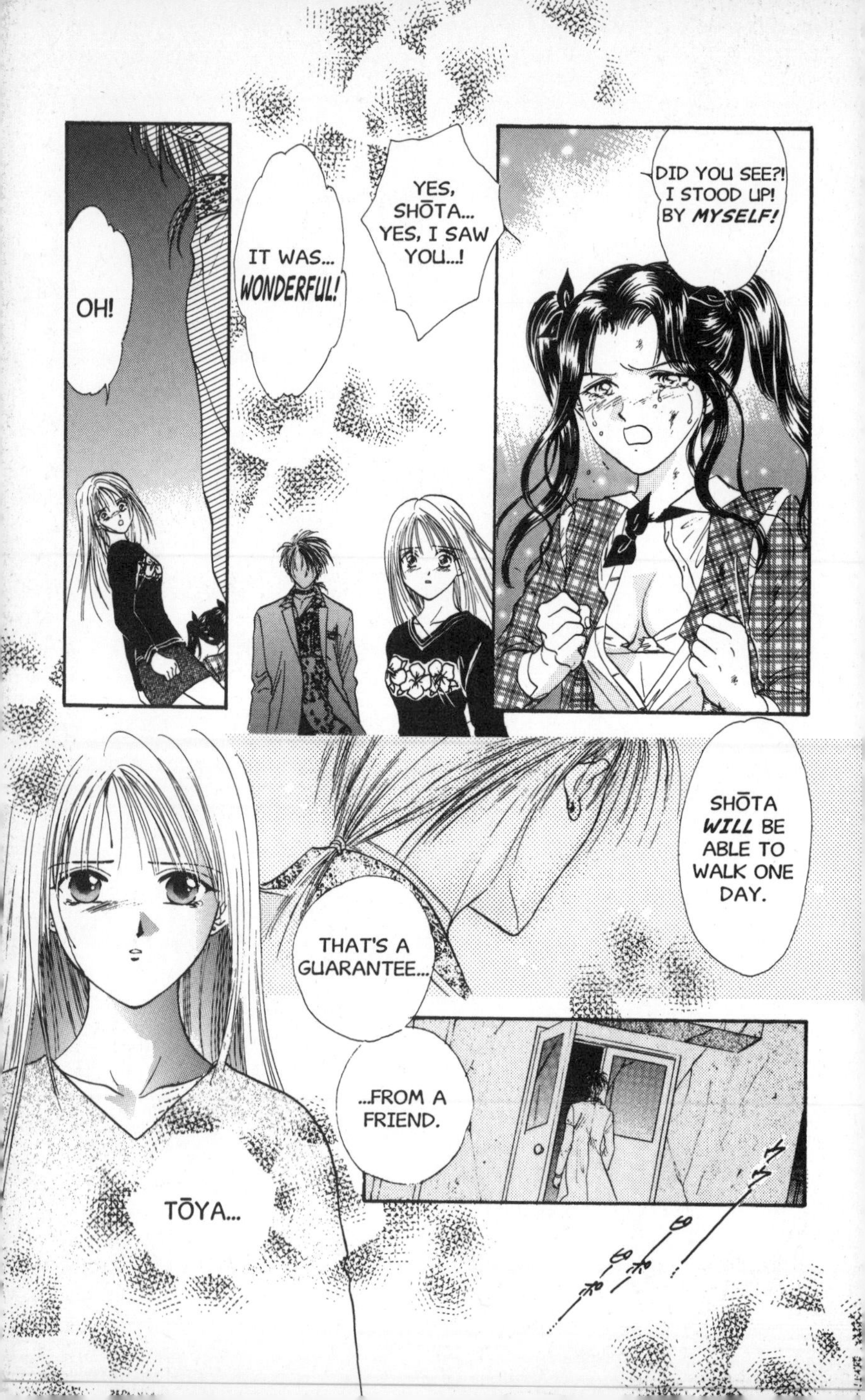
DID YOU SEE?! I STOOD UP! BY *MYSELF!*
YES, SHŌTA... YES, I SAW YOU...!
IT WAS... WONDERFUL!
OH!
SHŌTA *WILL* BE ABLE TO WALK ONE DAY.
THAT'S A GUARANTEE...
...FROM A FRIEND.
TŌYA...

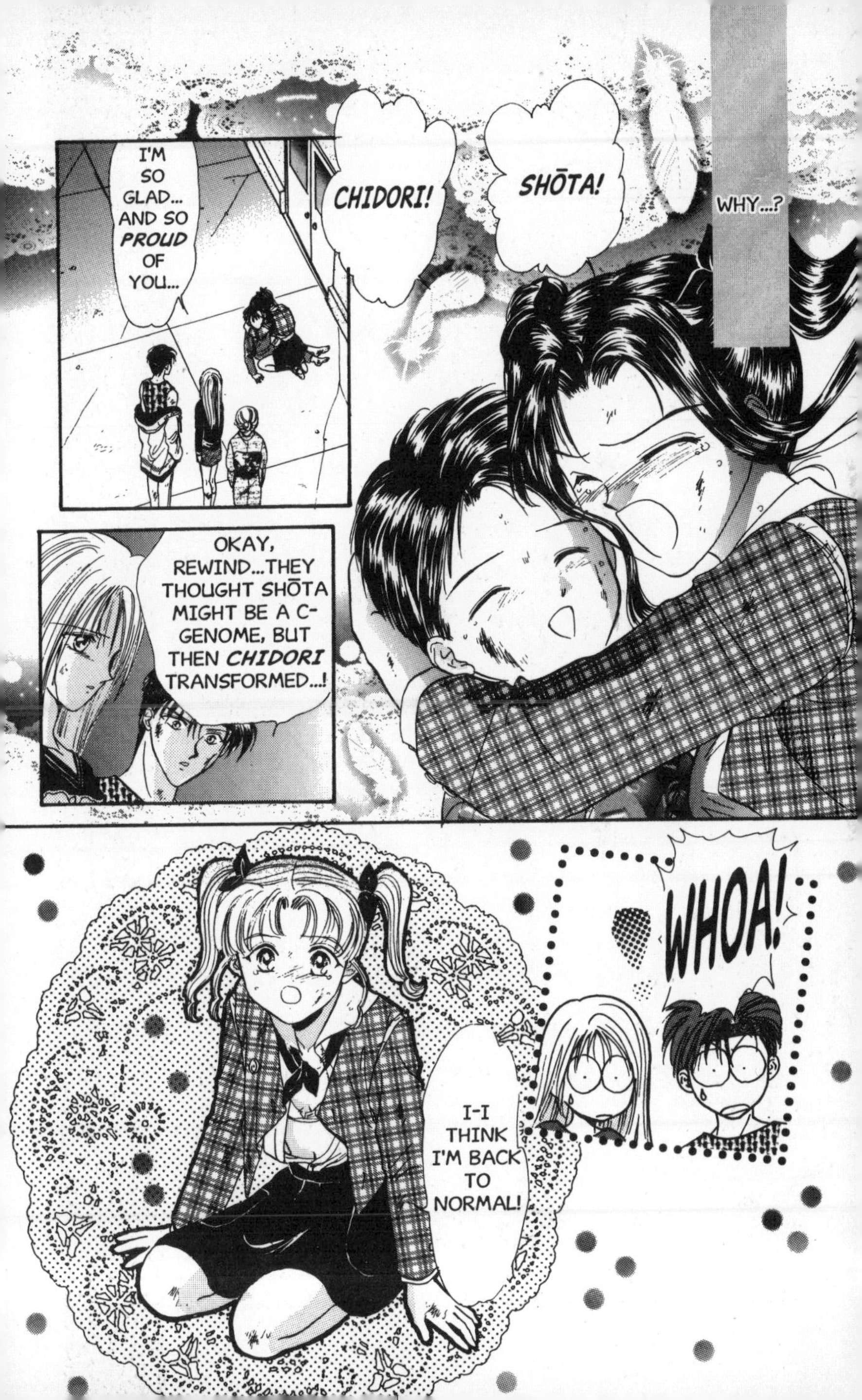
WHY...?
SHŌTA!
CHIDORI!
I'M SO GLAD... AND SO PROUD OF YOU...
OKAY, REWIND...THEY THOUGHT SHŌTA MIGHT BE A C-GENOME, BUT THEN CHIDORI TRANSFORMED...!
WHOA!
I-I THINK I'M BACK TO NORMAL!

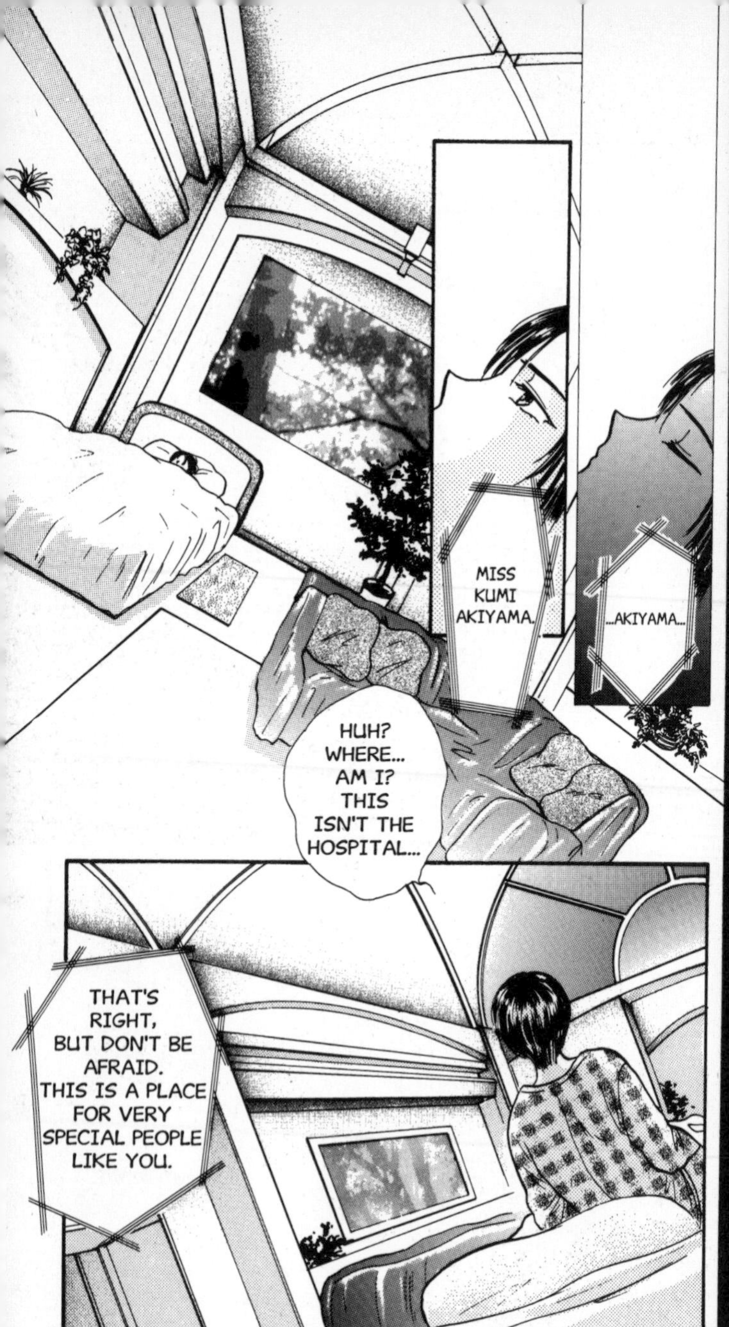
...AKIYAMA...
MISS KUMI AKIYAMA...
HUH? WHERE... AM I? THIS ISN'T THE HOSPITAL...
THAT'S RIGHT, BUT DON'T BE AFRAID. THIS IS A PLACE FOR VERY SPECIAL PEOPLE LIKE YOU.

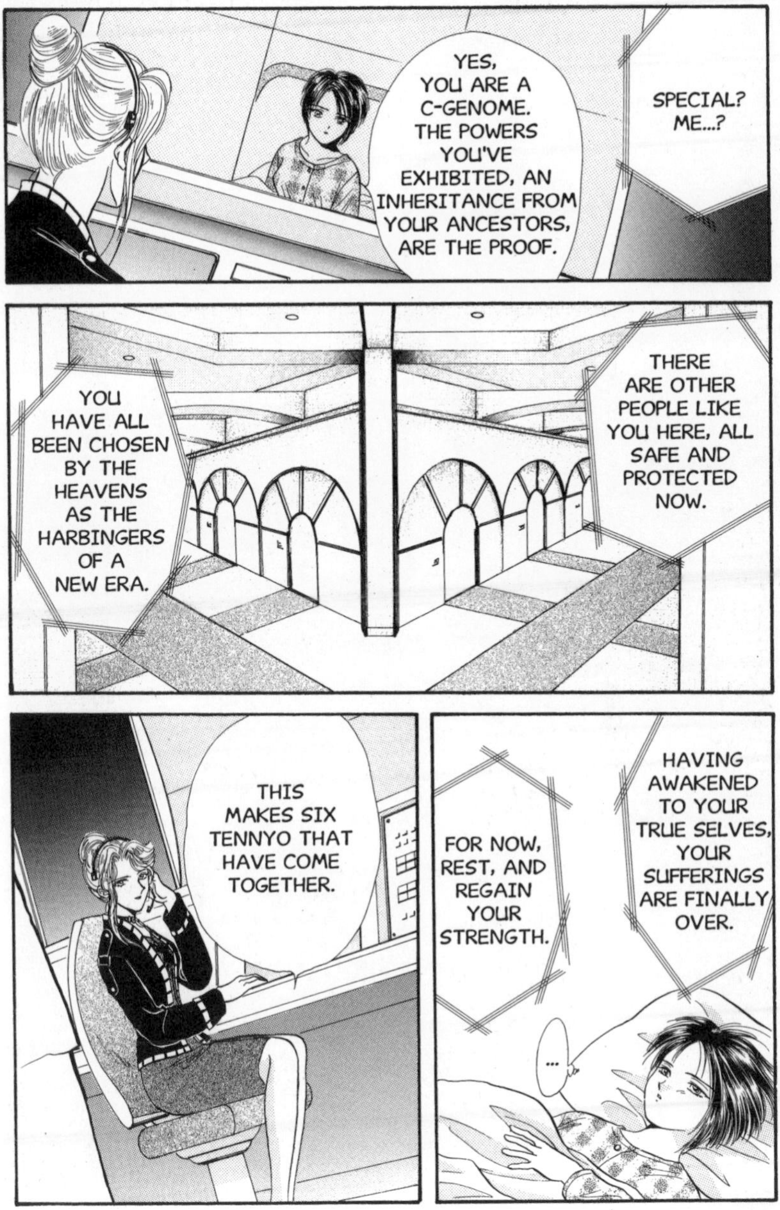
SPECIAL? ME...?
YES, YOU ARE A C-GENOME. THE POWERS YOU'VE EXHIBITED, AN INHERITANCE FROM YOUR ANCESTORS, ARE THE PROOF.
THERE ARE OTHER PEOPLE LIKE YOU HERE, ALL SAFE AND PROTECTED NOW.
YOU HAVE ALL BEEN CHOSEN BY THE HEAVENS AS THE HARBINGERS OF A NEW ERA.
HAVING AWAKENED TO YOUR TRUE SELVES, YOUR SUFFERINGS ARE FINALLY OVER.
FOR NOW, REST, AND REGAIN YOUR STRENGTH.
...
THIS MAKES SIX TENNYO THAT HAVE COME TOGETHER.

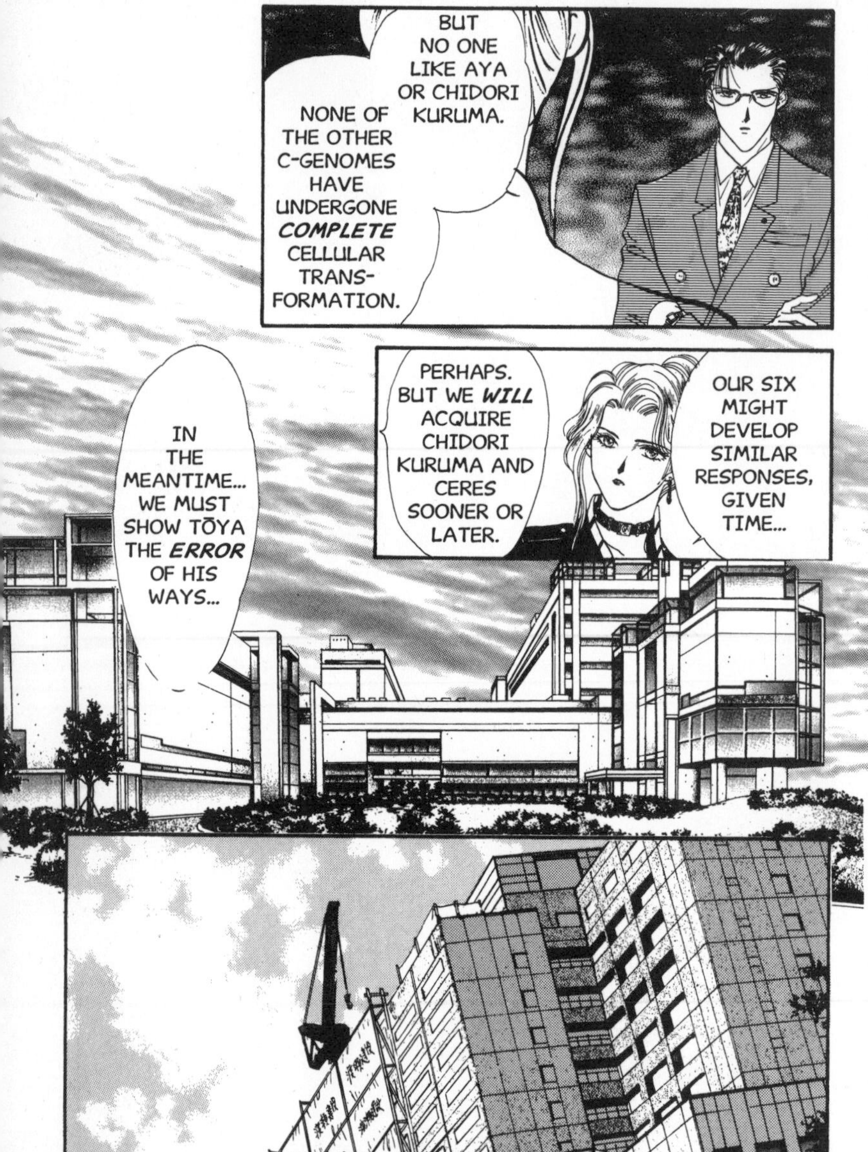
BUT NO ONE LIKE AYA OR CHIDORI KURUMA.
NONE OF THE OTHER C-GENOMES HAVE UNDERGONE ***COMPLETE*** CELLULAR TRANS-FORMATION.
OUR SIX MIGHT DEVELOP SIMILAR RESPONSES, GIVEN TIME...
PERHAPS. BUT WE ***WILL*** ACQUIRE CHIDORI KURUMA AND CERES SOONER OR LATER.
IN THE MEANTIME... WE MUST SHOW TŌYA THE ***ERROR*** OF HIS WAYS...

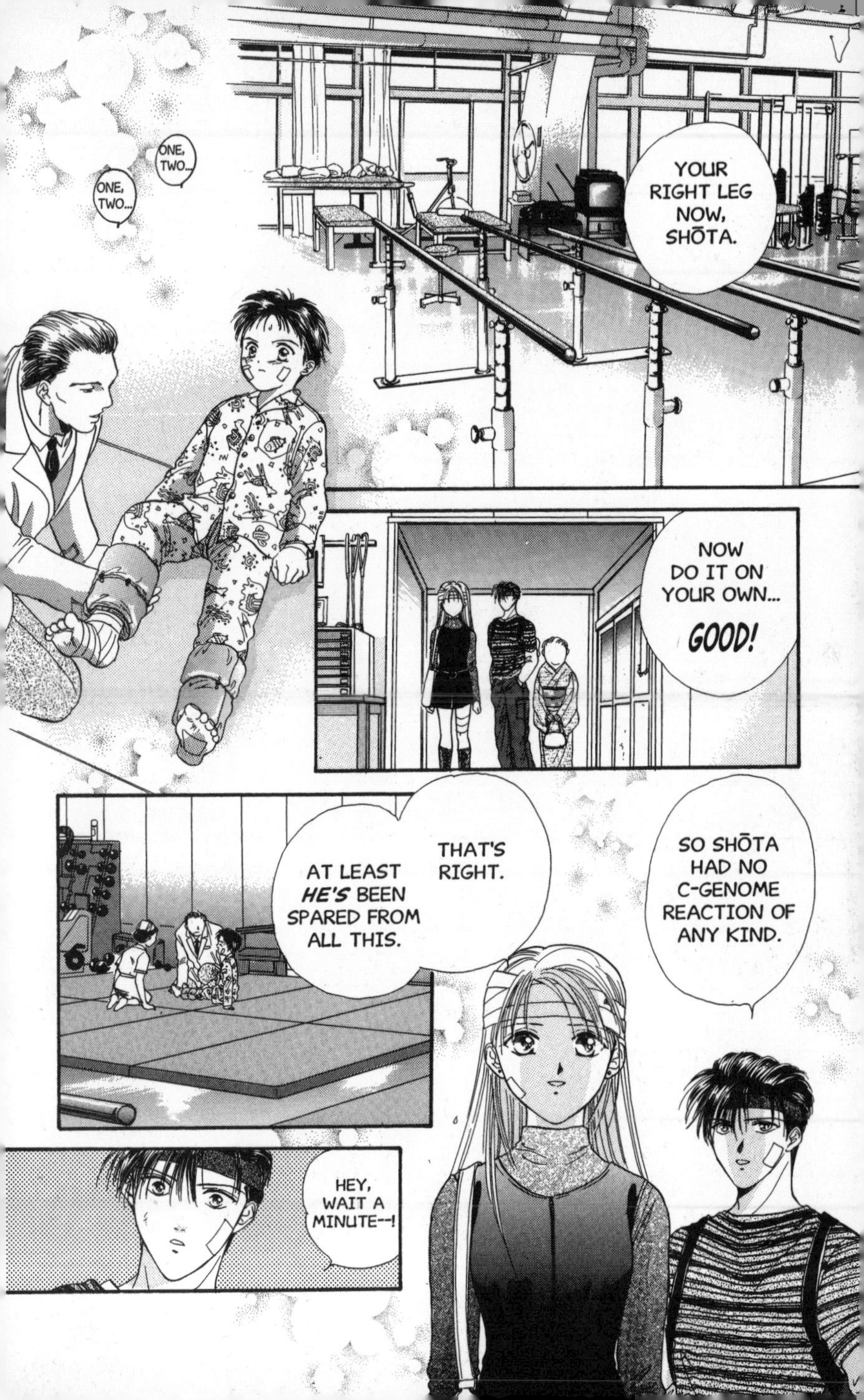
YOUR RIGHT LEG NOW, SHŌTA.
ONE, TWO...
ONE, TWO...
NOW DO IT ON YOUR OWN... GOOD!
SO SHŌTA HAD NO C-GENOME REACTION OF ANY KIND.
THAT'S RIGHT.
AT LEAST *HE'S* BEEN SPARED FROM ALL THIS.
HEY, WAIT A MINUTE--!

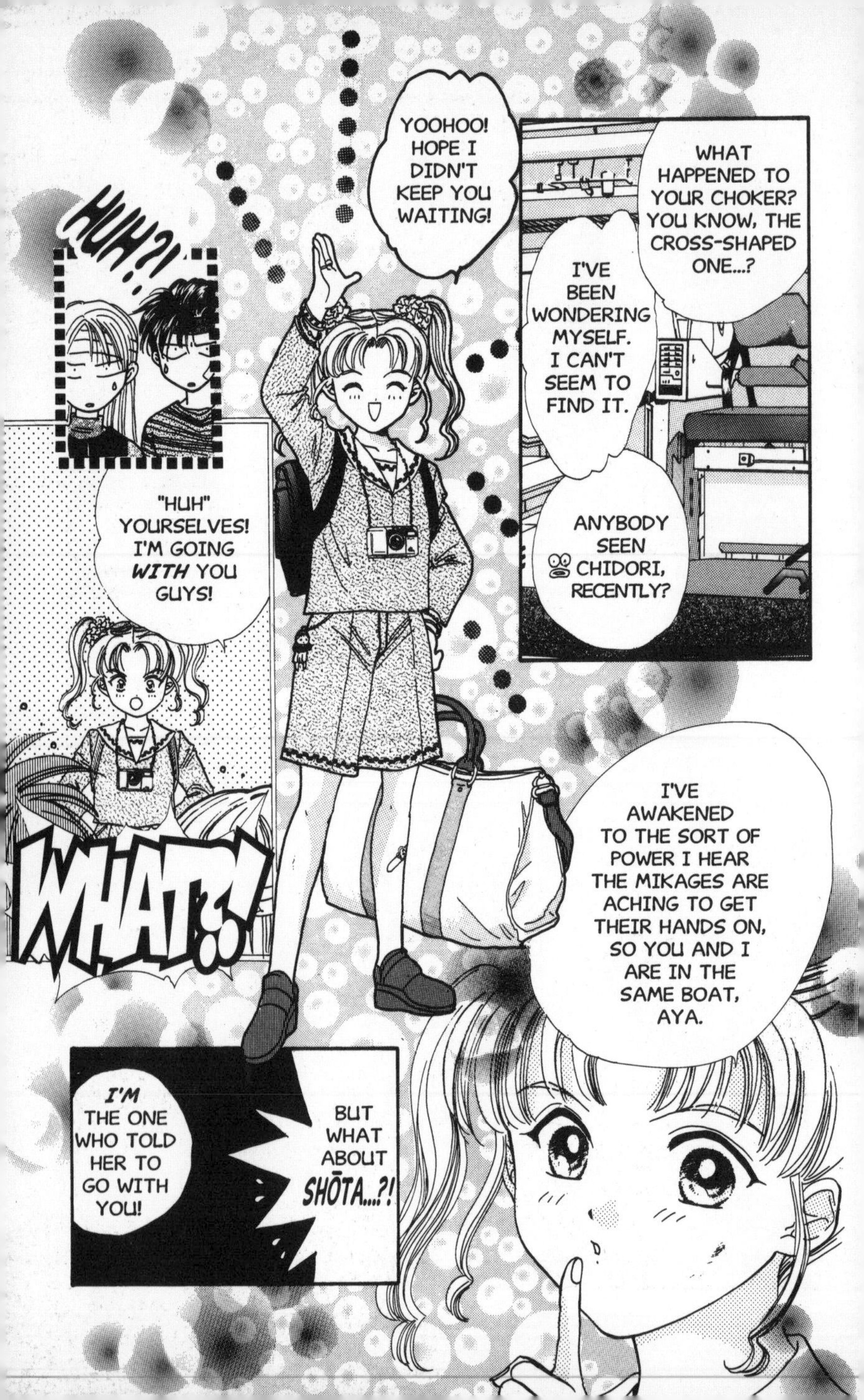
WHAT HAPPENED TO YOUR CHOKER? YOU KNOW, THE CROSS-SHAPED ONE...?
I'VE BEEN WONDERING MYSELF. I CAN'T SEEM TO FIND IT.
ANYBODY SEEN CHIDORI, RECENTLY?
YOOHOO! HOPE I DIDN'T KEEP YOU WAITING!
HUH?!
"HUH" YOURSELVES! I'M GOING *WITH* YOU GUYS!
WHAT?!
I'VE AWAKENED TO THE SORT OF POWER I HEAR THE MIKAGES ARE ACHING TO GET THEIR HANDS ON, SO YOU AND I ARE IN THE SAME BOAT, AYA.
BUT WHAT ABOUT SHŌTA...?!
I'M THE ONE WHO TOLD HER TO GO WITH YOU!

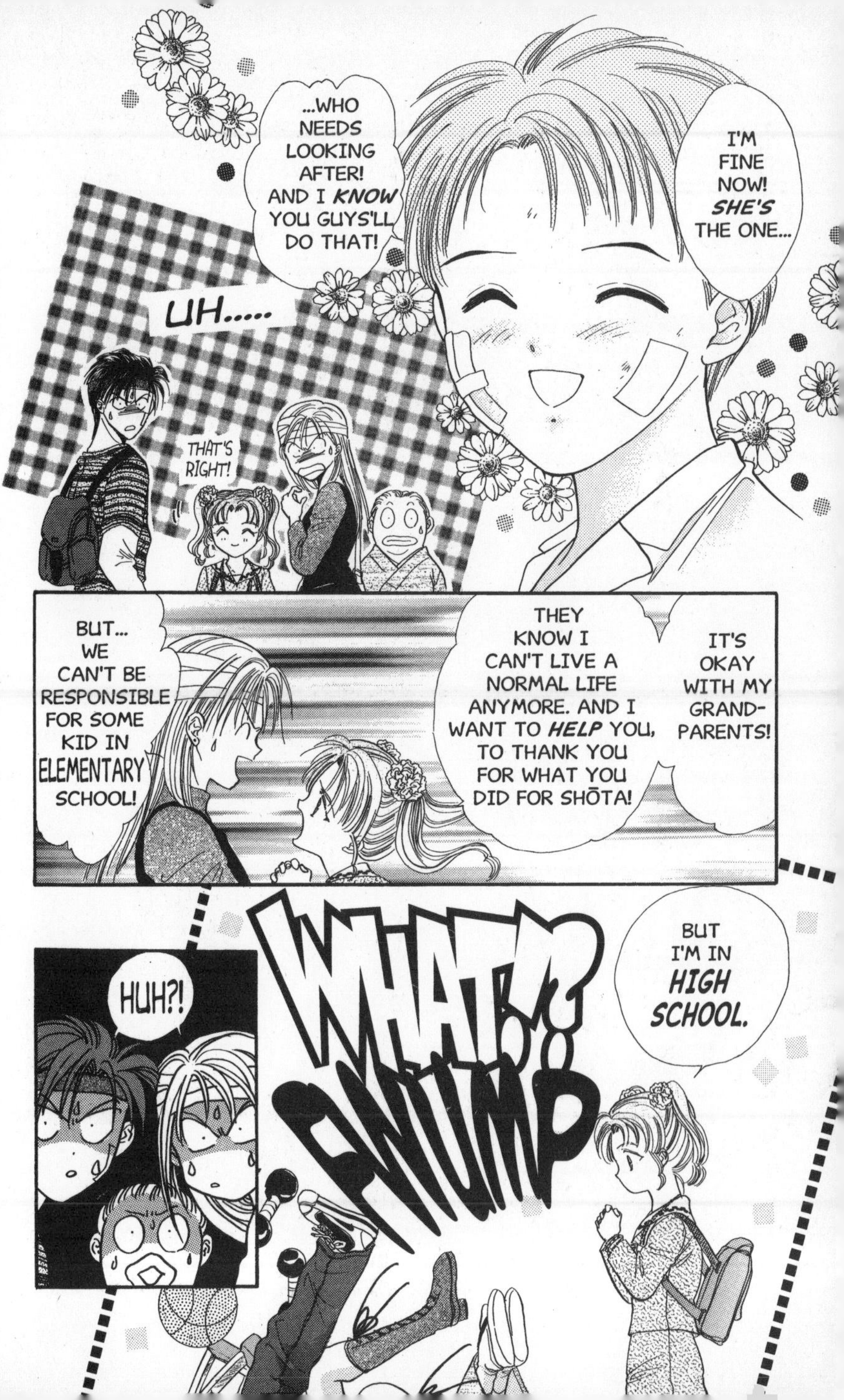
I'M FINE NOW! *SHE'S* THE ONE...
...WHO NEEDS LOOKING AFTER! AND I *KNOW* YOU GUYS'LL DO THAT!
UH.....
THAT'S RIGHT!
IT'S OKAY WITH MY GRAND-PARENTS!
THEY KNOW I CAN'T LIVE A NORMAL LIFE ANYMORE. AND I WANT TO *HELP* YOU, TO THANK YOU FOR WHAT YOU DID FOR SHŌTA!
BUT... WE CAN'T BE RESPONSIBLE FOR SOME KID IN ELEMENTARY SCHOOL!
BUT I'M IN *HIGH SCHOOL.*
WHAT?!
HUH?!
WHUMP

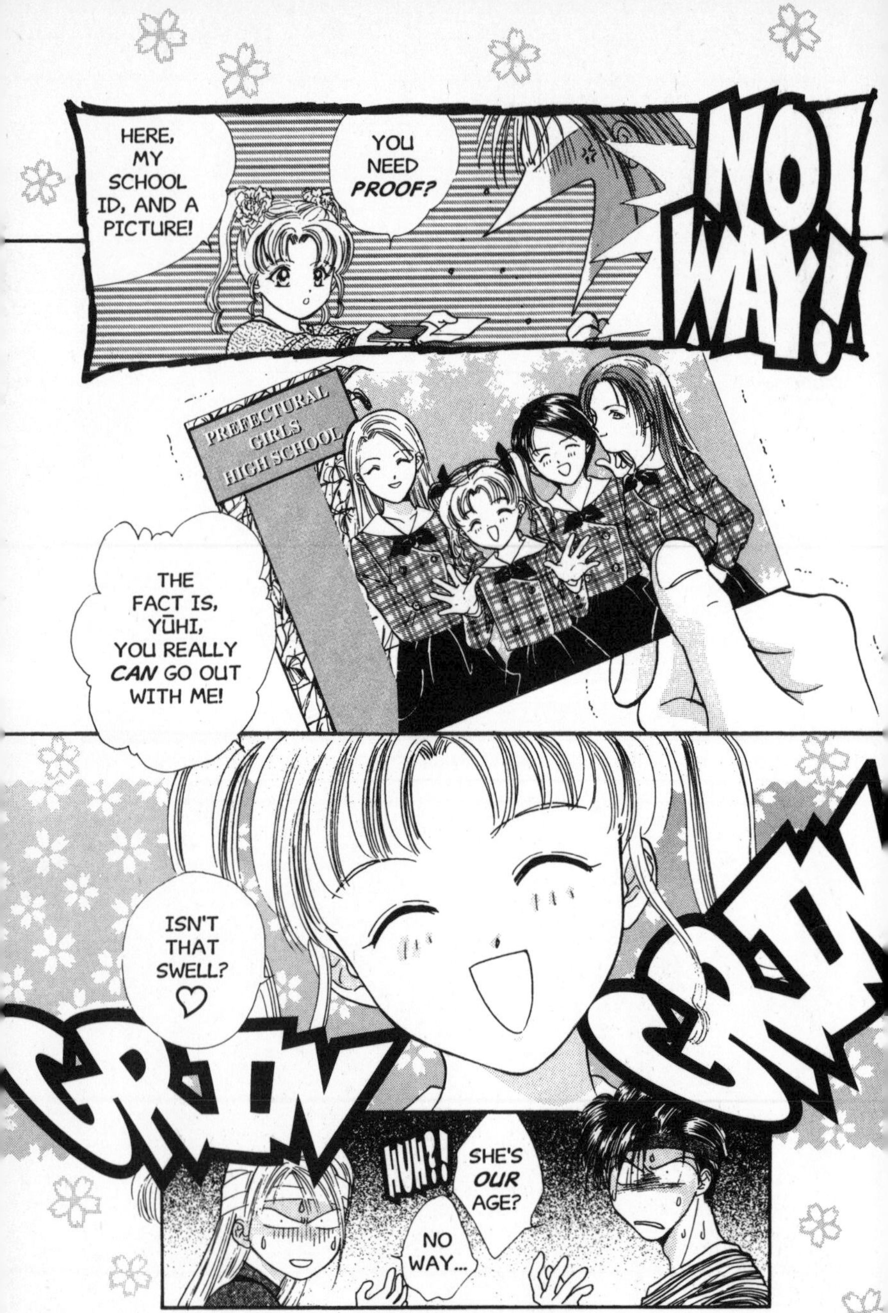
NO WAY!!
YOU NEED *PROOF?*
HERE, MY SCHOOL ID, AND A PICTURE!
PREFECTURAL GIRLS HIGH SCHOOL
THE FACT IS, YŪHI, YOU REALLY *CAN* GO OUT WITH ME!
ISN'T THAT SWELL? ♡
GRIN
GRIN
HUH?!
SHE'S *OUR* AGE?
NO WAY...

TO BE CONTINUED...

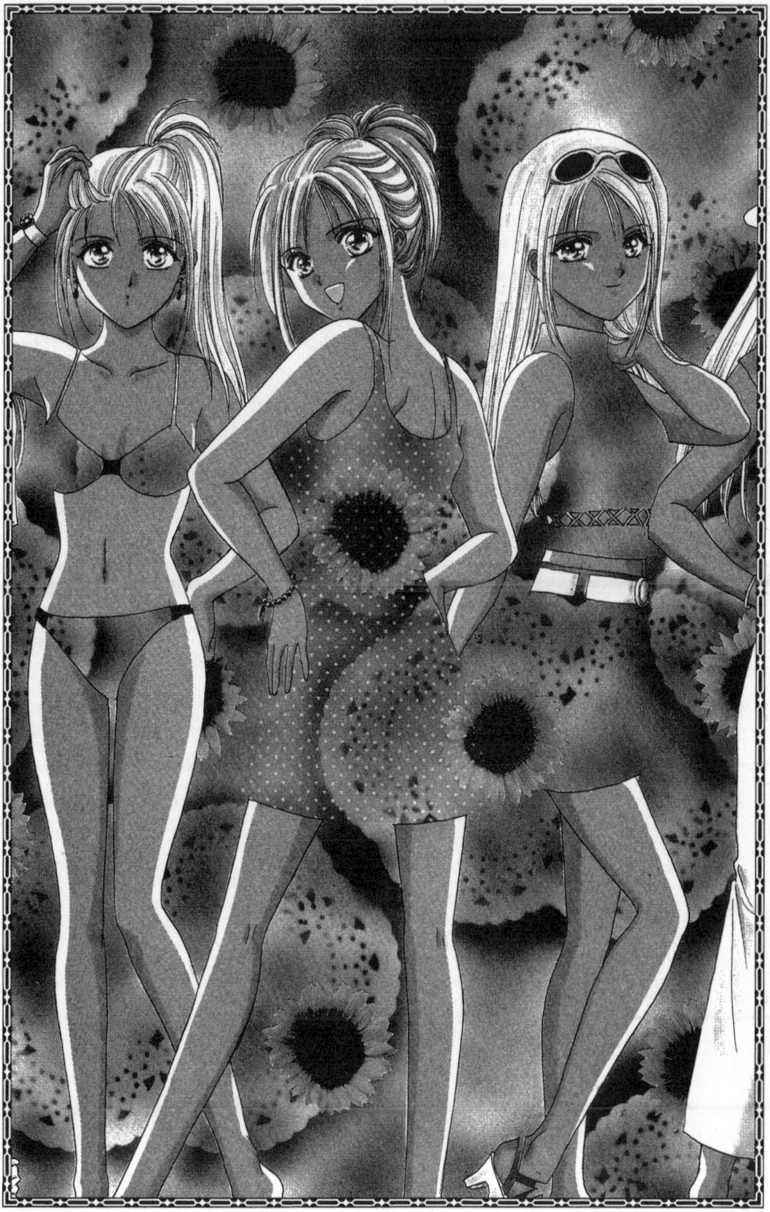

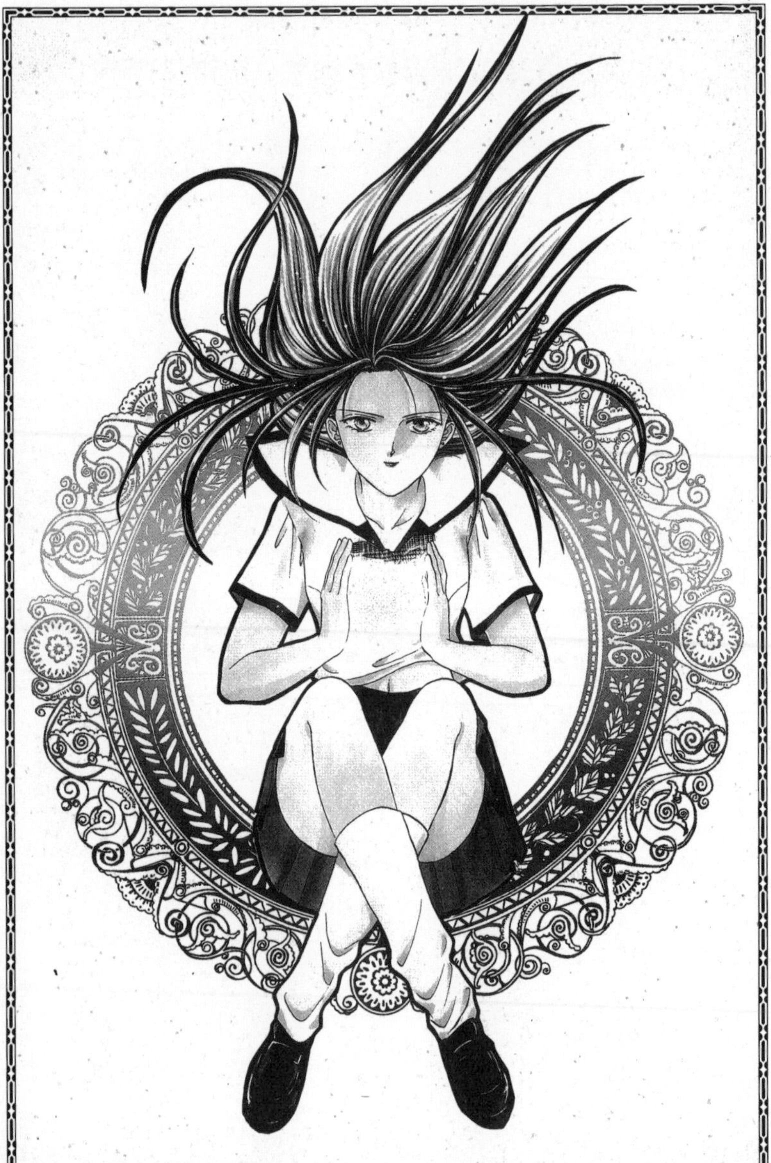

The Ceres Guide to Sound Effects

We've left most of the sound effects in CERES as Yû Watase originally created them – in Japanese.

VIZ has created this glossary to help you decipher, page-by-page and panel-by-panel, what all those foreign words and background noises mean. Use this guide to impress your friends with your new Japanese vocabulary.

The glossary lists the page number then panel. For example, 3.1 is page 3, panel 1.

5.3 FX: Doki... (ba-bump)

6.6 FX: Furu furu (tremble)

9.3 FX: Gyu... (squeeze)

10.1 FX: Ga (grip)
10.2 FX: Bikun (shudder)
10.6 FX: Gyu... (clench)

12.4 FX: Za (slash)

13.5 FX: Poto... (plop)

14.5 FX: Niko... (smile)

15.1 FX: Ka ka ka (tup tup tup)
15.2 FX: Ka ka ka (tup tup tup)

16.1 FX: Gako (shup)

17.6 FX: Ni (smirk)

18.1 FX: Fan fan (weeoo weeoo)

20.1 FX: Paa (fwish)
20.4 FX: Gyu (clench)

23.3 FX: Biku (flinch)

24.5 FX: Doki (ba-bump)

25.3 FX: Dokun dokun (ba-bump ba-bump)

27.5 FX: Kacha (kachook)

29.3 FX: Gaa (automatic door)
29.4 FX: Katsu (tump)

30.4 FX: Kashan (clack)

31.2 FX: Ga (stab)
31.5 FX: Kiri (cutting)

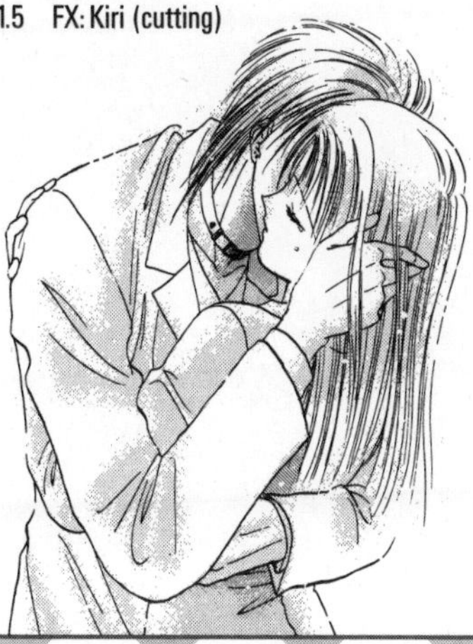

32.3 FX: Giri giri
(pushing into the wound)

33.2 FX: Gugu... (more pain)
33.4 FX: Ga (grip)

34.3 FX: Pa (changing back)

37.1 FX: Kururi (twirl)

41.4 FX: Teku teku teku
(pitter patter pitter patter)

42.4 FX: Ton ton ton (chop chop chop)

44.3 FX: Ji (stare)
44.4 FX: Jii (stare)
44.5 FX: Niko (smile)
44.6 FX: Gabaa (glomp)
44.6 FX: Don (thump)

45.4 FX: Suta suta suta (walking off)

47.2 FX: Jiro jiro (ogle ogle)

48.2 FX: Pashi (snap)
48.4 FX: Ba (fwip)

50.3 FX: Ban (slam)

51.6 FX: Gara (rattle)

52.2 FX: Haa haa (huff huff huff)

54.5 FX: Ka ka (tup tup)

55.3 FX: Koto (plunk)

56.1 FX: Katsu katsu (tump tump)
56.3 FX: Gyu... (squeeze)

57.5 FX: Ka (step)

59.3 FX: Ka ka ka (tup tup tup)
59.4 FX: Gyu (squeeze)
59.5 FX: Su (passing)
59.6 FX: Ka ka (tup tup)

60.1 FX: Ka ka (tup tup)
60.4 FX: Ka ka ka... (tup tup)

61.4 FX: Su (release)
61.5 FX: Ka ka ka (tup tup tup)

62.3 FX: Batan (slam)

65.4 FX: Gyu... (clench)

66.4 FX: Gyu (clench)

67.5 FX: Puchi puchi (snap snap)

68.1 FX: Basa (fwap)

69.3 FX: Gyu... (squeeze)

70.1 FX: Su (hands reaching)
70.1 FX: Biku (flinch)

73.2 FX: Pinpon panpon (ding dong)

74.4 FX: Kacha (click)

75.1 FX: Patan (slam)
75.2 FX: Ira ira (pacing)

104.1 FX: Piku (twitch)
104.5 FX: Suu (slide)

105.1 FX: Fura (stagger)
105.2 FX: Gu (urp)
105.3 FX: Geho (cough)
105.4 FX: A—!! (augh)

106.1 FX: Su (passing through)
106.3 FX: Zuru (slip)
106.4 FX: Tata (tup)

107.1 FX: Waaah (sob)

108.4 FX: Beki (smash)

112.4 FX: Kyu... (squeak)

116.6 FX: Katsu... (tump)

119.3 FX: Kasha (click)

120.1 FX: Piku (flinch)

121.1 FX: Doki doki (ba-bump ba-bump)

125.3 FX: Pi— pi— pi— (beep beep)

126.2 FX: Guwa (crash)

130.5 FX: Ga (slam)

131.4 FX: Bata bata (running)

132.1 FX: Zawa zawa (murmur murmur)

134.2 FX: Gachi (clench)

75.5 FX: Ira ira (pacing)

76.1 FX: Kasha (click)

78.4 FX: Niko (smile)

79.2 FX: Doh (donk)

81.1 FX: Gashi (hug)
81.1 FX: Ton ton (chop chop)
81.2 FX: Zakkuri (slice)
81.3 FX: Pasha (click)

83.6 FX: Niko (smile)

85.3 FX: Kotsu... (step)

86.4 FX: Takumo— (sheesh)

90.5 FX: Su (reaching hand)
90.6 FX: Chichichi (chirp chirp)

91.1 FX: Suu (drawing hand away)

96.3 FX: Don (slam)
96.4 FX: Buru buru (shudder shudder)
96.5 FX: Bibi (bzzt)

97.1 FX: Bachi bachi (zap crackle)

99.4 FX: Zaku zaku (hair flowing)
99.5 FX: Ga (grab)

100.1 FX: Za (fwoosh)

103.5 FX: Ban (smash)
103.5 FX: Pari—n (clink)

137.1 FX: Bata bata (running)
137.5 FX: Zuru (slip)

140.4 FX: Kakun (slump)

149.2 FX: Mishi (creak)

150.2 FX: Don (boom)

151.3 FX: Goohhh... (roar)

152.3 FX: Zu zuzu (drag)

153.1 FX: Peta peta... (tump tump)
153.2 FX: Peta peta (tump tump)
153.3 FX: Peta... (tump)
153.5 FX: Haa haa haa (huff huff huff)

154.1 FX: Haa haa (huff huff)
154.3 FX: Gu (clench)
154.4 FX: Biku biku (zap zap)
154.5 FX: Dokun (ba-bump)

155.1 FX: Fura (stagger)

160.3 FX: Biku (clench)
160.4 FX: Gaku gaku (tremble)

161.1 FX: Gu (squeeze)
161.3 FX: Doka (crash)

162.3 FX: Ban (slam)
162.4 FX: Pishi (crack)

163.3 FX: Gakun (slump)

165.4 FX: Bin (snap)

165.6 FX: Katsu katsu (tump tump)

168.1 FX: Pan (pop)
168.2 FX: Gara (clatter)

169.2 FX: Peta (slump)
169.5 FX: Bishi (snap)

170.4 FX: Su (taking out sword)

171.2 FX: Ban (zzak)
171.3 FX: Yoro (stagger)

173.1 FX: Beta (splat)

174.1 FX: Shuru (undoing chain)
174.6 FX: Ba (slash)

175.2 FX: Su (retreat)

176.1 FX: Fura (stagger)
176.2 FX: Dota (thump)
176.3 FX: Haa haa (huff huff)

177.6 FX: Oo– pi–po– pi–po–
(weeoo weeooo)

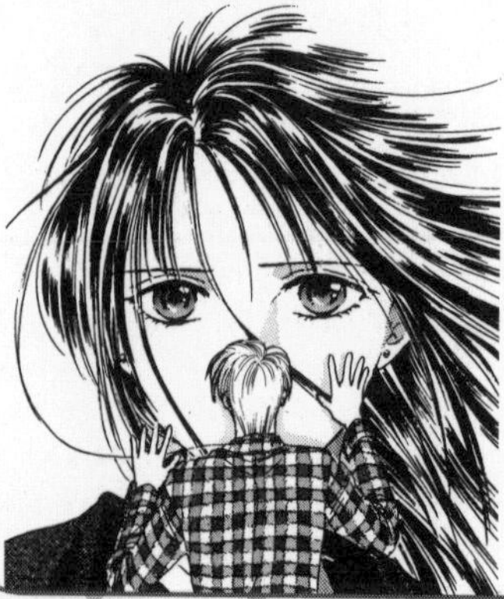

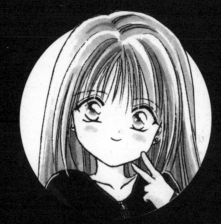

Yû Watase was born on March 5 in a town near Osaka, Japan, and she was raised there before moving to Tokyo to follow her dream of creating manga. In the decade since her debut short story, PAJAMA DE OJAMA ("An Intrusion in Pajamas"), she has produced more than 50 compiled volumes of short stories and continuing series. Her latest series, ZETTAI KARESHI ("He'll Be My Boyfriend"), is currently running in the anthology magazine SHÔJO COMIC. Watase's long-running fantasy/romance story FUSHIGI YÛGI and her most recent completed series, ALICE 19TH, are now available in North America published by VIZ. She loves science fiction, fantasy and comedy.

More Manga! More Manga!

If you like *CERES: CELESTIAL LEGEND*, here are some other manga VIZ recommends you read:

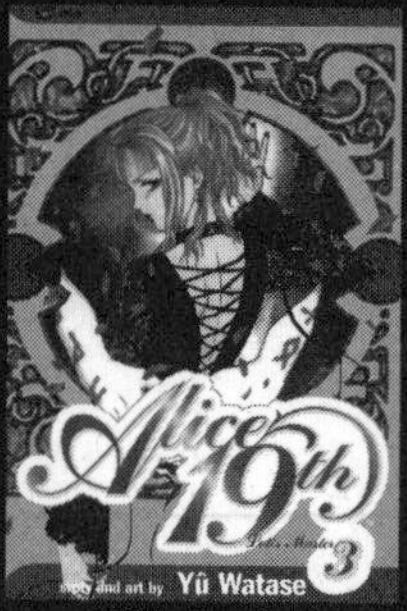
Alice 19th 3
Yû Watase

ALICE 19TH is the latest North American release from Yû Watase. Alice Seno is an ordinary high school girl living in the shadow of her older sister, Mayura. When a magical rabbit literally jumps into Alice's life, she quickly learns about the power of words. When Mayura is accidentally cast into a world of darkness, Alice must become a Lotis Words master in order to save her sister.

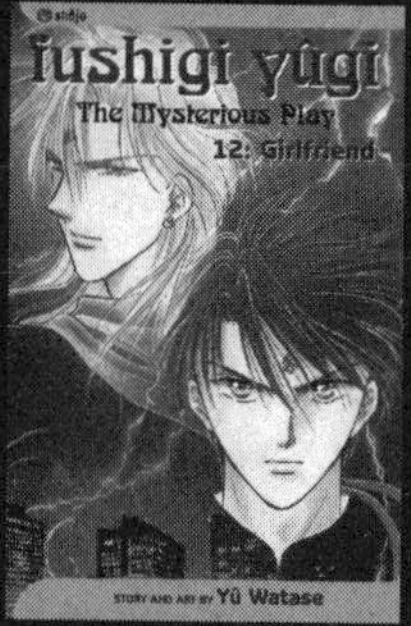
fushigi yûgi
The Mysterious Play
12: Girlfriend
STORY AND ART BY Yû Watase

FUSHIGI YÛGI is Yû Watase's popular fantasy shôjo series about a junior high school girl who suddenly travels to a fictional version of ancient China, where she finds love, betrayal and adventure.

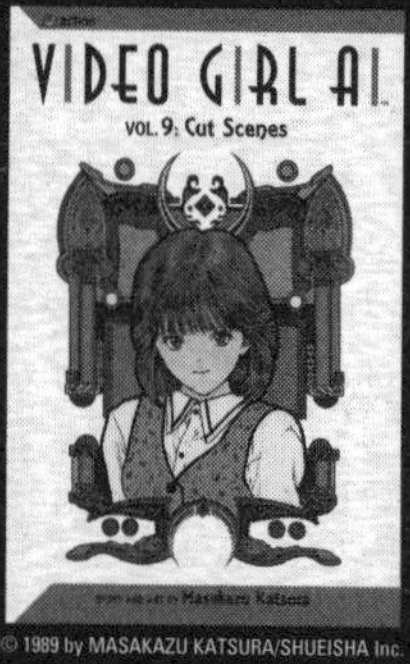
VIDEO GIRL AI
VOL. 9: Cut Scenes

VIDEO GIRL AI is a twist on the traditional love triangle. Yota Moteuchi's heart is broken when he finds out the girl he's in love with is in love with his friend. He wanders into a mysterious video store and picks up a rental starring cute, young Ai Amano. When he pops the tape into his broken VCR, Ai jumps from the screen into Yota's arms.

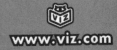

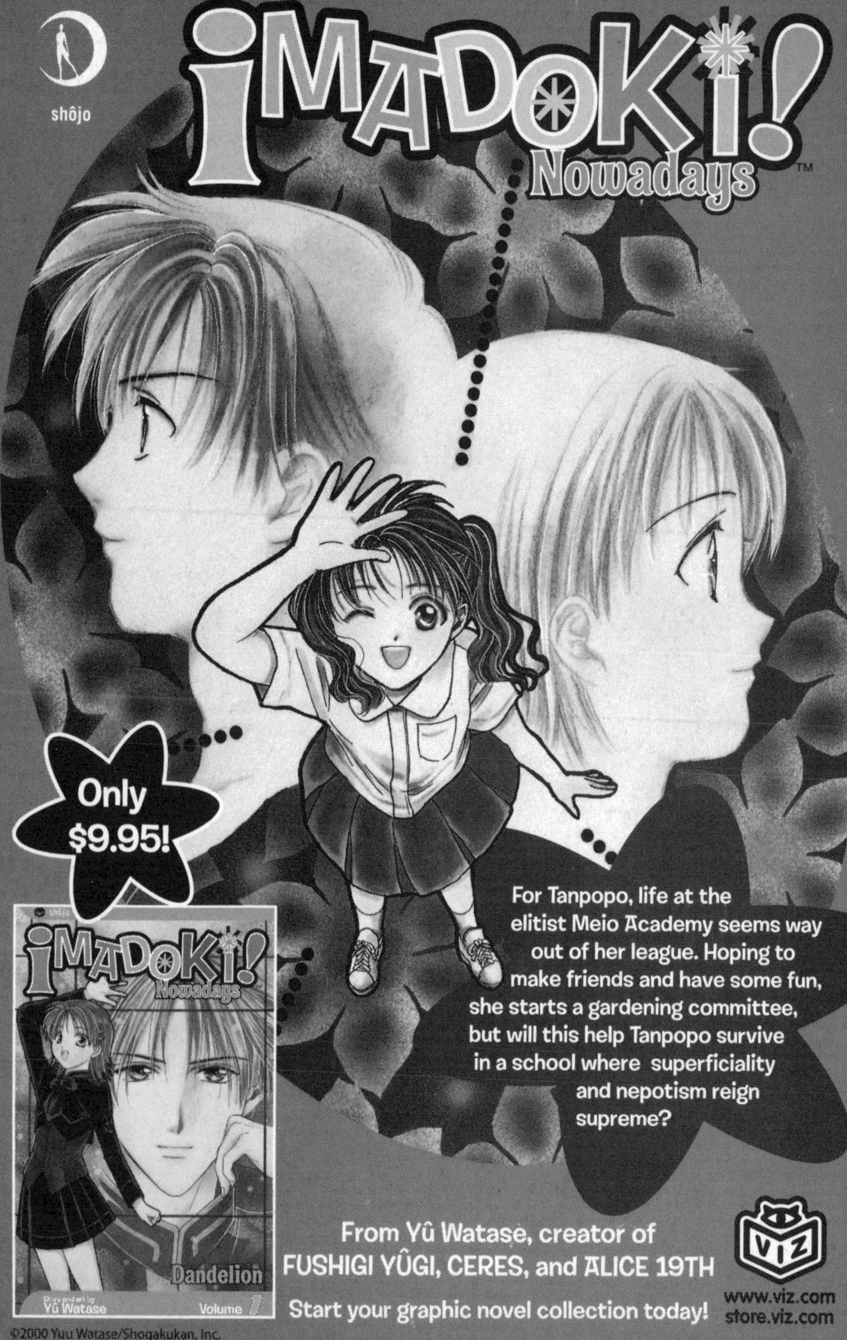
shôjo
IMADOKI! Nowadays™
Only $9.95!
IMADOKI! Nowadays
Dandelion
Yû Watase
Volume 1
For Tanpopo, life at the elitist Meio Academy seems way out of her league. Hoping to make friends and have some fun, she starts a gardening committee, but will this help Tanpopo survive in a school where superficiality and nepotism reign supreme?
From Yû Watase, creator of
FUSHIGI YÛGI, CERES, and ALICE 19TH
Start your graphic novel collection today!
VIZ
www.viz.com
store.viz.com

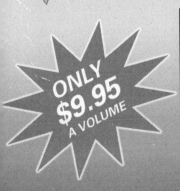
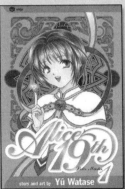

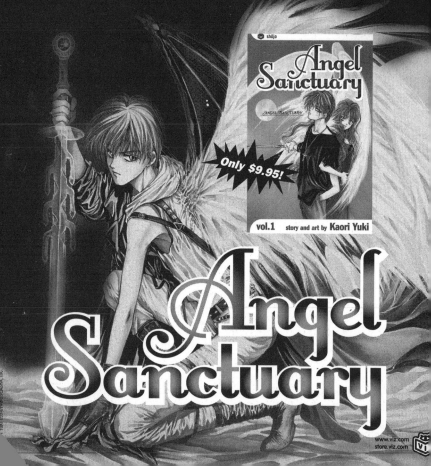

shôjo

AT THE HEART OF THE MATTER

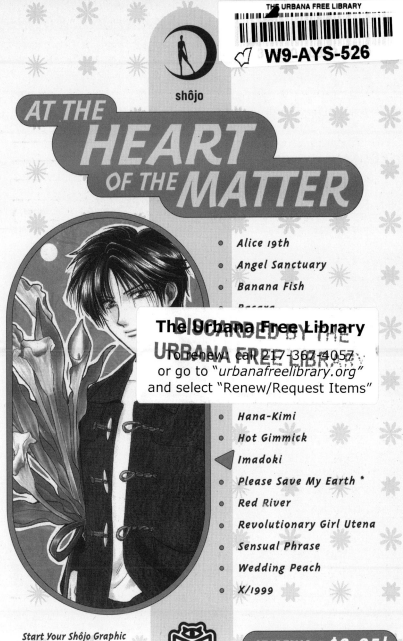

- Alice 19th
- Angel Sanctuary
- Banana Fish
- Basara

- Hana-Kimi
- Hot Gimmick
- Imadoki
- Please Save My Earth *
- Red River
- Revolutionary Girl Utena
- Sensual Phrase
- Wedding Peach
- X/1999

*Start Your Shôjo Graphic
Novel Collection Today!*

STARTING @ $9.95!

*Also available on DVD from VIZ

© 2000 YUU WATASE/SHOGAKUKAN, INC.

www.viz.com